123 Gill St.

YOU SAVED MONEY

This
BOOK
Belongs

To_____

_____

Thanks!

UNIVERSITY BOOK STORE
WHERE CRAZY TED PAYS THOSE CRAZY HIGH PRICES FOR YOUR USED BOOKS

Guiston 54 Answer B
55 " D
56 Answer BORO

24 $840

51072
04318
Timothy Lowenstein

Fundamentals of
Management
Functions, Behavior, Models

Fundamentals of
Management

Functions, Behavior, Models

JAMES H. DONNELLY, JR.
Associate Professor

JAMES L. GIBSON
Chairman and Associate Professor

JOHN M. IVANCEVICH
Associate Professor

All of the
Department of Business Administration
University of Kentucky

1971
BUSINESS PUBLICATIONS, INC. AUSTIN, TEXAS 78723
IRWIN-DORSEY LIMITED, GEORGETOWN, ONTARIO

© BUSINESS PUBLICATIONS, INC., 1971

First Printing, April, 1971

Library of Congress Catalog Card No. 76–146733
Printed in the United States of America

*This book is dedicated to
our parents and families*

Preface

The growth, stability, and quality of a society such as ours, which has evolved through specialization of labor and institutions, depend upon the decisions of those men and women who manage. It is they who allocate scarce resources to alternative, competing, and seemingly insatiable ends. Their skill, experience, and judgment determine the directions which institutions will take in society. For example, they have the power to build or close plants, to purify or pollute the environment, and to accept or reject proposals for capital expenditure programs. It is extremely difficult to identify anyone who is not either a manager or subject to the decisions made by a manager. Thus, to say that management is crucial and pervasive in our society is certainly no overstatement of the facts of everyday life.

Although managing people is such an important phenomenon, there is a lack of any specifically organized body of knowledge or universally accepted mechanism for coping with the ferment and changes in society. The truth of the matter is that a science of management is just starting to emerge. This book is an attempt to facilitate understanding of the fact that there exist many different techniques and theories about how to manage people in various institutions—businesses, government agencies, schools, and hospitals. The authors believe that the reader can acquire a more thorough and insightful understanding of management by using some systematic framework. In this book the framework consists of identifying three overlapping *schools* of management: the *Classical School,* the *Behavioral School,* and the *Management Science School.* We believe that the theories, concepts, and models found in each of these schools contribute positively to the total body of knowledge which comprises contemporary management.

We believe that using one school as a "strawman" in perpetuating another hinders the evolution of a science of management. This philosophy, however, does not preclude being critical about some of the theories, concepts, and models found in the various schools. If a manager is to cope effectively with the changes occurring in all fields of human endeavor, he should possess an understanding of the theories, concepts, and models in each of the schools. Hopefully, this book will show that the three schools of management are mutually supportive and not separate approaches that exist in a vacuum.

This book is certainly not intended to be the "only way" that management knowledge can be classified. Rather, it is designed to show that a contemporary and realistic manager can benefit by blending the approaches offered by the three schools of management. The manager who is able to use theories, concepts, and models from each of the three schools is designated as a reality-centered manager.

This book has been prepared for the first course in management at both the undergraduate and graduate level. Its use requires no previous study of management or administration. The materials in the text have been utilized and pretested at both the University of Maryland and the University of Kentucky.

The entire text or just sections of the book can be used, depending upon the orientation of the instructor or the objectives of the particular course. For example, some instructors may want to utilize only some of the chapters in the management science section or some of the chapters in the classical section. This certainly can be done without infringing upon the continuity of the book. The book was designed so that a complete effort to blend the three schools could be accomplished, or only a partial blending of various selected theories, concepts, and models could be undertaken.

The book is organized into four parts, plus an introductory chapter that discusses concisely the field of management. Part I, which includes Chapters 2–6, focuses upon the Classical Management School. In these chapters the contributions of a number of classical management scholars are discussed and three *functions* of management—planning, organizing, and controlling—are presented. These three functions were selected as being those which are most widely discussed and analyzed in the management literature.

Part II presents some theories, concepts, and models that are found in the Behavioral School. Chapters 7–12 focus upon such areas as the behavioral sciences in general, motivation, work groups, leadership, organizational design, and organizational change. The authors decided to organize this section in a manner in which "people factors" (e.g., motivation) are discussed before organizational design. A number of instructors may decide to discuss organizational design first so that a macro view of the firm is provided the reader and then look at specifics such as motivation and work groups. We believe that both approaches have merit, and it is possible to realign various chapters of Part II to meet the particular objectives of the class and the teaching approach of the instructor.

Part III includes Chapters 13–18. The material covered in this section can be comprehended by a reader with only a minimum background in mathematics and statistics. In fact, the reader with only a basic background in college algebra, statistics, economics, and accounting was kept in mind in preparing the entire section. The problems in each of the chapters and at the end of the chapters can be worked out if the reader honestly attempts to read the entire chapter. As stated previously, the materials in these chapters have been carefully pretested in the classroom and have been received favorably by students with only a minimum quantitative background.

Part IV includes one chapter on contemporary management. This chapter attempts to descriptively and graphically illustrate the overlap of the three management schools. In addition, three specific areas—information technology and organizational design, the multinational firm, and social responsibility—are discussed.

The authors are grateful to many individuals who have aided them in preparing this text. The numerous students who have read and critiqued various sections of the book are due a special note of thanks for their hours of work. Three University of Kentucky graduate students —Walt Bergmann, Steve Johnson, and William Routt—are due thanks for reading various chapters and critiquing them in detail.

The authors would like to acknowledge the permission received from Professor Rensis Likert, University of Michigan, to use his research instrument as an appendix to Chapter 12.

A very special note of gratitude is given to M. Gene Newport, University of Nebraska at Omaha, and Robert L. Trewatha, Southwest Missouri State College, for reading, editing, and commenting on the entire manuscript. These two professors have contributed a number of ideas to the text. Robert Miller of UpJohn Research Corporation has also contributed ideas that have been incorporated in the text.

We also wish to acknowledge Charles Haywood, Dean, and Joseph Massie, Associate Dean, both of the College of Business and Economics at the University of Kentucky, for providing an atmosphere of positive support for the authors' efforts. The typists who were an invaluable help in completing the text were Linda Arthur, Jacki Crowe, and Bobbi Oxnard.

March, 1971   JAMES H. DONNELLY, JR.
                                                      JAMES L. GIBSON
                                                      JOHN M. IVANCEVICH

Contents

ceptance. Second Phase: Decision-Making. Third Phase: Motivation. Fourth Phase: Control. Types of Groups in an Organization. *Command Group. Task Group. Interest Group. Friendship Group.* Characteristics of Work Groups. *The Emergent Leader. Status in a Group. Work Group Norms and Control.* Group Cohesiveness. *Size of Work Group. Dependence of Members upon the Work Group. Achievement of Goals. Status of Group. Management Demands and Pressure.* An End Result: Member Satisfaction. *Perceived Freedom to Participate. Perceived Goal Attainment. Status Consensus.* A Work Group Model. Techniques Offered by Behavioralists for Studying Groups. *Bales Laboratory Technique. The Who-to-Whom Matrix. Moreno's Sociometric Analysis.* Studies of Groups with Relevance to Organizations. *Van Zelst Construction Industry Study. A Field Study of Work Group Behavior. Group Cohesiveness Study.* Summary.

PART III. THE MANAGEMENT SCIENCE SCHOOL

INTRODUCTION

chapter one

The Field of Management

INTRODUCTION

A significant development during the years since the turn of this century is the emergence of a body of literature which constitutes the field of management, and which is the product of many scholars and practitioners who desire to expand and intensify our knowledge of management. This textbook is a survey of that literature. It was necessary for the authors to make decisions concerning the selection of material to be included in a survey of the fundamental theories, concepts, and research in the field of management. The authors' choice was based primarily upon the criterion of "general acceptability." Those materials are included which are regarded by most management scholars and practitioners as constituting the core of the field. The reader should recognize that the literature on management is voluminous; the authors hope that his study of this textbook will stimulate further reading in the field.

We should understand what we mean by the field of management. This understanding can be approached by answering a number of questions which, at the most general level, suggest the *scope* and *method* of the field.[1] The most basic questions dealing with scope are: What is

[1] The reader will recognize that these two questions are key issues which students of epistemology (the study of the nature and limits of knowledge) must confront. At this point in time, no management scholar has systematically confronted the epistemological problems of the field. Such an effort might be patterned after Philip H. Wicksteed, "The Scope and Method of Political Economy," in George J. Stigler and Kenneth E. Boulding (eds.), *Readings in Price Theory* (Homewood, Ill.: Richard D. Irwin, Inc., 1952), pp. 3–26, or Talcott Parsons, "The Prospects of Sociological Theory," *American Sociological Review*, Vol. 15 (February, 1950), pp. 3–16.

management? What is the phenomenon in the real world which is the focus of attention? The corollary questions are: Why should one study management? What justifies the considerable expenditures of energy and resources which have been and are being devoted to the field? This is the "So what?!" question and given the multiplicity of ends to which energy and resources can be allocated, it is a question that should be answered. Thus the scope questions direct attention (1) to that which is to be known and (2) to why it should be known.

The questions dealing with method are concerned with *how* one can acquire knowledge about the subject matter. The student should ask: "Given the nature of management and the relative importance of knowing about it, what are the appropriate means for acquiring knowledge about management?" A second way of stating the question is: "Given the various means of knowing (common sense, intuition, experience, and scientific inquiry in its various forms), which is appropriate for acquiring knowledge about management?" As the reader will discover in this introduction to management, all of these methods have been used in providing evidence to support a particular theory, principle, or practice. In fact, the student of management quickly learns that much of the literature in this field is devoted to methodology and its problems. There is also much disagreement on scope and content. Management as a field of study is relatively new and basic issues which have been tentatively resolved in more mature fields are still unanswered questions.

While some answers may be suggested in this first chapter, the entire balance of this book will be concerned with these questions. The authors hope that the reader will be better able to cope with them at its conclusion.

THE MANAGEMENT CONCEPT

Management is *the process by which individual and group effort is coordinated toward group goals.* This concept includes not only the content of the field, but also its importance. The latter is based upon the fact that modern society has developed through the creation of specialized institutions and organizations which provide the goods and services it desires. Moreover, these institutions are guided and directed by the decisions of one or more persons who are designated "managers" or "administrators." It is they who allocate scarce resources to alternative and competing ends. Their skill and judgment determine the means-ends relationships; they have the authority (as granted by society) and the responsibility (as accepted by them) to build or destroy cities, to wage peace or war, to purify or pollute the environment. They establish the conditions for the provision of jobs, incomes, products, services, protection, health care, and knowledge. It is difficult to identify anyone in an advanced society who is neither a manager nor subject to the decisions of a manager.[2]

This concept of management also directs our attention to the content of the field, specifically to those events, behaviors, and feelings arising from the nature of group activities. The formal study and systematic practice of management focus on the nature of group effort, various forms of coordination, and the manner of setting, ordering, and measuring goals. The management process is required whenever two or more persons combine efforts and resources to accomplish a goal which neither can accomplish by acting alone; the necessity for coordination follows from the fact that the actions of group participants constitute parts of a total task. If one person acts alone to accomplish a task, no managerial action is required, but once that person allocates a part of the task to a second or third person, the individual efforts must be coordinated *in some manner.*

The concept of the management process as defined here consists of all ongoing activities (personal and impersonal, subjective and objective, formal and informal) undertaken by one or more persons to affect the activities of one or more other persons so that some end is obtained. In a contemporary business organization the aim of these activities is to create a product or service that has a market value in excess of the costs of the product or service. The nature of the product or service and prevailing technology generally specify the tasks necessary to achieve the desired end. The business manager coordinates the specified tasks within the constraints imposed by the environment and the nature of the people in groups. The activity necessary to coordinate the group activity is the managerial process.

To provide the background for understanding some basic management concepts, let us see how the management process evolves in the context of a particular firm. In order to present management in a historical context, we will also briefly describe its evolution, with particular attention to the development of the literature which marked the early beginnings of the field of management.

The Evolution of Management in the Firm

The management of most contemporary organizations is specialized. Most students are aware of the various modifying adjectives preceding the noun *management:* top management, middle management, first-line management, general management, personnel management, production management, marketing management, and financial management. As an organization increases in size and complexity, the managerial process

[2] Robert Presthus, *The Organizational Society* (New York: Alfred A. Knopf, Inc., 1962).

adapts by becoming more specialized. The history of most long-lived business firms can be understood as a process by which the management has, in successive steps, moved from one manager with many subordinates to many managers with many subordinates.

The one-manager–many-subordinate firm is depicted in Figure 1–1.

FIGURE 1–1

No Specialization
of the Management Process

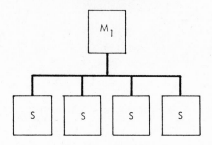

The manager, M_1, performs all the tasks necessary to coordinate the work of the subordinates, S's, toward the goals of the firm. If the firm is successful so that a larger volume of resources is available for allocation to more goals—more products, wider markets—the manager is confronted with the imperative of specialization. He may decide to specialize by

FIGURE 1–2

Horizontal Specialization
of the Management Process

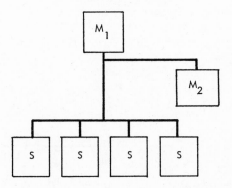

assigning certain tasks, such as the marketing of the product, to another man (Figure 1–2), or he may decide to assign the task of supervising subordinates to another man while he continues to concern himself with the marketing task (Figure 1–3). Whatever his decision, whether *hori-*

zontal specialization in the former or *vertical specialization* in the latter case, the managerial process is now shared, specialized, and more complex.

As the managerial structure of an organization evolves to a high degree of specialization, relationships among the members become more

FIGURE 1–3

**Vertical Specialization
of the
Management Process**

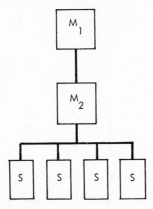

complex. In Figure 1–4, it is clear that each individual manager is concerned not only with coordinating the efforts of his group (his subordinates), but that he is the object of coordinative efforts by *his* manager as well. It is also apparent that, when the managerial process has been divided, the goals must be divided; that is, each subtask of management must be accompanied by a subgoal.

Vertical Specialization. The concept of specialized managerial tasks along the vertical dimension can be seen in Figure 1–4. The first digit of

FIGURE 1–4

Horizontal and Vertical Specialization of the Managerial Process

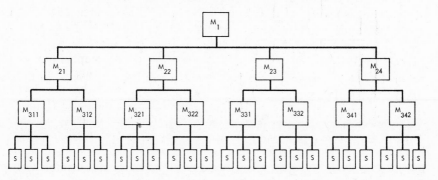

the subscript associated with each M refers to the position of that M in the scalar chain, i.e., the chain of command and accountability. The resultant system of tasks in graded order is the *hierarchy*. Accordingly, the scalar chain is $M_1 \rightarrow M_{2x} \rightarrow M_{3xx}$. The second and third digits of the subscripts refer to horizontal differentiation and are explained later.

In modern business parlance, M_1 is termed top management; M_{2x} are middle managers, and M_{3xx} are first-line managers, often referred to as supervisors or foremen. Each first-line manager derives authority from, and is accountable to, the appropriate middle manager who, in turn, derives authority from and is accountable to top management. Some obvious differences among the managerial tasks at each level can be noted.

First-line managers coordinate the work activity of others (S's), who are not themselves managers. The subordinates may be blue-collar workers, salesmen, clerks, or scientists, depending upon the particular tasks that the subunit must perform, e.g., production, marketing, accounting, or research. Whatever the case, the first-line manager coordinates the basic work of the organization according to plans and procedures provided by his superior, M_{2x}. He is in daily or near-daily contact with his subordinates. He is ordinarily assigned the task of first-line manager because of his ability to work with people—not only with his own subordinates but also with other first-line supervisors whose tasks are related to the task of his own unit. The first-line supervisor in contemporary business firms engages in upward, downward, and lateral relationships. He communicates and interacts with his own manager, with his subordinates, and with other first-line managers. The effectiveness of his coordinative efforts will depend as much, if not more, upon his human relations skills as upon his technical ability.

Middle managers, unlike first-line managers, coordinate the activity of other managers; yet, like first-line managers, they are subject to the coordinative efforts of a superior. The middle manager coordinates the activity of a subunit of the firm. The important characteristics of middle managers are described in terms of horizontal specialization.

Top management of a business firm coordinates the activity of the entire organization through the immediate subordinates. Unlike other managers, the top manager is accountable to no other manager, but instead to the owners of the resources utilized in the business. The form of the enterprise determines the exact manner in which this accountability is exercised. If the enterprise is a corporation, top management reports to the board of directors, which represents the stockholders; top management will report to the partners if it is a partnership; and to the proprietor, and perhaps to himself, if it is a proprietorship. Whatever the business form, society grants ultimate authority to the owners of property (resources) utilized in the firm.

The vertical dimension of management is defined, then, as the process by which the right to act and to use resources within specified limits (authority) is delegated downward. As this is effectuated in practice, managers can be described in terms of the extent and limits of authority at their disposal. The delegation of authority also prescribes differences in the on-job relationships of each manager.

Horizontal Specialization. The completion of a task requires the completion of a sequence of interrelated activities. As the sequence of activities is identified, and as the responsibility for completing each is assigned to a manager, the managerial process is horizontally specialized. Figure 1–4 illustrates horizontal specialization at two levels in the firm. The middle managers, M_{21}, M_{22}, M_{23}, and M_{24}, are responsible for the completion of major subtasks such as production, marketing, finance, and personnel. Each manager is at the same level in the hierarchy, as denoted by the first digit of the subscript, but each is responsible for completing a different part of the total objective, as denoted by the second digit of the subscript.

Similarly, the first-line managers are responsible for completing a subpart of the subpart. For example, M_{21}, the production manager, coordinates the activities of M_{311} and M_{312}, who may be the foreman of the fabrication department and the foreman of the finishing department. The successful completion of tasks assigned to the subordinates in these two departments, as coordinated by the foremen, results in the successful completion of the production manager's task. The manner in which the tasks are differentiated horizontally is a problem of organizational design.

The managerial process in contemporary business is assigned to numerous persons in the firm who have had specialized training and competence to deal with the assigned task. Descriptive labels promote some degree of understanding of what these persons do and are expected to do. Thus the layman understands, partially, the assignment of production managers, marketing managers, and personnel managers. There is general understanding of the distinction between top management and first-line management. Yet the specific nature of each managerial task is idiosyncratic to the firm within which the task is performed, due to the diversity of business as a social institution and to the unique character and history of each individual firm.

The Evolution of Management in Society

The practice of management is as old as man's history. Throughout time, men have joined with others to accomplish a goal, first in families, later in tribes and other more sophisticated political units. Ancient man constructed pyramids, temples, and ships; he created systems of government, farming, commerce, and warfare. These elaborated social achievements were created through the use of management techniques. Professor Claude S. George, Jr. has provided an interesting survey of the management practices of Sumerian temple priests, Egyptian pharaohs, and other functionaries of ancient civilization.[3] He observes that management was quite widespread throughout these civilizations, and that their literature made references to such managerial concepts as planning, staff assistance, division of labor, control, and leadership. But no efforts were made to accumulate and synthesize knowledge of management practice; what knowledge did exist was passed along from father to son or was learned through experience.

Management practices of considerable sophistication emerged during the eras of the Greek and Roman empires. These ancient city-states created organizations to carry on political, commercial, and military activities. As Professor George reports,[4] the Greeks recognized the relationship between efficiency in manual work and standard motions. Through the use of musical accompaniment, the Greeks introduced tempo and rhythm into the work place. The significant writings on the subject were those of Plato, Socrates, Aristotle, Xenophon, and a host of other philosophers. These insightful thinkers espoused principles of logic, economics, government, and science which are the foundations of Western civilization. Roman thinkers also contributed to this early literature as they documented and analyzed the problems of the Roman Republic and, later, the Roman Empire.

The administration of the far-flung Roman Empire required the application of managerial concepts. As James D. Mooney observed in his analysis of the historical development of management, "The real secret of the greatness of the Romans was their genius for organization."[5] Mooney's judgment derives from his investigation of the Roman's use of certain principles of organization to coordinate the diverse activities of the Empire. These principles stress the attainment of effective and efficient administration. Whether the decline and fall of the Roman Empire were due to the eventual neglect of these principles is for the historian to decide.

| The feudal system which evolved during the Medieval Period was an early experiment in decentralized government organization, and it is all the more interesting when compared to the centralized systems of Greece and Rome. The feudal system introduced all the usual problems associated with the management of a decentralized organization, including delegation of authority, decision-making, and accountability. The tenor of the times was not conducive to the literary arts; consequently,

---

[3] Claude S. George, Jr, *The History of Management Thought* (Englewood Cliffs, N.J.: Prentice-Hall, Inc., 1968), pp. 3–26.

[4] *Ibid.*, p. 15.

[5] James D. Mooney, *The Principles of Organization* (New York: Harper and Brothers, 1939), p. 63.

there is little written word to report the lessons in management to be learned from the feudal era. Niccolò Machiavelli did, of course, provide a treatise on the appropriate use of power. It is perhaps unfortunate that his ideas have been associated with despotism and the cynical use of power when, in fact, he may have provided the first codification of some basic managerial precepts.

The feudal system ultimately gave way to a recentralization of authority through mercantilism and, eventually, the industrial revolution. With the rise of the factory system and mass production, a need to rationalize the management process soon arose. Most students are well aware of the antecedents to modern manufacturing methods and institutions. It is sufficient to recall that the important developments were both technical and political. The development of steam power and the concept of interchangeable parts combined with a political philosophy of laissez-faire were the active ingredients of the industrialization of Western civilization. In an industrial society the management of business firms, *per se,* became the subject of specific analysis. It was during this period that practitioners began to evaluate the potential application of science to the management process. They also began to share insights through common associations and writings. Thus, even though the practice of management was present throughout history, the literature of management is barely 200 years old, with the most significant writings appearing in the last 50 years. Historical hindsight permits us to classify this literature on the basis of its primary thrust.

THREE SCHOOLS OF MANAGEMENT THOUGHT

The literature of management ranges over a wide variety of topics and has been produced by a wide variety of writers. The early writers were practitioners who described their own experiences, from which they generalized to broad principles. They were guided by pragmatic considerations; they wanted to share with others those practices which worked for them. A great deal of what is known about management comes from the autobiographies and memoirs of men who practiced management. On the other hand, there were other writers whose interest in management was (and is) solely scientific. Many social and behavioral scientists view the management of economic, political, military, and service institutions as an extremely important social phenomenon whose very existence justifies its study through scientific inquiry. As scientists using scientific methods, they make no value judgments regarding good or bad management practice; rather, their objective is to understand and to explain the subject of their analyses.

Between the extremes of pragmatism and scientism there are a great number of other writers who have contributed to literature on management. Their professional identifications cover a wide spectrum of knowledge, including engineering, sociology, anthropology, psychology, economics, law, accounting, mathematics, political science, and philosophy. The different points of view represented by these disciplines have been the bases for numerous attempts to provide classification schemes. For example, Koontz and O'Donnell identify six schools: (1) the operational school, (2) the empirical school, (3) the human behavior school, (4) the social system school, (5) the decision theory school, and (6) the mathematical school.[6] Haynes and Massie label six approaches: (1) quantitative approaches, (2) managerial economics and managerial accounting, (3) universals of management, (4) scientific management, (5) human relations, and (6) behavioral sciences.[7] The student can get an intuitive grasp of the kinds of material and subject matter discussed in management literature from the labels which have been used.

Our purpose is not to complicate matters by proposing yet another classification scheme. However, we believe that the discussion of the field of management can proceed quite well by means of a classification scheme which identifies only three schools: the *Classical School,* the *Behavioral School,* and the *Management Science School.* We believe that the ideas and concepts found in *each* school contribute positively to the total body of knowledge which comprises modern management thought, and that a student of management need not, in fact should not, emphasize one school and ignore the others. All three are mutually supportive; each adds to the total store of management knowledge without detracting from the other two. Through these three schools we can see an evolution of what is known and what should be known about management. At the same time, we have not written a text on the evolution of management theory, although the student of management should recognize and respect the fact that the field of management has historical origins and an extensive body of literature. Our classification scheme is for expository purposes only and, since it runs throughout the text, the student should at this point anticipate its general characteristics.

The *Classical School* of management is described in the literature which appeared primarily during the pre–World War II period. The writers of this era were seeking answers to quite fundamental questions. They were practitioners or scientists and engineers employed by business and government. At the most fundamental level the classicists were concerned with questions of efficiency, i.e., the maximization of output to input ratios. The technological insights of engineers were significant as

[6] Harold Koontz and Cyril O'Donnell, *Principles of Management,* 4th ed. (New York: McGraw-Hill Book Co., 1968), pp. 34–42.

[7] W. Warren Haynes and Joseph L. Massie, *Management,* 2d ed. (Englewood Cliffs, N.J.: Prentice-Hall, Inc., 1969), pp. 4–13.

business leaders sought to increase the productivity of workers. The efforts of these engineers led to the development of an extensive body of knowledge regarding plant and machinery design, work methods, materials flow, and the like. The basic orientation of this body of knowledge which was later termed "scientific management," was the application of scientific methods of inquiry to the problems of work and work management. The use of science to solve pragmatic problems placed management in the same category with engineering and medicine. However, the classicists were concerned not only with the management of work, but also with certain abstract questions that captured their attention.

The emergence of the Classical School coincided with the creation of large, complex organizations. Men who had practiced management within these organizations recognized that the management of organizations can be quite different from the management of work. Literature appeared which sought to explain management in terms of the functions of managers at every level of an organization. Thus the classical writers defined management as the process of coordinating group effort toward group goals. This is the definition used in this textbook. Moreover, through deductive reasoning the classicists identified (1) the *functions* which are necessary for coordination, namely, *planning, organizing* and *controlling;* and (2) the *principles* of effective managerial action. The culmination of the Classical School is an elaborate conceptual framework which relates these three basic, or organic, functions to logically identified subfunctions. The subsequent writers added to and modified the work of the classicists.

The *Behavioral School* has used the concepts of psychology, sociology, anthropology, and other behavioral sciences to extend our knowledge of human behavior in the work environment. The classical writers did not provide in-depth insights into human behavior. This was not due to their ignorance of the importance of the human element, but to their lack of sophisticated training. The writers of the Behavioral School have brought their research skills to bear on the *organizing* and *controlling* functions, beginning with the now classic Hawthorne Studies of the 1920s and continuing with vigorous attempts to test, by empirical research, the deductive insights of the Classical School.

The literature which we classify as belonging to the Behavioral School has two common characteristics. First, the focal point of the school is human behavior, managerial as well as nonmanagerial, in the context of work organizations. Secondly, the method of inquiry is essentially the scientific method, with emphasis on the discovery of causal relationships. The findings of behavioral research can be blended with the insights of the Classical School to extend our understanding of the managerial process.

The *Management Science School* in one sense is a modern version of scientific management. Its essential feature is sophistication in the use of mathematics and statistics in the construction of models to aid in resolving the operational problems of *planning* and *controlling.* The literature which we include in the Management Science School, then, focuses on technical (rather than behavioral) problems through the construction of quantitative models. The development of the computer has permitted analyses that were previously not possible because of their complexity. The computer has been of tremendous value to the growing importance of the Management Science School.

Our classification of management literature suggests the two main thrusts of management theory and practice since the Classical School. On the one hand there has been emphasis on behavioral problems; on the other hand, but coincidentally, there has been emphasis on technical problems. Rather than competing with the Classical School, this two-pronged attack is a natural extension of the earlier work.

CONTEMPORARY BUSINESS MANAGEMENT

The most powerful theoretical and practical insights into the nature and problems of business management take into account the entire range of knowledge. The contemporary business manager operates in an environment that is too complicated for easy, one-sided analyses. The manager must be able to blend the concepts, techniques, and models from each of the three schools. There are no easy solutions to the problems which he confronts. To select naively the approach of one of the schools to the exclusion of the others can only compound his difficulties. The modern manager faces diverse and often conflicting demands on his behavior. The sources of these demands are the many groups which have a vested interest in a firm, and include employees, customers, suppliers, creditors, owners, government officials, and the public at large. The demands of all these groups are seldom, if ever, completely satisfied by any management decision, a fact which results in the creation of dilemmas, situations requiring a choice between alternatives each of which may have unfavorable consequences. In recognition of this fact, managers must accept "second-best" solutions which rely upon knowledge from all three schools.

Contemporary society is the product of many complex and interrelated forces. No doubt the basic force has been the ability of man to convert scientific discoveries to practical use. Technological innovations in production, distribution, and communication processes have wrought irrevocable changes in business practice. The concommitant changes in the nature and composition of society, including organizations and the concentration of power, are likewise irrevocable, at least in the short

COLE, A. H. *Business Enterprise and Its Setting.* Cambridge, Mass.: Harvard University Press, 1959.

DRUCKER, P. *The Practice of Management.* New York: Harper and Row, 1954.

MEANS, G. *The Corporate Revolution in America.* New York: Crowell-Collier Press, 1962.

PETIT, T. *The Moral Crisis in Management.* New York: McGraw-Hill Book Company, 1967.

STEWART, R. *Managers and Their Jobs.* London: Macmillan & Company, 1967.

WALTON, C. C. *Ethos and the Executive.* Englewood Cliffs, N.J.: Prentice-Hall, Inc., 1969.

SELECTED MANAGEMENT AND RELATED PERIODICALS

Academy of Management Journal
Administrative Management
Administrative Science Quarterly
Advanced Management Journal
Business Management
California Management Review
Fortune
Harvard Business Review
Industrial and Labor Relations Review
Industrial Engineering
Industrial Management Review
Journal of Applied Behavioral Science
Journal of Applied Psychology
Journal of Business
Journal of Management Studies
Management of Personnel Quarterly
Management International Review
Management Review
Management Science
Organizational Behavior and Human Performance
Personnel
Personnel Journal
Personnel Psychology
Training and Development Journal

run. This means that managers, as the wielders of power, are called upon to answer to the grantors of that power.

In a traditional society consisting of many small and relatively insignificant firms, the legitimate function of business was to seek a profit through the production of goods and services. The rules of the game were only loosely drawn and seldom given force of law. The market place was counted on to provide the brake on the use of power. *Laissez-faire* and *caveat emptor* expressed the prevailing ideology of the times. Society granted considerable freedom to business in exchange for the creation of economic well-being. But, at the turn of the 20th century, the view of society as reflected by its laws was changing.

In the 1930s American society could be described more accurately in terms of large interdependent units than in terms of small independent units. Large firms confronted large unions, with the public interest represented by a large and expanding federal government. The "Great Depression" of the 1930s was a strong indication that all was not right with the way America did business. The stage was set for the enactment of reform and regulatory legislation that would permanently affect the function of the business manager.

The modern manager recognizes full well the legitimate necessity for complying with federal, state, and local legislation designed to regulate the use of economic power. The list of laws and acts will not be catalogued here. At a more subtle level, the manager is now being called upon to respond to a host of demands whose legitimacy is not so well established either in law or in practice. The Vietnam War, the "war on poverty," and the social revolution of various groups (Indian, Mexican, and Black Americans) have created problems that impinge in direct ways upon the activities of managers. These demands find expression in the nebulous and ill-defined phrase, "management's social responsibilities."

That society should have expectations for business that go beyond the provision of goods and services within the framework of legal constraints reflects the ambivalence of society toward business. On the one hand it expects the traditional business function; yet it also desires such non-traditional functions as the location of plants in ghettos and in depressed regions. It desires training programs for the hard-core unemployed, yet asks for restraint on price increases in the face of inflation. In the midst of these developments, management must act or not act without the benefit of a clear-cut framework of values.

The resolution of the dilemmas which society imposes will ultimately depend upon the manager's own value system. As he confronts the conflicting demands in situations where some freedom of choice exists, his system of values will attach relative weights to these demands. That he will err in the minds of some is inevitable; that he must act is likewise inevitable.

SUMMARY

Thus far we have made a number of fundamental points concerning the field of management.

1. We have provided a basis for the importance of management to the workings of society: society tends to organize its resources through specialized institutions.

2. The process of organizing necessitates some means for coordinating the organization's (group's) activities. This coordinating process is termed management.

3. The management process tends to become specialized as the organization becomes larger and more complex.

4. The literature of management has evolved as the importance of management as a field of study and analysis became more widely accepted.

5. A variety of perspectives and emphases has characterized management literature. We can introduce some clarity by identifying three mutually supportive schools—the Classical, Behavioral Science, and Management Science Schools.

6. Finally, the contemporary business manager cannot ignore the contributions of any of the three schools if he is to deal effectively with his environment.

The identification of the three schools and our belief that the modern manager must recognize the contribution of each one has dictated the arrangement of subsequent materials in this text. Specifically, we have grouped the chapters in three parts, as follows: Chapters Two through Six comprise our discussion of the Classical School. In these chapters we present the ideas of the classical writers, with some discussion of the techniques and methods which implemented these ideas. Consistent with our understanding of the Classical School we suggest that classical management theory is the combination of concepts of (1) those who analyzed the problems and the management of work (Chapter Two), and (2) those who analyzed the problems of the management of organizations (Chapter Three). We then discuss the three management functions—planning (Chapter Four), organizing (Chapter Five), and controlling (Chapter Six). These three chapters stress the contributions of the Classical School, but also include descriptions of the more important techniques which implement the functions.

The Behavioral School concepts are presented in Chapters Seven through Twelve. An overview and introduction (Chapter Seven) precedes the discussion of motivation (Chapter Eight), work groups (Chapter Nine), leadership (Chapter Ten), organizational design (Chapter Eleven), and organizational change (Chapter Twelve). We believe that

this outline of the school reflects the central concerns of its contributors. Throughout these chapters, the relationships between the classical and behavioral concepts are noted, with special attention to instances where the Behavioral School fills certain voids in the Classical School.

The next six chapters, Thirteen through Eighteen, present the basic materials of the Management Science School. An introductory chapter (Chapter Thirteen) is followed by decision theory (Chapter Fourteen) break-even analysis and inventory models (Chapter Fifteen), linear programming (Chapter Sixteen), the transportation method (Chapter Seventeen), and finally, network models (Chapter Eighteen). We have emphasized the conceptual materials in these chapters and deemphasized the mathematical manipulations, although some comprehension of the latter does, of course, contribute to understanding the former. We make explicit the manner in which the Management Science builds upon the Classical School. Our final chapter attempts to the reader with an approach to management which considers tributions of each of the three schools of thought and also sugge future directions of management thought and practice.

DISCUSSION AND REVIEW QUESTIONS

1. Explain why management is required to coordinate group

2. What is the social significance of the fact that contempor "an organizational society"?

3. Compare your school and a business firm that you know spect to the extent of horizontal specialization of mana

4. What are some of the problems you would anticipate as seek to coordinate the work of their units with the w

5. "Management is getting things done through people

6. What might be the relevant factors bearing on a management function should be horizontally or

7. What, in your opinion, are society's legitimate der havior?

8. What are the features of a value system which should not fire an elderly employee with 20 ye now technologically obsolete?

9. What do you understand by the phrase "soc agement"?

10. What is meant by the statement: "Manager

ADDITIONAL REFERENCES

CHEIT, E. F. (ed.). The Business Establishme Sons, Inc., 1964.

chapter two

Classical Theory:
The Management of Work

INTRODUCTION

The development of any field of study requires pioneers who pursue answers to basic questions which define the field and its relationship to other fields. The literature which ordinarily is produced by these efforts is typically termed "classical theory." The chapters which follow in this section concisely present the work of the classical theorists in the field of management. The authors' intent is to provide the student with the perspective to understand contemporary management theory.

Classical management theory is a significant part of the contemporary theories in this field since it provides some important insights into the nature and scope of management. Certainly time and circumstances have changed since the pioneers first undertook their analysis, yet the essence of their work has endured. Contributions to management theory by behavioral scientists, social scientists, and management scientists during the past 30 years are compatible with the work of their predecessors. The classical theorists left many questions unanswered, but the student must not lose sight of the significant fact that they provided answers to many fundamental management questions.

Classical theory defines management in terms of the functions of a manager. The essential nature of management lies in the unique *activities* of managers. These activities should be the focus of the field. At the same time, the classical writers were interested in *prescriptive* management theory; that is, they sought to discover how managers *ought* to perform their functions. This prescriptive approach is readily seen in the area of scientific management where management's function is to discover the "one best way" to do manual tasks and to train workers. This orientation toward the one best way is also found in the classicists' discussion of organization theory. According to their analyses, there is one form of organization that is appropriate for the firm, and one of the management functions is to discover that form.

The classicists identified three primary functions of management, namely, *planning, organizing,* and *controlling.* Each of these three can be broken down into smaller and smaller subfunctions. The classical analysis synthesizes the subfunctions and produces a grand scheme which describes the managerial process in detail.

The planning, organizing, and controlling concepts can be understood by using an analogy from sailing. The captain of a sailing craft predetermines his ship's destination. He must also allow for any contingencies that will affect the success of the voyage—for example, he must prepare for weather and water conditions. In anticipation of the future the captain must prepare policies that will guide the ship through the waters. As part of, but separable from, the planning function, the captain must predetermine the duties of each member of the ship's company to assure that the necessary tasks of sailing a ship are performed in the right manner at the right time; that is, the captain must organize the crew. Finally, the captain must assure that the ship's passage conforms to the predetermined plan; he must control the actual ongoing activities of the ship and the ship's company. The fact that these three functions go on continually and without obvious beginning and ending points complicates one's ready understanding of their significance.

In this section of the book, we present the basic elements of classical management theory. The remainder of this chapter describes the contributions of the scientific management approach, with emphasis on men and methods. The scientific management contributions are then combined in Chapter 3 with the work of a group of men who dealt with the problems of *top management* (as distinct from *shop management* which was the focus of scientific *management*). In Chapters 4, 5, and 6 the basic management functions—planning, organizing and controlling—are discussed.

This presentation of material is based upon the authors' belief that classical management theory is the product of two distinct, but compatible perspectives in the literature. The first is the perspective which focused on the management of work—*shop level management.* This body of literature has been labelled "scientific management," and the label is widely recognized and accepted. The second perspective focused on the management of organizations—*the total entity.* There is no generally accepted label for this literature; we have chosen to label it "classical organization theory," and we believe that no great damage ensues from our action. *Classical management theory is the blend of scientific management and classical organization theory.*

THE FOCUS OF SCIENTIFIC MANAGEMENT

In modern manufacturing the first-level manager is concerned with the day-to-day routine of coordinating the work of specialized labor. Each specialized worker does his job according to a set of rules and procedures designed to assure its completion. The rules and procedures result from analysis of the technical and human requirements of the job and of its relationship to other jobs. The state of the art dealing with work-doing is now highly developed, but this was not so at the turn of the 20th century. The breakthrough occurred when a group of engineers became interested in the techniques of work.

The body of literature which emerged from the efforts of these engineers provides the basis for scientific management, the dominant theme of which is that work-doing and the overseeing of work-doing are processes which can be analyzed from a "scientific" point of view. The engineers believed that objective analyses of facts and data collected in work-doing experiments should reveal the best way to do the work. Their analyses focused on tasks traditionally considered trivial, mundane, and menial—shoveling, pig-iron handling, and sheet-metal cutting, for example—yet such tasks were crucial to the industrial development of America.

Scientific management was based upon a definite ideology and, as is true of all ideologies, contained implicit assumptions. The ideology, simply put, stated that the cause of industrial conflict was inefficient use of scarce resources.[1] The claimants of the economic pie were continually at odds because one claimant's share could be increased only at the expense of another's. For example, wages could increase only at the expense of profit. But such is the case only if the total size of the economic pie is fixed. If the entire supply of economic goods and services is increased through more efficient use of resources, then the absolute shares of the claimants can increase without impinging upon one another.

The proponents of scientific management believed that the economic causes of labor-management disagreements can be eliminated by applying certain physiological and engineering principles to the jobs of blue-collar workers. Thus, at a time of serious social concern for economic growth and resource conservation, scientific management became an

---

[1] For a discussion of the historical setting and ideology of scientific management, see Samuel Haber, *Efficiency and Uplift* (Chicago: University of Chicago Press, 1964).

important social and economic doctrine. Contained within the doctrine were certain implicit assumptions about the human element. Specifically, scientific management adopted the assumption of classical economic theory that man is basically driven (motivated) by his desire for economic betterment. Classical economists believed man is perfectly rational in his choice of means to the end of economic betterment.[2] Thus it followed (according to scientific management) that, if managers and workers are taught new methods of work-doing which enhance their chances for economic well-being, they should be quick to adopt them.

The implementation of scientific management entailed the adoption of certain methods which would change the ways in which workers and managers had traditionally done their jobs. The major and lasting changes were to be in the ways in which men had historically done manual work. The suggested changes in the manager's job were minor in comparison and have not endured to any important extent. Scientific management was primarily shop management in that it dealt with problems of doing work at the lowest level in the firm.

MAJOR CONTRIBUTORS TO SCIENTIFIC MANAGEMENT

To appreciate fully the importance of scientific management as a philosophy and practice, one must understand the major contributors and the era in which they developed their ideas. We begin with Frederick W. Taylor, the "father" of scientific management.

Frederick W. Taylor

At the turn of the 20th century, the country was flexing its industrial muscle. Business was expanding, new products and new markets were being created, but labor was in short supply. To offset labor shortages, two solutions were available: (1) to substitute capital for labor, or (2) to use labor more efficiently. Both approaches reduce labor cost per unit of output and, ordinarily, the average cost. During the last quarter of the 19th century, considerable efforts were made to solve the problem of labor efficiency. Most notable was the work of members of the American Society of Mechanical Engineers (A.S.M.E.).

Frederick W. Taylor joined the A.S.M.E. in 1886 and used the organization as a sounding board for his ideas which had started to take shape while he was employed at various steel firms. It was at the Midvale Steel Company that he had observed the phenomenon of "soldiering," men producing far less than their capacities would permit. Taylor believed

---

[2] William F. Whyte, *Money and Motivation* (New York: Harper and Brothers, 1955), pp. 2–3; and James L. Gibson, "Organization Theory and the Nature of Man," *Academy of Management Journal,* vol. 9 (September, 1966), pp. 233–45.

that this great waste was due to ignorance of what constituted a "fair day's work." There were no systematic studies to determine expected daily output per man (work standards), and the relationship between work standards and the wage system. Taylor's personal dislike for waste caused him to rebel at what he interpreted as inefficient management practice which was based largely on hunch, rule of thumb, conventional wisdom, and ignorance. Taylor believed that ignorance on the part of both management and labor accounted for the great waste of resources.

As a foreman at the Midvale Steel Company, Taylor began an analysis of lathe work. Rather than accept soldiering and ignorance, he began the process of fact-gathering and objective analysis which was to be typical of his entire career.[3] He studied the work of an individual lathe worker to discover exactly what the worker did as he performed his task. He identified each element of the worker's job and measured every element that was susceptible to measurement. In short, he was seeking a science of metal-cutting. His objective was to provide the craftsman with an objective standard which would define a "fair day's" work.

Taylor sought means for combining the interests of both management and labor to avoid the necessity for "sweat shop" management. He believed that the key to harmony was to discover the "one best way" to perform a task, determine the optimum daily pace of the task, train workers to do the task in the prescribed way and at the prescribed pace, and reward successful completion of the task by using an incentive wage system. Thus, if workers and managers know what is expected and know the positive consequences of achieving mutual expectations, a close harmony between management and labor results since the interests of both parties should be satisfied: cooperation should replace conflict.

Consequently, Taylor undertook a series of studies to determine work standards. In some cases, he dealt with physical factors of work. He found, for example, that the optimum weight of a shovel load is 22 pounds and that there is an appropriate shape for each kind of shoveling job. In other instances, he and his associates dealt with the human factor of work. He trained a pig-iron handler to increase his tonnage loaded from $12\frac{1}{2}$ to $47\frac{1}{2}$ long tons per day.

As described by Taylor, there is a science of carrying which relates load weight, load time, and fatigue. The physiological soundness of Taylor's work is not an issue here. The important point is that his analysis of the task of lifting and carrying a 92-pound pig of iron up an inclined plane onto a flatcar suggested the existence of a science that could be used to improve the task. Accordingly, his "law of heavy laboring" states that, for each given exertion of energy under load, there must be re-

[3] Lyndall Urwick, *The Golden Book of Management* (London: Newman Neame Ltd., 1956), pp. 72–79, outlines Taylor's career and personal life. Also see Lyndall Urwick and E. F. L. Brech, *The Making of Scientific Management* (London: Sir Isaac Pitman and Sons, 1951).

cuperative time. Taylor applied the "law" to pig-iron handling and believed that a man moving 92-pound pigs can be under load only 43 percent of the time and must rest the remainder of the time. By closely supervising the work of a specially selected pig-iron handler, Taylor and his colleagues produced a remarkable 300 percent increase in production, and the workman's average daily wage increased from $1.15 to $1.85. The method was then learned by a number of workmen, all of whom increased their daily production and their daily wage.

The pig-iron episode illustrates the four principles of "scientific management" which, according to Taylor, are:[4]

First: Develop a science for each element of a man's work which replaces the old rule-of-thumb method.

Second: Scientifically select and then train, teach, and develop the workman, whereas in the past he chose his own work and trained himself as best he could.

Third: Heartily cooperate with the men so as to insure all of the work being done in accordance with the principles of the science which has been developed.

Fourth: There is almost an equal division of the work and the responsibility between the management and the workmen. The management takes over all work for which they are better fitted than the workmen, while in the past, almost all of the work and the greater part of the responsibility were thrown upon the men.

These principles urged managers to take a more systematic approach in performing their coordinative role. Specialization of labor cannot be left to the "invisible hand," as Adam Smith would have it. Rather, the management process requires that initiative be seized by managers to rationalize the process.

The principles define the basic operating characteristics of scientific management as Taylor proposed it. But there was another aspect of scientific management—the essence, according to Taylor. He stated in his testimony before a Special Committee of The House of Representatives that ". . . scientific management involves a complete mental revolution on the part of the working man . . . and it involves the equally complete mental revolution on the part of those on the management's side . . . ."[5] Taylor went on to explain that the mental revolution of which he spoke would shift the emphasis of both management and labor away from the division of economic values and toward increasing the size of the available values.[6] We referred to this earlier in the chapter as the

<hr>

[4] Frederick W. Taylor, *Principles of Scientific Management* (New York: Harper and Brothers, 1911), pp. 36–37.

[5] Frederick W. Taylor, "Taylor's Testimony before the Special House Committee," *ibid.*, p. 27.

[6] *Ibid.*, p. 30.

distribution of the economic pie. Taylor viewed scientific management as holding the promise for uplifting the economic well-being of society. But he believed that there could be no scientific management without the mental revolution.

Taylor developed a variety of methods and procedures to implement his concept of management. Prominent were work improvement and work measurement procedures to determine the best way and time for performing a task. His differential piece rate introduced the notion of "task and bonus" at the shop level whereby a worker was rewarded for producing more than the standard output.

Taylor also proposed that management itself could become more efficient through specialization. In his idea of *functional foremanship*, for example, he proposed that there should be at least eight foremen supervising each worker. Four would be in the planning room (consonant with Taylor's notion that planning and executing are separate processes) concerned with production routing, methods, time and cost, and discipline, while four would be on the shop floor where they would deal with the pace and quality of output and maintenance of machinery. According to Taylor, the economies and efficiences of specialization could be realized through application to management as well as to labor. However, functional foremanship was never widely adopted in industry.

In the final analysis, Taylor's lasting contributions to management are to be found in the way work is done at the shop level. His experiments with stopwatch studies and work methods stimulated his contemporaries to undertake similar studies in other work contexts. Two important contemporaries were Lillian and Frank Gilbreth.

The Gilbreths

The Gilbreths, a husband-and-wife team, made significant contributions to the emerging knowledge of scientific management. They combined their talents to produce important breakthroughs in motion study and job simplification. An untrained but insightful engineer, Frank Gilbreth was an apprentice bricklayer in his first job. His observations of skilled bricklayers' motions convinced him that many of the body movements could be combined or eliminated so that the procedure would be simplified and production increased.

Gilbreth's analysis of the sequence and path of basic movements enabled him to reduce the number of motions required to lay exterior brick from 18 to 4½. Craftsmen who used Gilbreth's method were able to increase their production by 200 percent. Economy in the use of human energy, combined with technological improvements such as an adjustable stand to eliminate stooping for the brick and a mortar of proper consistency to eliminate "tapping," resulted in a science of the ancient and honorable craft of masonry.[7] Gilbreth's work was quite compatible and consistent with that of Taylor's as each sought the elusive "one best way" to do a job.

To add precision to his analysis of fundamental hand and arm motions, Gilbreth invented a number of devices. The microchronometer is a clock with a sweep hand which is placed in the field of work being studied. Gilbreth would use a camera to record the work being done against the backdrop of the sweep hand. By such methods, he was able to identify not only the basic motions, but also the time required for each hand and arm movement. The result of his efforts was the identification of numerous distinct movements which he labeled "Therbligs" (Gilbreth spelled backward with transposition of one letter).

Henry L. Gantt

A close associate of Taylor at Midvale and Bethlehem Steel was a young graduate engineer, Henry L. Gantt. Like Taylor and the Gilbreths, Gantt dealt with problems of efficiency at the shop floor level, but at the same time he recognized the human element of production work. Gantt's contributions to scientific management are most often recalled in terms of his development of a chart which shows the relationship between work planned and completed on one axis and time elapsed on the other. This chart, referred to as a *Gantt Chart,* is still used in industry and is the forerunner of modern PERT charts.[8] Yet Gantt's contributions go beyond this.

Unlike Taylor, Gantt believed that wage systems ought to provide a fair remuneration regardless of output. He devised a task-and-bonus system in which a workman received a bonus in addition to his day's wage upon completion of an assigned task. If the workman did not complete the task, he was not penalized, but received the day wage. Taylor's differential piecerate system, on the other hand, was a pure incentive plan whereby each worker received a wage based solely on his daily production. There was no guaranteed day wage. Should the worker produce more than the standard output, the piecerate was increased for all units produced.

In other respects, Gantt made unique contributions to the literature of management. He was among the first to recognize that nonmonetary factors such as job security are powerful incentives. The task and bonus plan with its assured daily wage implements his belief. He argued strongly that a responsibility of management is to train workers to do their jobs. He also agitated for the acceptance of his concept of industrial

---

[7] Claude S. George, Jr., *The History of Management Thought* (Englewood Cliffs, N.J.: Prentice-Hall, Inc., 1968), p. 97.

[8] See Chapter 18 for a discussion of PERT.

responsibility whereby industry pursues a service objective rather than a profit objective. Such statesments were premature for the times, though they are commonplace today.

In retrospect, Gantt can be understood as a valuable contributor to the literature of scientific management. He shared the skeptical orientation of Taylor and the Gilbreths: he, like them, believed that the accepted way of doing things was usually the wrong way. Gantt believed that the best sources of improved efficiency were the work methods not of the laborer, but of management. He stated that expertise should be the sole criterion for the endowment of authority, and that managers, as the recipients of authority, have the moral obligation to make decisions by scientific methods, not by opinion. Thus Gantt broadened the scope of scientific management by including managerial responsibility as well as managerial methods as appropriate areas for analysis and change.

Harrington Emerson

The public became aware of Harrington Emerson in 1910, when he testified as an expert witness before the Interstate Commerce Commission that the railroads could save one million dollars per day through the use of the methods and philosophy of scientific management, and thus obviate the necessity for a requested rate increase. Emerson's ideas are embodied in a set of principles that define the manner in which the efficient use of resources is to be accomplished. His 12 principles implement the basic elements of the scientific management approach. In summary form, they state that the manager should (1) use scientific, objective, and factually based analysis; (2) define the aims of the undertaking; (3) relate each part to the whole; (4) provide standardized procedures and methods; and (5) reward individuals for successful execution of the task.

Emerson's contributions go beyond his 12 principles of efficiency, though they and his testimony before the ICC would have assured his place in management theory. In addition to these obvious contributions, Emerson also recognized the positive lessons to be learned from the military's use of formalized staff and advisory positions. In his capacity as one of the first management consultants, he proposed the creation of a strict organization whose activities would be defined by clear statements of goals and purposes. In this respect, Emerson moved away from the traditional scientific management concern for work-doing and anticipated many developments of classical organization theory.

Other Antecedents and Contributors to Scientific Management

The attention to Taylor, Gilbreth, Gantt, and Emerson does not preclude the importance of many other contributors to scientific management. Taylor and his colleagues did not begin their work in a complete vacuum of ideas; their antecedents were quite important to the creation and subsequent acceptance of their notions. Notable was Charles Babbage,[9] who first articulated the principle of scientific inquiry as the basis for efficient use of resources. Although a mathematician by training and a scientist by profession, Babbage produced many powerful insights into the nature of manufacturing management. He anticipated the use of time studies to determine a fair day's work. He also argued for the use of standardized methods. He placed the responsibility for improving production methods and for increasing labor productivity squarely upon management. So insightful were his ideas as to lead some students to suggest that Babbage was the real "father of scientific management."[10]

The work of other men also paved the way for Taylor's analyses. For example, Henry R. Towne may well have stimulated Taylor's interest. Towne, the president of Yale and Towne Manufacturing Company, explained his ideas to the A.S.M.E. in 1886, when he argued for the recognition of shop management as distinct from engineering management. Taylor was in the audience and may well have decided to respond to Towne's plea. We must also acknowledge the efforts of Morris L. Cooke to apply the techniques of scientific management to nonbusiness organizations. He evaluated university and municipal administration and discovered many instances of inefficient use of resources through inadequate or improper management. His work suggested the universality of the scientific management approach.[11]

THE METHODS OF SCIENTIFIC MANAGEMENT

The methods of scientific management evolved quite naturally from the philosophy of its proponents. This philosophy states simply that the economic well-being of society depends upon the efficient use of resources. The methods were then designed as means for achieving efficient resource allocation. The fact that many of these methods are widely used in contemporary business practice is strong evidence that they are sound and practical implements.

The systematic analysis of work is a principal aspect of scientific management. Taylor contributed time study and Gilbreth, motion study, and each contributed an incentive wage system. According to scientific management, the way to improve work, i.e., to make it more efficient, is to determine (1) the "best way" to do a task, (2) the appropriate time for completion of the task, and (3) the fair wage for completion of the

---

[9] Charles Babbage, *On the Economy of Machinery and Manufacturers* (London: Charles Knight, 1832).

[10] Urwick and Brech, *op. cit.*, p. 28.

[11] George, *op. cit.*, p. 119–20.

task during the prescribed (standard) time. The relationship between motion study and time study is so close that to distinguish between the two may be misleading. For example, as a part of his time studies, Taylor analyzed work from the standpoint of preferred motions. To determine the standard time for a task without first determining whether the task can be improved is wasted effort. Yet Taylor did not go into as much detail in his motion studies as did the Gilbreths.

The improvement of work involves an analysis of the entire context and environment within which the work is done. The objective of motion study is to determine a preferable work method with consideration to raw materials, product design, order of work, tools, equipment, workplace layout, and the hand and body motions required by the workman.[12] In this context motion study, and the concomitant timing of work motions, is only one part of the total process of work improvement. For motion and time study to be meaningful and fully effective, it must be integrated with studies of plant layout, material flows, machine engineering, and workplace design. The principles of motion and time study are specific applications of the general principles of standardization and specialization.

Motion Study

Motion study is the process by which a task is broken down into fundamental hand motions as related to the machines and tools required in conjunction with the man or men doing the work. This analytic-synthetic technique derives primarily from the Gilbreths' studies of work movements and work simplification, whereby the manager seeks to eliminate, combine, or change superfluous and redundant motions. The heart of the analysis consists of the 17 fundamental hand motions, "Therbligs," which are required for doing manual work; they are described in Table 2–1.

Each Therblig begins when the effort is made to achieve the objective of the motion and is completed when the objective is completed. Thus, *grasp* begins when a hand or body member touches the object, and ends when control is gained. It is necesssary to define beginning and ending points for each Therblig to identify and separate them in the analytical phase of the motion study.

Reference to Table 2–1 will reveal some important differences among the Therbligs. Therbligs 1 through 7 are called terminal Therbligs because they ordinarily occur at the end of a sequence of preparatory mo-

---

12 Marvin E. Mundel, "Motion and Time Study," in William G. Ireson and Eugene L. Grant (eds.), *Handbook of Industrial Engineering and Management* (Englewood Cliffs, N.J.: Prentice-Hall, Inc., 1955), p. 285.

tions; 8 through 11 are movement motions; 12 through 15 are delay Therbligs; 16 and 17 involve thinking. These differences are the bases for certain principles of motion economy; for example, *hold, unavoidable delay,* and *avoidable delay* are undesirable and should be eliminated as parts of the cycle and replaced by a rest pause away from the work. If the work

TABLE 2–1

	Therblig	*Objective*
1.	Grasp	To gain control of an object
2.	Position	To line up, orient, or change position of a part
3.	Pre-position	To line up part or tool for use in another place
4.	Use	To apply tool
5.	Assembly	To assemble parts or objects
6.	Disassemble	To separate objects
7.	Release load	To release a part or object
8.	Transport empty	To reach for something
9.	Transport loaded	To change location of an object
10.	Search	To seek to find an object
11.	Select	To locate an object from a group of objects
12.	Hold	To hold object in fixed position and location
13.	Unavoidable delay	To wait for other body member or machine as a part of the work movement
14.	Avoidable delay	To wait for other body member or machine not a part of the work movement
15.	Rest for fatigue	To remain idle as a part of the cycle to overcome fatigue
16.	Plan	To determine course of action
17.	Inspect	To determine quality of item

Source: Adapted from Mundel, *op. cit.*, pp. 296–98.

is accompanied by a machine, rest can occur during machine running time. Scientific management advocates assumed that analysis of the man-machine relationship from the standpoint of motion analysis would eliminate superfluous motions.

Time Study

After the analyst, usually an engineer, has isolated the fundamental elements of a task and recombined them to determine the preferred method, he must fix the appropriate time for its completion. Two timing methods are available which can be substituted for arbitrary guess or managerial intuition; they are *stopwatch* study and *predetermined-time* study.

Stopwatch studies require that the analyst examine a task to determine timing elements. A timing element may consist of one or a series of interdependent Therbligs. The important consideration is that each timing element is independent of the preceding and succeding element. Thus, securing and positioning an object in a machine may be a separate timing element, though it consists of two Therbligs.

The identification of timing elements results in the identification of timing points, i.e., points at which readings of elapsed time are taken and recorded. A series of readings of each timing element is recorded and an average is calculated to determine the *base time* for the element. Next, the analyst must use judgment to assess the relative skill and speed of the operator doing the work. If, for example, the analyst believes the operator to be somewhat slower than the "typical" or "average" worker, the base time will be reduced; if the operator is faster and more skilled than the "average," the base time will be increased. The time which results from this exercise of measurement and judgment is the *normal time* for the completion of the element.

The summation of normal times for all elements constitutes the normal time of the entire task. The engineer must now make allowance for unavoidable delays such as machine breakdown, interruption of material flow, routine maintenance, and operator fatigue. The task must be set at a pace that the worker can sustain throughout the day. Thus the normal time is increased by a percentage suggested by experience and judgment. The final result is the *standard time* for the completion of the task. The standard time is the basis for costing the product and for paying the employee.

Suppose that a man is assigned a task the standard completion time of which is ten minutes. If he works an eight-hour day and 40-hour week, he should complete the task 48 times per day and 240 times per week. Moreover, if he is paid "by the piece" at the rate of $0.40, he would earn $96.00 per week if he produces the standard output.

Predetermined Time Study

A modern method of motion and time study which derives quite naturally and logically from Taylor's and Gilbreth's beginnings is Methods-Time Measurement (MTM). The assumption of the MTM system is that prescribed times exist for all basic work movements regardless of situation or context. That is, a "three-inch reach" work movement should take the same amount of time regardless of the particular job or operator.

The MTM system analyzes any manual operation by identifying the basic motions required to perform it. The system assigns a time for each motion depending upon its basic nature and the conditions under which the motion is made. The basic MTM motions are comparable to Therbligs and they are described as follows:[13]

---

[13] Ralph M. Barnes, *Motion and Time Study* (New York: John Wiley & Sons, Inc., 1958), pp. 483–88.

Reach—The movement of the hand or finger to a destination. The standard time for the movement depends upon the nature of the object toward which the reach is directed, the length of the motion, and the type of reach, i.e., whether the hand is moving at either (or both) beginning and end of reach.

Move—The transportation of an object to a destination. The standard time for this element depends upon the same factors which determine the time for the reach element. At the same time, the move element must include allowance for the weight of the object and the force required to move it.

Turn—The rotation of the hand, either empty or loaded. The standard time depends upon the number of degrees in the turn and the weight factor.

Grasp—The securing of control of an object in order to perform the next required element. The time of the grasp element is determined by the nature of the object itself, the conditions surrounding the element, and the intention of the grasp movement, i.e., whether the object is simply picked up or whether it is transported.

Position—The alignment or engagement of one object with another object. The time allowed for this element depends upon whether the required fit is loose or exact, the relative difficulty of handling, and the symmetry of the movement.

Release Load—The loosening of control over an object by the fingers or hands. A fixed time is established for this element.

Disengage—The breaking of contact between one object and another. The time depends upon the tightness of the fit that must be broken and the relative difficulty of handling the object.

In addition to these seven basic work elements, the MTM system also identifies a number of body, leg, and foot motions. Standard times are based upon the same kinds of factors and considerations which determine standard times for the basic hand and finger movements. A further refinement is the recognition that manual work also requires eye movement and eye focus. The MTM system also provides standard times.

The MTM system is but one of several predetermined-time systems.[14] Though each has its own approach and definitions of elements, they all have in common the assumption that the basic nature of work can be viewed apart from the person performing the work. These systems are much used in industry. Their basic origins are to be found in the rudimentary efforts of Taylor and Gilbreth.

Incentive Wage Systems

A major point of controversy among the engineers in the early days of scientific management, and one which remains unresolved, is the ap-

---

[14] *Ibid.*, p. 460.

propriate incentive plan. The fundamental notion was that wages ought to be related in some way to production. Figure 2–1 shows a simple, linear wage system based upon the previous illustration. The piecerate is $0.40, the standard output is 240, and the standard wage is $96.00.

FIGURE 2–1
A Simple, Linear Incentive System

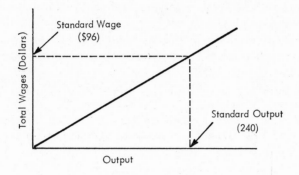

FIGURE 2–2
Taylor Differential Piecerate System

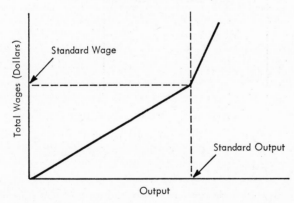

The critical issue in the creation of an incentive system is the exact relationship between wages and under-over standard production. There are, of course, many technical problems associated with incentive systems —the establishment of "standards," for example. We will not go into these problems here. Taylor believed that there should be two rates, one for production up to standard and a higher rate for production at and above standard.

Figure 2–2 illustrates Taylor's Differential Piecerate System; the piecerate is $0.40 for 0–239 pieces, but if 240 pieces are obtained, the rate is $0.42 for all pieces. A worker producing 239 units would be paid $95.60; one who produces 240 units would be paid $100.80. Thus, Taylor felt that wages should be related directly to production, that there should be no guaranteed "day" wage irrespective of output, and that high producers should be rewarded.

Gantt, on the other hand, believed that all workers should be paid a fixed and guaranteed living wage regardless of productivity. Gantt would reward high producers by paying a piecerate above the standard. Figure 2–3 illustrates the Gantt Task and Bonus System wherein the task is the completion of 240 units and all men are paid $96.00 for the effort to complete the assigned task. Men who produce more than the assigned 240 units are paid a bonus, say, $0.45 for each piece. Thus, production of 250 units would reward the worker by $96 + $0.45 (250–240), or $100.50.

FIGURE 2–3

Gantt's Task and Bonus System

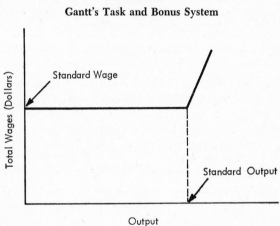

Selection and Training

Taylor's second principle stated that management's responsibility is to select by scientific means men who are capable of meeting the job demands, and then to train and develop these men to do the job in the prescribed way. When Taylor arrived on the scene, new workers learned their job from the older workers; traditional work habits were simply passed on from one worker to the next. Management did not accept training as its legitimate function. Taylor himself was no expert in the use of selection techniques beyond that of matching workers with tasks which required obvious physical characteristics, notably strength and endurance. Systematic, scientifically oriented selection methods were missing. By

1910, psychologists were beginning to see the possibilities for applications of their knowledge to the problems of selection.[15]

The field of industrial psychology began to take definite form with the work of Hugo Munsterberg, a German-born Harvard professor whose work established the beginnings of the field. The publication of his book, *Psychology and Industrial Efficiency*,[16] in 1913 was a landmark in the field. Psychological methods were developed for selecting workers whose mental and physical qualities would suit the demands of particular jobs. By 1915, tests were being used to select salesmen, telephone operators, and factory workers.[17] Perhaps the greatest stimulus to testing was World War I, during which more than one and a half million men completed psychological tests. With the end of the war, industrial psychology was firmly rooted in business practice.

Training workers to perform the job in the prescribed manner was an important part of scientific management. In fact, without training, the efforts to improve work would be wasted. Henry Gantt outlined the fundamentals in a paper before the A.S.M.E. at its December 1908 meeting.[18] In the paper, Gantt introduced the idea of using an instructor to train each individual worker in the preferred method. The idea that management should institute formal training programs was not widely accepted until the 1930s. This lag occurred partly due to incomplete knowledge about training methods and partly because management simply ignored the potential benefits of training. But by the beginning of World War II, training methods were widely represented in industry.

SCIENTIFIC MANAGEMENT IN RETROSPECT

If it were evaluated in terms of its impact on management practice at the time of its development, scientific management would receive a low grade. Its impact on contemporary management is more pronounced and significant. True, some firms adopted scientific management methods; yet the "mental revolution" which Taylor expected never occurred. Despite the fact that he, the Gilbreths, Gantt, Emerson, and others had provided a substantial, if unorganized body of knowledge which offered to bring harmony to all participants in economic life, strife between management and labor continued and the methods of scientific management were largely ignored.

[15] Loren Baritz, *The Servants of Power* (New York: John Wiley & Sons, 1960), p. 35.

[16] Hugo Munsterberg, *Psychology and Industrial Efficiency* (Boston: Houghton Mifflin Co., 1913).

[17] Baritz, *op. cit.*, p. 38.

[18] Henry Gantt, "Training Workmen in Habits of Industry and Cooperation," *Transactions of the American Society of Mechanical Engineers*, vol. 30 (1908), pp. 1037–48.

One cause of the seeming failure of scientific management is possibly found in the failure of its proponents to understand fully the psychological and sociological dimensions of work. Throughout Taylor's writing one finds the implicit assumption that man is motivated basically by economic considerations, and that, when given adequate information, man is able to choose rationally the alternative which maximizes his well-being. This assumption was reinforced by classical economic theory which enjoyed its height of popular acceptance at that time. In the context of the times, such an assumption was credible. Factory workers were by and large first-generation immigrants, ignorant of their surroundings and eking out a living on subsistence wages. Granted the historical justification for the assumption, there was another movement competing with scientific management to bring about industrial harmony, namely, unionism.

The union leaders of the time viewed scientific management as a threat to labor. Taylor's concept of separation of work-doing and work-planning threatened the prerogatives of labor, particularly of craftsmen. Union leaders anticipated the erosion of the importance of labor as each individual worker's contribution diminished. Workers lose control as work becomes more specialized and as each worker is more or less substitutable for any other worker. A second source of threat to unionism was the proposal that wage systems be determined solely by management decision of what constitutes "fair wages" for standard output. This would undercut the attempts of unions to have wages determined through collective bargaining. The conflict between unions and Taylorism was most apparent in 1909, when the federal government introduced an incentive system at the Watertown Arsenal. The union struck and was supported by Samuel Gomper's American Federation of Labor. The period of active antagonism between unionism and Taylorism waned with the entry of America into World War I, when the concern for "efficency at all cost" gave way to "production at any cost." The latter orientation prevailed throughout the 20s and ended in a crash with the Great Depression.

DISCUSSION AND REVIEW QUESTIONS

1. What is the traditional role of classical theory in any field of study, and particularly in management?
2. Why should one study classical management theory? Of what relevance is scientific management to the problems of the 1970s?
3. What is your understanding of the term "ideology" as applied to scientific management?
4. Was F. W. Taylor a realist or an idealist?
5. Do you believe that there is "one best way" to perform any task, including the work of a scientist?

6. Compare the concept of the "average worker" to professors' concepts of the "average student."

7. Is the "average worker" (or the average student) to be found in the real world?

8. Is "soldiering" so bad in today's world of affluence?

9. Evaluate the applicability of motion and time study techniques to the work of the President of the United States.

10. It is said that scientific management ignored the "human element" of work. Comment.

11. Was the development of industrial psychology compatible with scientific management?

12. Why did the "mental revolution" never occur? Or did it?

13. If scientific management promised the economic betterment of management and labor alike, why did *both* groups fight it?

14. "In the name of efficiency, we should strive for routinization and consistency in higher education." Comment.

ADDITIONAL REFERENCES

BRANDEIS, L. D. *Scientific Management and Railroads.* New York: The Engineering Magazine Co., 1911.

CHURCH, A. H. *The Science and Practice of Management.* New York: The Engineering Magazine Co., 1916.

DRURY, H. B. *Scientific Management: A History and Criticism.* New York: Longmans, Green and Co., 1922.

EMERSON, H. *Efficiency as a Basis for Operations and Wages.* New York: The Engineering Magazine Co., 1900.

EMERSON, H. *The Twelve Principles of Efficiency.* New York: The Engineering Magazine Co., 1913.

GANTT, H. L. *Industrial Leadership.* New Haven: Yale University Press, 1916.

GANTT, H. L. *Work, Wages and Profits.* New York: The Engineering Magazine Co., 1910.

GILBRETH, F. B. *Motion Study.* New York: D. Van Nostrand Co., 1911.

GILBRETH, L. M. *The Psychology of Management.* New York: Sturgis and Walton Co., 1914.

HOXIE, R. F. *Scientific Management and Labor.* New York: D. Appleton and Co., 1915.

MERRILL, H. F. (ed.) *Classics in Management.* New York: American Management Association, 1960.

MUNSTERBERG, H. *Business Psychology.* Chicago: LaSalle Extension University, 1918.

chapter three

Classical Theory:
The Management of Organizations

INTRODUCTION

Scientific management raised questions, undertook analyses, and provided prescriptions which were narrow in scope yet concrete in reality. Issues related to the coordination of large organizations and the managerial roles in these entities are much more complex and abstract. A body of literature emerged simultaneously with that on scientific management, dealing specifically with these issues. This literature on classical organization theory was affected by the same environmental and cultural conditions which, in turn, affected scientific management in such large measure. Indeed, as we shall see, the ideology and assumptions so apparent in the literature on scientific management are evident in the literature on classical organization theory.

The classicists raised two principal questions: (1) What are the basic principles which should guide the design, creation, and maintenance of an organization structure? and (2) What are the basic functions of management within the organization? An overriding objective, similar to that of scientific management, was to provide *prescriptive* guidelines for effective and efficient management. The classicists believed that the criterion against which management should assess results was goal accomplishment with the minimum use of resources; and for the business firm, the rate of profit was the ultimate measure of efficiency and effectiveness.

40

MAJOR CONTRIBUTORS TO CLASSICAL ORGANIZATION THEORY

Practitioners of management were the major contributors to the literature on classical organization theory. They brought their pragmatic orientation to bear on the problem of coordinating large-scale organizations. In this respect, these writers share the action-oriented background common to writers of scientific management. In this chapter, the work of Henri Fayol, James Mooney, Lyndall Urwick, and Chester Barnard is presented. The reader should keep in mind that the concepts with which these writers dealt are considerably more abstract than those of the preceding chapter. The reader should also remember that these writers dealt with both organization theory and managerial functions and that, in many instances, they made no sharp distinctions between the two issues.

Henri Fayol

Work experience as the managing director of a large coal mining company in France provided Henri Fayol with the background for his ideas about the managerial process. For 50 years, Fayol practiced and reflected upon the process of coordinating the diverse activities of the organization which he directed. His ideas were first committed to writing and became a part of the literature in 1916, when he contributed to the bulletin of a French industrial association. A more complete statement of his ideas appeared in 1925 with the publication of his book, but it was not until 1929 that the English translation appeared.[1]

Fayol sought to discover principles of management which determine the "soundness and good working order" of the firm. Such principles are flexible in their adaptation to circumstances and events. Fayol was not seeking fixed rules of conduct; rather, he sought guidelines to thinking. Deciding upon the appropriateness of a principle for a particular situation is the "art" of administration. Fayol believed that any number of principles might exist, and described only those which he most frequently applied in his own experience.

Fayol's chief desire was to elevate the status of administrative practice by supplying a framework for analysis. His framework included a statement of *principles* and *functions*. We shall discuss them in that order.

Management Principles. Fayol proposed 14 principles which *should guide the thinking of managers in resolving concrete problems* To reiterate, Fayol did not expound blind obedience to fixed courses of action; he relied upon managers' "experience and sense of proportion" to guide the

---

[1] Henri Fayol, *General and Industrial Management,* translated by J. A. Conbrough (Geneva: International Management Institute, 1929). All subsequent references in this text are to the more widely available translation by Constance Storrs (London: Pitman Publishing Corp., 1949).

degree of application of any principle in any situation. The principles are:[2]

1. Division of Work. |Specialization of labor is the natural means by which institutions and societies have progressed and developed.|It results in increased productivity through the reduction of job elements required of each worker. The process of specialization of labor was recognized by Adam Smith as an important condition for economical mass production; he described the production process in a pin factory as follows:

One man draws out the wire, another straights it, a third cuts it, a fourth points it, a fifth grinds it at the top for receiving the head; to make the head required two or three distinct operations; to put it on, is a peculiar business, to whiten the pins is another; it is even a trade by itself to put them into the paper; and the important business of making a pin is, in this manner, divided into about eighteen distinct operations, . . .

. . . I have seen a small manufactory of this kind where ten men only were employed, and where some of them consequently performed two or three distinct operations. . . . Those ten persons, therefore, could make among them upwards of forty-eight thousand pins in a day. . . . But, if they had all wrought separately and independently . . . they certainly could not each of them have made twenty, perhaps not one pin in a day; . . .[3]

Specialization of labor thus permits large-scale production at minimum cost. Additionally, the cost of training workers is considerably reduced since the content of each job has been greatly narrowed.

2. Authority and Responsibility.   Much confusion exists in current discussions of authority and responsibility. The terms are highly abstract and difficult to define in concrete terms.|Fayol recognized this difficulty; he defined *authority* as the "right to give orders and the power to exact obedience."|But Fayol went on to distinguish between the *official* authority which derives from holding an office, and *personal* authority which derives from the office holder's own personality, experience, moral worth, and other personal characteristics that enable him to influence the efforts of subordinates. Fayol stated that authority and responsibility should be equal; yet he recognized that, as one moves up in the administrative hierarchy, it becomes more and more difficult to fix exactly the responsibility of office holders. Fayol expected that the ultimate check on authority had to be the integrity and moral courage of administrators, and he fully recognized that such traits are "conferred neither by selection nor ownership."

3. Discipline.   The essence of discipline, according to Fayol, is obedience to agreements reached between parties in the firm. He believed that clear statements of agreements are necessary, but not sufficient for dis-

---

[2] This discussion of Fayol's principles is based upon his own discussion in *ibid.*, pp. 19–42.

[3] Adam Smith, *The Wealth of Nations* (Chicago: Henry Regnery Company, 1962), pp. 9–10.

cipline; he argued that the "state of discipline of any group of people depends essentially on the worthiness of its leaders," leaders who would judiciously apply sanctions in instances of breached discipline.

4. Unity of Command. Fayol believed that the existence of dual command (two supervisors, one subordinate) causes severe breakdowns in authority and discipline. Consequently he stated that an employee should receive orders from only one superior. He believed that recognition and observance of this principle would eliminate the causes of interdepartmental and interpersonal conflict arising out of jurisdictional issues. He also noted that the tendency of some superiors to bypass the chain of command and the difficulty of writing completely unambiguous job descriptions were principal causes of disruptions in the unity-of-command principle.

5. Unity of Direction. Each group of activities having the same direction should operate under one head and one plan. Fayol observed that this principle should not be confused with the unity-of-command principle. Unity of direction derives from a sound organizational structure which is departmentalized in an appropriate manner; the principle refers to the structure of the organization. Unity of command refers to the functioning of personnel within the structure. Unity of direction does not assure unity of command, but unity of command cannot exist without unity of direction.

6. Subordination of Individual Interest to General Interest. This principle states that the whole is greater than the sum of its parts, and that the overall objectives which the group seeks to achieve take precedence over the objectives of individuals.

7. Remuneration of Personnel. The remuneration of workers and managers for services rendered should be based on a systematic attempt to reward well-directed effort. Fayol regarded no particular wage system as a substitute for management competence. He discussed the advantages and disadvantages of various compensation plans, including piecerate, day rate, task rate, and profit-sharing plans.

8. Centralization. Fayol defined centralization as the degree to which the importance of subordinates' roles is reduced. He stated that the degree of centralization should be related to the character of the manager, the reliability of subordinates, and the conditions of the business. Fayol recognized that these circumstances are quite varied and that they change over time. It is the responsibility of managers to determine the appropriate balance which will "give the best overall yield."

9. Scalar Chain. The graded chain of authority from top to bottom through which all communications flow is termed the scalar chain. This chain implements the unity-of-command principle and provides for the orderly transmission of information. Yet Fayol recognized that strict adherence to the scalar chain can result in delay and frustrated employees.

Therefore he prescribed the use of "the gangplank principle," which authorizes persons at the same level to communicate directly, rather than through channels, so long as their superiors are aware of the situation and know in advance the kinds of issues to be resolved in this manner. Fayol introduced the problem of lateral communications and made explicit provision for carrying on such communications without threatening the integrity of the scalar chain.

10. *Order.* Fayol applied the principle of order to the material and human resources of the firm. This principle states that even as the material instruments of business must be arranged logically and neatly, so must the human instruments. To establish order in the human sphere, the manager must determine the exact nature and content of each job and demonstrate its relationship to the end product and to other jobs. These interrelationships appear in the form of an organization chart. All business concerns should have such a chart to guide the orderly arrangement of employees.

11. *Equity.* Fayol defined equity as the enforcement of established rules tempered by a sense of kindliness and justice. He believed that employees respond to equitable treatment by carrying out their duties in a sense of loyalty and devotion.

12. *Stability of Tenure of Personnel.* Fayol had observed that prosperous firms usually had a stable group of managerial personnel. He thus stated as a general principle that top management should implement practices which encourage the long-term commitment of employees, particularly of managers, to the firm.

13. *Initiative.* A principle corollary to those of unity of command and centralization states that employees must be encouraged to think through and implement a plan of action. Fayol believed that the opportunity to exercise initiative is a powerful motivator. The only limits on personal initiative should be the authority relationship defined by the scalar chain and by the employee's sense of discipline.

14. *Esprit de Corps.* Fayol defined *esprit de corps* as unity of effort through harmony of interests. In his view, the most effective means for achieving *esprit de corps* is through unity of command, and through oral rather than written communication. Many approaches to the creation of a sense of unity and harmony exist; Fayol suggested only those methods which seemed important to him.

Over the years, Fayol's principles were much discussed and much criticized in the literature on management. In any evaluation, the time and place in which they emerged should be kept in mind and should be an accurate reflection of Fayol's intent. He stated that the list of principles was not exhaustive, "This list has no precise limits;" the list of principles was not to endure regardless of time and place: "It [the list] seems *at the moment* especially useful . . . appropriate to concentrate general discussion." The principles do not answer questions of degree or specificity, but Fayol was not suggesting that the principles would absolve management from the responsibility for determining what he termed "the appropriate balance." Indeed, he emphasized time and again that the moral character of the manager would determine the ultimate outcome.

Management Functions. Fayol elaborated the managerial process by identifying five functions in which managers must engage as:

A. Planning   B. Organizing   C. Commanding
D. Coordinating   E. Controlling

Planning includes all those activities of a manager which result in a course of action. The manager should make the best possible forecast of future events that affect the firm and draw up an operating plan that guides future decisions.

Organizing includes all activities which result in a structure of tasks and authority. This managerial element determines the appropriate machines, material, and human mix necessary to accomplish the task. The manager will be successful in his performance of this function to the extent that he

1. Insures that the organization plan is judiciously prepared and carried out.
2. Sees that the organization structure is consistent with the resources and objectives of the firm.
3. Establishes a clear chain of authority from top to bottom.
4. Harmonizes and coordinates efforts and activities.
5. Formulates clear, distinct, and precise decisions.
6. Arranges for the efficient selection of personnel.
7. Defines duties clearly.
8. Encourages initiative and responsibility.
9. Develops a fair wage and salary system.
10. Uses appropriate sanctions to correct errors.
11. Maintains discipline.
12. Subordinates individual interests to the general interest.
13. Assures that for each man there is only one boss.
14. Supervises material and human order.
15. Has everything under control.
16. Discourages excessive use of regulations and red tape.

Fayol terms these 16 guides "Administrative Duties." They are based upon his own work experience and thus have an empirical, although modest, foundation.

Commanding activities are concerned with directing the activities of subordinates. To be successful, Fayol suggests, the manager should set a good example and know thoroughly the personnel and the agreements made between the personnel and the firm. The managers should have direct, two-way communication with subordinates. Furthermore, the manager should continually evaluate the organizational structure and subordinates, and he should not hesitate to change their structure if he considers it faulty, or to fire subordinates if they are incompetent.

Coordinating activities are those which bind together all individual efforts and direct them toward a common objective. Thus Fayol saw coordinating as simply another element of the total managerial process. The concept of management used in this textbook, on the other hand, suggests that coordination is the key element of the process.

Controlling activities are those which assure that actual activities are consistent with planned activities. Fayol did not expand the concept beyond stating that everything should be "subject to control."

Fayol's analysis provides a *means* (the five functions) for viewing the managerial process and *guides* (the principles) for implementing the process. The framework itself lacks logical clarity since it suggests nothing about the primacy of certain principles or the causality among these principles. It did, however, establish a basis for further elaboration by subsequent writers.

James Mooney

In 1931, James D. Mooney and Alan C. Reiley authored *Onward Industry,* which was revised in 1947 by Mooney and entitled *The Principles of Organization.*[4] This book is a most important part of the literature of classical management thought and, as will be seen, complements Fayol's work while also adding a new dimension.

Mooney viewed management as the technique, or art, of directing and inspiring other men. Organization, on the other hand, is the technique of relating specific duties or functions in a coordinated whole. The interrelationship between the two concepts is immediately apparent when we recognize that the duty of management is to provide its administrative instrument—an organization. Mooney's personal experience and his examination of organization in governmental, church, military, and industrial institutions were the bases for a framework of concepts which describes the essential nature of organizations.

The conceptual framework is based upon a system of logical argument which postulates that every *principle* has its *process* and *effect,* and that each process and effect (if correctly identified) will have a *principle, process, and effect.*[5] This analytical approach may appear unduly cumber-

---

[4] James D. Mooney, *The Principles of Organization* (New York: Harper and Brothers, 1947).

[5] This form of deductive reasoning was used by Louis F. Anderson, whose work Mooney acknowledged. The reader can consult Louis F. Anderson, *Logic and the Cosmic Order* (New York: The Theistic Society, 1940) for a complete description of this mode of logical reasoning.

some; yet it was important enough in the development of classical organization theory to warrant the student's best efforts to understand it. Essentially, it involves the definition of the supreme principle, or ultimate value, which underlies purposive activity. Such activity, or process, is observable behavior that leads to a definite and observable objective or effect. This framework, along with Mooney's labels, is shown in Table 3–1.

TABLE 3–1

	Principle	Process	Effect
Coordinating *Principle*	Authority	Processive Coordination	Effective Coordination
Scalar *Process*	Leadership	Delegation	Functional Definition
Functional *Effect*	Determinative Functionalism	Applicative Functionalism	Interpretative Functionalism

Mooney's analysis is explained as follows:

1. The primary, i.e., categorical, principle of organization is *coordination*, which "is the orderly arrangement of group effort to provide unity of action in the pursuit of a common purpose."[6] All other principles are subordinate to this primary one and are means by which coordination operates and becomes effective. The activity which implements coordination is the *scalar process*—the means by which a graded chain of authority is created. The result of implementing the scalar process is the *functional effect*, which constitutes the definition of the duties and responsibilities of each job and jobholder.

2. The coordinative principle, for completeness, must have its own principle, process, and effect. The principle is *authority*, the right to command derived from the appropriate legitimate source—the people, God, or private property. *Processive coordination* refers to all ongoing activities whose objective is to bring about unity and direction of each person's activity. The intended result of processive coordination is *effective coordination*, i.e., positive goal-directed effort.

3. The scalar process is the grading of individuals or units according to degrees of authority, i.e., it is vertical specialization. The determining principle of the scalar process is leadership, which is the personification of authority. The leader influences the group, and it is through his efforts that coordination is achieved. The means by which leadership achieves

[6] Mooney, *op. cit.*, p. 5.

coordination is *delegation*—the assignment of authority downward, upward, and outward.

To demonstrate the relationships between authority, leadership, and delegation, Mooney describes three different styles of leadership behavior. The first is represented by the leader who is very quick to delegate authority and, if possible, his own responsibility. Such a leader is one in name only, since he dislikes responsibilities and their obligations. The second style is one where the necessity for delegation of authority is recognized, but where the leader also recognizes that he can never rid himself of his own responsibility. Mooney identifies such men as the geniuses of organization. The third style of leader delegates responsibility only when it is physically impossible for him to do the job himself; however, he fails to delegate commensurate authority. Mooney suggested that there are other leadership styles, but that these three describe the most common instances.

The end result of the scalar process, *functional definition*, is the sum of delegated authority—the vertical chain of command. It is the basis by which supervisors are distinguished from blue-collar workers, sergeants from privates, bishops from priests, deans from professors. Each of these paired comparisons is distinguished in terms of "gradations in authority and is, therefore, scalar."[7] However, if we are to distinguish between two positions at the same level in the scalar chain, we must speak of differences in assigned duties, or functions.

4. *Functional effect* is the end result of the coordinative principle and the scalar process, and the concept refers to the acts which individuals are expected to perform, their job descriptions. Mooney referred to the distinctions that can be made between the production manager, the sales manager, and the finance officer at one level and between the setup man, machine operator, and shipping clerk at another level. Mooney observed that every organized activity which he had studied had three separate and distinct functions—*determinative, applicative,* and *interpretative.* The determinative function specifies the broad objectives—what is to be done, i.e., planning. The applicative function is the actual doing of what is to be done, i.e., executing. And the interpretative function is the analysis whether what was done conforms to expectations, i.e., controlling. All three functions are found in every organization, and in some degree in every job within the organization.

Mooney's analysis provides a framework of concepts, which are related through logical deduction. It is a basis for describing and understanding the management of organizations. Mooney made valuable contributions to management theory; his ideas were compatible with Fayol's, though

---

[7] *Ibid.*, p. 25.

each arrived at his ideas independently. The job of integrating their views was to be undertaken by Lyndall Urwick.

Lyndall Urwick

A most important landmark in the literature of management is Lyndall Urwick's *The Elements of Administration.*[8] Urwick combined and synthesized the ideas of Fayol, Mooney, and Taylor into one conceptual framework. It is with Urwick's analysis that scientific management and classical organization theory blend and classical management theory begins to emerge. It provided practitioners and students of management with the basis for understanding the managerial process as it relates to the total business enterprise. Its level of abstraction permits broad comprehension, yet it is concrete enough to provide insights into specific managerial functions.

The framework which Urwick devised uses Mooney's approach, and provides a complete description of the entire managerial process. Urwick's analysis moves through three levels of abstraction, beginning with the identification of basic business *operations:* security, accounting, financial, technical, administrative, and marketing. Each of these operations must be related through *plans* which provide appropriate objectives, appropriate resources, and appropriate organization.

Planning. The categorical principle of management as shown in Figure 3–1 is scientific *investigation* of facts for purposes of *forecasting.* The result (effect) of forecasting is a *plan* which directs the scope, nature, and interrelationship of each business operation.[9] Thus, the basic task or function of management is to deal effectively and efficiently with the future. This is the first level of analysis: to identify in broad terms the nature of management. Urwick moved on to a second level of analysis in which he described the concepts of *coordination* and *control,* as shown in Figure 3–2.

Coordination. Forecasting involves the determination of the appropriate mix of human and natural resources as required by the firm's objectives and as limited by its capacity to obtain resources. The resources must be related to one another in a system of activities (1) which are necessary for the completion of the plan and (2) which are arranged in groups and assigned to individuals, this being the process of organizing. The organization makes possible coordination of the diverse activities.

Urwick moved to a third level of analysis of coordination. The objec-

---

[8] Lyndall Urwick, *The Elements of Administration* (New York: Harper and Brothers, 1944).

[9] This discussion is based upon Urwick, *ibid.* The student is advised to follow carefully the discussion and refer to the figures for clarification.

tive of coordination is to provide a structure of tasks and authority which assures that the three types of functions identified by Mooney, *determinative, applicative*, and *interpretative*, are provided. Each business operation must include the appropriate balance of these functions. More specifically, each job must be defined in terms of its required activity and its assigned authority. The required activity, division of labor, is termed the

FIGURE 3–1

The Fundamental Principle—Process—Effect of Management:
The First Level of Analysis

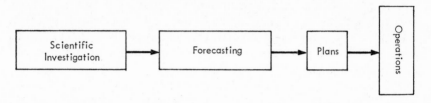

functional effect, and it results from the *scalar process*. At the same time, authority must be delegated in a manner which assures that the assigned tasks are completed; *leadership* is the essence of the process of delegating authority. The end product is termed *functional definition:* the specific delineation of duties in terms of assigned authority. Figure 3–3 demonstrates the relationships among these concepts.

The activation of the coordinative principle results in a structure of

FIGURE 3–2

Identification of Coordination and Control: The Second Level of Analysis

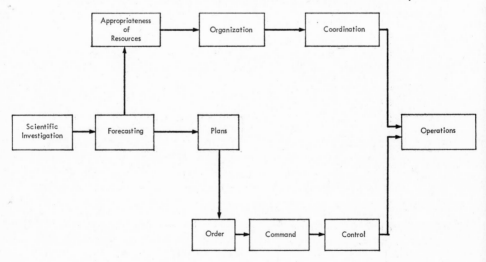

tasks and authority without regard to people. It is a "wiring diagram," an arrangement of activities and duties required by the technical demands of the firm's mission and constrained by the availability of resources. The problem of energizing the structure with material and human resources is confronted by the control function.

Control. A fundamental objective of planning is to provide systematic

FIGURE 3–3

The Coordinative Function: The Third Level of Analysis

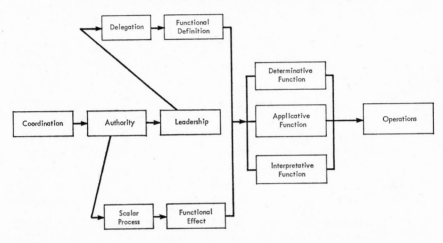

action directed toward accomplishing the objectives of the firm. To assure that all resources, human and physical, are directed to the prescribed ends, *order*, i.e., certainty or near-certainty, must exist as to the existence and function of all resources. From this principle, it follows that managerial action must be undertaken to implement order; such action is termed *command*. The result of this activity is goal-directed behavior or *control*, by all members of the firm. This analysis is shown in Figure 3–2 along with the previously discussed analysis of coordination. Urwick moved on to a third level of analysis of control as shown in Figure 3–4 and as described below.

Urwick was well aware of the necessity for acquiring the commitment of the job holders to the goals of the firm. Urwick proposed that the proper implementation of certain principles and processes will lead to a stable and unified staff which exercises initiative in the performance of its tasks, thus resulting in the desired commitment. Urwick termed these effects *stability, esprit de corps,* and *initiative.* Let us see how these results are to be achieved.

The control function is effectuated by *centralization, selection and placement,* and *equity.* Centralization as Urwick viewed it is the provision of ultimate authority for the resolution of conflicts that arise from the delegation of authority. To assure that such conflict is resolved, *staffing* must be guided by the need to acquire competent managerial personnel. The degree of unity or *esprit de corps* found in the firm depends directly upon the success of the staffing process. As Urwick states, "Organization

FIGURE 3–4

The Control Function: The Third Level of Analysis

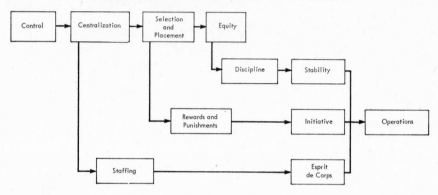

—the design on the drawing board—takes life and fire, becomes an organism, only through personality, a commander who can lead, helped by subordinates whose spirit is fused with his."[10]

The purpose of selection and placement is to provide the firm with a cadre of personnel who perform their tasks with a sense of *initiative.* The underlying process which determines the level and extent of initiative is the system of *rewards* and *sanctions.* Urwick recognized that a whole range of human motives exists which account for human behavior. Certainly, the financial reward system would be extremely important for the promotion of initiative, yet Urwick included more than financial rewards. He argued that the appropriate use of nonfinancial incentives is an important part of managerial command, and he recognized the need for much scientific investigation into the nature of human motivation.

To complete the classical model, Urwick developed the argument that staff *stability* results from the activation of the *equity* principle, in the form of *discipline.* Urwick followed Fayol's reasoning that stability is an important characteristic of successful firms. Furthermore, he believed that excessive turnover is the major outcome of management's failure to implement properly the system of discipline made necessary by the tasks to be undertaken. He warned against the imposition of disciplinary mea-

---

[10] *Ibid.,* p. 82.

FIGURE 3-5
The Conceptual Framework of Classical Management

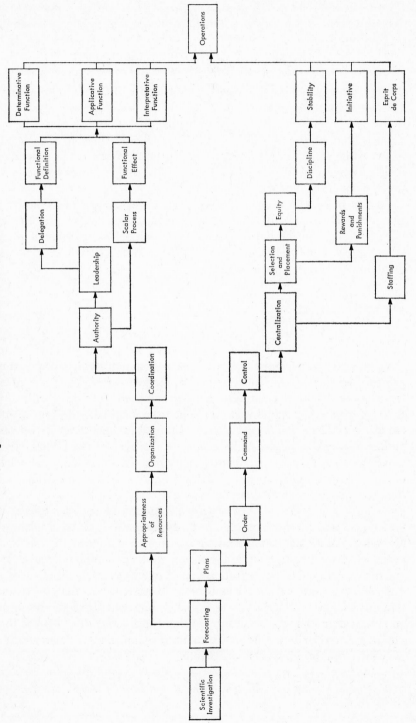

sures for their own sake, and he was particularly sensitive to the problem of "red tape," a phenomenon that he had observed during his military and civil service careers.

The result of Urwick's attempt to synthesize the work of his predecessors is the conceptual framework shown in Figure 3–5. Granted the limitations of the scheme, it does provide a description of the managerial process in an institution previously not subject to rigorous analysis—the individual business firm. Urwick's approach enables the analyst, whether a practitioner or an academician, to discover the relationship of each part to the whole by asking the following questions: What is the overriding issue (the principle)? How is the issue resolved operationally (the process)? What is the outcome (the effect)?

At this point, the student should be aware of the work of Chester I. Barnard, whose analysis of management and organization provides an effective link with the behavioral science approaches. Whether Barnard is a classicist is subject to debate; his contributions are, however, fundamental in the development of the field.

Chester I. Barnard

The insights of Chester I. Barnard have influenced the development of management thought in significant ways. In fact, his ideas are so pervasive that our efforts to condense and summarize them will surely not do justice to them. Barnard had a background similar to those of Fayol, Mooney, and Urwick. He was a practicing manager, an executive with New Jersey Bell Telephone, where he was president from 1927 until his retirement. He also shared his colleagues' interest in analyzing the function he was performing; he wanted to make "sense" of his job and to provide others with the concepts that make sense of management. His ideas were widely circulated in the form of papers, speeches, and books. The most important source of his ideas is *The Functions of the Executive*.[11]

Barnard, who believed that the basic function of the executive is to provide the basis for *cooperative* effort, defined organization as a system of goal-directed cooperative activities. Barnard went on to analyze management's functions to include the formulation of objectives and the acquisition of resources and efforts required to meet the stated objectives. This point of view is quite compatible with those of Fayol, Mooney, and Urwick. The new dimension that Barnard introduced was his emphasis on communications as means for acquiring cooperation. He believed that the system of communication within the organization is the means by which persons are induced to cooperate.

---

[11] Chester Barnard, *The Functions of the Executive* (Cambridge: Harvard University Press, 1938).

According to Barnard, the degree of employee cooperation depends upon the balance between inducements and contributions. Inducements include the sum total of financial and nonfinancial rewards which accrue to the individual in exchange for his efforts, i.e., his contributions. The purpose of communication is to provide the individual with the necessary information to evaluate the desired balance. At the same time, Barnard recognized that the communication system is the active process by which authority is implemented. Orders are transmitted downward as superiors seek to acquire certain behavior from their subordinates. He stated that the existence of the formal structure is no guarantee that subordinates would in fact follow orders.

Barnard challenged the wisdom of relying solely upon the authority structure to achieve compliance. Indeed, he stated a position that has become known as the *acceptance theory* of authority. This theory postulates that the subordinate himself will determine whether an order is legitimate, and whether to accept or reject it. He will accept the order only if he can understand it and is able to comply with it. Perhaps more importantly, he will accept it (even if understood) only if the required behavior is consistent with his view of the purposes of the organization *and his own* personal interests.

The ideas of Barnard have been woven into the practice and theory of modern management. It is now generally accepted that the manager must know a great deal about human behavior. As we shall see in subsequent chapters, the analysis of human behavior, singly and in groups, by behavioral scientists has added significant insights; but we must recognize the importance of Barnard as their forerunner.

SUMMARY OF CLASSICAL MANAGEMENT THEORY

Classical management theory defines management as the process of securing coordinated group effort through the application of planning, organizing, and controlling principles and techniques. We have emphasized the efforts of a selected few who participated in these early efforts to define and analyze the managerial process. What we have seen is the emergence of a rather elaborate scheme of logically and systematically related concepts. Some students may object to our regarding Urwick as the principal integrator of classical management theory, but we know of no one else who provided us with an integrated statement of the classical position.

The classical theory emphasizes structure and formal relationships, but does not ignore the human element. The classical writers understood that the human element could greatly affect the best-planned organization. They called upon others to devote time and energy to the development of knowledge about man at work; the classicists themselves did not have the basic training to develop a science of industrial psychology. We did observe in our discussion the efforts of Munsterberg to create such a science. We also acknowledged the implications of Chester Barnard's ideas regarding authority and communication. We shall see in later chapters how the work of behavioral scientists has added to classical management theory.

DISCUSSION AND REVIEW QUESTIONS

1. What do the authors mean when they say that classical organization theory deals with more complex and abstract problems than those which scientific management confronted?
2. Compare the ideologies of classical organization theory and scientific management.
3. What are "principles of management" as Fayol defined and explained them? Compare Fayol's and Mooney's ideas regarding principles.
4. What are the principles of being a "good student"?
5. "There must be a scalar process in all organized activity." Oh, yeah! How about a family? Comment.
6. Explain how Urwick combined scientific management and classical organization theory.
7. What new dimensions did Barnard add to classical theory?
8. How would a scientist go about testing classical management theory? How would a manager go about applying classical management theory? Which is more important to you personally—testing or applying?
9. Summarize classical management theory in a short paragraph.
10. "Classical management theory is planning, organizing, and controlling." Is that all there is? (With apologies to Peggy Lee.)

ADDITIONAL REFERENCES

BARNARD, C. I. *Organization and Management.* Cambridge: Harvard University Press, 1952.

DAVIS, R. C. *The Principles of Factory Organization and Management.* New York: Harper and Bros., 1928.

METCALF, H. C., AND URWICK, L. (eds.) *Dynamic Administration: The Collected Works of Mary Parker Follett.* New York: Harper and Brothers, 1942.

ROWNTREE, B. S. *The Human Factor in Business: Experiments in Industrial Democracy.* London: Longmans, Green and Co., 1921.

URWICK, L. (ed.) *The Golden Book of Management.* London: Newman Neame Ltd., 1956.

WEBER, M. *The Theory of Social and Economic Organization.* Glencoe, Ill.: Free Press, 1957.

chapter four

The Planning Function

INTRODUCTION

The fundamental and primary managerial activity is planning. As we discussed earlier, the organizing and controlling functions are derived from the planning function. The preeminent position of planning was recognized by both Taylor and Urwick. Taylor believed that planning and executing are separate functions, with management being responsible for the former and the worker being responsible for the latter. This theme was subsequently carried through in Urwick's interpretation of classical management theory, as we noted in the preceding chapter.

The planning function includes all the managerial activities which lead to the definition of goals and the determination of appropriate means to achieve these goals. The function can be broken down into four distinct phases:

Phase 1—Establishing goals and fixing their priority.

Phase 2—Forecasting future events which can affect goal accomplishment.

Phase 3—Making the plans operational through budgeting.

Phase 4—Stating and implementing policies which direct the firm's activities toward the desired ends.

Each phase must be completed and related to other phases in order to complete the planning process. The end result is an overall plan which guides the firm toward the predetermined goals. In the remainder of this chapter each phase is discussed and some of the more useful managerial planning techniques are described.

57

GOAL SETTING AND ORDERING

The planning function begins with analyses of the goals which the firm seeks to accomplish, without which the organization would be an aimless entity. Goals have at least three dimensions: *priority, time,* and *structure.*

Priority of Goals

Priority of goals implies that, at a given point in time, the accomplishment of one goal is relatively more important than others. For example, the goal of maintaining a minimum cash balance may be critically important to a firm having difficulty meeting payrolls and due dates on accounts. Priority of goals also says something about the relative importance of certain goals regardless of time. For example, survival of the firm is a necessary condition (objective) for the realization of all other goals.

Timing of Goals

The time dimension of goals implies that the firm's activities are guided by different objectives depending upon the duration of the action; it is traditional to speak of short-run, intermediate, and long-run goals. Short-run goals are those which extend for a period of less than a year; intermediate goals are those covering one to five years; and long-run goals are those extending beyond five years. The relationship between priority and timing of goals is quite close since the long-run goals tend to be stated in terms of "ultimates," that is, those objectives which must be accomplished in order to assure the long-run survival of the firm.

Structure of Goals

A third dimension of goals is structure. The process of breaking down the firm into units—for example, production, sales, and finance—requires that goals be assigned to each unit. Each unit is then given the responsibility for attaining an assigned goal. The process of allocating goals among various units creates the problem of potential goal conflict and suboptimization, wherein achieving the goals of one unit may jeopardize achieving the goals of another. For example, the production goal of low unit cost achieved through mass production of low-quality products may conflict with the sales goal of selling high-quality, high-markup products. The resolution of this problem is a careful balance of the goal for each unit, with the recognition that the goal of neither unit can be maximized. The result is a situation known as suboptimization of goals.

The problem of suboptimization of goals can be understood by recognizing a second aspect of goal structure.[1] If we view the business firm from the perspective of all those who have a stake in its operation, and if we recognize that the ends which each seeks in the firm's operation are potentially in conflict, we can readily understand the problem. Thus, at any point in time, stockholders (owners), employees (including unions), customers, suppliers, creditors, and governmental agencies are all concerned with the operation of the firm. The process of goal setting must recognize the relative importance of each of these groups, and the plans must incorporate and integrate their interests. The exact form and relative weight to be given to any particular interest group is precisely the nature of management's dilemma; yet it is precisely management's responsibility to make these kinds of judgments.

The management of the business firm must consider the expectations of these diverse groups because the firm's ultimate success depends upon them. For example, present and potential customers are the ultimate holders of power over the firm. If they are not happy with the price and quality of the firm's product, they withdraw their support (they stop buying), and the firm fails because of lack of funds. Suppliers have the power to disrupt the flow of their materials to express disagreement with the firm's activities. Governmental agencies have power to enforce the firm's accommodation to regulations which, in modern times, are affecting nearly every aspect of the firm's operation.[2] The existence of these interest groups and the fact of their power to affect the goal structure of the firm express the reality that the business firm is a social invention; the firm will exist only so long as it satisfies the larger society.

Profit-Seeking as a Goal

The widely recognized and understood fact that business firms, by their very nature, seek a wide range of goals has contributed to a generally blurred image of the role of profit-seeking as a goal. There is a general acceptance that firms do not seek maximum profits as hypothesized in classical economic theory. Such an objective is impossible to achieve since it requires not only perfect knowledge of all future events which affect the firm's cost and revenue, but also perfectly rational decision-makers at all levels in the organization.[3] Yet, even though one may dismiss

---

[1] See R. W. Morell, *Management: Ends and Means* (San Francisco, Calif.: Chandler Publishing Co., 1969), pp. 5–30, for a discussion of multiple goals and a suggested hierachy of goals.

[2] For a complete analysis of the relationship between power and goal setting, See A. D. Newman and R. W. Rowbottom, *Organizational Analysis* (Carbondale, Ill.: Southern Illinois University Press, 1968), pp. 101–8.

[3] The realization that maximum profit is an unrealistic goal has led to the suggestion that satisfactory profit is a reasonable goal to seek. See James G. March and Herbert A. Simon, *Organizations* (New York: John Wiley and Sons, 1958), pp. 140–41; and Herbert A. Simon, "Theories of Decision-Making in Economics and Behavioral Science," *American Economic Review*, vol. 19 (June, 1959), pp. 262–65.

"profit maximization" as a goal, one cannot also dismiss "profit seeking." Indeed, we must not lose sight of the primary mission of the business firm—to make a profit in exchange for the production of goods and services deemed desirable by society. Unless the firm satisfies this objective, it cannot accomplish any other.

At the same time, to say that profit is a *necessary* condition for the firm's survival is not to say that it is *sufficient* to insure it. A profitable firm earning a satisfactory return on stockholders' equity and paying a satisfactory dividend may not last long if it is not meeting the needs of employees for satisfactory working conditions or the demands of creditors for prompt payment of debt, or the insistence of governmental agencies

FIGURE 4–1

Goals of the Business Firm

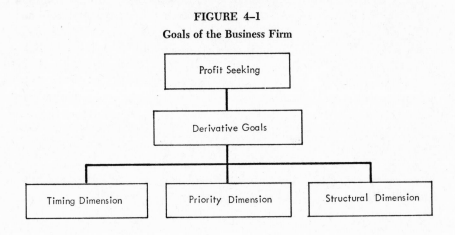

for appropriate response to regulatory legislation. Society expects much from the contemporary business firm, but its fundamental expectation is that the management will use scarce resources in an efficient manner in the production of goods and services. Profit is the principal means by which the firm's management is assessed. All other goals are derivatives of the basic goal of profit seeking.

Figure 4–1 summarizes the discussion up to this point. It demonstrates that profit seeking is the ultimate objective of the firm and that all other objectives are derived from and must be compatible with it. The various dimensions of goals which must be recognized in the goal-setting process are also shown. It should be pointed out that the final interpretation of the exact nature and mix of the firm's goals will depend in great measure upon the manager's personal goal structure as well as on his technical capacity to deal effectively with the problem. As Walton so neatly put it, *"What to make, what to charge,* and *how to market the wares* are questions that embrace moral as well as economic questions. The answers are conditioned by the personal value system of the decision maker and the institutional values which affect the relationships of the individual to the community."[4]

Studies of Actual Goals

A recent study sheds some light on the relative importance of goals, and at the same time reemphasizes the importance of profit seeking as the ultimate goal. George W. England[5] surveyed 1,072 American managers to obtain their judgments of the goal structure which they themselves viewed as important. The managers included in the survey considered profit and related goals of efficiency and productivity to be of supreme importance. The respondents ranked as secondarily important certain goals pertaining to growth and stability. From the perspective of profitability, such goals can be viewed as directly related and even corollary to profitability. Ranked third in importance is a set of goals which concern employee welfare; ranked fourth are goals dealing with the general public, namely, social and community interests. England's survey results support similar studies of management goals.[6] Furthermore, as Filley and House have observed,[7] the empirical research to date suggests that goal structures which give first priority to customer-market-profitability oriented objectives are characteristic of successful firms. This is not to say that successful firms respond only to profit-oriented goals, but only that such goals are dominant. It also does not say that the dominant position of this goal is constant over time. Indeed, the tendency in recent years has been toward a reordering of priorities as the public's expectations have changed and as the public has implemented its power through governmental agencies. The responsibility of business to society beyond that of providing goods and services will not subside in the years to come.

The discussion of goals to this point has emphasized their relatively abstract qualities. The implementation of goals requires that they be made concrete and specific, a requirement that raises two issues: (1) the clarity and unity of goals and (2) the measurement of goals.

---

[4] Clarence C. Walton, *Ethos and the Executive* (Englewood Cliffs, N.J.: Prentice-Hall, Inc., 1969), p. 192.

[5] George W. England, "Organizational Goals and Expected Behavior of American Managers," *Academy of Management Journal*, vol. 10 (June, 1967), pp. 107–17.

[6] See James K. Dent, "Organizational Correlates of the Goals of Business Management," *Personnel Psychology*, vol. 12 (August, 1959), pp. 365–93; and J. H. Healey, *Executive Coordination and Control* (Columbus, Ohio: Bureau of Business Research, Ohio State University, 1956).

[7] Alan C. Filley and Robert J. House, *Managerial Process and Organizational Behavior* (Glenview, Ill.: Scott, Foresman and Company, 1969), p. 146.

Clarity and Unity of Goals

Goals should be defined in terms that are understandable and acceptable to those who must produce the effort required to achieve them. In practice, effective managerial action requires goal setting in every area which contributes to the overall goals. One observer of business management, Peter Drucker,[8] has stated that subgoals must be set in at least eight areas, namely, (1) market standing, (2) innovation, (3) productivity, (4) physical and financial resources, (5) profitability, (6) manager performance and responsibility, (7) worker performance and attitude, and (8) public responsibility. Drucker's classification in no way implies relative importance; he is simply pointing out the necessity for considering the entire range of subgoals. The priority of each subgoal will depend upon the conditions confronting the firm at the particular point in time.

The manner in which the subgoals are allocated to personnel in the firm depends in large part upon the organizational structure, particularly the degree of horizontal specialization. The next chapter develops the organizing process; therefore we need not go into its discussion at this point. It must be recognized here that it is important to assign goals in a clear and unambiguous way, and that the ultimate test of clarity is the recipient's understanding of the goal statement. At the same time, this statement must not be so detailed that it becomes a straightjacket which restricts the freedom of the subunit manager to exercise initiative.

The person assigned the responsibility for goal achievement enters into the process in a very important way. He himself is the final arbiter as to the appropriateness of the goal. As Barnard[9] pointed out, each participant in an organization determines for himself the range of acceptable behavior, and if the activities required of him are outside this range, he will not pursue the objective. A production-line foreman can find all kinds of legitimate means to foil a production schedule if the meeting of that plan requires behavior unacceptable to him; for example, if it requires a heavy-handed approach to push his subordinates to levels of production beyond those which they themselves believe appropriate. Thus, the necessity for clarity of goals includes not only clear and unambiguous communication, but also consistency with the individual goals of the person assigned the responsibility for goal achievement.

The subunit goals must be compatible with and contribute to the overall goals. This is what is meant by "unity of direction." The relationship between each subgoal and the ultimate goal must be apparent to all

---

[8] Peter Drucker, *The Practice of Management* (New York: Harper and Brothers, 1954).

[9] Chester Barnard, *The Functions of the Executive* (Cambridge, Mass.: Harvard University Press, 1938).

concerned; otherwise the firm runs the danger of drift. The final test of the legitimacy and adequacy of each subgoal must be resolved in terms of the ultimate goal. Even so, if the goals are incapable of measurement, management's concern for clarity and unity will go for naught.

Measurement of Goals

As Drucker observed, "The real difficulty lies indeed not in determining what objectives we need, but in deciding how to set them."[10] The only approach, according to Drucker, is to determine *what* should be measured in each area, and *how* it should be measured. Immediately one can recognize the difficulty of measuring goals in certain areas. How, for example, does one measure manager and worker development, or public responsibility? The more abstract the goal, the more difficult it is to measure performance. Additionally, the measurement of abstract goals by quantitative means can lead to the problem of measurement orientation, i.e., the tendency to focus attention on the measurement and away from the substance of the goal. Those in academic fields are familiar with the manifestation of this problem in universities and colleges which measure teaching and research accomplishment in terms of quantity of students graduated and articles published.

Nevertheless, effective planning requires goal measurement. A variety of measurements exist for each area.

Profitability measures include profit return on sales, on total assets, and on capital (net worth). The tendency in recent years has been to emphasize the profit/sales ratio as the important test of profitability,[11] perhaps because both quantities required to calculate this measure are taken directly from the income statement, which management generally regards as a better test of performance than the balance sheet. However, many managers believe that the true test of profitability must combine the income statement and the balance sheet. Accordingly, such managers would use the profit/net-worth ratio. The arguments for and against the use of either of these two are basically due to differences in point of view as to whether *source* of capital is an important consideration. The profit/total-asset ratio measures the efficiency of management's use of all resources regardless of origin (i.e., creditors or owners), whereas the profit/net-worth ratio measures managerial efficiency only in terms of the use of the owners' contribution.

The resolution of the problem which profitability measure to select lies in the recognition that the measures are not mutually exclusive. All three can be used to set and evaluate profitability objectives, since each mea-

---

[10] Drucker, *op. cit.*, p. 64.

[11] *Ibid*, p. 79, and Neil W. Chamberlain, *The Firm: Micro-Economic Planning and Action* (New York: McGraw-Hill Book Co., 1962), p. 55.

sures a different, yet important aspect of the profit structure. However, the problem of the amount of profit remains to be solved, together with certain technical problems derived from the nature of accounting information. With respect to the amount of profit, we should recognize that the functions of profit are (1) to measure effectiveness, (2) to cover one cost element of being in business (return on invested capital), and (3) to provide funds for future expansion and innovation, either through retained earnings or through the capital market at rates made favorable because of the firm's history of profitability. Thus, the minimum profitability is that which assures the continuous stream of capital into the firm, given the inherent risks of the industry in which the firm operates.

A complete discussion of accounting theory as related to profitability measures is certainly beyond the scope of this book. However, it must be observed that the values assigned to balance sheet items are seldom true reflections of current or replacement cost values. The accounting convention of recording all assets at original cost results in the understatement of assets at future points in time during periods of inflation, and overstatement during periods of deflation. Measures of profitability must be based on accounting data that are adjusted for this distortion if one is to obtain relevant measures.

Marketing measures must relate products, markets, distribution, and customer service objectives. Figure 4–2 shows the matrix of decisions required in the analysis of products and markets. In each existing and potential market and for each existing and potential product, a specified goal must be established for total volume, market share, and profit. Coincidentally, management must develop an organization which will assure that resources are available to achieve the results.

FIGURE 4–2
Marketing Planning Matrix

	Existing Markets	New Markets
Existing Products	Target Volume Target Share Target Profit	Target Volume Target Share Target Profit
New Products	Target Volume Target Share Target Profit	Target Volume Target Share Target Profit

Productivity measures are basically ratios of output to input. Other factors being equal, the higher the ratio, the more efficient is the use of inputs. In traditional terms, productivity measures have related the output for certain inputs, for example, labor; these have been referred to as labor productivity. Yet, when different inputs are used together, it is quite difficult to identify which output is due to a particular input. Moreover, since the firm exists as an aggregation of resources which must be directed and coordinated to specified ends, the productivity measure should evaluate precisely that which results from the total effort, not the efforts of each part.

Drucker proposes that the *ratio of value added to sales and to profit* is the superior measure of productivity.[12] Furthermore, he states that the firm's objective should be to increase these ratios, and that units should be evaluated on the basis of these increases. His argument for value added, which he calls *contributed value,* is that it measures the increase in value of the purchased materials due to the combined efforts of the firm, since value added is equal to the difference between market value and purchased price of materials and supplies. Thus the efficiency of the firm's efforts is measured directly. Furthermore, this measure of productivity could be used for internal comparison of operating units.

Physical and financial measures reflect the firm's capacity to acquire resources sufficient for its larger objectives. The measurement of objectives in this area is comparatively easy due to the existence of quite a large number of accounting yardsticks which are appropriate for both physical and financial objectives. Rate-of-return measures are appropriate for setting objectives in decisions involving the acquisition of new plants and facilities. Liquidity and solvency measures are available for the measurement of financial objectives. Measures such as the current ratio, working capital turnover, the acid test, accounts receivable and inventory turnover, and debt to equity ratios can be used in setting objectives and evaluating results in the area of financial planning. These ratios are covered in greater detail in Chapter 6.

Subgoals in the areas of profitability, market standing, productivity, and physical and financial resources are amenable to measurement. Subgoals in areas such as innovation, management development, and public responsibility are not so easily identifiable and measurable in concrete terms. However, the important point to consider is that without some form of goal measurement subsequent evaluation, the control function, is necessarily quite inconclusive.

FORECASTING

The setting of goals must be implemented. The critical step in the implementation of goals is that of forecasting the future, the second phase

---

[12] Drucker, *op. cit.,* pp. 71–73.

of the planning process.[13] The results of the forecasts are included in budgets which are the major planning documents of the firm. The two basic issues that must be resolved through forecasting are: (1) what level of activity (short-run, intermediate-run, and long-run) can be expected during the planning period, and (2) what level of resources will be available to support the projected activity. The critical forecast upon which all others depend is the sales forecast.

Sales Forecasts

The projected future sales volume of the firm's product or service provides the basis for all other activities. The sales estimate sets the level of production and determines the level and timing of financial resources required to meet the sales volume. Because the sales forecast is so fundamental, we will discuss the methods for forecasting in the context of the sales forecast.

Forecasting is the process of using past and current information to predict future events. Thus the process involves information and techniques for information processing. There are four widely used methods, each of which requires its own type of data. These methods range in degree of sophistication from the hunches of experienced managers to econometric models.

Forecasting Approaches

Hunches are basically crude estimates of future events based upon past sales data, comments by salesmen and customers, and visceral reaction to the "general state of affairs." The hunch approach is relatively cheap and usually effective in firms whose market is stable or at least changing at a predictable rate.

Market surveys of customer intentions provided by the customer or by salesmen in the field can improve the accuracy of sales forecasts. At least, through the means of statistical sampling techniques, the forecaster can specify the range of projected sales and the degree of confidence that he has in his estimates. Of course, one should be very careful to evaluate the quality of information that goes into the market survey.

Time series analysis is a third technique of forecasting which, though it is a fairly complex statistical device, is no more effective than the good judgment of the analyst. Time series is nothing more than analysis of the relationship between sales and time, as shown in Figure 4–3. The chart shows points corresponding to the annual sales for each of the ten years.

---

[13] Refer to Harry D. Wolfe, *Business Forecasting Methods* (New York: Holt, Rinehart, and Winston, 1966) for a complete discussion of forecasting techniques.

A straight line is drawn through the points to show that there has been an upward pattern in the sales of the firm during the period.

The short-run question of sales during the first quarter of 1971 cannot be answered in Figure 4–3 if there is seasonality in the firm's sales pattern. If such were not the case, the quarterly sales would be approximately one quarter of the annual sales, but the sales of most firms are seasonal. If a company produces fishing equipment, the sharpest demand is during the spring and summer months, declining to quite low levels during the fall and winter. The prediction of annual sales can be at-

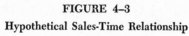

FIGURE 4–3

Hypothetical Sales-Time Relationship

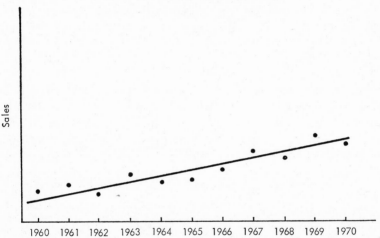

tempted from the annual data, provided one is willing to make the assumption that conditions which contributed to previous sales levels will prevail in the future. If not, the forecast must include variables other than time in the analysis.

The reader should not be led to believe that time series analysis is simply the naive projection of trend. It may be that in the hands of the unskilled, but if a skilled analyst is supplied with the right information, he can confront a whole range of questions. The movement of sales over time is due to at least three factors: seasonal, cyclical, and trend; that is, the firm's sales vary in response to seasonal factors, in response to cycles common to business activity generally, and to a trend of long-period duration. The management of a brewery knows that peak sales occur during the summer months, but is also aware of the cyclical nature of beer consumption as beer drinkers shift to liquor when their incomes increase, shifting back when their incomes decline. For long-term planning, the manager must also know something about the trend in beer consumption; consumer tastes change with time and with the introduction of new products. Yet, even the availability of these refinements does not undo the fact that time is the only determinant of sales included in the time-series analyses. Econometric models are means for systematically evaluating the impact of a number of variables on sales.

Econometric models are applications of multiple-correlation techniques to economic analysis. They permit the forecaster to discover the historical relationship between sales and a number of independent variables. These techniques are the most sophisticated of the methods, yet they offer no hope for the elimination of *all* uncertainty; management judgment is still needed.

The econometric approach begins with identification of those independent variables which would be expected to affect the sales of the firm's product. Among the obvious variables are price, competing products, and complementary products. Variables such as the age of existing stocks of the goods, availability of credit, and consumer tastes are less obvious. Measurements of these variables are obtained for previous years and matched with sales of the product for the same years. An equation is then derived which expresses the historical relationship between the variables. For example, if the sales volume of product Y is found to be related to variables X and Z, and the historical relationship is discovered to be

$$Y = 1.25X - 3.7Z,$$

then the forecaster need only predict the *future* values of X and Z to discover the future sales of Y. Now we see that the *forecast* of Y is derived from the *forecast* of X and Z.

No perfect method exists for projecting future sales. Hunches, surveys, and statistical analyses provide estimates which may or may not be reasonable. The estimates coming from these techniques can be no better than the information which goes into them. As technological breakthroughs in information processing occur, we can expect sales forecasts to become more accurate and consequently better guides for planning. At the present time, however, forecasting requires a great deal of managerial judgment.

The sales forecast, whether for one year or for ten years, is a prediction of the firm's level of activity. The prediction is conditioned by the availability of resources, general economic and social events beyond the province and control of management, and by the predetermined goals. The next phase of the planning process is the provision of resources necessary to sustain the forecasted level of activity. The principal means which management uses in this phase of the planning process are budgets.

BUDGETING

The third phase of the planning process is the creation of budgets for each important element of the firm. Budgets are widely used in business and government. A considerable body of literature exists dealing with budgeting techniques.[14] We should recognize the very close relationship between budgeting as a planning technique and budgeting as a control technique. In this section, we are concerned only with the preparation of budgets prior to operations. From this perspective, budgeting is a part of planning. However, with the passage of time and as the firm engages in its activities, the actual results are compared with the budgeted (planned) results. This analysis may lead to corrective action and this, as we shall see later, is the essense of controlling. The interrelationship between planning and controlling is well illustrated by the budgeting process.

Financial Budgeting

The financial budgeting process implements the income goals and objectives of the firm, and serves as the chief means for integrating the activities of all the various subunits. Budgeting can be viewed as an important method for coordinating the efforts of the firm.

The complexity of the financial budgeting process is revealed in Figure 4–4. The key position of the sales forecast is evident from the placement of the sales budget; all other budgets are related to it either directly or indirectly. For example, the production budget must specify the materials, labor, and other manufacturing expenses required to support the projected sales level. Similarly, the distribution expense budget details the costs associated with the level of sales activity projected for each product in each sales region. Administrative expenses also must be related to the predicted sales volume. The projected sales and expenses are combined in the financial budgets which consist of *pro forma* financial statements, inventory budgets, and the capital additions budget.

Two Budgeting Approaches

The usefulness of financial budgets depends mainly on the degree to which they are flexible to changes in conditions. The forecasted data are based upon certain premises or assumptions regarding the future. If these premises prove wrong, the budgets are inadequate. Two principal

---

[14] For example: Walter R. Bunge, *Managerial Budgeting for Profit Improvement* (New York: McGraw-Hill Book Co., Inc., 1968); Francis C. Dykeman, *Financial Reporting Systems and Techniques* (Englewood Cliffs, N.J.: Prentice-Hall, 1969); J. Brooks Heckert and James D. Willson, *Business Budgeting and Control* (New York: Ronald Press Co., 1967).

FIGURE 4–4

The Financial Budgeting Process*

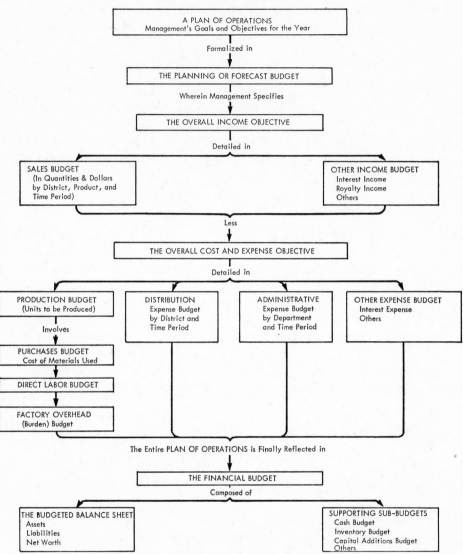

A PLAN OF OPERATIONS
Management's Goals and Objectives for the Year

Formalized in

THE PLANNING OR FORECAST BUDGET

Wherein Management Specifies

THE OVERALL INCOME OBJECTIVE

Detailed in

SALES BUDGET
(In Quantities & Dollars
by District, Product, and
Time Period)

OTHER INCOME BUDGET
Interest Income
Royalty Income
Others

Less

THE OVERALL COST AND EXPENSE OBJECTIVE

Detailed in

PRODUCTION BUDGET
(Units to be Produced)

DISTRIBUTION
Expense Budget
by District and
Time Period

ADMINISTRATIVE
Expense Budget
by Department
and Time Period

OTHER EXPENSE BUDGET
Interest Expense
Others

Involves

PURCHASES BUDGET
Cost of Materials Used

DIRECT LABOR BUDGET

FACTORY OVERHEAD
(Burden) Budget

The Entire PLAN OF OPERATIONS is Finally Reflected in

THE FINANCIAL BUDGET

Composed of

THE BUDGETED BALANCE SHEET
Assets
Liabilities
Net Worth

SUPPORTING SUB-BUDGETS
Cash Budget
Inventory Budget
Capital Additions Budget
Others

*Glenn A. Welsch, *Budgeting: Profit Planning and Control*, 2nd. ed., © 1964, p. 50. Reprinted by permission of Prentice-Hall, Inc., Englewood Cliffs, N.J.

means exist to provide flexibility, namely, variable budgeting and moving budgeting.

Variable budgeting accounts for the possibility that actual departs from planned output. It recognizes that certain costs are related to output (variable costs), while others are unrelated to output (fixed costs). Thus, if actual output is 20 percent less than planned output, it does not follow that actual profit will be 20 percent less than that planned. Rather, the actual profit will vary depending upon the quite complex relationship between costs and production. Figure 4–5 demonstrates a hypothetical situation.

FIGURE 4–5

The Relationship between Profit and Output

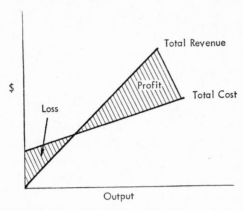

TABLE 4–1

A Hypothetical Variable Budget

Output (Units)		1000		1200		1400		1600
Sales @ $5.00		5000		6000		7000		8000
Variable Costs @ $3.00	3000		3600		4200		4800	
Fixed Costs	1000		1000		1000		1000	
Total Costs		4000		4600		5200		5800
Planned Profit		1000		1400		1800		2200

The relationships shown in Figure 4–5 take the form of the familiar break-even analysis which is explained in greater detail in a subsequent chapter. The point to be made here is simply that profit varies with output variations, but not proportionately. Table 4–1 shows a variable budget which allows for output variations and which demonstrates the behavior of costs and profits as output varies.

Variable budgeting requires adjustments in all supporting budgets for completeness. The production, distribution, and administrative budgets must likewise allow for the impact of output variation.

Moving budgeting is the preparation of a budget for a fixed period, say, one year, with periodic updating at fixed intervals, say, one month.

For example, the budget is prepared in December for the next 12 months, January through December. At the end of January, the budget is revised and projected for the next 12 months, February through January. In this manner, the most recent information is included in the budgeting process. Premises and assumptions are constantly being revised as the firm experiences reality.

Moving budgets have the advantage of systematic reexamination, but the disadvantage of becoming too costly to maintain. Budgets are important instruments for implementing the objectives of the firm; on the other hand, they must be kept in perspective and viewed as competing with other demands for managerial time.

POLICY-MAKING

The principal means by which management implements plans is through policy-making, the fourth phase of planning. *Policies are statements which reflect the basic objectives of the firm and which provide the guidelines for carrying out action throughout the firm.*[15] Policies, like plans, are both specific and general, abstract and concrete, short-run and long-run.

Policy-making is an important management tool for assuring that action taken by the firm is goal-oriented. Policies explain *how* the goals are to be achieved; they thus direct the behavior of persons in the firm. The interrelation among the managerial functions is reflected in the nature of policies. As we shall see, managerial *control* includes specification of action before the fact, and policies serve this end.

Effective policy-making requires recognition of the many dimensions and characteristics of policies. Ziegler[16] has suggested the following characteristics as important for creating effective policies:

1. *Flexibility.* A policy must strike a reasonable balance between stability and flexibility. Conditions change and policies must change accordingly. On the other hand, some degree of stability must prevail if order and a sense of direction are to be achieved. There are no rigid guidelines to specify the exact degree of requisite flexibility; only the judgment of management can determine the balance.
2. *Comprehensiveness.* A policy must be comprehensive enough to cover any contingency if plans are to be followed. The degree of comprehensiveness depends upon the scope of action controlled by the policy itself. If the policy is directed toward very narrow ranges of activity, for example, hiring policies, it need not be as comprehensive as a policy concerned with public relations.

---

[15] M. Valliant Higginson, *Management Policies I, AMA Research Study 76* (New York: American Management Association, 1966).

[16] Raymond J. Ziegler, *Business Policies and Decision Making* (New York: Appleton-Century-Crofts, 1966).

3. *Coordinative.* A policy must provide for coordination of the various subunits whose actions are interrelated. Without coordinative direction provided by policies, each subunit is tempted to pursue its own goals. The ultimate test of any subunit's activity should be its relationship to the policy statement.
4. *Ethical.* A policy must conform to the canons of ethical behavior which prevail in society. The manager is ultimately responsible for the resolution of issues which involve ethical principles. The increasingly complex and interdependent nature of contemporary society has resulted in a great number of problems involving ethical dimensions which are only vaguely understood.
5. *Clarity.* A policy must be written clearly and logically. It must specify the intended aim of the action which it governs, define the appropriate methods and action, and delineate the limits of freedom of action permitted to those whose actions are to be guided by it.

The ultimate test of the effectiveness of a policy is whether the intended objective is attained. If the policy does not lead to the goal, it should be revised. Thus, policies must be subjected to reexamination on a continual basis.

SUMMARY

The planning function is the fundamental managerial activity. It consists of four distinct subfunctions or elements: *goal setting, forecasting, budgeting,* and *policy-making.* We have seen that planning can have any time dimension ranging from the short to long run. We have also surveyed some of the more important forecasting and budgeting techniques. The student should not assume, however, that he has now surveyed the entire range of problems and issues associated with planning. At the same time, he should recognize that the essence of management is planning, and that all other functions are derived from planning.

DISCUSSION AND REVIEW QUESTIONS

1. Planning is *the* fundamental management function. Discuss.
2. A man designated by his employer as a "manager" says: "Plan? Hell, I never have time to plan. I live from day to day just trying to survive." Comment.
3. Planning involves goal setting and goal setting involves value judgments; planning then is the implementation of the manager's value system. True?
4. In what ways are the subgoals of a university suboptimized?
5. Describe potential conflicts between the goals of a production department and the goals of a sales department.

6. The planning function is only as good as the underlying forecasts. ¿Verdad?

7. Comment on the statement that budgeting is basically a political process.

8. How would you *measure* the results of programs designed to meet a firm's social responsibilities?

9. Do you believe that the basic social purpose is to provide goods or service at a profit?

10. Illustrate the misuse of policy statements from your own experience.

11. What is the only valid test of the appropriateness of a policy?

12. Review: What did Taylor, Fayol, and Urwick have to say about the planning function? Did what they say have any impact on management practice?

13. Suppose you were to find that the world's most successful manager (however identified) never looked beyond his nose; he lived for today and met tomorrow when it came. How could you justify the preeminence of planning in view of such evidence?

ADDITIONAL REFERENCES

ACKOFF, L. R. *A Concept of Corporate Planning.* New York: John Wiley and Sons, Inc., 1970.

ANSOFF, H. I. *Corporate Strategy.* New York: McGraw-Hill Book Co., 1965.

ANTHONY, R. N. *Planning and Control Systems.* Boston: Harvard Graduate School of Business, Division of Research, 1965.

BIERMAN, H. AND SMIDT, S. *The Capital Budgeting Decision.* New York: The Macmillan Co., 1966.

BRANCH, M. C. *Planning: Aspects and Applications.* New York: John Wiley and Sons, Inc., 1966.

EWING, D. W. *The Human Side of Planning.* New York: The Macmillan Co., 1969.

HENRY, H. W. *Long-Range Planning Practices in 45 Industrial Companies.* Englewood Cliffs, N.J.: Prentice-Hall, Inc., 1967.

HUGHES, C. L. *Goal Setting: Key to Individual and Organizational Effectiveness.* New York: American Management Association, 1965.

LeBRETON, P. P., AND HENNING, D. A. *Planning Theory.* Englewood Cliffs, N.J.: Prentice-Hall, Inc., 1961.

PAYNE, B. *Planning for Company Growth.* New York: McGraw-Hill Book Co., 1963.

STEINER, G. A. *Managerial Long-Range Planning.* New York: McGraw-Hill Book Co., 1963.

SWEET, F. H. *Strategic Planning.* Austin, Tex.: University of Texas, Bureau of Business Research, 1964.

THOMPSON, S. *How Companies Plan.* New York: American Management Association, 1962.

WARREN, E. K. *Long-Range Planning: The Executive Viewpoint.* Englewood Cliffs, N.J.: Prentice-Hall, Inc., 1966.

chapter five

The Organizing Function

INTRODUCTION

The organizing function is the means by which management coordinates material and human resources through the design of a formal structure of tasks and authority. The classicists demonstrated that each job in the formal structure has a vertical and a horizontal dimension. The vertical dimension (functional definition) specifies the job in terms of assigned authority, while the horizontal dimension (functional effect) does so in terms of its assigned activity. Management's responsibility is to design the organization structure in such a manner as to predetermine the vertical and horizontal dimensions of each job.

This chapter describes and illustrates the application of four classical principles of organization: (1) the principle of specialization of labor, (2) the principle of departmentalization, (3) the span-of-control principle, and (4) the unity-of-command principle. These principles, derived from Fayol and Mooney, direct attention to the four fundamental problems of organization, namely:

1) What should determine the nature and content of each job? The principle of specialization of labor addresses itself to this problem.

2) What should determine the way in which jobs are grouped together? The principle of departmentalization suggests bases for grouping jobs.

3) What should determine the size of the groups? The span-of-control principle provides guidelines for solving this issue.

4) How should authority be distributed? The unity-of-command principle is relevant to this issue.

Through the application of these principles a formal structure is created. We shall discuss the application of each principle and conclude the chapter with a summary which compares classical organization theory with the familiar bureaucratic organization.

THE PRINCIPLE OF SPECIALIZATION OF LABOR

Probably the most important single principle in an analysis of the classical approach to organizational design is specialization of labor. This principle affects everyone in society everyday. For example, in the construction of a single-family home, a number of divisions of work occur in every phase of construction. The workers perform tasks within a special-

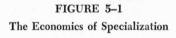

FIGURE 5–1

The Economics of Specialization

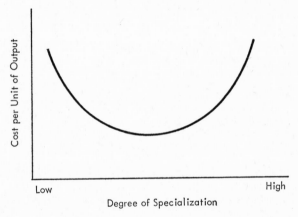

ized framework, and include bricklaying specialists, electrical specialists, plumbing specialists, and carpentry specialists. Each performs a narrow range of duties that he is trained and qualified to handle. The overall task of buiding the home is too large for any one group of specialists to handle within a reasonable period of time. The "jack of all trades" has moved aside for the "master" of a specialized task in home construction.

The narrow work capacity of one group of specialists (e.g., laborers) is one of many reasons why high degrees of division of labor are popular in the classical management approach. The overall production efficiencies generated by dividing labor are viewed as beneficial. This belief is certainly not new and is still accepted as valid.

The gains derived from narrow divisions of labor can be calculated in purely economic terms. Figure 5–1 shows this relationship. As the job is divided into ever smaller elements, additional output is obtained;

but more men and capital must be employed to do the smaller jobs. At some point, the costs of specialization (labor and capital) begin to outweigh the increased efficiency of specialization (output), and the cost per unit of output begins to rise.[1]

The problem of determining the appropriate degree of specialization becomes more difficult as the task becomes more abstract and less amenable to measurement. Nevertheless, the principle of specialization states that one must investigate the potential for gains due to specialization.

The end results of implementing the specialization-of-labor principle are job descriptions which define the *depth* and *scope*[2] of each job. The *depth* reflects the relative freedom that the job holder has in planning and controlling his duties. Ordinarily, one expects the depth of a job to increase as one moves up in the levels of the organization. An obvious contrast can be drawn between the work of the chief executive and the work of an assembly-line worker. But there can also be differences in job depth among persons at the same level. For example, a maintenance man has considerably more job depth than does a lathe worker. The *scope* of a job refers to the length of time of the job cycle; that is, the more often the job is repeated in a given time period, the more limited is its scope. We can expect to find differences in job scope among jobs at the same level and at different levels in the organization.

The principle of specialization of labor guides the manager in determining the content of individual jobs. From a different perspective, the principle also guides him in determining how jobs should be grouped together.

THE PRINCIPLE OF DEPARTMENTALIZATION

The classical-theory discussion of specialization of labor focuses upon the work of one specialist or of a small group of specialists. The principle of departmentalization applies the principle of specialization to determine how jobs should be grouped together.[3] The forms of departmentalization can be classified into two major groups. First, units specialized on the basis of *clients* or *output*[4] will be discussed. Second, the creation of de-

---

[1] Minimization of average cost is a solution under certain conditions; a generalized solution is to equate the marginal cost of specialization and the marginal gain of specialization. The reader who has had a course in basic economics will be familiar with the idea of marginal cost and gain.

[2] Alan C. Filley and Robert J. House, *Managerial Process and Organizational Behavior* (Glenview, Ill.: Scott, Foresman and Co., 1969), pp. 214–16.

[3] Luther Gulick, "Notes on the Theory of Organization," in Luther Gulick and Lyndall F. Urwick (eds.), *Papers on the Science of Administration* (New York: Columbia University, 1947), pp. 15–30.

[4] Materials for this section are based largely on the excellent discussion offered by Joseph A. Litterer, *The Analysis of Organizations* (New York: John Wiley & Sons, Inc., 1965), pp. 173–82.

78 Fundamentals of Management: Functions, Behavior, Models

partments based upon specific *internal* operations within the organization will be presented.

1. Output: Product Departmentalization. In many organizations, the activities necessary to manufacture a product or product line are grouped into departments. As the organization grows in size, it becomes difficult for managers to coordinate the activities of the expanding product lines. One commonly adopted strategy is to establish departments based upon product. The grouping of activities along product lines permits the utilization of the specialized skills of those people affiliated with a particular product or product line. An example of this type of departmentalization is presented in a partial organization chart format in Figure 5–2.

FIGURE 5–2

Departmentalization along Product Lines

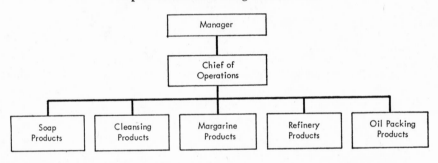

2. Client: Customer Departmentalization. In some organizations, various activities are grouped together based upon the customers served. For example, a company may have two sales departments that deal with two major groups of customers. One department may service the general public, while the other may be designed to provide goods to an industrial group of customers. The customer departmentalization design is presented in Figure 5–3.

3. Output: Geographical Departmentalization. Grouping activities on the basis of location is popular in organizations that have physically dispersed markets to serve. The assumption is that, if markets are widely dispersed, an improved cost-and-profit situation will result if all activities affecting a product or product line in a specific geographical region are grouped together. Figure 5–4 illustrates an example of geographical departmentalization.

The first classification for grouping work, i.e., product, customer, and geography, is oriented toward factors which are external to the actual operations of the firm. For example, the customer is a factor "out there" in the market. The geographical territory is also "out there," as is the distribution of the product. Another major classification for grouping work centers around the actual operations of the organization.

4. Internal Operations: Operational Departmentalization. Some organizations are designed on the basis of the operations performed by a

FIGURE 5–3

Departmentalization along Customer Lines

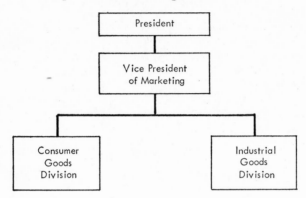

FIGURE 5–4

Departmentalization along Geographical Lines

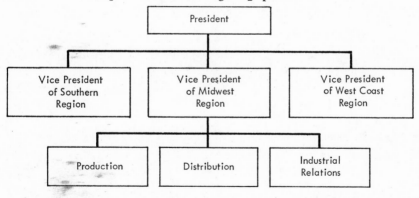

unit. For example, in a food-processing firm, all job-related activities involved in recruiting and selecting management trainees might be assigned to the personnel department, all marketing-related activities to the marketing department, and all activities concerned with the actual production of goods would be grouped in the production department. The operational organization design is used to some extent in manufacturing firms. Figure 5–5 illustrates the operational design in schematic form.

5. Internal Operations: Process Departmentalization. Another departmentalization method divides work along process lines. This is often referred to as division according to technical functions. For example, the manufacturing of a product may include cutting the materials on a lathe, heat-treating the materials, and finally cutting it into its final shape. The same type of technical functional division of work may be found in an of-

FIGURE 5–5

Departmentalization along Operational Lines

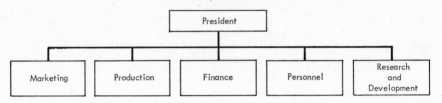

fice of a business administration department at a college. A number of typists may be assigned specific duties to perform. One girl types manuscripts, another typist is concerned with correspondence, and the third handles the telephone and the typing of classroom materials. In Figure 5–6, the division of work along process lines is presented.

FIGURE 5–6

Departmentalization along Process Lines

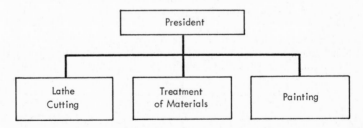

A Final Word on Departmentalization

The methods cited above for dividing work are not exhaustive; there are many other ways. Furthermore, in most large business organizations a number of different methods of dividing work are used at the same time. For example, at the upper levels of management, the vice presidents reporting to the president represent different product groups. At the level directly below the vice presidents, the managers may be part of a particular operational function. At the next level in the organization, there may be a number of different technical classifications. This approach of a multiple division of work in organizational design is illustrated in Figure 5–7.

The principle of departmentalization specifies the general objective to be followed in grouping activities, but the basis actually chosen is a matter of balancing advantages and disadvantages. For example, the advantage of departmentalizing on the basis of customers or products is that of bringing together under the control of a single manager all the resources necessary to make the product and/or service for the customers.

FIGURE 5–7

Organizational Design Employing a Number of Divisions of
Work Approaches

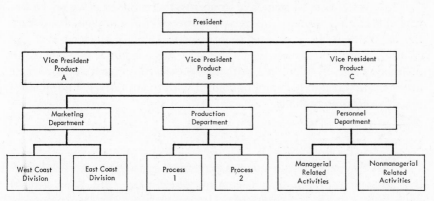

Additionally, the specification of goals is considerably easier when the emphasis is on the final product. Yet, at the same time, the ease of goal identification and measurement can encourage the individual departments to pursue their own goals at the expense of company goals; we referred to this possibility in the discussion of goal structure and the problem of suboptimization in Chapter 4. A second disadvantage of product and customer departmentalization is that the task of coordinating the activities tends to be more complex. Reporting to the unit manager are the managers of the various functions, product, sales, and finance, for example, whose diverse but interdependent activities must be coordinated.

Departmentalization based upon internal operations (process departments) have advantages as well as disadvantages. The primary advantage is that such departments are based upon specific skills and training; and activities assigned to the department emphasize the skills which individual members bring to the job. The managerial task of coordinating the activities of process departments is considerably less complex than in the product department because of the similarity of the subordinates' tasks. At the same time, the disadvantages of process departments must be recognized, the principal disadvantage being the difficulty of providing job depth for the managers of such groups. Since process departmentalization involves breaking up a natural work flow and assigning parts of this flow to different departments, each departmental manager must coordinate his task with those of other departmental managers. As shown in Figure 5–6, the president must necessarily limit the freedom of the managers of each of the three process departments in order to coordinate their activity.

THE PRINCIPLE OF SPAN OF CONTROL

The span-of-control principle concerns the number of subordinates who directly report to a supervisor; it therefore determines the size of the department. In a general sense, classical theory suggests that the span of control of a supervisor should be kept small. A number of individuals typically identified with the classical approach support their interpretation of limited span of control with quantitatively and qualitatively based presentations.

Graicunas' Theory of Limited Span of Control

A. V. Graicunas, a Lithuanian management consultant, applied deductive reasoning to the span-of-control phenomenon and then applied mathematics to his display of logic.[5] He demonstrated that, as the number of subordinates reporting to a supervisor increases arithmetically, the number of potential interactions between the subordinates and the supervisor increases geometrically. As shown in Figure 5–8, the manager could relate to W_1 and W_2 at different times (direct). He could interact with a group in which W_1 is the leader $\left(\begin{matrix} W_1 \\ W_2 \end{matrix}\right)$ or with a group in which W_2 is the leader $\left(\begin{matrix} W_2 \\ W_1 \end{matrix}\right)$. Finally he could receive information that flows from $W_1 \rightarrow W_2$ or from $W_2 \rightarrow W_1$ (cross).

If the number of subordinates is increased from two to three, the number of potential relationships increases from six to 18. Graicunas developed the following formula which is used to ascertain the number of potential contacts of a manager with an increasing number of subordinates:

$$C = N\left[\frac{2^N}{2} + N - 1\right].$$

---

[5] A. V. Graicunas, "Relationship in Organization," in Gulick and Urwick (eds.), op. cit., pp. 183–87.

FIGURE 5-8

Potential Relationships between a Supervisor and His Subordinates

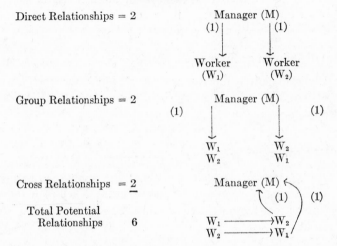

Direct Relationships = 2

Group Relationships = 2

Cross Relationships = 2

Total Potential
Relationships   6

C designates the total potential contacts and N, the number of subordinates reporting directly to the manager. Table 5-1 clearly shows the geometric increase in the number of possible relationships if the number of subordinates increases arithmetically.

If it is assumed that each of the potential relationships is important for successfully managing a group of subordinates, then the argument in favor of limiting the span of control gains some credence. It is, of course,

TABLE 5-1

Potential Relationships with Variable Number of Subordinates*

Number of Subordinates	Number of Relationships
1	1
2	16
3	18
4	44
5	100
6	222
7	490
8	1,080
9	2,276
10	5,210
11	11,374
12	24,708
18	2,359,602

* From Harold Koontz and Cyril O'Donnell, *Principles of Management*, 4th ed. (New York: McGraw-Hill Book Co., 1968), p. 246.

unlikely that each of the potential relationships occurs on a daily basis. However, the Graicunas presentation of geometric increases in potential relationships provides a striking example of the increase in complexities as the span of control increases.

R. C. Davis' Opinion on Span of Control

R. C. Davis, one of the most prestigious classical management scholars, distinguishes between two categories of span of control.[6] He discusses an *executive span* and an *operative span*. It is Davis' contention that the executive span includes the middle and top management positions in an organization structure. The span for managers at these levels should vary from three to nine, depending upon the nature of the manager's job and responsibilities and the rate of growth of the company, among other factors. The operative span applies to the lowest level of management. Davis proposes that the operative span can be effective with as many as 30 subordinates.

Urwick's Opinion on Span of Control

Urwick contends that managers should have a limited span of control because man in general has a limited span of attention.[7] That is, a limit exists as to the number of other people or objects to which a person can attend at the same time. Urwick recognizes that, though a manager with ten subordinates can be involved with over 5,210 contacts, he typically does not enter into every potential contact in the course of a day. However, if only a portion of the potential 5,210 relationships actually occurs in a day, there is a definite limit on the manager's time. Based upon his interpretation of span of control and the potential relationships, Urwick proposes that the ideal span for top management is four but that, at other supervisory levels, the number may be eight to twelve.

The classical version of the span-of-control principle is thus seen to be flexible in specifying the exact span. Both Davis and Urwick recognize that the optimum span depends upon a number of considerations. A latter-day statement of the principle recognizes that the span is related to at least the following variables:[8]

---

[6] Ralph C. Davis, *Fundamentals of Top Management* (New York: Harper and Row, 1951).

[7] Lyndall F. Urwick, "The Manager's Span of Control," *Harvard Business Review*, vol. 35 (May–June, 1956), pp. 39–47.

[8] Harold Steiglitz, *Organization Planning* (New York: National Industrial Conference Board, 1966), p. 15.

1. The competence of both the superior and the subordinates.
2. The degree of interaction between the units or personnel being supervised.
3. The extent to which the supervisor must carry out nonmanagerial responsibilities and the demands on his time from other people and units.
4. The similarity or dissimilarity of the activities being supervised.
5. The incidence of new problems in his unit.
6. The extent of standardized procedures.
7. The degree of physical dispersion.

Depending upon the relative importance of each of these factors, the optimum span of control could vary quite considerably. Classical management theory leaves unanswered the manner in which the optimum can be determined for any particular situation. Such determination had to await the development of more sophisticated analyses than were available to the classicists. It is fair to say, however, that the tendency in classical theory is toward a narrow span of control, for the emphasis in classical literature is on stability and predictability.

THE PRINCIPLE OF UNITY OF COMMAND

One of the most fundamental relationships presented in the classical approach to organizational design is that existing between superior and subordinate. The classical interpretation of unity of command can be described easily once the concept of chain of command is understood. The chain-of-command relationship is viewed as a series of superior–subordinate relationships. Starting at the top of the organization with the president and progressing down to the unskilled employee, the managerial chain of command in the classical school is viewed as a pyramid. Figure 5–9 depicts the chain of command in a hypothetical managerial hierarchy.

Chain of Command

The chain of command is the formal channel which determines authority, responsibility, power, and communications, among other organization-related phenomena. It is postulated that, because of the complexity of these phenomena, no individual should be subject to the direct command of more than one superior in performing his job tasks, as defined by the unity-of-command principle. Thus, in a simplistic way, unity of command stresses that a subordinate is delegated authority and decision-making power from, and communicates with, one superior.

The classical management reasoning for advocating the unity-of-command principle is that receiving commands from two or more superiors is likely to bring about confusion and frustration. According to the classicists, which superior's command should be followed first poses a frustrating and confusing dilemma for the subordinate which should be avoided whenever possible.

The unity-of-command principle is directly related to the *scalar process* which specifies that an unbroken chain of command must be instituted from top to bottom. At the same time, the classicists recognized the need for providing the opportunity to bypass the formal chain when conditions warrant this. Fayol had this in mind when he proposed that a subordinate should be empowered to communicate directly with a peer

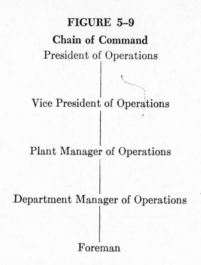

FIGURE 5–9

Chain of Command

President of Operations

Vice President of Operations

Plant Manager of Operations

Department Manager of Operations

Foreman

outside the chain, provided that the appropriate superiors approve beforehand the circumstances which permit the crossovers. Figure 5–10 shows a bridge between F and G which D and E have approved. Under special circumstances, F and G may communicate directly without going through channels, yet neither F nor G would be accountable to anyone but their immediate superiors—in this case, D and E.

Unity of Command and the Staff Function

The classicists also invoked the unity-of-command principle to guide the use of staff personnel. An important point in examining organizational design in terms of the classical theory is to distinguish between line and staff. The list of experts providing definitions for line and staff is endless.[9]

---

[9] Koontz and O'Donnell, *op. cit.*, pp. 291–326.

FIGURE 5–10
Fayol's Bridge

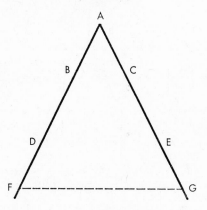

Perhaps the most concise and least confusing citation for line and staff is offered by Scott.[10] He perceives *line* as deriving from operational activities in a direct sense—creating, financing, and distributing a good or service, while *staff* is viewed as an advisory and facilitative function for the line. The crux of this viewpoint of line and staff is the degree to which the function contributes directly to the attainment of organizational objectives. The *line function* contributes directly to accomplishing the firm's objectives, while *staff* functions facilitate the accomplishment of the major organizational objectives of the firm in an indirect manner. Figure 5–11 illustrates a line-and-staff organizational design of a hypothetical firm.

Assuming that the organization depicted in Figure 5–11 is a manufacturing firm would enable one to conclude which of the positions illustrated are line and which are staff. Using the criterion that the line function contributes directly to the firm's objectives would lead to the conclusion that the marketing and production departments perform activities directly related to the attainment of a most important organizational goal—placing an acceptable product on the market. The activities of the managers of environmental control and engineering are advisory in nature. That is, they are helpful in enabling the firm to produce and market their product, but do not directly contribute to the process. Thus they are considered to be staff departments in this particular firm.

The unity-of-command principle quite clearly defines the appropriate role of the staff specialist in the organization: The staff advises and pro-

---

[10] William G. Scott, *Organization Theory* (Homewood, Ill.: Richard D. Irwin, Inc., 1967), p. 107. Our choice of this particular distinction is arbitrary. For a complete discussion of various line-staff conceptualizations, see Robert T. Golembiewski, *Organizing Men and Power: Patterns of Behavior and Line-Staff Models* (Chicago: Rand McNally and Co., 1967).

FIGURE 5–11

A Line and Staff Design
(partial organization chart)

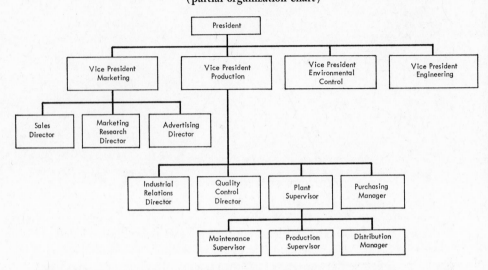

vides information, but has no authority over the work of a particular line manager's subordinates. To place a subordinate under the jurisdiction of a staff official as well as of his line manager would violate the span-of-control principle and would weaken the chain of command.

THE CLASSICAL APPROACH TO DESIGN: A SUMMARY

The classical approach emphasizes the design of the formal structure of the organization to achieve coordinated effort. Various principles of management such as division of labor, span of control, unity of command, departmentalization, and scalar authority provide the cornerstones of the classical approach. It is generally concluded that the main emphasis of classical design theory, which employs these principles is upon the anatomy of the formal organization.[11]

It has also been observed that the classical theory of organizing includes certain assumptions about the participants. These assumptions in turn greatly influenced the classical approach.[12] Douglas McGregor referred to them as Theory X and described them as follows:[13]

---

[11] Scott, op. cit., p. 102.

[12] For a survey of the literature with emphasis on the underlying assumptions of various theories of organization, see James L. Gibson, "Organization Theory and the Nature of Man," Academy of Management Journal, vol. 9 (September, 1966), pp. 233–45.

[13] Douglas McGregor, The Human Side of Enterprise (New York: McGraw-Hill Book Co., 1960).

1. *The employees of the firm inherently dislike their jobs and will resort to many secretive and disruptive practices to avoid work.* This assumption illustrates a mistrust of the employee since productivity is a desired goal of the Theory X advocate and, consequently, if work is disliked and avoided when possible, the hoped-for goal may not be achieved.

2. *Since employees dislike work, most people must be coerced, controlled and literally threatened with punishment if the firm's desired goals are to be achieved.* This contention is a logical extension and result of the first assumption. If people dislike and avoid work, they must be brought in line by the formal authority system within the organization.

3. *Most workers in an organization want to be directed by a formal leader and want to avoid job responsibilities whenever possible.* This assumption stresses the importance of structuring work in such a manner that the workers will be led and directed by a recognized authority figure in the organization.

4. *Most workers want security above all other factors which can be associated with their work.* McGregor included the security factor in his third assumption; however, since it is such an important concept today, the security item is viewed here as a separate assumption. It suggests that managers believe that, in motivating workers or organizing work, they can derive more positive results in performance by considering the high levels of insecurity among the work force.

We can understand how these assumptions influenced classical organization theory by examining them in the context of bureaucratic organization. The bureaucracy as described by Max Weber is a highly structured, formalized, and impersonal organization.[14] Weber, writing at the same time as the classical management theorists, argued that the bureaucracy is the most efficient form of organization for achieving goals such as production efficiency. He recognized that the degree of bureaucratization varied widely in practice; but he proposed that certain characteristics define the most efficient organization, which he termed the "ideal" type. Scott has listed these characteristics as follows:[15]

1. A clear division of labor exists, so that each task to be performed by employees is systematically established and legitimatized by formal recognition as an official duty.

2. The functions within the organizational system are officially arranged in a hierarchical manner. That is, a chain of command from the top down is established. This is referred to in the management literature as the *scalar principle*.

3. The actions of employees are governed by rules and procedures which are formally prescribed and which are utilized in a uniform manner in every situation.

---

[14] Max Weber, "The Essentials of Bureaucratic Organization: An Ideal-Type Construction," In Robert K. Merton, *et al.* (eds.), *A Reader in Bureaucracy* (Glencoe, Ill.: The Free Press, 1952), pp. 18–27.

[15] Scott, *op. cit.*, pp. 249–50.

4. The officials of the bureaucracy apply the rules and procedures as impersonally as is humanly possible. The "people" element of the organizational system is given consideration after the entity itself.

5. Admission to the bureaucracy is based upon rigid selection criteria which apply uniformly and impersonally to each candidate applying or being considered for a position. The criteria for selection are based upon objective standards for the job which have been established by the formal officials of the organization.

Examination of these five characteristics shows that they are similar in many ways to classical organization principles, and that they implement Theory X assumptions. In Theory X, it is assumed that human behavior requires a systematic organizational system which is developed and operated by officials. The bureaucratic form of organization is most compatible with the desires of people who are characterized by Theory X. Table 5–2 demonstrates this compatibility.

TABLE 5–2

Theory X and Bureaucracy

McGregor	Weber Characteristics Satisfying the People Desires
1. People dislike work	Division of labor
2. People need to be controlled, coerced, and threatened	Chain of command
	Specified rules and procedures
3. People need to be directed	Impersonality
4. People need security	Rigid selection criteria

In Table 5–2, the chain of command is connected to three McGregor assumptions: (1) dislike of work; (2) control, coercion, and threats, and (3) direction. This indicates how the chain-of-command concept may be viewed as overcoming and satisfying the characteristics of people postulated by McGregor. Further, the rules and procedure requirement of Weber is related to two McGregor assumptions. This is due to the reasoning that rules and procedures give some people the security they desire and the control mechanisms they need. The other relationships in the table should be interpreted in a similar manner.

The Theory X set of assumptions and the "ideal" bureaucracy characteristics offer insight into the principles of management and concepts employed in the classical theory of organization and design. As discussed in this chapter, the organizing process in classical theory is concerned with providing a formal structure within which work takes place. However, the structure does not guarantee that the desired activities will automatically be realized. The program undertaken by management to assure that actual activity conforms to planned activity constitutes the control function. Control from the classical viewpoint is discussed in the final chapter of Part I.

DISCUSSION AND REVIEW QUESTIONS

1. What are the objectives of the organizing function?
2. How are organizing and planning related?
3. Use the classical organizing approach to evaluate your fraternity, a club, or any particular group to which you belong. How would you explain the fact that your analysis could indicate violations of the basic principles, and that your group (perhaps) nevertheless gets along just fine?
4. What are the bases of departmentalization in the college in which you are enrolled? What alternative bases might be used to group faculty together? Which one is the "best"?
5. How does the manager know that he has designed the right organization structure?
6. The critic of capitalism states that the cost of specialization of labor is alienation from the workplace. Is he correct? If he is, so what? What is the alternative?
7. How can the use of staff personnel conflict with the unity-of-command principle? How could such conflicts be resolved?
8. What is the relationship between Taylor's "functional foremanship" and the use of staff?
9. Classical organization theory stresses structure. Comment.
10. Do you believe that Theory X describes the nature of man? Do you believe that classical organization theory is based upon Theory X?
11. What is the meaning of bureaucracy to a political scientist?
12. "All organizations have elements of bureaucracy." True?

ADDITIONAL REFERENCES

BAKER, A. W. AND DAVIS, R. C. Ratios of Staff to Line Employees and Stages of Differentiations of Staff Functions. Columbus: Ohio State University, Bureau of Business Research, 1954.

BROWN, A. Organization of Industry. Englewood Cliffs, N.J.: Prentice-Hall, Inc., 1947.

DALE, E. Planning and Developing the Company Organization Structure. New York: American Management Association, 1952.

DALE, E. AND URWICK, L. F. Staff in Organization. New York: McGraw-Hill Book Company, 1960.

DAVIS, R. C. The Fundamentals of Top Management. New York: Harper and Brothers, 1951.

FOX, W. M. The Management Process. Homewood, Ill.: Richard D. Irwin, Inc., 1963.

HALL, C. L. *The Management Guide*. Standard Oil Company of California, Department of Organization, 1948.

HOLDEN, P. E., FISH, L. S. AND SMITH, H. L. *Top-Management Organization and Control*. New York: McGraw-Hill Book Company, 1941.

PFIFFNER, J. M. AND SHERWOOD, F. P. *Administrative Organization*. Englewood Cliffs, N.J.: Prentice-Hall, Inc., 1960.

chapter six

The Controlling Function

INTRODUCTION

The third management function which is identified and analyzed in classical theory is controlling. This function includes *all activities which the manager undertakes in attempting to assure that actual operations conform to planned operations.* We can see that control was the emphasis of scientific management. The development of standard methods was the result of concerted efforts by Taylor, the Gilbreths, and others to implement managerial control. They recommended a complete separation of duties between workers and managers, with workers executing tasks in consistent and uniform ways as defined by management.

The control function was elaborated in considerable detail by Urwick, who synthesized the previous work of Fayol, Mooney, and Taylor to arrive at a framework for analyzing the controlling function. According to Urwick, the desired effect of managerial control is a *stable* work force which pursues its prescribed (planned) activities with a spirit of *initiative* and a *sense of unity.* The means to this end include staffing the firm with competent managers, and selection and placement of qualified workers, augmented by the use of rewards and sanctions. The classicists emphasized structural means for control, but they stressed that the competence of managers crucially determines the outcome of control efforts. We have discussed these aspects of control in Chapter 3.

Here we shall rely upon the work of Professor R. C. Davis, who expanded the classical concept of control. Professor Davis's analysis permits us to study the control function by breaking it down into subfunctions and relating each to the total concept. At the same time, we are able to relate controlling to planning and organizing. Finally, we can demonstrate the relationship of certain well-known and widely used accounting, financial, and production control methods to the classical-management form of control. The remainder of this chapter expands each of these considerations. We must first, however, recognize that the successful implementation of control methods depends upon the provision of three basic conditions.

NECESSARY CONDITIONS FOR CONTROL

The implementation of control requires three basic conditions: (1) *standards* must be established, (2) *information* which compares actual results (standards) must be provided, and (3) *action* to bring about correction of any deviations between actual and standard must be possible. The logic is evident: without standards, there can be no basis for evaluating the adequacy of actual performance; without information there can be no way of knowing the situation; without provision for action to correct deviations, the entire control process becomes a pointless exercise.

Standards are derived from goals and have many of the characteristics of goals. Like goals, they are targets; to be effective, they must be clearly stated and logically related to the larger goals of the unit. Standards are the criteria against which future, current, or past actions are compared. They are measured in a variety of ways, including physical, monetary, quantitative and qualitative terms. The various forms which standards can take will be made clear in subsequent discussions of control methods.

Information which reports actual performance and which permits appraisal of the performance against standards must be provided. Such information is most easily acquired for activities which produce specific and concrete results; for example, production and sales activities have end products which are easily identifiable and for which information is readily obtainable. For example, the performance of the legal department, the research-and-development unit, and the personnel department are quite difficult to appraise because of the nature of their activities.

Action to correct deviations results from the discovery of the need for action and from the ability to implement the desired action. One person responsible for taking the corrective steps must know that he is indeed responsible and that he has the assigned authority to take the action. Unless the job and position descriptions include specific statements which clearly delineate these two requirements, the control process will surely fall short of its objective.

The control function, then, involves the implementation of methods which provide answers to three basic questions, namely: What are the planned and expected results? By what means can the actual results be compared to planned results? What corrective action is appropriate from which authorized person? Let us go on to describe more specifically the relationship between controlling, planning, and organizing by identifying three major types of control.

THREE TYPES OF CONTROL[1]

The controlling function can be broken down into three types on the basis of the focus of control activity. Figure 6–1 describes the three types.

Preliminary control focuses on the problem of preventing deviations in the quality and quantity of resources used in the firm. Human resources

FIGURE 6–1
The Controlling Function

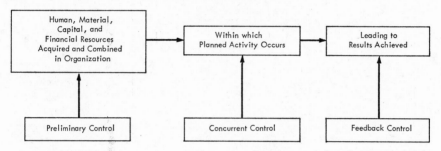

must meet the job requirements as defined by the organization structure; employees must have the capability, whether physical or intellectual, to perform the assigned tasks. The materials must meet acceptable levels of quality and must be available at the proper time and place. In addition, capital must be on hand to assure the adequate supply of plant and equipment. Finally, financial resources must be available in the right amounts and at the right times. A number of methods exist which enable management to implement preliminary control. Some of these are described in this chapter.

Concurrent control monitors actual ongoing operations to assure that objectives are pursued. The principal means by which *concurrent control* is implemented are the directing or supervisory activities of managers. Through personal, on-the-spot observation, the manager determines whether the work of others is proceeding in the manner defined by policies and procedures. The delegation of authority provides him with the power to use financial and nonfinancial incentives to affect concurrent

---

[1] In this section we identify *feedback* control as a separate type. Many students will recognize that feedback can also be viewed as part of the broader concept of control where it refers to the information which reports results to the manager.

control. The standards guiding ongoing activity are derived from job descriptions and from policies which result from the planning function.

Feedback control methods focus on end results. The corrective action, if taken, is directed at improving either the resource acquisition process or the actual operations. This type of control derives its name from the fact that *historical* results guide *future* actions. An illustration of feedback control is a thermostat, which automatically regulates the temperature of a room by constantly measuring actual temperature and comparing it with the desired temperature. Figure 6–2 shows feedback control applied to the temperature example.

FIGURE 6–2

A Simple Feedback Control System

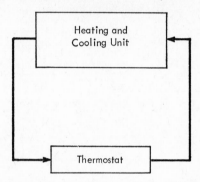

Since the thermostat maintains the preset temperature (objective) by constantly monitoring the actual temperature, future results (temperature) are directly and continually determined by actual results (again, temperature). The feedback methods employed in business include analyses of budget, standard costs, financial statements and quality control.

CONTROL IN CLASSICAL THEORY

Classical theory distinguishes between preliminary and concurrent control. A distinction is based upon the relationship of the execution of control efforts to the operation, or variable, to be controlled. Classical theory delineates the eight subfunctions of control and identifies the normal sequence and the organizational assignment of the subfunctions.

According to Davis,[2] control consists of two types (preliminary and concurrent), which in turn can be broken down into eight subfunctions.

---

[2] Ralph C. Davis, *The Fundamentals of Top Management* (New York: Harper and Brothers, 1951), p. 407.

Furthermore, the normal sequence and organizational assignment (line or staff) of the eight subfunctions can be identified. Davis's ideas are illustrated in Figure 6–3.

FIGURE 6–3

Classical Control Concepts

Preliminary Control Subfunctions

1. Routine Planning.......... Staff Assignment
2. Scheduling............... Staff Assignment
3. Preparation.............. Staff Assignment
4. Dispatching.............. Staff Assignment

Concurrent Control Subfunctions

5. Direction................ Line Assignment
6. Supervision.............. Line Assignment
7. Comparison.............. Staff Assignment
8. Corrective Action......... Line Assignment

Davis defined the eight subfunctions as follows:[3]

Routine Planning (RP). A secondary, routine provision of information concerning the plan.
Scheduling (S). The determination when, or at what rate, the principal phases of the plan must be completed to meet the final time objective of the undertaking.
Preparation (P). The function of assuring that the factors and conditions required for the execution of the plan will be available as needed.
Dispatching (D). The maintenance of coordination through control of the release of the authority to act.
Direction (DN). The function of instruction concerning the requirements for proper execution of the plan.
Supervision (SN). The function of assuring that current execution is taking place in accordance with plans and instructions.
Comparison (C). The function of determining the extent of agreement between actual and planned results.
Corrective Action (CA). The removal of interferences with planned execution and the restoration of effective, coordinated action.

Davis demonstrated the relationship between the management levels and the operative level where the activity is executed, as illustrated in Figure 6–4. This figure shows the sequence of control subfunctions being performed at the two management levels; it also shows the release of authority (1) from top management to middle and departmental management and the release of authority (2) from middle and departmental management to the operative level. It may be noted that top management executes direction and supervision over the entire control process under-

---

[3] *Ibid.*, p. 407.

FIGURE 6–4

The Subfunctions of Control within the Organization*

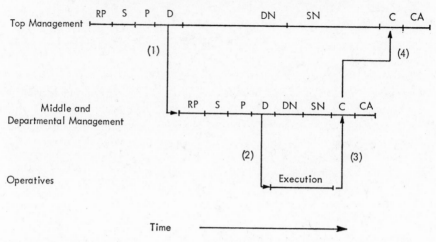

* Based upon *ibid.*, p. 651.

taken at the second level, and that management in the second level directs and supervises the execution of the activity at the operative level. Information flows up the line [see (3) and (4) in Figure 6–4]. This line reports the status of the assigned task and serves as the basis for comparison and corrective action.

The corrective-action phase of preliminary control and concurrent control adjusts that which is being measured. Preliminary control adjusts

FIGURE 6–5

The Three Types of Control as Distinguished by Focus of Corrective Action

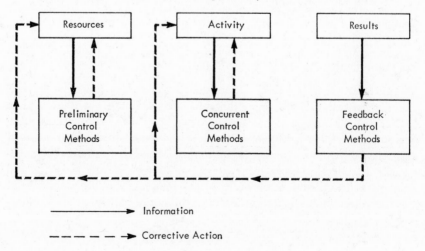

the quality and quantity of resources, based upon information pertaining to these resources; concurrent control adjusts the actual operations based upon information pertaining to these operations. On the other hand, the focus of feedback corrective action is not the variable being measured (results). Rather, corrective action is taken at either or both the resources and activity phases of the cycle, as is shown in Figure 6–5, opposite. Though it is not identified *per se* in classical theory, the importance of feedback control in modern industry suggests that it should be discussed separately.

Up to this point, we have identified the necessary conditions for effective control and defined three types of control depending upon the focus of the corrective action. We shall next discuss certain control methods in terms of the three types.

PRELIMINARY CONTROL PROCEDURES

Preliminary control procedures include all managerial efforts whose purpose it is to increase the probability that future actual results will compare favorably with planned results. From this perspective, we can see that policies are important means for implementing pre-control, since policies are by nature guidelines for future action. Yet we want to distinguish between *setting* policies and *implementing* them. The former is included in the planning function, whereas the latter is a part of the control function. Similarly, we might include job descriptions in the control function since job descriptions predetermine the activity of the job-holder. At the same time, however, we want to distinguish between *defining* and *staffing* the task structure. The former is a part of the organizing function, and the latter of the control function.

Preliminary Control of Human Resources

The organization structure defines the job requirements and predetermines the skill requirements of the job holders. These requirements vary in the degree of specificity depending upon the nature of the task. At the shop level the skill requirements can be specified in terms of physical attributes and manual dexterity. On the other hand, the job requirements of management and staff personnel are more difficult to define in terms of concrete measurements.

As implied in Chapter Five, preliminary control is effected through procedures which include the selection and placement of managerial and nonmanagerial personnel.[4] We should distinguish between those

----

[4] This phase of preliminary control is an aspect of personnel management. See Leon C. Megginson, *Personnel: A Behavioral Science Approach to Administration*

procedures which are designed to obtain qualified subordinate managers (staffing) and those which are designed to obtain qualified nonmanagers and operatives (selection and placement). The basic procedures and objectives are essentially the same; yet classical theory makes the distinction because of its emphasis upon managerial competence as the fundamental determiner of the organization's success.

The candidates for positions must be recruited from inside or outside the firm and the most promising applicant selected from the list of candidates. The selection decision is based upon the congruence of the applicant's skills, personal characteristics, and the job requirements. The successful candidate must be trained in methods and procedures appropriate for the job—a managerial responsibility that is clearly defined in classical theory by Taylor. Most modern organizations have elaborate procedures for providing training on a continual basis.

Preliminary Control of Materials

The raw material which is converted into the finished product must conform to standards of quality. At the same time, a sufficient inventory must be maintained to insure a continuous flow to meet customer demands. The techniques of inventory control are discussed in a later chapter; at this point, we should only be concerned with the quality of incoming materials.

The principal means for assuring quality is inspection. In recent years numerous methods have been devised which use statistical sampling to control the quality of materials by the inspection of samples rather than of the entire lot. These methods are less costly in terms of inspection time, but there is the risk of accepting defective material if the sample does not happen to contain any of the defectives.

A complete discussion of statistical sampling is beyond the scope of this text, but the essence of the procedure can be understood easily.[5] Suppose, for example, that management sets a standard three percent level of defective items as the maximum that it will accept from the supplier. The material is then inspected by selecting a random sample and calculating the percentage of defective items in that sample. The decision that must then be made, based on the sample, is whether to accept or reject the entire order, or to take another sample. Errors can be made in

(Homewood, Ill.: Richard D. Irwin, Inc., 1967); Paul S. Greenlaw and Robert D. Smith, *Personnel Management* (Scranton, Pa.: International Textbook Co., 1970); Arthur R. Prell, *Recruiting and Selecting Personnel* (New York: Regents Publishing Co., 1969).

[5] See Lloyd A. Knowler, *Quality Control by Statistical Methods* (New York: McGraw-Hill Book Co., 1969); Eugene L. Grant, *Statistical Quality Control* (New York: McGraw-Hill Book Co., 1952); Acheson J. Duncan, *Quality Control and Industrial Statistics* (Homewood, Ill.: Richard D. Irwin, Inc., 1959).

sampling so that a lot is accepted when in fact it contains more than three percent defectives, or a lot is rejected when in fact it contains less than three percent defectives. The control system will be constructed based upon a careful balancing of the relative costs of these two errors.

The characteristics of materials pre-control are illustrative of control systems which are quite routine. The decision to accept or reject materials recurs frequently and must be made on a fairly routine basis. The standard is easily measured and information (the sample) is readily available. The decision to accept or reject (or take another sample) is based upon straightforward instruction; given the sample results, the decision is automatic. The inspector's instructions may read: "If sample defectives are equal to or less than three percent, accept the lot; if sample defectives are equal to or more than five percent, reject the lot; if sample defectives are between three and five percent, take another sample." If a second sample is required, the inspector's actions will be determined by another set of instructions.

Preliminary Control of Capital

The acquisition of capital results from the need to replace existing equipment or to expand the firm's productive capacity. Capital acquisitions are controlled by establishing criteria of potential profitability which must be met before the proposal is authorized. Such acquisitions are ordinarily included in the *capital budget*, which is an intermediate and long-run planning budget that details the alternative sources and uses of funds. The decisions to be made by the manager, which involve the commitment of present funds in exchange for future funds, are termed *investment decisions;* and the methods which serve to screen investment proposals derive from economic analysis.[6] In this section a number of methods in widespread practice will be discussed. Each of these methods involves the formulation of a standard which must be met in order to accept the prospective capital acquisition.

The Payback Method. The simplest and apparently most widely used method is the payback method. This appraisal calculates the number of years needed for the proposed capital acquisition to repay its original cost out of future cash earnings. For example, a manager is considering a machine which will reduce labor costs by $4,000 per year for each of the four years of its estimated life. The cost of the machine is $8,000 and

---

[6] The analysis of investment opportunities is a highly developed topic in financial management. See Adolph E. Grunewald and Erwin E. Nemmers, *Basic Managerial Finance* (New York: Holt, Rinehart, and Winston, 1970); Curtis W. Symonds, *Basic Financial Management* (New York: American Management Association, 1969); Harold Bierman and Seymour Smidt, *The Capital Budgeting Decision* (New York: The Macmillan Co., 1966).

the tax rate is 50 percent. The additional after-tax cash inflow from which the machine cost must be paid is calculated as follows:

Additional before tax cash inflow		
(labor cost savings)		$4,000
Less additional taxes:		
Additional income	$4,000	
Less depreciation (8,000 ÷ 4)	2,000	
Additional taxable income	2,000	
Tax rate	.5	
Additional tax payment		1,000
Additional after-tax cash inflow		$3,000

After additional taxes are deducted from the labor savings, the paycheck period can be calculated as follows:

$$\frac{\$8,000}{\$3,000} = 2.67 \text{ years.}$$

The proposed machine will repay its original cost in two and two-thirds years; if the standard requires a payback of at most three years, the machine would be deemed an appropriate investment.

The payback method suffers many limitations as a standard for evaluating capital resources. It does not produce a measurement of profitability and, more importantly, it does not take into account the time value of money, that is, it does not recognize that a dollar today is worth more than a dollar at a future date. Other methods can be employed which include these important considerations.

Rate of Return on Investment. One alternative which produces a measure of profitability and which is parallel to methods ordinarily employed in accounting is the simple rate of return. Using the above example, the calculation would be as follows:

Additional gross income		$4,000
Less depreciation ($8,000 ÷ 4)	$2,000	
Less taxes	1,000	
Total additional expenses		3,000
Additional net income after taxes		$1,000

The rate of return is the ratio of additional net income to the original cost:

$$\frac{\$1,000}{\$8,000} = 12.5\%.$$

The calculated rate of return would then be compared to some standard of minimum acceptability, and the decision to accept or reject would depend upon that comparison.

The measurement of the simple rate of return has the advantage of being easily understood. It also has the disadvantage, however, of not including the time value of money. The discounted rate of return overcomes this deficiency.

Discounted Rate of Return. A measurement of profitability which can be used as a standard for screening potential capital resources and which takes into account the time value of money is the discounted rate of return. This method is similar to the payback period in that only cash inflows and outflows are considered. The method itself is not widely used because of its apparent complexity and difficulty, yet it is considered the "theoretically correct" method for calculating the rate of return. It proceeds as follows, based upon the above example:

$$\$8,000 = \frac{\$3,000}{(1+r)} + \frac{\$3,000}{(1+r)^2} + \frac{\$3,000}{(1+r)^3} + \frac{\$3,000}{(1+r)^4};$$
$$r = 18\%.$$

The discounted rate of return (r) is 18 percent, which is interpreted to mean that an $8,000 investment which repays $3,000 in cash at the end of each of four years yields a return of 18 percent.

The rationale of the method can be understood by thinking of the $3,000 inflows as cash payments received by the firm. In exchange for each of these four payments of $3,000 the firm must pay $8,000. The rate of return, 18 percent, is the factor which equates future cash inflows and present cash outflow.

The time value of money is explicitly considered in the method in the following way: If we remember that 18 percent is the rate of return and that there are four distinct and separate future receipts of $3,000, we can see that $8,000 is the *present value* of the future proceeds.[7]

$2,542 = present value of $3,000 to be received in 1 year
   or $2,542 × (1.18) = $3,000
$2,155 = present value of $3,000 to be received in 2 years
   or $2,155 × (1.18)² = $3,000
$1,826 = present value of $3,000 to be received in 3 years
   or $1,826 × (1.18)³ = $3,000
$1,547 = present value of $3,000 to be received in 4 years
   or $1,547 × (1.18)⁴ = $3,000
$8,070 = Total present value.[8]

Preliminary Control of Financial Resources

An adequate supply of financial resources must be available to assure the firm's meeting current obligations arising from current operations. Materials must be purchased, wages paid, interest charges and due dates met. The principal means of controlling the availability and cost of

[7] For a complete discussion of the relationships between discounted rate of return and present value, see Bierman and Smidt, *ibid.*, pp. 39–43; and G. David Quirin, *The Capital Expenditure Decision* (Homewood, Ill.: Richard D. Irwin, Inc., 1967) pp. 39–55.

[8] Not exactly equal to $8000 because of rounding errors.

financial resources is budgeting—particularly cash and working capital budgets.[9]

These budgets anticipate the ebb and flow of business activity when materials are purchased, finished goods are produced and inventoried, goods are sold, and cash received. This cycle of activity, the operating cycle, results in a problem of *timing* the availability of cash to meet the obligations. The simple relationship between cash and inventory is shown in Figure 6–6. As inventories of finished goods increase, the supply

FIGURE 6–6

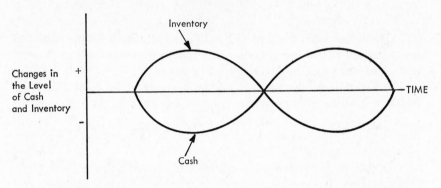

of cash decreases while materials, labor, and other expenses are incurred and paid. As inventory is depleted through sales, cash increases. Pre-control of cash requires that cash be available during the period of inventory buildup and be used wisely during periods of abundance. This requires the careful consideration of alternative sources of short-term financing during inventory buildup and of alternative short-run investment opportunities during periods of inventory depletion.

To aid in the process, attention is given by managers to certain financial ratios. For example, the pre-control standard may be in terms of the working capital ratio (the ratio of current assets to current liabilities) and a minimum and a maximum is set. The minimum ratio could be set at 2:1, and the maximum, at 3:1, a practice which recognizes the cost of both too little and too much investment in liquid assets. The control would be in terms of corrective action when the actual working capital ratio deviates from the standard. Other financial ratios which contribute

[9] Yair E. Ogler, *Cash Management* (Belmont, Calif.: Wadsworth Publishing Co., Inc., 1969); William J. Vatter, *Operating Budgets* (Belmont, Calif.: Wadsworth Publishing Co., Inc., 1969); Colin Park and John W. Gladson, *Working Capital* (New York: The Macmillan Co., 1963); Walter Rautenstrauch and Raymond Villers, *Budgetary Control* (New York: Funk and Wagnalls, 1968).

to pre-control of financial resources include the acid test ratio, inventory turnover, and average collection period. These ratios are discussed in greater detail in the section on feedback control methods.

CONCURRENT CONTROL PROCEDURES

Concurrent control consists of methods which monitor the actual execution of plans. In most cases, the focus of concurrent control is the work of subordinates. The direction and supervision phases of the control function encompass all activity of the subordinates. The responsibility of the manager when directing and supervising subordinates is (1) to instruct them in the proper methods and procedures and (2) to assure that they are following instructions.

The direction function follows the formal chain of command since the responsibility of each superior is to interpret for subordinates the orders received from higher echelons. The relative importance of direction depends almost entirely upon the nature of the tasks which are ordinarily performed by subordinates. The forearm of an assembly line which produces a simple component part requiring relatively simple manual operations may seldom engage in direction. On the other hand, the manager of a research-and-development unit must devote considerable time to direction. Research work is inherently more complex and varied than manual work, thus requiring more interpretation and instruction.

The scope and content of the direction function varies, depending upon the nature of work being supervised, as noted above. We can also distinguish a number of other factors which describe differences in the form of direction. For example, if we recognize that direction is basically the process of personal communication, then we can see that the amount and clarity of information are important factors. Subordinates must receive sufficient information to carry out the task and must understand the information that they receive. On the other hand, too much information and too much detail can be damaging. We should also recognize that the manager's mode and tone of expression greatly influence the direction function.

Supervision is the process of overseeing the work of subordinates. The purpose is to assure that plans are being carried out in accordance with instructions. Supervision is "primarily a mental activity that involves face-to-face leadership."[10] This recognition permits us to place supervision within the context of a leadership framework. Our objective at this stage is to identify the place of supervision (leadership) in management theory: it is a subfunction of concurrent control.

---

[10] Davis, *op. cit.*, p. 709.

FEEDBACK CONTROL PROCEDURES

The distinguishing feature of feedback control methods is focusing corrective action upon historical outcomes which are used then to correct *future* actions. For example the financial statements of a firm are used to evaluate the acceptability of historical results and to determine the desirability of making changes in future resource acquisitions or operation procedures (activity). In this section we outline three feedback control methods which are widely used in business; they are: financial statement analysis, standard cost analysis, and quality control. Our objective is to demonstrate the general features of all feedback control techniques through these three examples.

Financial Statement Analysis

A principal source of information from which managers can evaluate historical results is the firm's accounting system. Periodically, the manager receives a set of financial statements which usually includes a balance sheet, an income statement, and a sources and uses of funds statement. These statements summarize and classify the effects of transactions in terms of assets, liabilities, equity, revenues, and expenses—the principal components of the firm's financial structure.[11]

A detailed analysis of the information contained in the financial statements enables management to ascertain the adequacy of the firm's earning power and its ability to meet current and long-term obligations; i.e., the manager must have measures of and standards for profitability, liquidity, and solvency. The various measures of profitability were discussed in Chapter 4. The planning discussion described the various profitability measures and presented arguments for each. Whether the manager prefers the rate of return on sales, on owner's equity, or on total assets, or a combination of all three, it is important to establish a meaningful norm—one that is appropriate to the particular firm, given its industry and stage of growth. An adequate rate of return will negatively affect the firm's ability to attract funds for expansion, particularly if a downward trend over time is evident.

The measures of liquidity reflect the firm's ability to meet current obligations as they become due. The widest known and most often used measure is *working capital*, the ratio of current assets to current liabilities. The standard of acceptability depends upon the particular firm's own

---

[11] See John N. Meyer, *Financial Statement Analysis* (Englewood Cliffs, N.J.: Prentice-Hall, Inc., 1969); S. Winston Korn and Thomas Boyd, *Accounting for Management Planning and Decision-Making* (New York: John Wiley and Sons, 1969).

operating characteristics. Bases for comparison are available from trade associations which publish industry averages. A more rigorous test of liquidity is the *acid test ratio,* which relates only cash and near cash items (current assets excluding inventories and prepaid expenses) to current liabilities.

The relationship between current assets and current liabilities is an important determinate of liquidity. Equally important is the *composition* of current assets. Two measures which indicate composition and which rely upon information found in both the balance sheet and income statement are the *accounts receivable turnover* and the *inventory turnover.* The accounts receivable turnover is the ratio of credit sales to average accounts receivable. The higher the turnover, the more rapid is the conversion of accounts receivable to cash. A low turnover would indicate a time lag in the collection of receivables, which in turn, could strain the firm's ability to meet its own obligations; the appropriate corrective action might be a tightening of credit standards or a more vigorous effort to collect outstanding accounts. The inventory turnover also facilitates the analysis of appropriate balances in current assets. It is calculated as the ratio of cost of goods sold to average inventory. A high ratio could indicate a dangerously low inventory balance in relation to sales with the possibility of missed sales or production slowdowns; conversely, a low ratio might indicate an overinvestment in inventory to the exclusion of other, more profitable, assets. Whatever the case, the appropriate ratio must be established by the manager based upon the firm's experience within its industry and market.

Another financial measure is solvency, the ability of the firm to meet its long-term obligations—its fixed commitments. The solvency measure relates the claims of creditors and owners on the assets of the firm. An appropriate balance must be maintained—a balance which protects the interests of the owners, yet does not ignore the advantages of long-term debt as a source of funds. A commonly used measure of solvency is the *ratio of net income before interest and taxes to interest expense.* This indicates the margin of safety to managers and, ordinarily, a high ratio is preferred. However, a very high ratio combined with a low debt to equity ratio could indicate that management has not taken advantage of debt as a source of funds. The appropriate balance between debt and equity depends upon a great number of factors; and the issue is an important topic in financial management. But, as a general rule, one can say that the proportion of debt would vary directly with the stability of the firm's earnings.

The ratios discussed above are only suggestive of the great number and variety of methods used to evaluate the financial results of the firm. Accounting as a tool of analysis in business management has a long

$$y = ax^2 + bx + c \qquad \frac{-b \pm \sqrt{b^2 - 4ac}}{2a}$$

history predating scientific management.[12] Our point here is that financial statement analysis as a part of the management process is clearly a feedback control method.

Standard Cost Analysis

Standard cost accounting systems date from and are considered a major contribution of the scientific management era. A standard cost system provides information that enables management to compare actual costs with predetermined (standard) costs. Management can then take appropriate corrective action or assign the authority to take action to others. The first use of standard costing was affecting control over manufacturing costs; but, in recent years, standard costing has been applied to selling, general, and administrative expenses. Here we discuss standard manufacturing costs.

The three elements of manufacturing costs are: direct labor, direct materials, and overhead. For each of these, an estimate must be made of the element's cost per unit of output. For example, the direct labor cost per unit of output consists of the standard usage of labor and the standard price of labor. The standard usage derives from time studies which fix the expected output per man-hour; the standard price of labor will be fixed by the salary schedule appropriate for the kind of work necessary to produce the output. A similar determination is made for direct materials. Thus, the standard labor and standard materials cost might be as follows:

Standard labor usage per unit	2 hours
Standard wage rate per hour	$3.00
Standard labor cost (2 × $3.00)	$6.00
Standard material usage per unit	6 pounds
Standard material price per pound	$ .30
Standard material cost (6 × $.30)	$1.80

The accounting system produces information which enables the manager to compare incurred costs and standard costs. For example, if during the period covered by the report, 200 units of output were produced, the standard labor cost is $1,200 (200 × $6.00) and the standard material cost is $360 (200 × $1.80). Assume that the actual payroll cost for that same time period was $1,500 and the actual material cost was $400. That is, there was an *unfavorable labor variance* of $300 and an *unfavorable material variance* of $40. Management must determine the reasons for the variances and decide what corrective action is appropriate.

Assuming that the standards are correct, the manager must analyze the variance and fix the responsibility for restoring the balance between

---

[12] A. C. Littleton, *Accounting Evolution to 1900* (New York: Russell and Russell, 1966).

standard and actual costs. It is obvious that if actual labor cost exceeds standard cost, the reason for the difference is found in labor usage and labor wage rates. Either actual labor usage exceeded standard labor usage or actual wage rates exceeded standard wage rates, or both, or some combination of both. Suppose that, in this example, the accountant reports the actual payroll consisted of 450 actual hours at an average wage rate of $3.33. The questions management must resolve are now narrowed to two: what happened during the period to cause output per man-hour to go down (to produce 200 units of output should require 400 labor hours); and, why was the average wage rate more than the standard wage rate. The answers to these questions are found in the resources and activity stages of the cycle (see Figure 6–1).

Similar analyses are made to discover the causes for the unfavorable material variance. The first step is discovering the relationships between actual and standard usage and between actual and standard price. As with the labor, the manager may find actual material usage exceeded that specified by standard; and/or the manager may find the actual price exceeds the standard price. Once the cause is isolated, the analysis must proceed to fix responsibility for corrective action.

The analysis of manufacturing overhead variances is considerably more complicated than that for labor and material. A complete discussion would carry us far afield.[13] Suffice to say that it is necessary to isolate the causes through comparisons with standards and budgets.

Quality Control

A final illustration of feedback control is quality control of the finished product. This approach uses information regarding attributes and characteristics of output to ascertain whether the manufacturing process is "in control," that is, producing acceptable output. To make this determination, the manager must specify the product characteristic that is considered critical. This may be weight, length, consistency, or defects. Once the characteristic is defined, it must be measured.

For an example, consider one problem of a manufacturer of peanut butter: maintaining a minimum quantity of peanut butter in each comtainer, say 12 ounces. One approach would be to weigh each container when it is filled, that is, 100 per-cent of the output could be inspected. An alternative is to inspect samples of output to make inferences about the process based upon the sample information. The latter approach is termed

---

[13] The reader can consult any text in cost accounting and managerial accounting for elaborate discussions of standard cost analysis. For example, see: Charles T. Horngren, *Cost Accounting: A Managerial Emphasis* (Englewood Cliffs, N.J.: Prentice-Hall, Inc., 1967); Harold Bierman, *Topics in Cost Accounting and Decisions* (New York: McGraw-Hill Book Co., Inc., 1963); Carl L. Moore and Robert K. Jaedicke, *Managerial Accounting* (Cincinnati, Ohio: South-Western Publishing Co., 1967).

statistical quality control. This method makes use of statistical sampling theory and, since the amount of time devoted to inspection is reduced, the cost of inspection is also reduced.

SUMMARY

In this chapter, we have seen that the control process can be subdivided into preliminary control, concurrent control, and feedback control. Furthermore, we have seen that the techniques used in each of these three subdivisions necessitate the establishment of standards, the provision of information, and the implementation of corrective action. These three requirements are necessary for the effective functioning of any control technique.

This chapter completes our discussion of the three management functions. We have not attempted to go into great detail in our descriptions of the various planning, organizing, and controlling techniques. Our objective was simply to provide the student a framework for understanding what management is in terms of what managers do. This concept of management is a significant contribution of classical management theory. The next section provides the student with information to understand some of the contributions of behavioral scientists to the theory and practice of management.

DISCUSSION AND REVIEW QUESTIONS

1. "The term 'control' connotes restriction of freedom and such terms should be avoided in management literature." Discuss.
2. What is the relationship between policies, standards, and goals?
3. Why are preliminary control and concurrent control methods so widely used in organizations such as universities and other nonmarket institutions?
4. Research the term "cybernetics" and relate it to feedback control.
5. What is the relationship between the controlling function and the organizing function?
6. Why should payback, rate of return, and discounted rate of return measures of investment acceptability exist coincidently? Surely, one must be correct and the others incorrect.
7. Distinguish between direction and supervision. Are such distinctions useful?
8. "Financial ratios don't lie, but liars figure financial ratios!" Now what does that mean?!
9. Under what circumstances would feedback control methods be inappropriate?

10. Review: What did Fayol, Mooney, and Urwick say about the controlling function?

11. Research the concept "responsibility accounting" and relate it to the discussion in this chapter.

ADDITIONAL REFERENCES

DUNCAN, A. J. *Quality Control and Industrial Statistics.* Homewood, Ill.: Richard D. Irwin, Inc., 1965.

EMERY, J. C. *Organizational Planning and Control Systems: Theory and Technology.* New York: Macmillan, 1969.

FOULKE, R. A. *Practical Financial Statement Analysis.* New York: McGraw-Hill Book Co., 1957.

GARDNER, F. V. *Profit Management and Control.* New York: McGraw-Hill Book Co., 1955.

JEROME, W. T. *Executive Control—The Catalyst.* New York: John Wiley and Sons, Inc., 1961.

KING-SCOTT, P. *Industrial Supervision.* London: Sir Isaac Pitman and Sons, Ltd., 1969.

MARTINDELL, J. W. *The Appraisal of Management.* New York: Harper and Row, 1962.

ROSE, T. G. *Top Management Accounting.* London: Sir Isaac Pitman and Sons, Ltd., 1958.

ROSE, T. G. AND FARR, D. E. *Higher Management Control.* New York: McGraw-Hill Book Co., 1957.

part **II**
THE BEHAVIORAL SCHOOL

Human Relations and Behavioral
  Science Foundations
Motivation
Work Groups in the Organization
Leadership
Organizational Design
Organizational Change

chapter seven

Human Relations and
Behavioral Science Foundations

INTRODUCTION

As noted in the previous section, a major limitation of the classical approach to management was that the classical writers did not rigorously analyze the human element. Therefore it is not surprising that a school of thought developed which added to the already established classical theories. This school has been described in several ways; we shall entitle it the Behavioral School of Management.[1] Its first phase may be identified as the "human relations" branch. The human relations movement became popular in the 1940s and early 1950s. The second branch was the "behavioral science" approach, which came into popular use in the early 1950s and today receives much emphasis in the literature of management. This is illustrated diagrammatically in Figure 7–1. Both phases will be discussed in this chapter, in which we shall touch briefly upon the foundations of the behavioral school of management.

HUMAN RELATIONS THEORY

Human relations theory brought to the attention of management the important role played by individuals in determining the success or

---

[1] Some writers describe this school as the "human relations" or "neo-classical" school and distinguish it from the behavioral science school, which they consider as part of "modern" management theory. However, in this text the human relations and behavioral science theories will be examined under the general heading of the Behavioral School of Management.

failure of an organization. This theory dealt with the critical task of compensating for some of the deficiencies in classical theory. Basically, the human relations approach accepted the major premises of the classical school. However, it showed how these premises should be modified because of differences in individual behavior and the influence of work groups upon the individual, and *vice versa.* Thus, human relations theory

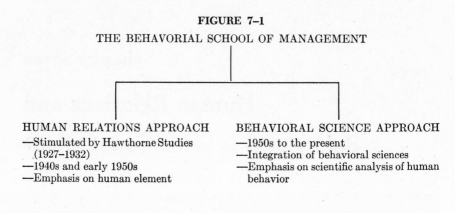

FIGURE 7-1

THE BEHAVORIAL SCHOOL OF MANAGEMENT

HUMAN RELATIONS APPROACH
—Stimulated by Hawthorne Studies
  (1927–1932)
—1940s and early 1950s
—Emphasis on human element

BEHAVIORAL SCIENCE APPROACH
—1950s to the present
—Integration of behavioral sciences
—Emphasis on scientific analysis of human behavior

concentrated on the social environment surrounding the job, whereas classical writers were concerned mainly with the physical environment.

The Hawthorne Studies

The human relations approach began when a group of researchers from Harvard University was invited to conduct studies at the Chicago Hawthorne Plant of Western Electric.[2] The researchers originally set out to study the relationship between productivity and physical working conditions.

The general progression of the research at Hawthorne can be grouped in four phases.[3] However, it should be noted that each of the last three developed as an attempt on the part of the researchers to answer questions raised by the previous phase. The four phases were:

1. Experiments to determine the effects of changes in illumination on productivity.
2. Experiments to determine the effects of changes in hours and other working conditions (e.g., rest periods, refreshments) on productivity (Relay Assembly Test Room Experiment).

---

[2] For a complete account of these studies, see Fritz J. Roethlisberger and W. J. Dickson, *Management and the Worker* (Boston: Harvard University Press, 1939).

[3] Paul R. Lawrence and John A. Seiler, *Organizational Behavior and Administration* (Homewood, Ill.: Richard D. Irwin, Inc., 1965), p. 165.

3. Conducting a plant-wide interview program to determine worker attitudes and sentiments.
4. Determination and analysis of social organization at work (Bank Wiring Observation Room Experiment).

Experiments in Illumination

In the first series of experiments a sample group of workers was chosen and placed in two separate groups. One group was exposed to varying intensities of illumination. Since this group was subjected to experimental changes, it was termed the *experimental* group. Another group, the *control* group, continued to work under constant intensities of illumination. Surprisingly, the researchers found that, as they increased the illumination in the experimental group, both groups increased production. When the researchers decreased the intensity, output continued to rise for both groups. Finally, the illumination in the experimental group was reduced to that of moonlight. Then, and only then, was there a significant decline in output. The researchers concluded that illumination in the workplace had little or no effect on the productivity of the two groups.

Relay Assembly Test Room Experiment

In the second phase of the study, several persons volunteered to work under controlled conditions isolated from the other workers. Several changes in the conditions of the job were made (e.g., refreshments, workplace, temperature) with little effect on productivity.

In another phase, a group of women employees was placed together in an isolated part of the assembly department. The experimental group was given a special group incentive, a wage payment. In this case, output increased for each operator.

Overall, the relay assembly test room experiment was designed to determine the effect of changes in various job conditions on group productivity. The researchers concluded that these factors had little or no effect.

Employee Interviews

After the first two phases, the researchers concluded that their attempt to relate physical conditions of the job to productivity did not produce any significant results. They therefore postulated that the human element in the work environment apparently had a significantly greater impact on the rate of productivity than the technical and physical aspects of the job. The researchers summarized this as follows:

In brief, the increase in the output rate of the girls in the Relay Assembly Test Room could not be related to any change in their physical conditions of work, whether experimentally induced or not. It could, however, be related to what can only be spoken of as the development of an organized social group and a peculiar and effective relation with its supervisors.[4]

On the basis of their extensive interview program, the researchers proposed the premise that the work group as a whole determined the production output of individual group members by enforcing an informal norm of what a fair day's work should be.

Bank Wiring Observation Room Experiment

In order to test the premise formulated at the conclusion of the interview program, the researchers decided to conduct a final experiment. The procedure in this part of the study was similar to that in the relay assembly test room procedure, except that nine male operators who assembled terminal banks for telephone exchanges were used.

In this experiment, an attempt was made to determine the effect of a group piecework incentive pay plan, assuming that the workers would seek their own economic interests by maximizing their productivity and that faster workers would pressure the slower ones to improve their efficiency. However, the researchers found that pressure was actually a form of social behavior. In order to be accepted in the work group, the worker had to act in accord with group norms and not be a "rate buster" by overproducing, or a "chiseler" by underproducing. The group defined what constituted a day's work, and as soon as they knew that they could reach this output level, they slacked off. This process was more marked among the faster than the slower workers.

The researchers concluded that the social standards of the work group set the fair rates for each of its members. They found no relationship between productivity and intelligence, dexterity, and other skills. They concluded that the wage incentive plan was less important in determining an individual worker's output than group acceptance and security.

A Review of the Hawthorne Studies

Probably the major contribution of the Hawthorne studies is that they generated a great deal of interest in human problems of the workplace. They were also the catalyst for a number of future studies of human behavior in organizational settings.

The Hawthorne studies have been widely criticized by some behavioral scientists because of the lack of use, or misuse, of the scientific method in arriving at conclusions. Some critics feel that there was a great deal

---

[4] *Ibid.*, p. 173.

of bias and preconception on the part of the researchers. One writer developed a detailed comparison between the conclusions drawn by the researchers and the evidence they presented, and found that their conclusions were almost entirely unsupported.[5] He asks the question ". . . how it was possible for studies so nearly devoid of scientific merit, and conclusions so little supported by evidence, to gain so influential and respected a place within scientific disciplines and to hold this place for so long."[6]

Other criticisms have also been leveled at the Hawthorne studies,[7] for example:

1. The Hawthorne researchers did not give sufficient attention to the attitudes that people bring with them to the workplace. They did not recognize such forces as class consciousness, the role of unions and other extra-plant forces on attitudes.

2. The Hawthorne plant was not a typical plant because it was a thoroughly unpleasant place in which to work.

3. The Hawthorne studies look upon the worker as a means to an end, not an end in himself. They assume acceptance of management's goals and look on the worker as someone to be manipulated by management.

Although they have been criticized, the Hawthorne studies had a significant impact on management practice. As a result of the studies, human relations training programs became extremely popular in industry after World War II. These training programs were a spill-over from the Training Within Industry Program of the War Manpower Commission. This was a supervisory training program to make up for the shortage of civilian supervisory skills during the war. Many of these programs had as an underlying rationale the belief that a happy worker would be a productive worker. It was not until later that behavioral science research found that such training programs might have no influence on productivity.

While we do not hold up the Hawthorne studies as a model in the application of scientific methodology to problems of human behavior, it does represent a benchmark in such studies. If it did nothing else, it stimulated an interest in the human problems of management. Although the assumptions and methods of human relations and behavioral science are not the same, it was the human relations branch that provided the impetus for the present-day behavioral science emphasis in management theory.

---

[5] Alex Carey, "The Hawthorne Studies: A Radical Criticism," *American Sociological Review*, vol. 32 (June, 1967), pp. 403–16.

[6] *Ibid.*, p. 403.

[7] Henry A. Landsberger, *Hawthorne Revisited* (Ithaca, N.Y.: New York State School of Industrial and Labor Relations, Cornell University, 1958).

HUMAN RELATIONS MODIFICATIONS
OF SELECTED PRINCIPLES OF ORGANIZATION

The human relations approach to management regarded the classical principles of organization as given. However, an attempt was made to modify classical doctrine by injecting the human element either through individual behavior or through the influence of the work group. Let us examine these modifications of the principles of classical management theory.[8]

1. *Division of Labor.* The division of labor received a great deal of attention from human relations writers. Special attention was given to the isolation of the worker and his feelings of anonymity, resulting from his insignificant job and lack of feeling of task completion because of his negligible contribution to the final product.

Human relations writers generally assumed that, as the division of labor increases, the need for managerial motivation and coordination of the activities of others arises. Thus a large volume of their writing focuses upon the consequences of dividing work into smaller and smaller units. The emphasis of many of these writers is on procedures that can be used to minimize some of the negative consequences (e.g., boredom, fatigue) of the division of labor.

2. *Scalar and Functional Processes.* The human relations writers believed that the scalar and functional processes are theoretically sound, but break down once the human element enters the picture. They believed that the classical writers assumed perfection in the delegation and functionalization processes, but that human problems resulted through imperfections in the manner in which these processes are handled.

For example, too much or not enough delegation may render a manager incapable of action; or the failure to delegate sufficient authority, or to delegate authority and responsibility equally, may cause frustration for the delegatee. These and other human-relations implications of the scalar and functional processes were examined and discussed by human relations writers.

3. *Structure.* The human relations writers were quick to point out that human behavior can disrupt the best-laid organizational plans. Once the human element entered the picture, much of the neatness and the logical relationships set forth in the formal structure changed. They also noted the internal frictions that can develop among people who perform different functions. One of the often-mentioned areas of friction was that between line and staff functions. The human relations writers offered prescriptions for the management of conflict within the organization

[8] The following discussion is based upon William G. Scott, "Organization Theory: An Overview and an Appraisal," *Journal of the Academy of Management,* vol. 4 (April, 1961), pp. 7–26. Also see William G. Scott, *Human Problems in Management* (Homewood, Ill.: Richard D. Irwin, Inc., 1962).

structure. Two of the most frequently mentioned prescriptions were participation and better communication. The latter, however, was not necessarily a new prescription since classical writers such as Fayol, Mooney, and Barnard were also interested in communications.

4. Span of Control. The human relations writers believed that it was not possible to reduce the problem of span of control to an accurate, universally applicable ratio. They were concerned with the various human factors that affect span of control, believing that the key determinants were individual differences in managerial abilities, the kind of people and the type of function supervised, and the effectiveness of communication between superior and subordinate.

Another problem related to the question of span of control was examined: that of the type of structure which develops. In other words, is a tall structure with a short span of control or a flat structure with a wide span of control more conducive to high morale and good human relations? Here also they concluded that the answer is situational; that is, because of differences in the people or the organization, one is sometimes more effective than the other.

The reader can see that the human relations branch basically accepted the postulates put forth by the classical theorists. However, the human relations approach added to classical theory by introducing the human element and indicating how this modified the principles developed by the classical theorists. As we mentioned previously, it also provided the impetus for the present behavioral science approach.

In addition to modifying the principles of organization, human relations writers also focused attention on the informal work group, which the classical writers did not thoroughly analyze. By informal groups we mean natural formations of people in the work situation, not specified in the formal organization. The Hawthorne studies stimulated interest in the study of groups in the work situation. Human relations writers, and later behavioral science writers, began to examine the underlying determinants, types, characteristics, and roles of work groups. We shall devote an entire chapter to work groups in the organization.

THE BEHAVIORAL SCIENCE APPROACH

As was noted earlier, the behavioral science approach to management became popular in the early 1950s. It was at this time that an organization known as the Foundation for Research on Human Behavior was established. The goals and objectives of this organization were to promote and support behavioral science research in business, government, and other types of organizations. We shall define the behavioral science approach to the study of management as follows:

. . . the study of observable and verifiable human behavior in organizations, using scientific procedures. It is largely inductive and problem centered, focusing on the issue of human behavior, and drawing from any relevant literature, especially in psychology, sociology and anthropology.[9]

The advocates of the behavioral science approach were bothered by the fact that both practitioners and scholars had accepted without scientific validation so much of the management theory that preceded them. Their own scientific approach has added greatly to the earlier body of knowledge, since they provided a means to test the earlier theories. Through their work some aspects of the prior theory have been modified while others withstood the test of scientific validation. Because of the emphasis on the behavioral sciences and on science itself, let us examine each of these.

The Behavioral Sciences

First we must distinguish between the behavioral sciences and the social sciences. The term "social sciences" usually refers to six disciplines: anthropology, economics, history, political science, psychology, and sociology. When we use the term "behavioral sciences," we refer to the disciplines of anthropology, psychology, and sociology.

Psychology is the study of human behavior. There are many branches of general psychology which have provided concepts and theories useful to the study of management, for example, *social psychology*, which deals with behavior as it relates to other individuals. It studies how groups and individuals influence and modify each other's behavior. *Organizational psychology* is a relatively new branch which deals with man's behavior and attitudes within an organizational setting. It studies the effect of the organization upon the individual and the individual's effect upon the organization. It is easy to see that these areas of psychology have direct relevance to the field of management.

Of all the behavioral sciences, psychology has probably played the biggest role in influencing management thought. Psychologists have shown that people have a great variety of needs which they attempt to satisfy at work. In a later chapter in this section, we shall see that these include social and psychological as well as economic needs.

Sociology attempts to isolate, define, and describe human behavior in groups. It strives to develop laws and generalizations about human nature, social interaction, culture, and social organization.

One of the major contributions of sociologists to management thought has been their focus on small groups, which are often treated in the management literature as the informal components of organization. We shall see that much has been learned about the behavior of small groups, the

---

[9] Alan C. Filley and Robert J. House, *Managerial Process and Organizational Behavior* (Glenview, Ill.: Scott, Foresman and Company, 1969), p. 8.

influence they have on members, and their impact on the formal organization.

Sociologists also have an interest in formal organizations, which they approach as the study of bureaucracy, focusing on bureaucratic behavior as well as the structural relationships in bureaucratic organizations. Sociologists have provided management with knowledge regarding leader and follower roles and the patterns of power and authority in formal organizations.

Anthropology examines all the behaviors of man which have been learned, including all of the social, technical, and familial behaviors which are a part of the broad concept of "culture." This is the major theme of cultural anthropology, the science devoted to the study of different peoples and cultures of the world, and is a key concept in the behavioral sciences. In fact, the entire way in which an individual behaves, the priority of needs he attempts to satisfy, and the means he chooses to satisfy them are functions of his culture.

While psychology and sociology have had a greater impact in shaping management thought, cultural anthropology has made significant contributions regarding the impact of culture on formal organizations. In the future, as firms expand their activities overseas, anthropology will undoubtedly provide management with valuable insights as they attempt to perform the management functions of planning, organizing, and controlling in different cultural environments.

Science and Human Behavior

Thus far, we have emphasized that the behavioral science approach to management attempts to study human behavior in organizations by using scientific procedures. Hence it is necessary to examine the nature of science as it is applied to human behavior. We do not, however, intend to get into arguments whether (1) there can be such a thing as a science of human behavior, (2) management is a science or not, and (3) the same scientific procedures used so successfully in the natural sciences can be adapted to the study of humans, especially humans in an organizational setting. The authors merely assume that science is applicable to management and behavioral studies. We fully realize that there are means other than scientific procedures (e.g., observation, intuition) which have provided insights into human behavior.

The scientific approach, however, has a great deal to offer in the study of human behavior. First, it has made great strides in many other fields such as the physical sciences. In addition, it has produced information about human behavior that has become established knowledge. The greatest advantage of the scientific approach has been summarized as follows:

The scientific approach has one characteristic that no other method of attaining knowledge has: self-correction. There are built-in checks all along the way to scientific knowledge. These checks are so conceived and used that they control and verify the scientist's activities and conclusions to the end of attaining dependable knowledge outside himself.[10]

Most writers agree that there is no single scientific method,[11] but rather several methods that scientists can and do use. Thus it is probably better to say that there is a scientific approach.

Characteristics of the Scientific Approach

While only an "ideal" science would exhibit each of the following characteristics, they nevertheless are the hallmarks of the scientific approach.[12]

1. The Procedures Are Public. This means that a scientific report contains a complete description of what was done, to enable other researchers in the field to follow each step of the investigation as if they were actually present.

2. The Definitions Are Precise. The procedures used, the variables measured, and how they were measured must be clearly stated. For example, if we were examining motivation among employees in a given plant, it would be necessary to define what we mean by motivation and how we measured it (e.g., number of units produced, number of absences).

3. The Data-Collecting Is Objective. Bias in collecting data as well as in the interpretation of results has no place in science. Objectivity throughout is a key feature of the scientific approach.

4. The Findings Must Be Replicable. This enables any researcher in the field to test the findings or results of a study by attempting to reproduce them.

5. The Approach Is Systematic and Cumulative. This relates to one of the underlying purposes of science, to develop a unified body of knowledge. Thus, a major purpose of the behavioral science approach to management is to develop an organized system of verified propositions about human behavior in organizations.

6. The Purposes Are Explanation, Understanding and Prediction. Every scientist wants to know "why" and "how." If he determines "why" and "how" and is able to provide proof, he can then predict the particular conditions under which specific events (behavior in this case) will occur.

---

[10] Fred N. Kerlinger, *Foundations of Behavioral Research* (New York: Holt, Rinehart, and Winston, Inc., 1964), p. 7.

[11] *Ibid.*, p. 7.

[12] Bernard Berelson and Gary A. Steiner, *Human Behavior: An Inventory of Scientific Findings* (New York: Harcourt, Brace and World, Inc., 1964), pp. 16–18.

This is the ultimate objective of behavioral science, as it is of all science.

These six characteristics exhibit the basic nature of the scientific approach. Throughout the discussion we have stressed the objective, systematic, and controlled nature of the scientific approach, which enables others to have confidence in research outcomes. What is important is the overall fundamental idea that the scientific approach is a controlled rational process.

Methods of Inquiry

Just as other scientists have certain tools and methods for obtaining data, so does the behavioral scientist. These are usually referred to as designs. In broad terms, there are three basic designs used by behavioral scientists: the experiment, the sample survey, and the case study.[13]

1. The Experiment. An investigation that can be considered an experiment must contain two elements—manipulation of some variable by the researcher and observation or measurement of the results. There are several different forms which an experiment can take, but we shall not examine them here.[14] An example of a simple experiment might be one in which management is trying to determine the effect of increases in piecerates on productivity. Since they already have existing measures of productivity, they would have a "before" measure with which to compare the results. Their first step would be to assign workers randomly to two groups. The *experimental* group would have its piecerates altered while the *control* group would continue working under the existing rates. After a period of time (e.g., six months), the output of both groups would be compared with their productivity before the experiment began. This might give some idea as to the effect of a higher piecerate on productivity. This experiment is an oversimplification used for illustrative purposes. Obviously, there would have to be provisions made to keep the results from being distorted (e.g., workers being aware that they are participating in an experiment). However, this example does illustrate the two major elements of an experiment, manipulation of some variable by the researcher (piecerates) and observation or measurement of the results (productivity).

Obviously, the practical aspects of a business would often preclude experimentation in an actual setting or in an ongoing business system. As a result, many of the findings of behavioral scientists which are being applied in the field of management have resulted from experimental studies outside the business organization. However, in many cases experimentation has also been possible within the business organization.

---

[13] *Ibid.*, pp. 18–27.

[14] The interested reader should consult Kerlinger, *op. cit.*, Chapters 15–19.

2. The Sample Survey. In this type of study, the collection of data is from a limited number of units which are assumed to be representative of an entire group. For example, suppose we decide to study college students. This is the group or "population" we are concerned about. We then select a sample (e.g., randomly) of this group and collect some measures on particular characteristics in which we are interested (e.g., attitudes toward big business). It should be clear that there are certain kinds of questions (e.g., attitudes of college students toward big business) that can only be answered by a sample survey. However, it is often necessary to develop provisions to handle changes in attitudes over time in order to improve the usefulness of the findings.

3. The Case Study. Unlike the sample survey which attempts to measure one or more characteristics in many people, usually at one point in time, the case study attempts to examine numerous characteristics of one person or group,[15] usually over an extended time period. A behavioral scientist who spends time living with a mountain tribe or working with a group of blue-collar workers will usually report his results in the form of a case study (e.g., the key factors and incidents leading up to a wildcat strike). While this method is extremely valuable in answering questions concerning development (e.g., factors leading up to a strike) and for exploratory purposes, its major limitation is that the ability to generalize from it is uncertain, since the results are usually based on a sample of one. Perhaps, in another firm, the same incidents may not result in a wildcat strike. A case study as such usually does not prove or disprove anything.[16]

Management's Use of Behavioral Science Theory

One of the vital tasks performed by a manager is decision-making. To make decisions he must have possible alternatives from which to choose, authority to implement the alternative he chooses, and information. This last factor is our concern in this section. The manager needs two kinds of information: First, he must have facts about the particular system, the men and machines involved, and the cost. Second, he needs theory to aid in explaining what will happen if he alters one variable, and he must know how the different variables are related to each other. The behavioral school of management focuses upon the theory and research concerning human behavior in organizations developed by behavioral scientists.

If theory is to be useful to the manager, it must be programmatic, that is, it must tell him what to do in problem situations, provide him with a description of his environment, or provide him with a conceptual framework on which to rely in problem solving situations to help him explain

---

[15] Berelson and Steiner, *op. cit.*, p. 27.
[16] *Ibid.*, p. 27.

his organizational environment. In other words, theory must provide him with guides for problem definition, problem solving, explanation of behavior, and control of variables. In order to be useful, theory must make him a better practitioner.

In the following chapters we shall examine areas such as motivation, work groups, leadership, organizational design, and organizational change. Throughout our discussions we shall draw upon material from each of the behavioral sciences. While the disciplines may differ, the findings drawn upon will, for the most part, have a common thread. They will have been arrived at using the methods which we have described as the scientific approach.

This section should in no way be viewed as excluding the classical management school. Instead, it should be regarded as an addition to the classical management functions of *organizing* and *controlling*. The authors contend that the classical approach without the behavioral orientation is as sterile as the behavioral approach without the classical foundations. The sole purpose in presenting the behavioral material in the following chapters is to provide the reader with knowledge from the behavioral sciences that will make him a better organizer and a more effective controller. Since the functions of management include organizing and controlling, the findings of the behavioral scientists must assist him in performing these functions. Otherwise they would be of little value to the manager and would have no place in this text.

DISCUSSION AND REVIEW QUESTIONS

1. Discuss the underlying reasons for the development of the behavioral school of management.

2. The Hawthorne studies are considered to have provided the impetus for human relations theory. Discuss in detail the four phases of the Hawthorne studies.

3. The Hawthorne studies have been widely criticized on several points. Discuss in detail each of these criticisms.

4. The human relations writers sought to modify classical doctrine by integrating the human element either through individual behavior or the influence of the informal group. Discuss how they modified each of the principles of classical management theory.

5. How does the behavioral science approach differ from the human relations approach?

6. Discuss the major characteristics of the scientific approach.

7. Assume that the dean at your school has asked you to study the problem of student motivation. You have decided to use the scientific approach. What are some questions that would have to be answered before you could begin the study?

8. Discuss the three basic study designs used by behavioral scientists. Give an example of each type, other than those provided in the chapter.

9. A popular magazine features an article entitled, "Study and Social Habits of College Females." Upon reading the article you find that it is based on a case study of the members of a sorority at a private school in the eastern part of the country. Evaluate this study based upon your knowledge of the characteristics and methods of scientific inquiry.

10. Of what value is theory to the practicing manager?

ADDITIONAL REFERENCES

Athos, A. G. and Coffey, R. E. *Behavior in Organizations: A Multidimensional Approach*. Englewood Cliffs, N.J.: Prentice-Hall, Inc., 1968.

Bass, B. M. *Organizational Psychology*. Boston: Allyn and Bacon, Inc., 1965.

Barnard, C. I. *The Functions of the Executive*. Boston: Harvard University Press, 1938.

Cyert, R. M. and March, J. G. *A Behavioral Theory of the Firm*. Englewood Cliffs, N.J.: Prentice-Hall, Inc., 1963.

Flippo, E. B. *Management: A Behavioral Approach*. Boston: Allyn and Bacon, Inc., 1970.

Hodge, B. J. and Johnson, H. J. *Management and Organizational Behavior: A Multidimensional Approach*. New York: John Wiley and Sons, Inc., 1970.

Koontz, H. (ed.). *Toward a Unified Theory of Management*. New York: McGraw-Hill Book Company, Inc., 1964.

Likert, R. and Hayes, S. P., Jr. (eds.). *Some Applications of Behavioral Research*. Paris: UNESCO, 1957.

March, J. G. and Simon, H. A. *Organizations*. New York: John Wiley and Sons, Inc., 1958.

Mayo, E. *The Human Problems of Industrial Civilization*. New York: Macmillan and Company, 1933.

Mayo, E. *The Social Problems of an Industrial Civilization*. Boston: Harvard University Press, 1945.

Roethlisberger, F. J. *Management and Morale*. Boston: Harvard University Press, 1941.

chapter eight

Motivation

INTRODUCTION

Motivation is concerned with the "why" of human behavior, what it is that makes people do things. Why does Harry have frequent run-ins with the boss, or why does Tom work so much harder than Jim? These questions can be partially answered with an understanding of human motivation. Obviously, an understanding of motivation is a necessity for the student of management. It is an area which receives a great deal of attention from the behavioral school of management. Behavioralists are concerned with the relationship between the satisfaction of individual needs and the workplace. They believe that, in order to perform his functions effectively, a manager must understand why people are motivated to behave as they do. In this way the manager can make the kinds of decisions which will encourage subordinates to direct their efforts toward achievement of organizational goals.

THE NATURE OF MOTIVATION

Before examining the elements of motivation, it is vital that we clearly understand exactly what the term means. Berelson and Steiner define motivation as "all those inner striving conditions described as wishes, desires, drives, etc. . . . . It is an inner state that activates or moves."[1]

More specifically, the term motivation has often been called an *inter-*

---

[1] Bernard Berelson and Gary A. Steiner, *Human Behavior: An Inventory of Scientific Findings* (New York: Harcourt, Brace, and World, 1964).

vening variable.[2] Intervening variables are internal and psychological processes which are not directly observable and which, in turn, account for behavior.[3] Thus motivation is an intervening variable; for it cannot be seen, heard, or felt, and is inferred from behavior. Thus we can judge a person's motivation by observing his behavior, whereas we cannot measure it directly because it is an unobservable entity. This means that we can only measure presumed indicants of motivation, but not motivation itself. For example, if we observe a pieceworker and determine that he is producing more than any of his co-workers, we infer that he is being motivated. However, we did not measure motivation directly; we observed a presumed indicant of motivation and made inferences from our observations. Before this could be done, we had to define operationally what motivation would be—i.e., the number of units produced on the piecerate system.

Motivation and Behavior

Psychologists generally agree that all behavior is motivated, and that people have reasons for doing the things they do or for behaving in the manner that they do. In other words, all human behavior is designed to

FIGURE 8–1

The Process of Motivation

achieve certain goals and objectives. Such goal-directed behavior revolves around the desire for need satisfaction.

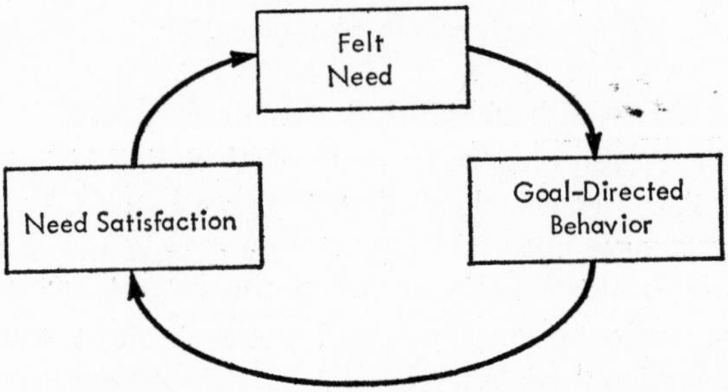

A felt need is the starting point in the process of motivation. It is a deficiency of something within the individual and provides the spark which begins the chain of events leading to behavior. An unsatisfied need

---

[2] E. Tolman, *Behavior and Psychological Man* (Berkeley, Calif.: University of California Press, 1958), pp. 115–29.

[3] Fred N. Kerlinger, *Foundations of Behavioral Research* (New York: Holt, Rinehart, and Winston, Inc., 1964), p. 44.

causes tension within the individual, leading the individual to engage in some kind of behavior (seek a means) to satisfy the need, and thereby to reduce the tension. Note that this activity is directed toward a goal; arrival at the goal satisfies the need, and the mechanism of motivation is complete. For example, a thirsty person *needs* water, he is *driven* by thirst, and *motivated* by a desire for water in order to satisfy his need.

Thus, the continuous process begins with a felt need and ends with need satisfaction with goal-directed behavior as a part of the process. This can be illustrated in a diagram (Figure 8–1). Since needs are such an important part of the process of motivation, let us examine them in more detail.

THE NEED HIERARCHY AND MOTIVATION

As we have already mentioned, felt needs are the starting point in the process of motivation. These needs may be classified in different ways.

Classical Management School Motivation Theory

Many of the early writers on management emphasized monetary incentives as prime means for motivating the individual. These men were undoubtedly influenced by the classical economists who placed chief emphasis on man's rational pursuit of economic objectives. They believed that economic behavior was characterized by rational economic calculations. Most psychologists agree that, while money is obviously an important motivator, man seeks to satisfy other than purely economic needs. In fact, Freud was the first psychologist to hypothesize that much of man's behavior may not even be rational, but that it may be influenced by motives of which the individual is not aware.

While most psychologists agree that man is motivated by the desire to satisfy many needs, there is a wide difference of opinion as to what these needs and their relative importance are. Most, however, take the pluralistic view, emphasizing many different types of needs the satisfaction of which is a key determinant of behavior. Let us now examine one of the most widely adopted theories of human motivation.

The Hierarchy of Needs

A widely adopted pluralistic framework is that presented by psychologist A. H. Maslow.[4] His theory of motivation stresses two fundamental premises:

---

[4] Abraham H. Maslow, *Motivation and Personality* (New York: Harper and Brothers, 1954), Chapter 5.

1. Man is a wanting animal whose needs depend on what he already has. Only needs not yet satisfied can influence behavior; a satisfied need is not a motivator.
2. Man's needs are arranged in a hierarchy of importance. Once one need is satisfied, another emerges and demands satisfaction.

Maslow hypothesizes five classes of needs in the order of their prepotency. These needs are (1) physiological, (2) safety, (3) belongingness, (4) esteem, and (5) self-actualization.[5] He placed them in a formal framework referred to as the *hierarchy of needs* because of the different levels of importance indicated. This framework is presented diagrammatically as Figure 8–2.

Maslow states that, if all of a person's needs are unsatisfied at a particular time, satisfaction of the most prepotent needs will be more pressing than the others. Those which come first must be satisfied before a higher need comes into play, and only when they are sufficiently satisfied are the next ones in line significant. Let us briefly examine each need level.

Physiological Needs

This category consists of the primary needs of the human body such as food, water, and sex. Physiological needs will dominate when all needs are unsatisfied. In such a case, no other needs will serve as a basis for motivation. As Maslow states, "a person who is lacking food, safety, love, and esteem would probably hunger for food more strongly than for anything else."[6]

Since these types of situations probably do not arise often these days, particularly in the United States, the important needs, at least from a managerial standpoint, would appear to be those higher in the hierarchy.

Safety Needs

With the physiological needs met, the next higher level assumes importance. Safety needs include protection from physical harm, ill health, and economic disaster, and avoidance of the unexpected. From a managerial standpoint, safety needs can be seen in attempts to insure job security and attempts to move toward greater financial support. For example, in the early days of labor unions, the primary demands which

---

[5] Less described, and hence not as well known are the cognitive and aesthetic needs hypothesized by Maslow. Examples of cognitive needs are the need to know or to understand, and the manipulation of the environment as the result of curiosity. The aesthetic needs are satisfied by moving from ugliness toward beauty. Maslow did not include them in the formal hierarchy framework. *Ibid.*, pp. 93–98.

[6] *Ibid.*, p. 82.

FIGURE 8–2

Hierarchy of Needs

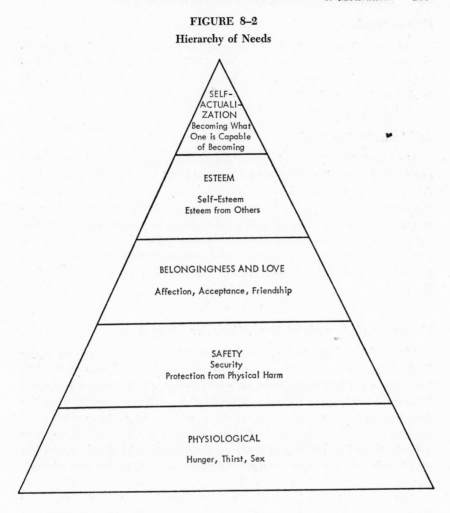

SELF-
ACTUALI-
ZATION
Becoming What
One is Capable
of Becoming

ESTEEM

Self-Esteem
Esteem from Others

BELONGINGNESS AND LOVE

Affection, Acceptance, Friendship

SAFETY
Security
Protection from Physical Harm

PHYSIOLOGICAL

Hunger, Thirst, Sex

unions presented to management consisted of monetary increases. Today, however, many unions are making demands on management for such things as fringe benefits and job security, with less emphasis on increases in pay.

Belongingness and Love Needs

These needs are related to the social and gregarious nature of man and his need for companionship. This level in the hierarchy is the point of departure from the physical or quasi-physical needs of the two previous levels. Nonsatisfaction of this level of need may affect the mental health of the individual.

Esteem Needs

These needs consist both of the need for the awareness of importance to others (self-esteem) and the actual esteem from others. The latter must also be felt as warranted and deserved. Satisfaction of these needs leads to a feeling of self-confidence and prestige.

Self-Actualization Needs

Maslow defines this need as the "desire to become more and more what one is, to become everything one is capable of becoming."[7] This means that the individual will fully realize the potentialities of his talents and capabilities. Obviously, as the status and role of the individual vary, so will the external aspects of self-actualization. In other words, whether the person is a college professor, a corporate manager, or a mother, the drive is to be effective and efficient in the particular role. Maslow assumes that satisfaction of these needs is possible only after the satisfaction of all the needs.

Management's Use of the Need-Hierarchy Concept

Maslow's need hierarchy has attracted a great deal of attention in the field of management both within and outside the academic circle. We have discussed McGregor's "Theory X" (Chapter Five) and will discuss "Theory Y" (Chapter Eleven). Examination of these suggests that the foundation of McGregor's theory is the need hierarchy. Many other writers also use this hierarchy when they discuss motivation in the business organization.[8] Later in this chapter we shall see that Maslow's model has also been used as a basis for a great deal of research in the area of motivation.

This motivation model is also widely referred to by practitioners, for it is easy to comprehend, has a great deal of "common-sense" validity, and points out some of the factors that motivate people in a business organization. Business organizations in the United States have been extremely successful in satisfying lower-level needs. Through the salary he receives, the individual is able to satisfy the physiological needs of himself and his family. The firm aids in satisfying security or safety needs through both salary and fringe benefit programs. Finally, it aids in satisfying the individual's social and affiliation needs by allowing interaction and association with others on the job. In one way, all of this may have created a

---

[7] *Ibid.*, p. 92.

[8] For representative examples see W. Warren Haynes and Joseph L. Massie, *Management: Analysis, Concepts, and Cases* (Englewood Cliffs, N.J.: Prentice-Hall, Inc., 1969); and Alan C. Filley and Robert J. House, *Managerial Process and Organizational Behavior* (Glenview, Ill.: Scott, Foresman and Company, 1969).

future problem for management. Since human behavior is primarily directed toward fulfilling unsatisfied needs, how successful a manager is in the future in motivating his subordinates may be a function of his ability to satisfy their higher-level needs.

While Maslow's need hierarchy does not provide a complete understanding of human motivation or the means to motivate people, it does provide an excellent starting point for the student of management. We shall use it in this chapter as the foundation for an understanding of motivation in business organizations.

NON-SATISFACTION OF NEEDS

We have said that needs are the starting points for the understanding of motivation. However, many times an individual is unsuccessful in his attempts to satisfy his needs. In order to improve our understanding of motivation, it is necessary to explore what happens when needs are not satisfied.

As was indicated previously, unsatisfied needs produce tensions within the individual. (The reader is encouraged to think of these unsatisfied needs as occurring at any level in the need hierarchy. An unsatisfied social need can produce as much tension as an unsatisfied physiological need such as hunger.) These unsatisfied needs motivate the individual to behavior which he feels will help him relieve the tension. When the individual is unable to satisfy his needs (and thereby reduce the tension), he experiences *frustration*. The college male who plots conscientiously for half a semester to secure a date with a co-ed in his management class only to have her refuse is an example of an individual who would probably be quite frustrated. His goal of getting a date, the attainment of which would have brought the satisfaction of several needs (e.g., social, prestige, status) has been blocked.

Just as the importance of different needs, and the means used to satisfy the same need, will vary from person to person, so will the reaction to frustration vary from person to person. Some people will react in a positive manner (constructive behavior), and others in a negative manner (defensive behavior). Let us examine each of these reactions to frustration.

— HERE

Constructive Behavior

The reader is undoubtedly familiar with the constructive adaptive behavior in which a person engages when faced with frustration in his attempts to satisfy his needs. An assembly-line worker frustrated in his attempts for recognition because of the nature of his job may seek recognition off the job by seeking election to leadership posts in fraternal or civic organizations. In order to satisfy social and belonging needs, a worker may conform to the norms and values of the work group of which he is a member. (The strong attraction of work groups will be discussed later in Chapter Nine.) Finally, the college male mentioned previously may settle for a date with a less attractive co-ed or attend a party without a date but with some friends. Each of these is an example of constructive adaptive strategies which the individuals involved employed to reduce their frustration and satisfy their needs.

Defensive Behavior

When an individual is blocked in his attempts to satisfy his needs or achieve his goals, he may evoke one or more defense mechanisms instead of adopting constructive strategies to solve his problems. All of us employ defense mechanisms in one way or another, because they perform an important protective function for the individual in his attempt to cope with reality. In most cases, they do not handicap the individual to any great degree. Ordinarily, however, they are not adequate for the task of protecting the self. As a result, adults whose behavior is continually dominated by defensive behavior will usually have great difficulty in adapting to the responsibilities of work and of other people.

What happens when needs are not satisfied is a complex area of inquiry still being investigated by psychologists. However, there are some general patterns of defensive behavior which have been identified, some of the most common being:

Withdrawal. One obvious way to avoid reality is to withdraw or avoid those situations which will prove frustrating. The withdrawal may be physical (leaving the scene), but more than likely will be internalized and manifested in apathy. Workers whose jobs provide little in the way of need satisfaction may "withdraw" in the form of excessive absences, latenesses, or turnover.

Aggression. A very common reaction to frustration is aggression. In some cases, there may be a direct attack on the source of the frustration. However, this may often not be possible (e.g., to fight the boss). Unfortunately, all too often the aggression is directed toward another object or party. This is known as *displacement.* Thus, a foreman may displace his aggression on a subordinate production worker who, in turn, might displace his aggression on his wife.

Substitution. This occurs when the individual puts something else in the place of the original object. A middle manager frustrated in his attempts to be promoted within the organization may substitute a civic group to achieve leadership status. The frustrated college male previously referred to may substitute another co-ed for the original one.

Compensation. When a person goes overboard in one area or activity to make up for deficiencies in another, he is evoking this defense mechanism. A superior who realizes that he has a disagreeable personality may overcompensate in his attempts to practice good "human relations" with his subordinates.

Repression. Many times the individual will repress a situation and a problem in order to keep frustration down. At times repression is an almost automatic response whereby the individual loses awareness of incidents that would cause anxiety or frustration if allowed to remain at the conscious level of his mind. Thus an unpleasant situation with his superior may be quickly "forgotten" by a subordinate.

Regression. When confronted with frustration, some individuals will revert back (regress) to childlike forms of behavior in their attempts to avoid the unpleasant reality. In the work situation, this often manifests itself in some form of horseplay.

Projection. This involves attributing one's own feelings to someone else. A subordinate may dislike his superior for some particular reason and attempt to make the superior appear ineffective whenever possible. The subordinate will attempt to justify this by saying, "My boss never liked me from the moment I got here."

Rationalization. This occurs when an individual presents a reason for his behavior which he sees as less ego-deflating or more socially acceptable than the true reason. An example of this popular defense mechanism is an employee perceiving his poor performance as the result of obsolete equipment rather than of his own deficiency.

Since every individual relies to some extent on defense mechanisms, this kind of behavior is difficult to eliminate completely in business organizations. In fact, it performs a useful role in maintaining mental health. However, its occurrence may be minimized at least to the extent that managerial decisions provide conditions under which employees experience minimum frustration. In addition, understanding of such behavior gives the future manager greater empathy in his everyday interactions with superiors and subordinates, and makes him aware that an individual's behavior may not be a true indication of the type of person with whom he is dealing, since defense mechanisms may hide the true personality of the individual.

We can summarize what we have said thus far about motivation in the schematic model presented in Figure 8–3. The diagram indicates that a felt need results in tensions within the individual and motivates him to search for ways to relieve the tension. The diagram indicates that, if he is successful in achieving his goal, the next felt need emerges. If, however, his attempts are met with frustration, he either engages in adaptive behavior (note the plus sign to indicate its constructive nature), or he

FIGURE 8–3

A Motivational Model

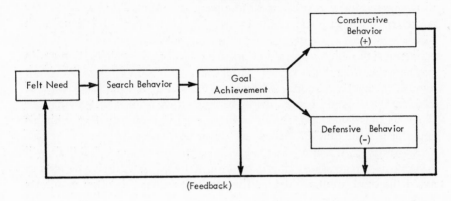

(Feedback)

resorts to defensive types of behavior (indicated with a minus sign because of its often dysfunctional effects). In either case, the individual returns to the next felt need which emerges.

PERSONALITY, BEHAVIOR, AND MOTIVATION

In the previous section we presented a conceptual framework for the relationship between needs and motivation. It is obvious that this is a general behavioral model which does not consider individual differences in motivation and behavior; otherwise, based on this model, one should be able to predict behavior. The reader should see that this is not possible: Given similar needs, different people react in different ways, not only in the goals they select and the means they choose to achieve them, but also in their reactions to frustration. Evidently there is some element missing in our explanation of motivation. This important element is the individual personality. Though each of us may be motivated to fulfill similar kinds of needs, the particular patterns of motivation and behavior we choose will differ from those of others. We shall now examine the relationship between personality, behavior, and motivation.

Personality

The term personality means many things to behavioralists. We shall define it as the general sum of traits or characteristics of an individual. The reader should note that, when we use the term, we do not mean what people often refer to when they describe an outstanding aspect of the impression which an individual creates on others. Personality is a conglomerate of forces within the individual and can be thought of as a dynamic system.

Determinants of Personality. Man is like all other men, and yet like no other man. One of the unique areas of his development is the personality. In order to understand how personality relates to motivation and behavior, let us first examine the determinants of personality.

The formation of the human personality is influenced by the mutual interaction of many factors. While the list could be unending, experts agree that there are four general classifications of influencing factors.[9]

1. *Constitutional Determinants.* These are inborn characteristics which the individual inherits. For example, different genetic structures result in varying potentials for learning, energy, activity, and tolerance for frustration. Sex and age are also important constitutional determinants of personality. These characteristics influence an individual's needs and expectations.

2. *Group Membership Determinants.* Different individuals within any culture are exposed to beliefs, values, and mores of the culture in different ways. These are usually transmitted to the individual through the various groups (e.g., family, education, religious) with which he comes into contact. The relationships which the individual develops are likely to have a lasting influence on his personality and his ways of viewing life.

3. *Role Determinants.* In a sense, role determinants of personality can be considered a special class of group membership determinants. Each of us has a number of different roles which he plays at different times. This is because the roles an individual plays to fulfill a given position are determined by the group within which the position exists. For example, the roles of a husband and father are determined by the cultural environment within which the position exists, while the roles of a military officer or college professor are determined by their reference groups. While it is incorrect to accept a person's behavior in a particular situation (e.g., a college professor's in his office) as representative of his total personality, the role which a person plays every day in his life can have a great influence upon his personality.

4. *Situational Determinants.* Situational determinants of personality include the unique factors which influence an individual's personality. For example, a student who is undecided which functional area of business to major in while at college may have in his first marketing course a dynamic, persuasive marketing executive as a guest speaker. While this event may not directly and immediately alter the student's personality, it may put into motion events which will be decisive in influencing his personality.

---

[9] Clyde Kluckhohn and Henry A. Murray, *Personality* (New York: Alfred A. Knopf, Inc., 1956), Chapter 2.

While each of the determinants discussed has an important influence on personality development, it is necessary to recognize their interdependence rather than considering them as isolated factors. In other words, it is incorrect to view a single determinant as the cause of personality. Instead, the personality of an individual is conditioned by several mutually interdependent and interacting variables.

Personality and Motivation. In our earlier discussion of motivation, we constructed a motivational model which indicated that most behavior is directed toward satisfying a felt need and that, whenever need gratification is blocked, the individual experiences frustration. We saw that the individual may react to frustration either by engaging in some kind of constructive behavior to solve his problem or evoking one or more defense mechanisms. Now that we have discussed personality, how does this important determinant of behavior fit into the motivational model? Personality differences influence the motivational model in the following ways:[10]

1. *Strength of Needs.* The strength and importance of various needs will differ from one individual to another depending on the individual's personality. For example, some people have strong esteem needs which lead them to buy a whole different range of products or seek different kinds of employment than people whose esteem needs are less prepotent. The same will be true of people with strong security needs.

2. *Aspiration Level.* Aspiration levels differ among individuals depending upon the strength of their needs. One individual may not be satisfied until he reaches a position of power and influence in a firm, while another may be quite satisfied in a middle management position.

3. *Types of Behavior.* Although individuals may experience the same needs, the strategies or types of behavior which an individual utilizes to achieve satisfaction of his needs are a function of his personality. For example, one person may satisfy his esteem needs by gaining on-the-job recognition, while another may satisfy the same needs by becoming a leader in civic and community activities.

4. *Reaction to Frustration.* How a person reacts to non-satisfaction of needs is also a function of his personality. Personality differences affect the types of situations which cause frustration, the degree to which defense mechanisms are evoked, and the kinds of defense mechanisms resorted to.

We have discussed a motivational model similar to those found in the behavioral school of management, based upon the need-hierarchy framework. We have also noted that both motivation and behavior will vary from person to person as a result of differences in personality structure.

---

[10] Max D. Richards and Paul S. Greenlaw, *Management Decision Making* (Homewood, Ill.: Richard D. Irwin, Inc., 1966), pp. 112–15. The discussion here is based on their work.

TWO-FACTOR THEORY OF MOTIVATION

Before leaving the subject of motivation, let us examine another theory which is based to a great extent on the need hierarchy. However, it differs from the need hierarchy in that it is more specifically related to motivation on the job. This theory, often referred to as the "two-factor" theory of motivation, was first advanced by Frederick Herzberg, who based his theory on a study of need satisfactions and the reported motivational effects of these satisfactions on 200 engineers and accountants.[11]

In this study, Herzberg and his associates asked each individual employee to think of a time when he felt especially good and a time when he felt especially bad about his job. Each employee was then asked to describe the conditions which led to these particular feelings. It was found that the employees named different kinds of conditions which caused each of the feelings. For example, if recognition led to a good feeling about the job, the lack of recognition was seldom indicated as a cause of bad feelings.

Based on this research, Herzberg reached the following two conclusions:

1. There are some conditions of the job which operate primarily to dissatisfy employees when they are not present. However, the presence of these conditions does not build strong motivation. Herzberg called these factors *maintenance* or *hygiene* factors since they are necessary to maintain a reasonable level of satisfaction. He also noted that many of these factors have often been perceived by managers as motivators, but that they are, in fact more potent as dissatisfiers when they are absent. He concluded that there were ten maintenance factors, namely,

a) company policy and administration,
b) technical supervision,
c) interpersonal relations with supervisor,
d) interpersonal relations with peers,
e) interpersonal relations with subordinates,
f) salary,
g) job security,
h) personal life,
i) work conditions, and
j) status.

2. There are some job conditions which, if present, operate to build high levels of motivation and job satisfaction. However, if these conditions are not present, they do not prove highly dissatisfying. Herzberg described six of these factors as *motivational* factors or satisfiers:

[11] See Frederick Herzberg, B. Mausner, and B. Snyderman, *The Motivation to Work* (New York: John Wiley and Sons, Inc., 1959).

a) achievement,
b) recognition,
c) advancement,

d) the work itself,
e) the possibility of growth,
f) responsibility.

The maintenance factors cause much dissatisfaction when they are not present, but do not provide strong motivation when they are. On the other hand, the factors in the second group lead to strong motivation and satisfaction when they are present, but do not cause much dissatisfaction when they are absent.

The reader has probably noted that the *motivational factors* are job-centered; that is, they relate directly to the job content itself, the individual's performance of it, his responsibilities, and the growth and recognition he obtains from it. *Maintenance factors* are peripheral to the job itself and more related to the external environment of work. Another important finding of the study is that, when employees are highly motivated, they have a high tolerance for dissatisfaction arising from the peripheral factors. However, the reverse is not true.

One limitation of Herzberg's original study and conclusions is that the subjects consisted of engineers and accountants. The fact that these individuals were in such positions indicates that they had the motivation to seek advanced education and expect to be rewarded for it. The same may not hold true for the nonprofessional worker. In fact, some testing of Herzberg's model on blue-collar workers showed that some of the factors considered as maintenance factors by Herzberg (pay, job security) are considered by blue-collar workers to be motivational factors.[12]

Another limitation of Herzberg's work has been cited by Vroom.[13] He believes that Herzberg's inference concerning qualitative differences between dissatisfiers and motivators cannot be completely accepted, and that the differences between stated sources of satisfaction and dissatisfaction in Herzberg's study may be the result of defensive processes within those responding. Vroom points out that people are apt to attribute the causes of satisfaction to their own achievements, but more likely to attribute their dissatisfaction to obstacles presented by company policies or superiors than to their own deficiencies.[14]

Another group of writers believes that the two-factor theory is an oversimplification of the true relationship between motivation and dissatisfac-

---

[12] Michael R. Malinovsky and John R. Barry, "Determinants of Work Attitudes," *Journal of Applied Psychology,* vol. 49 (December, 1965), pp. 446–51. Also see M. Scott Myers, "Who Are Your Motivated Workers?" *Harvard Business Review,* vol. 42 (January–February, 1964), pp. 73–88, for a detailed study of maintenance and motivating factors at Texas Instruments.

[13] Victor H. Vroom, *Work and Motivation* (New York: John Wiley and Sons, Inc., 1964), pp. 128–29.

[14] *Ibid.*

FIGURE 8–4

A Comparison of the Maslow and Herzberg Models*

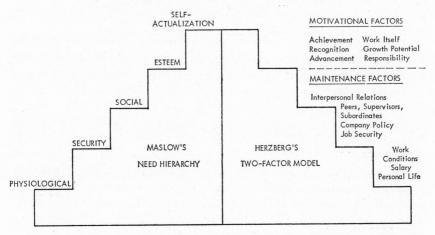

* Also see Keith Davis, *Human Relations at Work* (New York: McGraw-Hill Book Co., 1967), p. 37.

tion as well as between the sources of job satisfaction and dissatisfaction.[15] They reviewed several studies which showed that one factor can cause job satisfaction for one person and job dissatisfaction for another. In addition, they pointed out that intrinsic job factors are more important to both satisfying and dissatisfying job events. They concluded that further research is needed to be able to predict in what situations worker satisfaction will produce greater productivity.[16]

This discussion indicates that Herzberg's theory has generated a great deal of criticism. Therefore the reader should view this theory not as a panacea for all motivation problems in organizations, but as a starting point which he can use when attempting to develop his own approach to the motivation of employees.

Comparison of the Two-Factor Model and the Need Hierarchy Model

There is much similarity between Herzberg's and Maslow's models. A close examination of Herzberg's theory indicates that what he is actually saying is that professional and managerial employees may have achieved a level of social and economic progress in our industrial society such that the higher-level needs of Maslow (esteem and self-actualization) are the primary motivators. However, they still must satisfy the lower-level

[15] R. J. House and L. A. Wigdor, "Herzberg's Dual-Factor Theory of Job Satisfaction and Motivation: A Review of the Evidence and a Criticism," *Personnel Psychology,* vol. 20, (Winter, 1967), pp. 369–89.

[16] *Ibid.,* pp. 388–89.

needs for the maintenance of their current state. Thus, we can see that money would still be a motivator for nonmanagement workers (particularly those at a minimum wage level) and for some managerial employees. In addition, Herzberg's model adds to the need hierarchy model because it draws a distinction between the two groups of motivational and maintenance factors, and points out that the motivational factors are often derived from the job itself. Figure 8–4 shows a diagrammatic comparison of the two models.

TWO MANAGEMENT TECHNIQUES DESIGNED TO INCREASE MOTIVATION

Interest in improving the performance and overall contribution of organization members has been growing ever since behavioral scientists have provided evidence that certain appraisal and motivational programs yield positive results. Two of these programs, management by objectives and job enrichment, are excellent examples of the types of motivation techniques being espoused by the behavioralists.

Management by Objectives

One management technique which has acquired a legion of advocates since it was first introduced in the early 1950s is management by objectives (MBO). Exactly what MBO entails has been presented in slightly different styles by those who advocate its use. For example, Peter Drucker who first introduced the concept of MBO describes it as follows:

. . . the objectives of the district manager's job should be defined by the contribution he and his district sales force have to make to the sales department, the objectives of the project engineer's job by the contribution he, his engineers and draftsmen make to the engineering department. . . .

This requires each manager to develop and set the objectives of his unit himself. Higher management must, of course, reserve the power to approve or disapprove these objectives. But their development is part of a manager's responsibility; indeed, it is his first responsibility. . . .[17]

Drucker believes that the greatest advantage of MBO is that it allows the manager to control his own performance. This self-control is interpreted to mean stronger motivation to do the best rather than just to get by.

Another slightly different presentation of the basic fundamentals and overall philosophy of MBO is provided by Odiorne:

---

[17] Peter Drucker, *The Practice of Management* (New York: Harper and Brothers, 1954), pp. 128–29.

. . . a process whereby the superior and subordinate managers of an organization jointly identify its common goals, define each individual's major areas of responsibility in terms of the results expected of him, and use these measures as guides for operating the unit and assessing the contribution of each of its members.[18]

An important factor, in Odiorne's viewpoint, is for the subordinate and superior to have an understanding regarding the subordinate's major areas of responsibility, what will constitute an acceptable level of performance, and what needs to be done to improve performance. A common thread found in both the Drucker and Odiorne conceptions is that MBO should lead to improved motivation of participants.

Other well-known scholars have also written extensively on MBO.[19] Their contentions are similar to those offered by Drucker and Odiorne. Synthesizing the works of these experts enables one to develop a set of three guidelines which will provide the reader with an operational understanding of the approach of management by objectives. The guidelines emphasize that, in MBO programs,

1. superiors and subordinates meet and discuss goals (results) for the subordinates which are in line with overall organizational goals;

2. the superior and subordinate jointly establish attainable goals for the subordinate;

3. the superior and subordinate meet again after the initial goals are established, and evaluate the subordinate's performance in terms of the goals. The essential feature is that *feedback* on performance is provided the subordinate. The subordinate knows where he stands with regard to his contribution to his organizational unit and the firm.

The exact procedures employed in implementing the goal-setting and performance evaluation program will vary from firm to firm or from organizational unit to organizational unit. The anticipated end results, however, will be the same: (1) improved participant contribution to the firm, (2) improved morale and attitudes of the participants toward the firm, and (3) reduced employee anxiety resulting from ambiguity as to where he stands with his superior.

Some Research Findings

A number of firms have implemented MBO-type programs on a company or departmental basis. A number of recent studies report some of the effects of such programs.

---

[18] George Odiorne, *Management by Objectives* (New York: Pitman Publishing Co., 1965), p. 26.

[19] See Douglas McGregor, "An Uneasy Look at Performance Appraisal," *Harvard Business Review*, vol. 35 (May–June, 1957), pp. 89–94; and E. C. Schleh, *Management by Results* (New York: McGraw-Hill Book Co., 1961).

A two-part study of a form of MBO program referred to as "Goal Setting and Self-Control" was undertaken during 1965 and 1966 at the Purex Corporation.[20] The result of the research was that, after the goal-setting program had been initiated, participants at Purex were more concerned about and aware of the firm's goals and future activities. In the initial study it was also found that the goal-setting procedure improved communications and understanding among those involved.

The follow-up study showed that many of the participants perceived the program as being a weak incentive for improving the performance level of participants. They had changed their attitudes about the program after it had been in operation over a four-year period. Their reasons for changing their opinions about the program were divided into five categories:[21]

1. Managers reported that the program was used as a whip.
2. The program increased the amount of paperwork.
3. The program failed to reach the lower managerial levels.
4. There was an overemphasis placed on production.
5. The program failed to provide adequate incentives to improve performance.

Another study was made on the effects of a form of MBO program known as "Work Planning and Review."[22] An experimental and a control group of managers were included in the research design. The control group operated under a traditional performance appraisal system. This involved an annual appraisal of a subordinate's performance by his manager. The experimental group was encouraged to prepare a set of goals for achieving improved job performance and to submit them for the superior's review and approval.

Managers using the goal-setting program (i.e., work planning and review) were compared to those operating under the traditional appraisal program. The managers using the goal-setting program expressed significantly more favorable attitudes. Specifically, their attitudes changed in a favorable direction over the one-year study in the following areas:

1. extent to which the managers made use of their abilities and experiences;
2. ability of the managers to plan;
3. degree to which the managers were receptive to new ideas and suggestions; and

---

[20] Anthony P. Raia, "Goal Setting and Self Control," *Journal of Management Studies,* vol. 2 (September, 1965), pp. 34–53; and Anthony P. Raia, "A Second Look at Management Goals and Controls," *California Management Review,* vol. 8 (Summer, 1966), pp. 49–58.

[21] *Ibid.*

[22] Herbert H. Meyer, Emanuel Kay, and John R. P. French, Jr., "Split Roles in Performance Appraisal," *Harvard Business Review,* vol. 43 (January–February, 1965), pp. 21–27.

4.) degree to which they felt the goals for which they were aiming were what they should be.

A more recent study dealt with managerial reactions to management by objectives in a large manufacturing firm.[23] The researchers were concerned with the manager's perceptions associated with the MBO approach. The rationale of the program most cited by participants was that the objectives-setting process was intended to link the evaluation of an individual to his actual performance rather than to personality or other characteristics. It was also found that a majority of the participating managers believed that the most significant advantage of the program was that one was more likely "to know what was expected of him by his boss." A major problem cited by the managers was that excessive formal requirements were imposed because of the program; that is, the need to process, complete, and update forms, and to provide other data to the coordinator of the program were major irritants.

In the studies cited thus far, it was attempted to determine some of the effects of MBO programs rather than the impact of MBO upon managers. A recent study, however, was designed to determine the impact of MBO on participant job satisfaction.[24] In the study, the researchers administered a psychological test which measures an individual's perceived need satisfactions. It was found that the need satisfaction of participants was probably influenced by the MBO program. However, the findings indicated that the manner in which MBO was implemented in the two companies studied had some impact on the perceived need satisfactions of the participants. More will be said about this in the following section.

Implementing MBO Programs

Despite the purported advantages of MBO, there are several key factors which should be considered in the implementation phase. For example, managers who are about to engage in MBO programs must first be conditioned and psychologically prepared.[25] With the introduction of MBO, changes will often occur in organizational variables such as the flow of communications horizontally and vertically, the intensity of intergroup interaction, and the number of personal contacts between superiors and subordinates. Thus, the dynamic nature of these variables and

---

[23] Henry L. Tosi, and Stephen J. Carroll, "Managerial Reaction to Management by Objectives," *Academy of Management Journal,* vol. 11 (December, 1968), pp. 415–26.

[24] John M. Ivancevich, James H. Donnelly, Jr., and Herbert L. Lyon, "A Study of the Impact of Management by Objectives on Perceived Need Satisfactions," *Personnel Psychology,* vol. 23 (Summer, 1970), pp. 139–51.

[25] Henry L. Tosi, Jr., "Management Development and Management by Objectives —An Interrelationship," *Management of Personnel Quarterly,* vol. 4 (Summer, 1965), p. 24.

their impact on the functioning of the organization necessitate complete understanding of MBO by managers, to insure that managerial resistance to implementation and participation is minimal.

Another critical factor in the implementation of MBO programs is the supportive managerial climate which pervades the organization. In a study previously cited, two important conclusions were reached concerning implementation:[26]

1) Top management must not assume a passive role. The most effective manner to implement MBO is to allow the top-level executives to explain, coordinate, and guide the program. When top managers were actively involved, the philosophy and mechanics of the program filtered through and penetrated the entire organization. Thus, a possible motivation strategy to improve need satisfaction at lower levels of management would be to involve the top-level management group in the MBO program.

2) Improvements in need satisfaction were higher in the company where the MBO program was instituted by upper-level executives than in the company where it was implemented by the personnel department.

Management by objectives is not being offered here as a cure-all for motivation problems in business organizations, but it is an approach which warrants careful consideration, especially since some evidence of its effectiveness is available.

JOB ENRICHMENT

Earlier in this chapter, we discussed the motivational and maintenance factors model of motivation developed by Herzberg. In a recent discussion, Herzberg has gone farther and attempted to increase employee motivation through building up the motivational factors in a job. He has reported the successful application of his approach involving stockholder correspondents employed by a large corporation.[27] He refers to his approach as job enrichment, which, as he describes it,

. . . seeks to improve both task efficiency and human satisfaction by means of building into people's jobs, quite specifically, greater scope for personal achievement and recognition, more challenging and responsible work, and more opportunity for individual advancement and growth. It is concerned only incidentally with matters such as pay and working conditions, organizational structure, communications, and training, important and necessary though these may be in their own right.[28]

---

[26] Ivancevich, Donnelly, and Lyon, *op. cit.*, pp. 148–50.

[27] Frederick Herzberg, "One More Time: How Do You Motivate Employees?" *Harvard Business Review*, vol. 46 (January–February, 1968), p. 53.

[28] William J. Paul, Jr., Keith B. Robertson, and Frederick Herzberg, "Job Enrichment Pays Off," *Harvard Business Review*, vol. 47 (March–April 1969), p. 61.

This article reported the results of five studies carried on in various British firms to determine among other things the generality of Herzberg's original findings.[29] The five studies covered widely different business areas and company functions as well as many types and levels of jobs. The five groups of workers covered were laboratory technicians in an R&D department, sales representatives, design engineers, production foremen on shift work, and engineering foremen on day work. There were three main features to the study:[30]

1. The hygiene factors were held constant. This means that no deliberate changes were made in pay, security, and other maintenance factors, because the researchers were only interested in determining gains which were brought about through change in job content.

2. An "experimental" group was formed for whom the specific changes in job content were made, and a "control" group was formed whose job content remained the same.

3. The fact that the studies were being done was kept confidential. This was done to avoid the well-known tendency of people to behave differently when they are aware that they are part of a controlled study.

The researchers sought to measure job satisfaction and performance for both groups over the study period, which generally lasted one year. Performance measures were specific to the group concerned and were determined by the local management of the participating company.

How were the jobs in the experimental group "enriched"? Rather than examine all five groups, let us review the program of action devised and implemented for the sales representatives.

Sales representatives were no longer obliged to write reports on every customer call. They were asked simply to pass on information when they thought it appropriate or request action as they thought it was required.

Responsibility for determining calling frequencies was put wholly with the representatives themselves, who kept the only records for purposes such as staff reviews.

The technical service department agreed to provide service "on demand" from the representatives; nominated technicians regarded such calls as their first priority. Communication was by direct contact, paperwork being cleared after the event.[31]

Following the changes in job content of the sales representatives, there resulted an increase in sales of 19 percent over the same period of the previous year for the experimental group. In the control group, sales declined during the study period by 5 percent. The equivalent change for both groups the previous year had been a decline of three percent.

[29] Ibid., p. 61.
[30] Ibid., p. 62.
[31] Ibid., p. 66.

The content of the jobs in the remaining four groups was "enriched" in a similar fashion as for the sales representatives. The specific changes are not detailed here. However, it is necessary to note that similar positive results were found for each of the other four types of jobs when specific changes were made in the job content of the workers in each "experimental" group. The researchers concluded among other things that "tasks have to be motivational—i.e., the more they draw upon the motivators, the more likely they are to produce an effective contribution to business objectives."[32]

Texas Instruments Program

Over a period of years a study of motivation in the work place has been conducted at Texas Instruments, Inc. (TI).[33] The company grew by leaps and bounds during the 1950s from a firm with 1,700 to one with 17,000 employees. The management of the company and consultants believed that they could best cope with this significant growth by implementing a management philosophy that encouraged individual self-actualization. The basic premise was that TI goals could be achieved more readily by providing opportunities for employees to attain their personal goals.

In 1961, scientific research began at TI on motivational problems. A number of randomly selected employees participated in research which used Herzberg's motivational model as a cornerstone for determining maintenance and motivation factors. Five classifications of employees were included in the sample—scientists, engineers, manufacturing supervisors, technicians, and female assemblers.

All of the five occupational groups, except female assemblers, were largely comprised of actual or potential motivation seekers. That is, they sought achievement, recognition, and growth among other things. The scientists were the group most oriented toward motivational factors, while the group most oriented toward maintenance factors (e.g., pay, supplemental benefits) was that of the female assemblers.

Based upon these and other research findings, TI has implemented a program which attempts to make supervisors aware of the two-factor (Herzberg) theory so that it can aid them in designing jobs. For example, the supervisors analyzed the functions performed by their subordinates in terms of the potential for serving maintenance or motivation needs. The company implemented a training program for supervisors to facilitate the understanding of employee motivation. Group meetings were used so that skills in motivating people could be developed. Thus, the

---

[32] *Ibid.*, p. 77.

[33] For an excellent discussion of a six-year study of motivation at Texas Instruments, see Myers, *op. cit.*

TI research has led to an attempt to implement Herzberg's theory over a period of time so that it is integrated into the total management system.

SUMMARY

We have examined an area of prime importance in the behavioral school of management. We have seen that motivation is closely related to needs and to the individual personality. A knowledge of these behavioral concepts provides the business manager with insight into the complex area of human motivation.

We have also examined two management techniques—management by objectives and job enrichment—whose supporters believe that they can lead to many positive consequences if utilized correctly. The authors do not contend that either of these techniques are free of limitations for business managers. There are many additional management techniques not discussed in this text for lack of space. We do not mean to imply by omission that these other techniques will not result in positive consequences if they are utilized.

One final comment is in order: The reader should note that a common thread (participation by subordinates in planning and goal setting) can be found in both the MBO and job enrichment approaches. We shall see in the following chapters that advocates of the behavioral school of management place a great deal of emphasis on the participative approach.

DISCUSSION AND REVIEW QUESTIONS

1. Discuss the following statement: "Motivation can be directly and accurately measured."

2. "I believe that money is the best of all possible motivators. You can say what you please about all the other factors, but when it comes down to it, if you give a guy a raise, you'll motivate him." In light of what was discussed in the chapter, comment on this statement.

3. Do you feel it is necessary for managers to be familiar with the fundamental needs of man in order to motivate employees successfully?

4. What is the significance of the physiological and safety needs in the U.S. today? Can you think of some circumstances where these needs would become important?

5. From your own experience, discuss a situation where two individuals reacted differently to frustration under the same circumstances, and where the difference in reaction might be attributed to personality differences between the individuals.

6. Differentiate between maintenance factors and motivational factors. Can you apply this approach to the classroom? Develop a list of motivational factors for your professor.

7. Outline the basic elements of management by objectives (MBO).

8. Outline the basic elements of job enrichment.

9. Compare and contrast job enrichment and MBO.

10. Assume that you have completed college and have recently accepted a job with a large corporation. Discuss the factors you feel would motivate you during your first three years. Do the same thing again, except assume you have been out of college for 15 years.

ADDITIONAL REFERENCES

BENNIS, W. G. *Changing Organization.* New York: McGraw-Hill Book Co., Inc., 1966.

BOLLES, R. C. *Theory of Motivation.* New York: Harper and Row Publishers, 1967.

CLARK, J. V. "Motivation in Work Groups: A Tentative View," *Human Organization,* Vol. 19 (1960–1961), 199–208.

DALTON, G. W. AND LAWRENCE, P. *Motivation and Control in Organizations.* Homewood, Ill.: Richard D. Irwin, Inc., and The Dorsey Press, Inc., 1970.

GELLERMAN, S. W. *Motivation and Productivity.* New York: American Management Association, 1963.

HERZBERG, F. *Work and the Nature of Man.* New York: World Publishing Co., 1966.

KELLY, J. *Organizational Behaviour.* Homewood, Ill.: Richard D. Irwin, Inc., and The Dorsey Press, Inc., 1969.

LEAVITT, H. T. *Managerial Psychology.* 2nd ed. Chicago: University of Chicago Press, 1964.

LIKERT, R. *The Human Organization.* New York: McGraw-Hill Book Co., Inc., 1967.

McCLELLAND, D. C. *The Achieving Society.* Princeton, N.J.: Van Nostrand Company, 1961.

MASLOW, A. H. *Eupsychian Management.* Homewood, Ill.: Richard D. Irwin, Inc., and The Dorsey Press, Inc., 1965.

PORTER, L. W. AND LAWLER, E. E. *Managerial Attitudes and Performance.* Homewood, Ill.: Richard D. Irwin, Inc., and The Dorsey Press, Inc., 1968.

VROOM, V. H. *Work and Motivation.* New York: John Wiley and Sons, Inc., 1964.

chapter nine

Work Groups in the Organization

INTRODUCTION

Few management scholars question the existence of work groups in the formal organization structure. Work groups exist within what is called the formal organization and also within informal organizations. This chapter is concerned with the general concept of groups in all types of organizations. Beginning with the famous Hawthorne studies of the 1920s, behavioralists have paid special attention to the processes occurring within groups which affect individuals and the formal organization. Thus, any presentation of a behavioral approach to management would certainly be incomplete if the reader were not provided with a framework for understanding the nature and characteristics of work groups in organizations.

The purpose of this chapter is to provide (1) a classification system which can be used to sort the different types of work groups; (2) some knowledge about the reasons for formation of work groups; (3) some explanation of methods utilized to study work groups; (4) some insights into the results of group membership; (5) an understanding of some of the structural characteristics of groups; and (6) a brief presentation of some studies on groups which are relevant to actual organizational situations.

An appropriate definition of the term "work group" is essential to an analysis of the way in which the behavioralist discusses groups in the management literature. The list of elaborate definitions proposed by individuals studying work groups is endless. However, a concise definition which is appropriate for the present chapter is as follows: *A work group is a collection of employees (managerial or nonmanagerial), sharing certain norms, who are striving toward member need satisfaction through the attainment of a group goal(s).*

Many individuals ask why work groups should be studied in a management text. There are, of course, many different answers which can be provided. Some of the more relevant responses are:

1. The formation of work group(s) are inevitable and ubiquitous.[1] Consequently, no matter how rewarding or satisfying it is to work in a particular organization, it is almost certain that work groups will be formed. Thus it is in management's interest to understand what happens within work groups because they are found throughout the organization.

2. Work groups strongly influence the overall behavior and performance of members. To understand the forces of influence exerted by the group requires a systematic analysis.

3. Group membership can have both positive and negative consequences as far as the organization is concerned. If executives are to avoid the negative consequences generated by work groups, it behooves them to learn about groups.

These three answers are typical of the numerous explanations provided when writers are attempting to justify or support their discussion of work groups. The common thread found in most answers is that groups exist and are a force which affect the performance and behavior of employees. This is the most obvious and pragmatic reason for the study of groups; no further justification or explanation is needed.

REASONS FOR THE FORMATION OF WORK GROUPS

An explanation of the reasons for group formation can center around a number of factors which may be physical, economic, and socio-psychological. All of these factors can be viewed as categories of determinants for group formation.

Location

When people are put in close proximity to each other, there is a tendency for them to interact and communicate with each other. If workers

---

[1] Dorwin Cartwright and Ronald Lippett, "Group Dynamics and the Individual," *International Journal of Group Psychotherapy*, vol. 7 (January, 1957), p. 88.

are not able to do this on a fairly regular basis, there is less tendency to form a group.[2] This is not to say that workers must communicate daily or hourly before a work group forms. Instead, it should be obvious that some degree of interaction and communication is necessary.

In organizations, it is a typical procedure to locate workers in similar occupations together. For example, in the construction of a home, the bricklayers perform their jobs in close proximity to each other. The same situation exists in offices where secretaries are located next to each other.[3]

Economic Reasons

In some cases, work groups form because individuals believe that they can derive more economic benefits on their jobs if they form into groups. For example, individuals (strangers) working at different stations on an assembly line may be paid on a group incentive basis. Whatever the particular group produces determines the wages for each member. Because of the interest of the workers in their wages, they would interact and communicate with each other. By working as a group instead of as individuals, the employees may perceive and actually obtain higher economic benefits.

Another example of the economic motive for work group formation could definitely exist in a non-union organization, where the workers may form into a group to bring pressure against management for more economic benefits. The group members have a common interest—increased economic benefits—which leads to group affiliation.

A number of older workers may form into a work group because of economic motives, such as the administration and payment of their pensions after retirement. Assuming that they wanted to handle discussions of the pension plan outside the jurisdiction of their union (if they are in a unionized plant), they would be considered a work group.

Socio-Psychological Reasons

Workers in organizations are also motivated to form work groups so that their needs can be more adequately satisfied. The security, social, esteem, and self-actualization needs can be satisfied to some degree by workers if they belong to work groups.

Security. Work groups protect members from outside pressures such as management demands for better quality and quantity of production, punching the clock on time, and recommendations for changing the in-

---

[2] William G. Scott, *Organization Theory* (Homewood, Ill., Richard D. Irwin, Inc., 1967), p. 86.

[3] *Ibid.*, p. 87.

dividuals' work area layout. By being a member of a group, the employee can immerse himself in the group activities and openly discuss these management demands with individuals who usually support his viewpoint. Without the group to lean on when various management demands are made, the employee often assumes that he is standing alone facing management and the entire organization system. This "aloneness" leads to a degree of insecurity.

The interactions and communications existing between members of a work group serve as a buffer to management demands. Another form of security need satisfaction occurs in instances when an individual is a new employee and is asked to perform a difficult job task over an extended period of time. The employee may not want to continually contact his supervisor for help in correctly performing his job; therefore he depends largely upon the group. This reliance can certainly be interpreted as providing the new employee with a form of security need satisfaction. New employees are often very concerned with performing well so that they can continue on the job. Thus, continually requesting help from the supervisor is thought of by some new employees as indicating that they are not able to handle the job. Consequently they turn to the group for help so that their new position is not threatened. Whether the supervisor believes that a subordinate continually asking for help is a sign of inability to perform the job is not the main issue. The important point is how new workers perceive their situation and job security.

Social. Employees often join work groups because of an intense need for affiliation. The basis of affiliation ranges from wanting to interact with and enjoy other employees to more complex desires for group support of self-image.[4] A management atmosphere which does not permit interaction and communication is suppressing the desire of employees to feel a sense of belongingness.

The desire to belong and to be a part of a group points up the intensity of the social needs of employees within the United States. An excellent discussion of the social needs of Americans is offered by Edgar Schein. He discusses the concern which was voiced about the behavior of United States prisoners of war in North Korea. Since there were few escapes and numerous instances of apparent collaboration, many citizens of the U.S. were distressed. Schein suggests that one of the reasons for the POW situation was the manner in which prisoners were treated.[5]

In the North Korean POW camps, officers (supervisors) were sepa-

---

[4] David R. Hampton, Charles E. Summer, and Ross A. Webber, *Organization Behavior and the Practice of Management* (Glenview, Ill.: Scott, Foresman and Company, 1968), p. 275.

[5] Edgar Schein, "The Chinese Indoctrination Program for Prisoners of War," *Psychiatry*, vol. 19 (May, 1956), pp. 149–72.

rated from enlisted men (subordinates). Groups were systematically broken up and prisoners were regularly transferred between barracks to forestall the development of an informal organization. The fact that informal organizations could not be formed on a continuing basis could explain the low escape rate: because the men could not get organized, they could not develop the type of plan that was needed by POW's to break free. Also, they could not develop the trust in each other that is so essential for escape. Without the required trust, the "belongingness" urge was reduced and so was the overall morale in the POW camps.

Schein's discussion of POWs certainly has implications for managers in organizations. Work groups appear to satisfy an individual's social needs. The group affiliation enables the individual to identify himself and to deal with his environment (e.g., POW camp or the organization). Small-group research findings indicate that employees who are isolated from each other because of plant layout report that their jobs are less satisfying than those of group members who are able to socialize on the job.[6]

Esteem. Some employees are attracted toward joining a work group because they perceive themselves as having more prestige by being inside the group. In an organization, a particular group may be viewed by employees as being a top-notch work group. Consequently, membership in the elite group bestows prestige upon the members which is not enjoyed by nonmembers. This prestige is conferred on members by other employees (nonmembers), and this often leads to more gratification of the esteem needs. By sharing in the activities of a high-prestige work group the individual identifies more closely with the group. This form of identification is valued highly by some employees.

Self-Actualization. The desire of individuals to utilize their skills to maximum efficiency and to grow and develop psychologically on the job is interpreted as the self-actualization need (see discussion in Chapter 8). Employees often believe that rigid job requirements and rules imposed by decision-making executives do not enable them to satisfy this need sufficiently. One reaction to rigid requirements, rules, and regulations is to join a work group, which is viewed as a vehicle for communicating among friends about the use of a job-related skill. The jargon utilized and the skill employed are appreciated by the knowledgeable group members. This appreciation can lead to a feeling of accomplishing a worthwhile task. This feeling, and other similar feelings which are related to a belief that one is creative and skillful, often lead to more satisfaction of the self-actualization need.

---

[6] Elton Mayo, *The Human Problems of an Industrial Civilization* (Boston: Graduate School of Business Administration, Harvard University, 1946), pp. 42–52.

A Final Note on Work Group Formation

The above reasons for group formation are by no means to be interpreted as being mutually exclusive or the only specific reasons for group formation. They do, however, have a behavioral overtone, and this is why they are presented. The main theme in the discussion of the reasons for group formation is that group membership is closely related to individual satisfaction. This is not meant to be an indictment that the formal organization does or cannot sufficiently provide an atmosphere of work conducive to high levels of satisfaction. Although this may be true in many cases, it would seem that both the formal organization and the work groups can be compatible and provide the employee with opportunities to satisfy their needs. In fact, it should be remembered that groups exist in both the formal and informal type of organization.

DEVELOPMENT OF WORK GROUPS

The development of work groups is distinctly related to learning—learning to work together, to accept each other, and to trust each other. Bass has succinctly presented a four-phase group development schedule which points out clearly some of the problems and frustrations inherent in group development.[7]

First Phase: Mutual Acceptance

Employees in an organization are often hampered by their mistrust of each other, of the organization, and of their superiors. They are fearful that they do not have the necessary training or skill to perform the job or to compete with others on the job. These feelings of insecurity motivate employees to seek out others in the same predicament, and to begin to express their feelings openly. A group results, and the mistrust is significantly reduced. Thus, after an initial period of uneasiness and learning about the feelings of others, individuals begin to accept each other.

Second Phase: Decision-Making

During this phase, open communication and expression of thoughts concerning the job are the rule. Problem-solving and decisions are the order of the day. The workers trust each other's viewpoints and beliefs and develop strategies to make the job easier or to help members perform more efficiently.

---

[7] The discussion of the development of groups is based largely upon Bernard Bass, *Organizational Psychology* (Boston: Allyn and Bacon, Inc., 1965), pp. 197–98. A number of alterations were made by the authors.

Third Phase: Motivation

The group has reached maturity and the problems of its members are known. It is accepted that it is better for the group to have cooperation instead of competition from the members. Thus, the emphasis is on group solidarity in the form of cooperating with each other so that the job is more rewarding both economically and socio-psychologically.

Fourth Phase: Control

The group has successfully organized its work, and members are performing tasks according to their abilities and interests. The group exercises sanctions when control is needed to bring members into line with the group's norm of production.

The structures and processes which are found in work groups develop over a period of time. The motivation of members or the control of output is not an overnight occurrence in the work place. The four phases of development show that a learning process is involved. Performance and motivation of group members depend on individual learning and on the degree to which the group coordinates the efforts and desires of members.

TYPES OF GROUPS IN AN ORGANIZATION

Both managers and nonmanagers belong to a number of different groups within the formal organization.[8] The membership in these groups often overlaps. In some instances, the individual employee is a member of a group because of his formal position in the organization. However, through the contacts he makes in the group, he begins to affiliate with some of its members and other nonmembers on an informal basis. The overlapping form of groups is illustrated in Figure 9–1.

There are five overlapping groups presented in Figure 9–1:
Group 1—John, Ralph, Mike, George;
Group 2—Ralph, Sam, Tony, Nick;
Group 3—Ralph, Nick, Bob;
Group 4—George, Stu, Phil;
Group 5—Mike, George, Pete, Stu.

Group 1 is a formal organization group which causes John, Ralph, Mike, and George to communicate with each other. By position, John is the leader in this group. The leaders of the other four work groups which have formed are not indicated. Any one of the individuals in these overlapping groups may be the leader. In some groups an indi-

[8] Rensis Likert, *New Patterns of Management* (New York: McGraw-Hill Book Company, 1961), Chapter 8.

FIGURE 9-1

Group Overlay

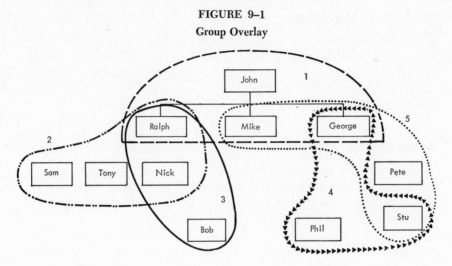

vidual will emerge as a leader and, in others, he will be one of many followers.

In examining groups in a general framework, it becomes apparent that formal organizational demands and processes lead to the formation of different types of work groups. One classification system used to describe groups is the command, task, interest, and friendship framework.[9]

Command Group

The command group is specified by the formal organization chart. The subordinates who report directly to a given supervisor make up a command group. The relationship between the department manager and the four foremen in a machine shop is spelled out in the organization chart (Figure 9-2).

As the span of control of the department manager increases, his command group increases in size.

Task Group

A number of employees that work together to complete a project or job task are considered a task group. A manufacturing or office work process that requires a great deal of interdependency is an example of a

---

[9] This is the widely used and insightful framework offered by Leonard R. Sayles, "Research in Industrial Human Relations," *Industrial Relations Research Association* (New York: Harper and Row, 1957), pp. 131–45.

task group. Assume that three office clerks are required for (1) securing a file of an automobile accident claim; (2) checking the accuracy of the claim by contacting persons involved; and (3) typing the claim, securing the required signatures of those involved, and refiling the claim.

The activation of the file and the steps required before the claim is refiled constitute required tasks. These activities create a situation in which three clerks must communicate and coordinate with each other if the file is to be handled properly. Their activities and interactions facilitate the formation of the task group.

Interest Group

In discussing the economic determinant of group formation, an example of older workers grouping together to present a united front was

FIGURE 9–2

Command Group Structure

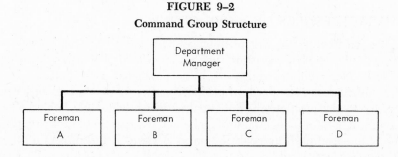

cited. This type of group can be viewed as an interest group, for the members have joined together to achieve some objective such as an equitable pension payment. The members of the group may or may not be members of the same command or task group.

When the desired objective has been achieved or is thought to be within reach, the interest group might disband. Thus, this type of group typically exists for a shorter period of time than the other three group categories.

Friendship Group

In the workplace, employees, because of some common characteristic such as age, ethnic background, political sentiment, interest in sports, or desire to drink coffee in the cafeteria at 10:30 A.M., often form a friendship group. These groups often extend their interaction and communication to off-the-job activities. For example, they get to know each other in the workplace because of friendship and then bowl together, or attend sporting events together, or take their families on picnics.

If an individual's affiliation patterns are reviewed, it becomes readily apparent that managerial and nonmanagerial personnel belong to many different and occasionally overlapping groups. Membership in command and task groups is designated by the formal organization, which specifies who will be the superior and who will be the subordinate in the command group. The flow of work specified by management and the job description designate the composition of task-type groups.

The membership patterns of interest and friendship groups are not tightly controlled by the organization. However, managerial actions such as laying out a work area, allowing workers to take coffee breaks at a specified time, and demanding a certain level of productivity influence the interaction and communication patterns of employees, causing individuals to affiliate with each other so that interest and friendship groups emerge.

CHARACTERISTICS OF WORK GROUPS

The creation of an organization system and of informal organizations results in characteristics such as specified relationships between subordinates, superiors, and peers, leaders assigned to positions, communication networks, standards of performance, and a status rank order according to the position an individual is filling. The logic behind these formally and informally established characteristics is that, if the organization is to accomplish its goals, retain its personnel, and project a favorable image to the public, it must have structure and a favorable work atmosphere (i.e., the employees must enjoy going to work to some extent). The term *structure* refers to the standards of conduct applied by the total group, the communication system, and the reward and sanction mechanisms of the group.[10] This definition implies that structure is a set of work group boundary and guideline characteristics. Some of these characteristics of groups are discussed below.

The Emergent Leader

As a group strives to complete some objective and the individual members begin to know each other, members begin to fill one or more of the many group roles. One of the most important roles is that of the group leader. The leader is accepted by the group members and emerges from within. In the formal organization, the leader is appointed.

The leader in the formal organization is followed and obeyed because employees perceive him as possessing power and influence to reward or

---

[10] Leonard R. Sayles and George Strauss, *Human Behavior in Organizations* (Englewood Cliffs, N.J.: Prentice-Hall, Inc., 1966), pp. 90–100.

punish them for not complying with his requests. The formal leader possesses the power to discipline and/or fire members of a work group. On the other hand, the informal group leader does not possess this power.

The informal leader emerges from within because he serves a number of facilitating functions. First, any group of individuals that does not have a plan or some coordination becomes an ineffective unit. The individuals are not directed toward the accomplishment of goals, and this leads to a breakdown in group effectiveness. The leader serves to initiate action and provide direction. If there are differences of opinions on a group-related matter, he attempts to compromise differences of opinion and move the group toward accomplishing its goals.

Second, some individual must communicate the group's beliefs about policies, the job, the organization, the supervision, and other related matters to nonmembers. The nonmembership category could include members of other groups, supervisory personnel, and the union. In effect, the group leader communicates the values of the group. As long as he is able to communicate effectively what the group's opinions are on relevant issues, he remains in the leadership role.

A number of research studies have been reported which focus upon the personal characteristics of group leaders. The findings about work group leaders have been presented broadly and generally. The above discussion represents some of the general findings concerning leaders, which can be summarized as follows:

1. The leadership role is filled by an individual if he possesses the attributes which the members perceive as being critical for satisfying their needs.
2. The leader embodies the values of the group from which he emerged. He is able to perceive these values, organize them into an intelligible philosophy, and verbalize them to nonmembers.[11]
3. The leader is able to receive effectively and decipher communication relevant to the group and effectively communicate important information to group members. He can be thought of as an information center.[12]

Status in a Group

The manager in an organization system is accorded status because of his position in the management hierarchy; that is, the top management group of the firm has more prestige or status than middle managers in the organization, while middle managers have more prestige or status than lower-level managers. The basic cornerstone of status in the formal organization system is a comparative process. The top-level positions em-

[11] Scott, *op. cit.*, p. 97.
[12] *Ibid.*

body more authority, responsibility, power, and influence, and thus are accorded more status. In effect, a status hierarchy emerges with the top-level positions listed first and the lower-level positions listed last.

In a work group a similar type of status system develops. For many different reasons, an individual is accorded status by the groups in which he interacts and communicates. The individuals performing in leadership roles possess prestige because of their role. Consequently they are ranked by group members as being at a particular level in the group status hierarchy.

There are a number of other factors which influence the status systems developed by groups. The seniority of a member is a factor which many groups consider to be important. If a worker has more seniority, he is often thought of as being "organizationally intelligent"; that is, he knows how to adapt to the demands of supervisors, subordinates, or peers. This ability to adjust is an important status factor with group members.

The skill of an individual in performing a job is another factor related to status. An individual who is an expert in the technical aspects, managerial or nonmanagerial, of the job is given a high status ranking in some groups. This type of status does not mean that the individual actually utilizes his skill to perform more efficiently, but that the group members perceive him as having this skill.

Thus, the status system in a work group is formed on the basis of such factors as whether the member is a leader, his seniority, and his skill. These and other factors are weighted differently by each type of work group; the varying amount of importance placed on them affects the status system.

Work Group Norms and Control

Throughout a person's lifetime, he is influenced significantly by group norms. A *norm* is an agreement among the group membership as to how members in the group should behave.[13] The more an individual complies with norms, the more he is accepting the group's standards of behavior. The teen-age girl who dresses exactly like her friends at school is being influenced by the group norm concerning dress behavior.

Work groups also utilize norms to bring about job performance that is acceptable to the group. In the workplace a number of different production-related norms are evident. The following are typical: (1) Don't agree with management in its campaign to change the wage structure; (2) present a united front to the supervisor concerning the displeasure of the group about firing Mr. Jones; (3) resist the suggestions of the new college graduate assigned to the group's work area; (4) do not produce

---

[13] Joseph A. Litterer, *The Analysis of Organizations* (New York: John Wiley and Sons, Inc., 1965), p. 108.

above the group leader's level of production; (5) help members of the group to achieve an acceptable production level if they are having difficulty and you have time; and (6) don't allow the union steward to convince you to vote for his favorite union presidential candidate in the upcoming election.

Three specific social processes bring about compliance with group norms,[14] namely, group pressure, group review and enforcement, and the personalization of norms.

Group Pressure. The process of group pressure is clearly illustrated by Asch in a series of experiments[15] in which he was concerned with studying how social forces constrain opinions and attitudes. Asch utilized groups of college students to conduct a "psychological experiment" in visual judgment. The experimenter informed the members of the group that they would be comparing the lengths of lines. Two sets of white cards, similar to those presented in Figure 9–3, were used for each comparison.

FIGURE 9–3

Asch-Type Comparisons

Card I   Card II

The individuals tested had to choose the line on the second card that matched the line on the first card in length. These comparisons were made a number of times.

Prior to the actual visual observation of the lengths of lines on various sets of cards, the experimenter "rigged" the results. He informed all but one member of the group that they should choose on the third comparison a line that did not match the length of the line shown on the first card of the set. The reaction of the uninformed member in each group of students was observed and recorded.

The results of the Asch experiments showed that, when an individual was confronted with only one other group member who was giving incorrect matching responses, he continued to stick with his correct answer. When the opposition (those giving incorrect answer) was increased to two, the group pressure influence became noticeable: The uninformed group member accepted the incorrect answer 13.6 percent of the time.

---

[14] *Ibid.*, pp. 109–12.

[15] Solomon E. Asch, "Opinions and Social Pressures," *Scientific American,* vol. 193 (November, 1955), pp. 31–35.

Under the group pressures provided by three incorrect responses, the uninformed members gave incorrect responses 31.8 percent of the time.

This experiment illustrates how group pressures and having support for one's viewpoint are related. If an individual stands alone, he is inclined to succumb to group pressures; but when he finds his attitude supported by even one group member, he resists pressure to change.

Individuals who value their group membership highly and who satisfy some combination of personal needs by being a part of a group allow group pressures to influence their behavior and performance. This premise leads to a second type of group process designated here as group review and enforcement.

Group Review and Enforcement. When an individual becomes a member of a group, especially the task group, he quickly becomes aware of group norms. The group position on such matters as production, absenteeism, and quality of output is communicated. The group members then observe the actions and language of the new member to determine whether the group norms are being followed.

If individual members, both oldtimers and newcomers, are not complying with generally accepted norms, a number of different approaches may be employed. A "soft" approach would be a discussion between respected leaders and those persons deviating from the norm. If this does not prove effective, more rigid corrective action such as the membership scolding the individual or individuals both privately and publicly is used. The ultimate type of enforcement would be to ostracize the nonconforming members, which may take the form of not communicating with them.

These are only a few of the numerous strategies which may be implemented to bring deviants back into line. Other, more severe techniques such as sabotaging the nonconformers' performance have also been utilized in organizations. It should be made clear that review and enforcement occur at the managerial levels in a form similar to that in the nonmanagerial ranks.

Personal Values and Norms. The behavioral patterns of an individual are influenced significantly by his value system.[16] The values of a person are influenced by the events occurring around him; they are learned and become personalized. For example, the norm of a work group to which a person belongs may encourage the group member to treat college graduates and non-college individuals equally and courteously. This norm may be accepted by the individual as morally and ethically correct. Prior to the individual's group affiliation, he may have displayed little interest in a "fair treatment of all" philosophy. However, based on a latent feeling of fairness, he personalizes this group-learned norm. It becomes a standard of conduct which is correct from a group and society vantage point.

---

[16] Litterer, *op. cit.*, p. 111.

In some, but definitely not in all instances, group pressures, group review and enforcement, and personalization of norms may conflict with organizational objectives such as higher production, improved quality of output, lower absenteeism, and loyalty to the firm. The emphasis here is on the word "some." It is nonsense to assume that all groups are established to resist the achievement of organizational goals.

Communication Network. In classical organization theory, the specified communication network is represented by the superior-subordinate relationships shown in the organization chart. The formal communication network follows the chain of command (Figure 9–4).

FIGURE 9–4

Formal Communication Flow

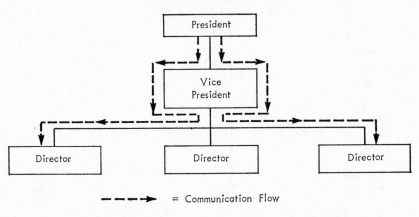

‒ ‒ ‒ ➤   = Communication Flow

In work groups the communication patterns are not rigidly set. In the formal organization system, the top-level executives possessing the most status direct their messages to lower-status members. However, research conducted within groups generally indicates that low-status group members direct more communication toward higher-status group members.[17]

A detailed study by Bavelas clearly illustrated some of the communication networks that can exist in groups. He was interested in the efficiency with which groups completed their tasks. In the Bavelas experiments, members of a group were isolated so that no cross-communication could occur, as illustrated in the diagram, Figure 9–5 (ⓧ designates the leader).

Bavelas provided some interesting insights into the results of these four networks on leaders and problem-solving abilities. The location of a

---

[17] Harold H. Kelly, "Communication in Experimentally Created Hierarchies," *Human Relations,* vol. 4 (February, 1951), pp. 39–56.

person in a central position (e.g., the circled ⓧ in the chain network of five individuals) produces group leaders. The centrally located person is in the best position to facilitate the smooth flow of information among group members.

It was also determined that, when simple problems had to be solved, the wheel network was the fastest and most efficient. The members of the group fed information to the central figure, and it was acted upon rapidly. When difficult tasks had to be solved and interaction and exchange of ideas were important to task completion, the circle arrangement proved fastest.

Although the Bavelas research was conducted in a laboratory situa-

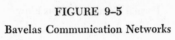

FIGURE 9–5

Bavelas Communication Networks

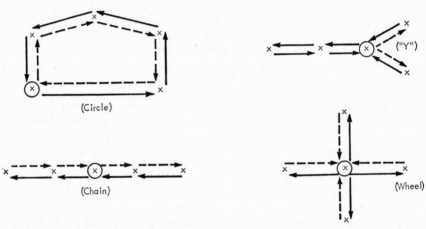

tion, it indicates clearly some of the events that may occur in small group communication networks. The leader is at the center of the group and is a facilitator. The networks are similar to the formal organization chain-of-command pattern and enable problems to be solved efficiently. This suggests that a less rigid form of communication can lead to effective problem solving.

In reviewing the characteristics of work groups, it becomes apparent that many similarities and some differences exist between the formal and informal organizations. Characteristics such as leaders, status systems, norms and control mechanisms, and communication networks are found in both types of organization. The major differences between the formal and informal organization are that the leader of the formal organization is appointed and that the status, norms, and communication systems flow from this pre-established structuring. Because an individual is a formal leader possessing a certain degree of status, he is expected to perform at a norm which is established by the organization. In the informal group, a leader emerges and is given a status ranking by the members. Because he is the emergent leader, he helps in setting acceptable group norms.

GROUP COHESIVENESS

Cohesiveness is another important group concept which must be understood if the behavioral analysis of groups is to be complete. In a simplistic manner, this concept involves the "stick-together" characteristics of groups and their impact on group members. In a more refined definition, group cohesiveness is stated as the attraction of members to the group in terms of the strength of forces on the individual member to remain active in the group and to resist leaving it.[18]

All of the above characteristics of groups are influenced in some degree by the cohesiveness within the group.[19] For example, the greater the attraction within the group, the more likely it is that the membership will adhere closely to a group norm such as production level.

Research findings have allowed those interested in work group cohesiveness to isolate some of the more important factors which affect it. Some of the conditions which influence cohesiveness are schematically presented in Figure 9–6. The factors which are identified in Figure 9–6 are only examples of some of the variables uncovered in research studies, but they are representative of the types of factors that can enhance or reduce cohesiveness.

Size of Work Group

One of the important and necessary conditions for the existence of a group is that members interact and communicate with each other. If the group is so large that members do not get to know each other, there is little likelihood that the group will be high in cohesiveness. This is a logical assumption that would be made by those who understand the difficulties of communicating in large groups.

Research studies found in behavioral literature indicate that the logical assumption is accurate, and that an inverse relationship does exist between size of group and group cohesiveness.[20] As the size of a group increases, its cohesiveness decreases.

---

[18] This definition is based upon the group cohesiveness concept presented by Stanley E. Seashore, *Group Cohesiveness in the Industrial Work Group* (Ann Arbor, Mich.: University of Michigan, Institute for Social Research, 1954).

[19] Sayles and Strauss, *op. cit.*, p. 101.

[20] Seashore, *op. cit.*, pp. 90–95. This study will be discussed in more detail later in the chapter.

FIGURE 9–6

Factors Contributing to Group Cohesiveness

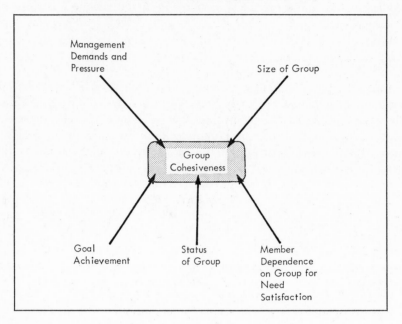

Dependence of Members upon the Work Group

As stated previously, individuals join groups because they perceive the group as a unit which can help them satisfy economic and socio-psychological needs. A group that is able to satisfy a significant portion of an individual's needs will appear attractive to that individual. Group processes such as communication and overall friendship make the group a key factor in the individual's life. Thus, what the group stands for, its norms, and its membership are bonds which relate the individual to the group. These are examples of the forces of attraction discussed by be-havioralists. The greater the individual's dependency upon the group, the stronger these bonds of attraction will be.

Achievement of Goals

The attainment of some set of group-established goals (e.g., better production than another group) has an influence on members. For ex-ample, a work group that attains a highly desired rating for completing a task enhances the value of being a group member; individuals within the group feel a pride in being members of a work group that has performed in such a manner that they are recognized as being superior. The group has proved through task completion efforts that it possesses the individual skills and coordination necessary for organizational performance that is viewed as successful.

Work groups that have successfully attained pre-established goals are likely to be highly cohesive units, the members tending to be more attracted toward each other because they have worked together in the past and because their efforts have resulted in achieving a desired goal. Thus, success and cohesiveness are interrelated: Success in goal achievement encourages cohesiveness, and cohesive work groups are more likely to attain pre-established goals. It is important to consider that, although group cohesiveness can lead to successful achievement of goals, it can prove detrimental when group and organization goals are not congruent.

Status of Group

In an organizational setting work groups are typically ranked in a status hierarchy. An intergroup status hierarchy may develop for many different reasons, including the following:
1. One group is rated higher than another in overall performance; this is a measure of success in the organization.
2. To become a member of the group, individuals must display a high level of skill.
3. The work being done by the group is dangerous or financially more rewarding or more challenging than other work.
4. The group is less closely supervised in comparison to other groups.
5. In the past, members of the group have been considered for promotion more often than members of other groups.
These are only some of the criteria which affect the status hierarchy of groups.[21] Generally, the higher a group ranks in the intergroup status hierarchy, the greater its cohesiveness. However, the higher-status groups appear attractive only to some nonmembers. Individuals on the outside of the group may not want to become members of a high-status group because membership entails close adherence to group norms.

Management Demands and Pressure

The last determinant of group cohesiveness discussed in this section should not be viewed as the least significant factor because of its ranking in our discussion. It is certainly true in many organizations that management or superiors have a significant impact on group cohesiveness. The

---

[21] For a listing of other status criteria, see Sayles and Strauss, *op. cit.*, p. 102.

member of work groups tend to "stick together" more when they are pressured by superiors to conform to some organizational norm (e.g., punching in at 8:00 and not 8:05 A.M., or producing at least 125 units per week).

The group cohesiveness attributed to managerial demands may be a short-run or long-run phenomenon. In some cases, a group may be loosely knit (low in cohesiveness), and a company policy statement may be interpreted as a threat to the job security of group members. Consequently the members of the group become a more cohesive and unified whole in order to withstand the perceived management threat. After the danger is past (i.e., the policy statement is rescinded), the group gradually drifts back toward low cohesiveness. In other cases, the cohesiveness may be a longer-lasting phenomenon. The important point to grasp is that demands and pressures can create an atmosphere in which members of groups are attracted toward each other so that the outside pressure forces eventually confront a cohesive work group.

AN END RESULT: MEMBER SATISFACTION

A desired end result or consequence of group membership is increased satisfaction of members. Social psychologists have, in recent years, increased their efforts to unravel some of the mysteries of member satisfaction within groups. Perhaps the most provocative integrative analysis of work group member satisfaction is presented by Heslin and Dunphy.[22] They report on a survey of thirty-seven studies which show specific relationships between work group member satisfaction and (1) perceived freedom to participate, (2) perceived goal attainment, and (3) status consensus.

Perceived Freedom to Participate

Heslin and Dunphy, through their analysis of small-group studies, indicate that a member's perception of his freedom to participate influences his need satisfaction. The individuals who perceived themselves as active participators reported themselves more satisfied,[23] while those who perceived their freedom to participate to be insignificant typically were the least satisfied members in a work group.

The freedom-to-participate phenomenon is related to the entire spectrum of economic and socio-psychological needs. For example, the perceived ability to participate may lead an individual to believe that he

---

[22] Richard Heslin and Dexter Dunphy, "Three Dimensions of Member Satisfaction in Small Groups," *Human Relations*, vol. 17 (May, 1964), pp. 99–112.

[23] This was indicated in Bavelas' experiments with communication networks in Bavelas, *op. cit.*, p. 81.

is a valued member of the group. This assumption can lead to satisfaction of security, esteem, and self-actualization needs.

Perceived Goal Attainment

A number of behaviorally oriented studies indicate that a group member's perception of progress toward the attainment of desired goals is an important factor which is related to member satisfaction. Groups under study who progressed toward the attainment of goals did indicate higher levels of satisfaction, while members of groups not adequately progressing toward the attainment of group goals showed a lower satisfaction level.

Status Consensus

This concept is defined as agreement about the relative status of all group members. Several studies reviewed by Heslin and Dunphy indicate that, when the degree of status consensus is high, member satisfaction tends to be high; where status consensus within the group is low, member satisfaction tends to be low.

It is also concluded that status consensus is more readily achieved in groups where
1. the group task specialist is perceived to be competent by the membership,
2. a leader emerges who plays a role that is considered an important group task, and
3. a leadership role emerges and is filled by an individual who concentrates on coordinating and maintaining the activities of the group.

The insightful review of Heslin and Dunphy suggests that the perception of the membership concerning freedom to participate, movement toward goal attainment, and status consensus significantly influences the level of need satisfaction attained by group members. Their review also clearly indicates that, when an individual member's goals and needs are in conflict with the goals and needs of the overall group, lower levels of membership satisfaction are the result.

A WORK GROUP MODEL

Our discussion of work groups now enables us to develop a schematic representation of work group behavior. This representation is shown in Figure 9–7. The diagram has a distinct behavioral character, since it contains the "why," "how," and "when" of work groups as found in the behavioral literature. Figure 9–7 succinctly summarizes what has been discussed concerning reasons for group formation, the types of groups, the characteristics of group membership, and one of the major end results, membership satisfaction.

Another important phase of the work group framework is the feedback cycle. As designated in Figure 9–7, feedback on the end results of group membership influences each of the stages in the framework. For example, the perceived goal attainment opportunities in a work group

FIGURE 9–7

A Model of Work Group Behavior

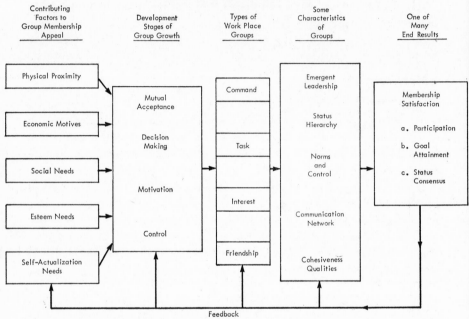

influence its cohesiveness. As stated previously, groups that achieve or are moving toward success (goal attainment) have the greatest attraction (cohesiveness) within the group.

TECHNIQUES OFFERED BY BEHAVIORALISTS FOR STUDYING GROUPS

The behavioralists believe that systematic research is needed if managers and researchers are to continue acquiring vital knowledge about factors such as characteristics of group structure, the impact of groups on the attitudes of members, and how the membership influences phenomena like group culture and attractiveness. The methods typically suggested by behavioralists have, in most instances, proved successful in studying group behavior in a laboratory setting. The college classroom, management development seminar, or boys' day camp is used as settings for investigating group phenomena. Although these settings are not exactly similar to a company office or production department work area, there are many perceptive insights provided by laboratory group behavior studies. For example, the flow of communication and personal interaction, the emergence of leaders, and the exercise of pressure upon members are some of the phenomena that can be examined in laboratory settings.

There are several popular group behavior study methods proposed in the behavioral literature. The two methods, developed over a decade ago, yet continually found in contemporary literature are Bales' interaction analysis method and Moreno's sociometric analysis.

Bales Laboratory Technique

R. F. Bales developed interaction profile analysis to obtain work group behavior data by observing directly what is occurring within a group. He studied groups attempting to reach a group decision on a full-fledged problem (e.g., solving a business case). After studying groups in the laboratory setting, Bales concluded that group behavior can be classified as task-oriented and human-relations-oriented. Bales proposed that, through group interaction, a number of task and human-relations reactions occur in both positive and negative forms.[24]

Bales observed the interactions through one-way mirrors and recorded the group discussion that occurred in leaderless groups attempting to analyze a Harvard University case in human relations. He identified 12 categories of interaction which occurred within the groups as they attempted to resolve the case. The 12 categories were briefly described as follows:[25]

I.   Human Relations   Shows solidarity, gives
     (Positive)   help, reward.
                          Shows tension release,
                          jokes, laughs.
                          Understands, concurs,
                          complies.

---

[24] R. F. Bales and F. L. Strodbeck, "Phases in Group Problem Solving," *The Journal of Abnormal and Social Psychology,* vol. 46 (October, 1951), pp. 485–95. For a complete discussion of the interaction analysis, see R. F. Bales, *Interaction Process Analysis: A Method for the Study of Small Groups* (Cambridge, Mass: Addison-Wesley, Inc., 1950).

[25] *Ibid.*

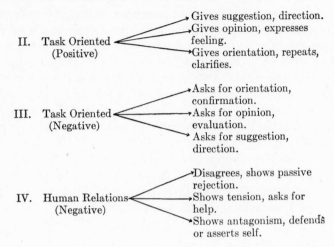

II.   Task Oriented
      (Positive)

→ Gives suggestion, direction.
→ Gives opinion, expresses feeling.
→ Gives orientation, repeats, clarifies.

III. Task Oriented
      (Negative)

→ Asks for orientation, confirmation.
→ Asks for opinion, evaluation.
→ Asks for suggestion, direction.

IV.   Human Relations
      (Negative)

→ Disagrees, shows passive rejection.
→ Shows tension, asks for help.
→ Shows antagonism, defends or asserts self.

After the group case-solving sessions, members fill out a questionnaire asking about their reactions, their satisfactions, their relations to each other, and their opinions about their discussion group. From the questionnaire answers and from observation, Bales developed an interaction profile of satisfied and dissatisfied case-solving groups using the twelve-category descriptive system he developed.

The Who-to-Whom Matrix

Another procedure developed by Bales for acquiring a better understanding of work group behavior and interaction is the who-to-whom matrix. Bales tabulated the number of discussions going on between individuals, who initiated the discussion, and who addressed discussion to the group as a whole.

Bales found that the patterns of discussion varied under different circumstances. For example, groups with no designated leader generally tend to have more equal participation than groups with designated leaders of higher status. It was also found that the size of the group is an important factor affecting within-group discussion patterns. The leader in groups larger than five tends to speak considerably more to the group as a whole than to specific members. All other members tend to speak more to specific individuals than to the group as a whole. As groups increase in size, a larger and larger proportion of the activity tends to be addressed to the leader, and a smaller and smaller proportion to other members. In effect, the communication pattern tends to "centralize" around the leader.

In addition to tracing communication patterns in his small-group analysis, Bales also studied the roles of group members. Specifically, he investigated the roles of the best idea man, best guidance man, best liked, and scapegoat. The man who had the best ideas and gave the most guidance was classified as the group task specialist, while the best liked person was viewed as the group human relations specialist.

By using the task specialist and human relations specialist classification, Bales introduced an interesting analysis of what could happen if, for example, the human relations specialist attempts to take over the group from the task specialist. This type of internal struggling can disrupt the activities and overall performance of the group. The implication of this part of the Bales analysis is that groups work more effectively with two members filling the two separate leader roles.

Bales' interaction process analysis furnishes a valuable technique for analyzing small-group functioning in laboratory settings. The findings and insights of his research provide business managers at all levels of the managerial hierarchy with insights about communication patterns, roles, and the relationship between communication initiation and the status systems within work groups. Thus, although it would be extremely difficult, if not impossible, to perform interaction process analysis in an office or on the production floor, the laboratory-based findings provide needed knowledge about groups. The vital questions regarding what makes a group "tick," what is the pattern of group communications, and who is the task leader and human relations leader can be coped with more effectively if research findings similar to those of Bales are common knowledge among business managers.

Moreno's Sociometric Analysis

The sociometric-analysis method of studying work group behavior and structural characteristics involves the use of self-reports from group members. These reports indicate the preference and repulsion patterns of group members. Based on the preferences and repulsion choices of members, insights about the leaders and status hierarchy of the group and about communication patterns can be provided to those interested in such phenomena.[26]

Sociometric Choice and Sociogram. For the purpose of understanding the complex communication patterns and interactions of groups, Moreno developed questions which asked group members whom they liked and disliked within the group,[27] enabling Moreno to gain knowledge about group relations. From the data collected by interview and/or questionnaire, Moreno was able to construct a *sociogram.*

The *sociogram* is a diagram which illustrates the interpersonal relation-

[26] J. L. Moreno, "Contributions of Sociometry to Research Methodology in Sociology," *American Sociological Review,* vol. 12 (June, 1947), pp. 287–92.

[27] J. H. Jacobs, "The Application of Sociometry to Industry," *Sociometry,* vol. 8 (May, 1954), pp. 181–98.

ships existing within a group. Figure 9–8 presents a simple sociogram based upon feelings of attraction reported by a group of production workers. The line from Nick to Jim represents an expressed choice by Nick. That is, Nick likes to work with Jim. The Jim-to-Nick line shows that Jim likes to work with Nick. This is a mutual choice pair (Nick to Jim and Jim to Nick). The relationship reported between Bob and Nick, however, is a single choice pattern: Bob likes to work with Nick. The same type of procedure can be used to depict rejections, that is, asking with whom someone dislikes working would show rejection choices.

FIGURE 9–8

Sociogram Patterns of Attraction

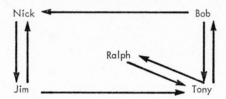

Questions concerning the choice by group members when they have technical problems with their work can help management identify those members with respected technical expertise. Assumed sociometric-choice data concerning individuals whom the group members contact in their informal task work group are analyzed and summarized in Figure 9–9.

FIGURE 9–9

Technical Expert Preferences

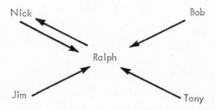

Ralph is the overwhelming choice of the group members. Other similar patterns of choice and rejection can identify isolates and scapegoats of groups. The isolate would not be the choice of other group members; and the scapegoat would be designated verbally as a poor group member.

The sociometric procedures recommended by Moreno have potential value for introducing structural, personnel, and technological changes in an organization. For example, if a manager could identify the leader(s) of the group, he could hopefully work with the leader(s) in bringing about change. Of course, many factors such as the type of change being introduced, the groups' past relations with management, and the influence of the leader within the group would be critical to the success of dealing with work group leaders. Sociometric analysis has been used on a small scale in business organizations; however, this does not detract from its potential value to managers.[28]

STUDIES OF GROUPS WITH RELEVANCE TO ORGANIZATIONS

The amount of research carried out on groups has filled entire books. Group studies have involved college students, housewives, children, religious sects, business executives, military personnel, and many other segments of society. There have been a few studies involving business organizations that stress some of the group characteristics discussed in this chapter. These studies show how group characteristics influence the on-the-job performance of individuals within an organizational setting. Three such studies are briefly presented.

Van Zelst Construction Industry Study

In the building trades, work groups are typically formed on a piece-meal basis. For example, bricklayers are sent to a job location from the union hall and are assigned work by the supervisor. The task group is structured by management and, once the job is completed, the group is generally disbanded.

Van Zelst theorized that, if construction workers were allowed to select their own partners and form their own groups, overall group performance would improve.[29] He used two groups of workers, namely, carpenters and bricklayers, to test his theory. These workers were allowed to select their partners, and work assignments were rearranged to conform to these preferences—first into mutual-choice teams of two (Moreno sociometric choice, Figure 9–8); then, when technically necessary, these pairs were combined into larger work teams.

The group established by the usual methods and those established by allowing workers to select their partners were compared on such meas-

---

[28] For an excellent discussion of some of the limitations of sociometric analysis (e.g., inadequate attention to the selection of sociometric criteria), see Gardner Lindzey and Edgar F. Borgatta, "Sociometric Measurement," in Gardner Lindzey (ed.), *Handbook of Social Psychology* (Reading, Mass.: Addison-Wesley, Inc., 1954), pp. 405–48.

[29] R. H. Van Zelst, "Sociometrically Selected Work Teams Increase Production," *Personnel Psychology*, vol. 5, (Autumn, 1952), pp. 175–85.

ures as job satisfaction, turnover, labor cost, and material cost. The results clearly indicated that the groups established on the basis of peer selection were far superior on each of these measures.

The results of Van Zelst's investigation should not be interpreted as a "one best way" answer to establishing task groups. In some instances, for example, those workers selecting each other may be low producers and/or troublemakers who, by getting together, can cause more disruption in the workplace than if they were apart. These employees may have goals of interacting and socializing, while a basic organizational goal such as higher productivity is not achieved. Thus the feasibility and wisdom of allowing workers to select their task group partners can result in positive or negative consequences for an organization.

A Field Study of Work Group Behavior

The artificial connotation associated with laboratory studies of work group behavior causes many practicing business managers concern. They fear that what is being observed and analyzed at some university is not what is occurring in their company. However, an interesting study conducted by Whyte[30] in restaurants illustrates how many of the group characteristics discovered through interaction process analysis and sociometric analysis are also found in an ongoing business operation.

Whyte studied such factors as the work flow in the restaurant, the group status hierarchies, the communication patterns between members of different status groups, and conflict between members of different groups. He discovered that the flow of work begins when the customer places an order with the waitress. Figure 9-10 depicts the work-flow pattern.

FIGURE 9-10
Restaurant Work Flow

1. Customer enters ——→	2. Order taken by ——→ waitress	3. Order taken to pantry where it is assembled (salad) or may not be assembled (meat)
4. Runner assigned to take meat requests ——→	5. Runner informs ——→ cook of customer meat request	6. Cook prepares meat
7. Runner takes meat to pantry to complete order ——→	8. Waitress has order ——→ checked by individual to see that portions are the proper size	9. Waitress delivers completed order to the customer

[30] William F. Whyte, *Human Relations in the Restaurant Industry* (New York: McGraw-Hill Book Co., 1948).

In observing the work flow, Whyte recognized that the highest-status employees in the restaurant kitchens are the cooks, while the lowest-status persons are the runners. Many times conflict arose between these two groups. During rush hours, the cooks had difficulty meeting orders, and the runners had to ask that special dishes be prepared. In effect, the lowest-status runners initiated communication with the highest-status cooks. Heated arguments occurred and this conflict led to a slowdown in filling customer orders.

Whyte further observed that social groups existed throughout the restaurant. These groups tended to form around members of the same age, sex, and outside interests. These friendship and interest groups served to satisfy the social needs of restaurant employees.

This excellent study and its documentation by Whyte indicate that group characteristics are more than a laboratory myth perpetuated by behavioral scientists. They exist and influence member behavior and overall organizational effectiveness (e.g., slowdown in filling orders).

Group Cohesiveness Study

In the early 1950's, Seashore studied work group cohesiveness (defined as attraction to the group or resistance to leaving it) and various measures of group member attitudes and productivity.[31] He reached a number of insightful conclusions based on responses to questions concerning cohesiveness and on production records.

First, Seashore reports that high group cohesiveness is associated with less anxiety about job-related matters. For example, high cohesive group members were significantly less likely than low cohesive group members to report (1) feeling under pressure for higher productivity, (2) feeling lack of supportiveness (i.e., individual sees his on-the-job experiences as contributing to or maintaining his sense of personal worth), (3) feeling "jumpy" or "nervous" about the job. The anxiety finding is concisely summarized in Figure 9–11.

Seashore's results suggest that, if an employee is a member of a highly cohesive group, he receives the type of support that reduces typical workplace anxieties (pressure to produce). The group serves as an anxiety-reducing mechanism.

Secondly, it was found that, the greater the cohesiveness of the group, the greater the influence which the goals of the group have on the performance of members. In work groups with high cohesiveness, the variation in productivity among members is less than in groups with low cohesiveness. Seashore concluded that, on the average, highly cohesive

---

[31] Seashore, *op. cit.*, p. 20.

groups are somewhat more productive than low cohesive groups. However, a key factor specified by him is that those groups that tend to support company goals and also are cohesive produce at higher levels. Thus, an important qualification is that the cohesive group perceive as supportive both management and company goals.

Seashore's productivity findings are summarized in Figure 9–12. It shows that a cohesive work group can produce significantly below industrial-engineering-established norms, especially if the group is cohesive and perceives management as being nonsupportive.

FIGURE 9–11

Group Cohesiveness as Related to Anxiety

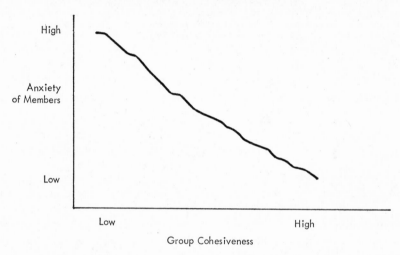

The Seashore studies indicate that cohesiveness factors influence behavior (anxiety) and productivity. They imply that the supervisor who can foster a cohesive work group that perceives the company and him as being supportive should be rewarded with higher levels of productivity. The difficulty, of course, lies in determining group cohesiveness initially. Like so many behavior concepts, group cohesiveness is difficult to measure. Also, it is certainly difficult to examine productivity indices for many groups. For example, how do we measure the productivity of group members engaged in managerial work, or in work where it is difficult to determine the output of each individual member? Despite these perplexing problems, the findings of Seashore, Van Zelst, and Whyte clearly indicate that group phenomena observed in the laboratory also exist in the workplace. Consequently, to supervise more effectively, it is

FIGURE 9–12

Cohesiveness and Productivity

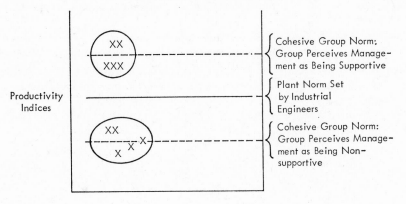

in management's best interest to learn more about group processes and influence.

SUMMARY

The behavioral approach to management is replete with discussions, theories, and research findings concerning work groups. The intense interest in groups displayed by behavioralists is based upon premises such as (1) groups are ubiquitous; (2) groups influence an employee's perceptions and attitudes; (3) groups influence productivity of employees; (4) groups aid an individual in satisfying unfulfilled needs; and (5) groups facilitate communications.

The interest in groups and their dynamics has not waned and is not expected to do so. What has been and is presently being learned about group phenomena is being put to greater use in business organizations (e.g., Van Zelst, Seashore, and Whyte). Awareness of the practical importance of groups to the continued effectiveness of an organization should generate more scientific research studies which should lead to additional understanding of group behavior and group influence in organizational settings.

DISCUSSION AND REVIEW QUESTIONS

1. Distinguish between status hierarchy and status among different groups.
2. Why would it be difficult to utilize the Bales interaction analysis method and the sociometric analysis technique of Moreno in an actual organizational setting?

3. What would be some of the reasons for an individual to become an isolate (a member not in good standing) in a work group?

4. Should management encourage and aid in the development of cohesive work groups?

5. What organizational factors other than those shown in Figure 9–6 could possibly lead to the development of cohesive work groups?

6. Would behavioralists agree that the emergent leaders of work groups would typically utilize democratic leadership in their roles of leading the group? Why?

7. Discuss and compare the reward procedures utilized by informal groups and by the formal organization.

8. In what type of work would it be feasible to utilize the sociometric peer choice arrangement used by Van Zelst in his construction industry study?

9. It is generally agreed that a group influences individual behavior. Can an individual significantly influence a group's overall behavior? Why?

10. Why is it difficult to achieve status consensus in some work groups?

ADDITIONAL REFERENCES

BRIDGES, E. M., et al., "Effects of Hierarchical Differentiation on Group Productivity, Efficiency, and Risk Taking," Administrative Science Quarterly, 13 (1968), 305–19.

BUCKLOW, M. "A New Role for the Work Group," Administrative Science Quarterly, 7 (1962), 236–57.

FOREHAND, G. A. AND GILMER B. "Environmental Variation in Studies of Organizational Behavior," Psychological Bulletin, 62 (1965), 361–82.

HARE, A. PAUL. Handbook of Small Group Research. New York: The Free Press of Glencoe, 1962.

HOMANS, G. C. The Human Group. New York: Harcourt, Brace & World, 1950.

PATCHEN, M. "The Effect of Reference Group Standards on Job Satisfactions," Human Relations, 11 (1958), 303–14.

PATCHEN, M. "Supervisory Methods and Group Performance Norms," Administrative Science Quarterly, 7 (1962), 275–94.

SLATER, P. E. Microcosm: Structural, Psychological and Religious Evolution in Groups. New York: John Wiley & Sons, Inc., 1966.

STOGDILL, R. M. Individual Behavior and Group Achievement. New York: Oxford Press, 1959.

THOMAS, E. J. AND FINK, C. F. "Effects of Group Size," Psychological Bulletin, 60 (1963), 371–84.

chapter ten

Leadership

INTRODUCTION

Managerial scholars and practitioners have been perplexed for years by the phenomenon of leadership in organizations. Concerted effort has been expended to describe and analyze the relationships between the way in which a leader functions and the way in which his followers perform in their job tasks.

Behavioralists have attempted to apply their logic and methodologies to clarify some of the variables normally associated with leading people. However, although some of the many leadership variables have been clarified, numerous incongruities and contradictory theories and research findings still exist in behavioral literature. In this chapter, some of the theories and findings are organized into a manageable leadership framework. The material presented here shows that no one behavioral theory of leadership is universally accepted. It will show, however, that many of the theories of leadership overlap. Although the terms used are different, the underlying rationale, premises, and tentative conclusions of the various theories are similar.

WHAT IS LEADERSHIP?

Some behavioral theories and research findings have projected the impression that leadership is a synonym for managership. The realities of formal and informal organizational life indicate that this assumption is not correct. Leaders are found not only in the managerial hierarchy, but also in informal work groups. The discussion in this chapter is directed toward the exercise of leadership by individuals in the formal managerial hierarchy.

In the behavioral management literature, there are many definitions of leadership. Listed below are a few of the more popular ones:

(1) Leadership is one form of dominance, in which the followers more or less willingly accept direction and control by another person.[1]

(2) Leadership is the process of influencing the activities of an organized group in efforts toward goal setting and goal achievement.[2]

(3) Leadership is the process by which an agent induces a subordinate to behave in a desired manner.[3]

(4) Leadership is an influence process the dynamics of which are a function of the personal characteristics of the leader and his followers and of the nature of the specific situation.[4]

A review of the four leadership definitions indicates that, although (1) was stated in 1946 and (4) was proposed in 1966, they are very similar. The common thread running through these four definitions is that leadership is a process whereby one individual exerts his influence over others in his group. The important implication of this common feature is that leadership occurs only when there is interaction between individuals. Thus, instead of adding to an already adequate list of definitions of leadership, we only want to stress two words—*influence* and *interaction*.

AN INFLUENCE THEORY

Several attempts have been made to clarify and depict the basis upon which a superior might influence a subordinate or a group of subordinates. One of the most concise, but insightful approaches is offered by French and Raven.[5] These researchers define power in terms of influence—the control which a person possesses and can exercise on others.

It is proposed by French and Raven that there are five different bases of power:

---

[1] K. Young, *Handbook of Social Psychology* (London: Routledge & Kegan Paul Ltd., 1946).

[2] Ralph M. Stogdill, "Leadership, Membership and Organization," *Psychological Bulletin*, vol. 52 (January, 1950), p. 4.

[3] Warren G. Bennis, "Leadership Theory and Administrative Behavior: The Problem of Authority," *Administrative Science Quarterly*, vol. 4 (December, 1959), p. 261.

[4] Max D. Richards and Paul S. Greenlaw, *Management Decision Making* (Homewood, Ill.: Richard D. Irwin, Inc., 1966), p. 135.

[5] John R. P. French and Bertram Raven, "The Bases of Social Power," in Dorwin Cartwright and A. F. Zander (eds.), *Group Dynamics* (2nd ed.; Evanston, Ill.: Row, Peterson, and Company, 1960), pp. 607–23.

1. *Coercive Power.* This is power based upon fear. A subordinate per-
    ceives that failure to comply with the wishes of his superior would
    lead to punishment (e.g., a poor work assignment, a reprimand).
    Coercive power is based upon the expectations of individuals that
    punishment is the consequence for not agreeing with the actions, at-
    titudes, or theories of a superior.
2. *Reward Power.* This is the opposite of coercive power. A subordinate
    perceives that compliance with the wishes of his superior will lead
    to positive rewards. These rewards could be monetary (increases in
    pay) or psychological (a compliment for a job well done).
3. *Legitimate Power.* This type of power derives from the position of a
    manager in the organizational hierarchy. For example, the president
    of a corporation possesses more legitimate power than the vice presi-
    dent, and the department manager has more legitimate power than
    the first line foreman.
4. *Expert Power.* An individual with this type of power is one with some
    expertise, special skill, or knowledge. The possession of one or more of
    these variables gains for the possessor the respect and compliance of
    peers or subordinates.
5. *Referent Power.* This power is based on a follower's identification
    with a leader. The leader is admired because of one or more personal
    traits, and the follower can be influenced because of this admiration.

This fivefold framework offers the student of management a conceptual
distinction between the bases of power. These can be reclassified into
two major categories: (1) power based primarily on organizational
factors, and (2) power based on individual factors.

Coercive, reward, and legitimate power are specified primarily by the
individual's position in the organization. The foreman in an organization is at a lower managerial level in the firm than the department manager, and consequently his coercive, reward, and legitimate power bases
are significantly less than those of the department manager. Upper level
managers are allowed various company facilities and resources, while
managers at the lower levels cannot utilize these. Position also affects the
use of power in regard to the discipline process. A foreman can reprimand
his subordinates (coercive power), while the department manager can
reprimand the foreman.

The degree and scope of a manager's referent and expert power bases
are dictated primarily by individual characteristics. Some managers
possess specific qualities (e.g., skills or attributes) that make them attractive to subordinates, although the managers are working within an
organizational system. Thus, the individual manager controls the referent
and expert power bases while the organization controls the coercive,
reward, and legitimate power bases.

A book by Katz and Kahn[6] has added another concept to the fivefold power framework for studying leadership. They propose an incremental influence category in the following manner:

> . . . we consider the essence of organizational leadership to be the influential increment over and above the mechanical compliance with routine directives of the organization.

The incremental influence factor could be described in the French and Raven approach as a combination of the referent and expert bases.[7] The essence of the influence theory is that the organizational and individual characteristics of managers are related to each other. Thus, the act of influencing or leading others depends on the organization system itself and on the perceptions which subordinates hold of their leaders, among other things.

The influence framework can be utilized to identify the functions which a leader is supposed to perform in an organization. Many distinct behavioral viewpoints of leadership functions are espoused by individuals studying leadership behavior. Two of the most controversial interpretations of what the leader should and must do in the organization have been classified as the psychological view and the sociological view.[8]

The Leadership Job: Psychological Overview

The identification and clarification of the job which leaders are expected to perform in any organizational system is a controversial issue. The behavioral approach to leadership has not yet clearly explained the organizationally related functions of a leader. One behavioral perspective of the functions of a leader is designated as the *psychological overview*.

The psychological overview proposes that the primary function of a leader is to develop effective motivation systems. The leader must be able to stimulate his subordinates in such a manner that they contribute positively to organizational goals and are also able to satisfy various personal needs.

The Maslow need hierarchy could serve as a model for the leader in developing the most effective motivation system. The need hierarchy approach was discussed in Chapter 8. The leader, by being familiar with the premise that "man does not live by bread alone" but is interested in

---

[6] Daniel Katz and Robert L. Kahn, *The Social Psychology of Organizations* (New York: John Wiley and Sons, Inc., 1966), p. 302.

[7] Kurt R. Student, "Supervisory Influence and Work-Group Performance," *Journal of Applied Psychology*, vol. 52 (June 1968), pp. 188–94.

[8] This terminology has been proposed by Harold Koontz and Cyril O'Donnell, *Principles of Management* (New York: McGraw-Hill Book Co., 1968), pp. 615–16.

psychological growth, can develop programs that achieve optimum contribution from subordinates. A program that focuses upon the entire need spectrum—physiological, security, social, esteem, and self-actualization —is assumed to have a higher probability for motivating successfully than a partial program.

In the psychological overview, the French and Raven power theory is an integral part. To consider only organizationally controlled power sources—coercive, reward, and legitimate—leads to the development of incomplete and often misdirected motivational programs. The leader must also consider his referent and expert power bases when developing motivation programs intended to help employees satisfy their needs.

The theme stressed in the psychological overview of the leader's job is this aiding of subordinates in satisfying their various needs. The satisfaction of these needs in such a manner that the organization is more successful and the employees happier is the function which a leader must perform. Any leader not accomplishing this complex task is rated low on a hypothetical leadership effectiveness scale.

The Leadership Job: Sociological Overview

Another group of behavioralists perceives the leadership function as a facilitative activity. For example, the leader establishes goals and reconciles organizational conflict between followers, exerting his influence by performing these activities.

The establishment of goals provides the direction which followers often require. It provides the followers with guidance so that they know what type of performance or attitude is expected of them. The goals also influence the interaction patterns that develop between followers. This leads to specific group characteristics such as communication networks, cohesiveness, and status hierarchies.

Conflict among followers can become so disruptive that nothing positive is contributed to the firm. When this occurs, a leader's influence must be exercised to minimize the disruptive conflict within or between groups.

These two categorizations of leadership functions are much too broad and general. The psychological view assumes that a unique motivation strategy exists, and that it can be implemented by leaders. Only a cursory review of the behavioral management literature indicates that *an ideal* motivation strategy is nonexistent. Differences in people, leaders, and organizations diminish the validity of the psychological view.

The sociological view can also be criticized from a pragmatic viewpoint. While it is accurate to assume that leaders facilitate the activities of followers, it is misleading to contend that leaders can always set goals and resolve conflict. These are large orders for any leader, which are once again made more difficult by differences in people, and by leadership ability and situations.

In summary, the psychological and sociological views are much too broad to be of much value to those interested in learning about leadership behavior. A much better system for studying leadership would be one which is narrower and is based, if possible, on a more scientific foundation.

SELECTED LEADERSHIP THEORIES

Recent efforts by behavioralists have indicated that there is interest among them to organize the numerous theories. Instead of creating more theories of leadership behavior, the focus here is upon systematically organizing and categorizing what is already available. There appear to be three broad leadership theory categories that have evolved from the recent stop-and-organize efforts. They are (1) the trait theories,

FIGURE 10–1

Overlap of Theories of Leadership

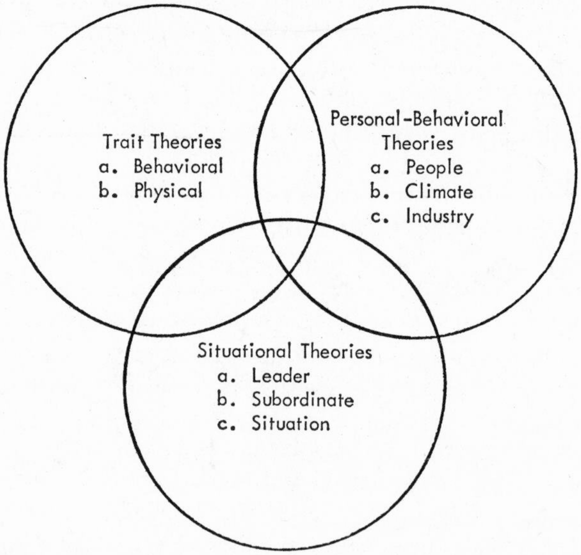

(2) the personal-behavioral theories, and (3) the situational theories. Figure 10–1 illustrates that the trait and personal-behavioral approaches can be integrated to some degree to yield the situational approach. Some of the situational theories emerging have borrowed from the trait ap-

proaches and from various personal-behavioral approaches. Therefore it is best to consider each of the approaches as having many similarities and some differences.

Trait Theories

The identification of various personal traits of leaders as criteria for describing or predicting success has been used for some time. Many executives engaged in recruitment and selection of managers believe that the trait approach is as valid as any other method available and use it instead of ink blots or other techniques. However, the comparison of leaders by various physical, personality, and intelligence traits has resulted in little agreement among researchers.

Physical Traits. There are advocates of the trait theory who contend that the physical stature of a person affects his ability to influence followers. For example, in an extensive review of 12 leadership investigations, Stogdill determined that in nine of the studies leaders were found to be taller than followers; two found them to be shorter, while one other concluded that height was not the most important factor.[9]

Personality. A research study by Ghiselli[10] reports on several personality factors that are related in most, though not all cases to leadership. He found that leaders who have the drive to act independently and are self-assured (e.g., have confidence in their leadership skills) are successful in achieving organizational goals.

The work of Fiedler suggests that successful leaders may be more perceptive than nonsuccessful leaders.[11] He found that effective leaders are more proficient in differentiating between their best and poorest followers than are the less effective supervisors. The leaders of the more effective groups indicate that they maintain greater psychological distance between themselves and their followers than do leaders of less effective groups.

Intelligence. After surveying the literature, Stogdill concluded that leadership ability is associated with the judgment and verbal facility of the leader.[12] Ghiselli also, after conducting research, concluded that an individual's intelligence is an accurate predictor of managerial success within a certain range. Above and below this range the chances of successful prediction significantly decrease.[13]

---

[9] Ralph Stogdill, "Personal Factors Associated with Leadership," *Journal of Applied Psychology,* vol. 25 (January, 1948), pp. 35–71.

[10] Edwin E. Ghiselli, "Managerial Talent," *American Psychologist,* vol. 18 (October, 1963), pp. 631–41.

[11] Fred Fiedler, "The Leader's Psychological Distance and Group Effectiveness," in Cartwright and Zander (eds.), *op. cit.,* pp. 586–605.

[12] Stogdill, *op. cit.*

[13] Ghiselli, *op. cit.*

There are some shortcomings in the method of employing a trait approach and assuming that, if a man is confident, independent, and intelligent, he has a higher probability of succeeding. First, the trait theory of leadership ignores the subordinates. The followers have a significant effect on the job accomplished by the leader. Second, trait theorists do not specify the relative importance of various traits. Should a firm attempt to find managers who are confident or those who act independently—which should be weighted more? Third, the research evidence is inconsistent. Finally, though endless lists of traits have already been uncovered, the list grows annually, so that the numerous traits already uncovered suggest that others will be found in the future. The cumbersome listings lead to confusion and disputes, and provide little insight into organizational leadership. Perhaps the most significant limitation is that trait-related research findings do not allow us to generalize such findings from one situation to another.

Personal-Behavioral Theories

The personal-behavioral approach to the examination of organizational leadership contends that leaders may best be classified by personal qualities (styles) or behavioral patterns. A number of individuals have presented theories of leadership which fit into the personal-behavioral (P-B) category. The P-B theories of leadership focus upon an analysis of what the leader does in carrying out his managerial job.

A Continuum of Leadership. Tannenbaum and Schmidt postulate that the manager in an organization often has difficulty in deciding what type of leadership action is most appropriate for handling a particular problem.[14] He is not sure whether to make the decision himself or to delegate the decision-making authority to one of his subordinates. To provide insight into the meaning of leadership behavior with regard to decision-making, Tannenbaum and Schmidt suggest a continuum.

Figure 10–2 presents this leadership continuum. Leadership actions are related to the degree of authority used by the manager, and to the amount of freedom available to the subordinates in reaching decisions. The managerial actions depicted on the left characterize the manager who maintains a high degree of control, while those on the right designate a manager who delegates decision-making authority. The continuum clearly illustrates that there are a number of leadership styles that can be employed. Perhaps the type of leader who would be most effective would be the one who is adaptable, that is, who can delegate authority effectively because he considers his capabilities, his subordinates' capabilities, and the goals to be accomplished. Thus, Tannenbaum and Schmidt imply

---

[14] Robert Tannenbaum and Warren H. Schmidt, "How to Choose a Leadership Pattern," *Harvard Business Review,* vol. 36 (March–April, 1958), pp. 95–101.

FIGURE 10–2

Continuum of Leadership Behavior

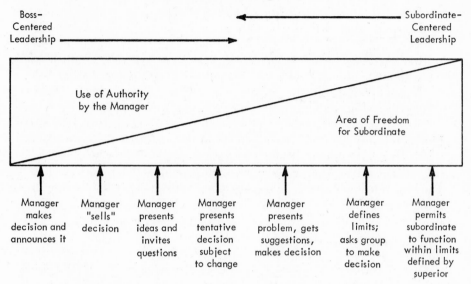

that a leader should not choose a strict "autocratic" or "democratic" style, but should be flexible enough to cope with different situations.

Benevolent Autocracy.   McMurry believes that the cold realities of organizational life have doomed what is referred to as democratic leadership.[15] The democratic leader and the autocratic leader both must set objectives and guide subordinates. However, the democratic leader encourages two-way communication between himself and his subordinates. The benevolent autocrat is interpreted to be a powerful and prestigious manager who can be communicated with and is personally interested in his subordinates' problems. This type of manager is perceived as being able to take prompt remedial action for activities within his jurisdiction.

To support the benevolent-autocrat theory, McMurry offers the following reasons for the demise of democratic leadership:

1. The climate within organizations is unfavorable. The "captains" of industry have worked hard to attain their positions in the managerial hierarchy. Thus they are likely to be hard-driving and would like to control the destiny of their firms. These individuals are not likely to favor delegation of decision-making power.

2. Since most organizations must make rapid and difficult decisions, it is in their best interest to maintain the control of operations in a

[15] Robert N. McMurry, "The Case for Benevolent Autocracy," *Harvard Business Review,* vol. 36 (January–February, 1958), pp. 82–90.

centralized group of managers. Thus, freedom of action is constrained by the need to make rapid decisions, and democratic leadership is not feasible because it encourages freedom of action.

3. Democratic leadership concepts are relatively new and unproven. The historical folklore of successful firms (e.g., profits) have followed traditional bureaucratic principles. These are generally compatible with autocratic and not with democratic leadership. Once a firm has begun to follow bureaucratic guidelines and develop autocratic leaders, these leaders begin to perpetuate themselves.

These three reasons, among others, are the evidence offered by Mc-Murry to justify his claim that the benevolent autocrat is the most effective leader. This type of leader structures his subordinates' work activities; he makes the policy decisions affecting them; he enforces discipline. The benevolent autocrat may encourage participation in the planning of a course of action, but he is the "chief" in executing a decision. Briefly, the benevolent autocrat is concerned about his subordinates' feelings, attitudes, and productivity; but despite these humanistic feelings he runs his operation by using rules, regulations, and specified policies.

Over a decade has passed since McMurry first stated his leadership approach. What has occurred in society recently seems to indicate that the climate, centralization, and folklore arguments have weakened. It appears that there are growing numbers of organizations willing to attempt leadership approaches that are more humanistic and less benevolently autocratic. This is not to say that the benevolent autocrat is not found in organizations or is not successful in the modern corporation. Evidence suggests that he is effective in some situations and the democratic leader in others.

Job-Centered–Employee-Centered Leaders. The Tannenbaum and Schmidt and McMurry theories are based upon opinion. They do not offer the type of performance data being demanded by executives. Since 1947, Likert and his associates at the Institute for Social Research at the University of Michigan have conducted studies of leadership.[16] They have studied leaders in industry, hospitals, and government, obtaining data from thousands of employees.

After extensive analyses, the leaders studied were classified as job-centered or employee-centered. The *job-centered manager* structures the job of his subordinates, closely supervises to see that designated tasks are performed, uses incentives to spur production, and determines satisfactory rates of production based on procedures such as time study.

The *employee-centered manager* focuses his attention on the human aspects of his subordinates' problems and on building effective work

---

[16] Rensis Likert, *New Patterns of Management* (New York: McGraw-Hill Book Company, Inc., 1961). Figures 10–3 and 10–4 are based upon Likert's research findings.

groups with high performance goals. He specifies objectives, communicates them to subordinates and gives his subordinates considerable freedom to accomplish their job tasks and goals. Figure 10–3 presents the findings from one study which compared employee-centered and job-centered managers.

FIGURE 10–3
Number of Supervisors Who Are:

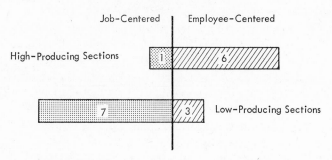

As indicated, the majority of high-producing sections were led by managers who displayed an employee-centered style. In a study of clerical workers the employee-centered manager was described as a general supervisor and the job-centered manager as a close supervisor. Once again, productivity data clearly indicated that the general type of

FIGURE 10–4
Number of Supervisors Who Are:

Under Close Supervision | Under General Supervision

High-Producing Sections   1   9

8   4   Low-Producing Sections

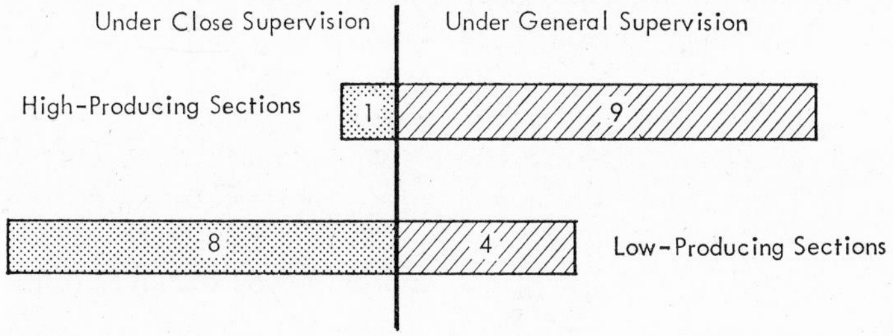

supervision (employee-centered) was more effective than the close supervision style (job-centered). Figure 10–4 presents a summary of the clerical worker data.

Based on his extensive research, Likert suggests that data show that the type of leadership style used significantly influences various end-result variables. Such variables as productivity, absenteeism, attitudes, turnover, and defective units were found to be more favorable from an organizational standpoint when employee-centered or general supervision was utilized. Likert implies that the choice is of the either–or variety, that is, a manager can be categorized and practice as an employee-centered or a job-centered leader. His recommendation is to develop employee-centered managers whenever possible.

Two-Dimensional Theory. In 1945, a group of researchers at Ohio State University began extensive investigations of leadership. Their work uncovered many provocative insights concerning leadership behavior. Perhaps the most publicized aspect of the Ohio State leadership studies was the isolation of two dimensions of leadership behavior, identified through statistical analysis as "consideration" and "initiating structure."[17]

These two dimensions were used to describe leadership behavior characteristics in organizational settings. They assessed how the supervisor thinks he should behave in his leadership role (Leadership Opinion Questionnaire). A second questionnaire attempted to ascertain subordinate perceptions of supervisory behavior (Leader Behavior Description Questionnaire). Analyses of responses to these questionnaires allowed the Ohio State researchers to score a leader on "consideration" and "initiating structure."

A leader who scored high on the "consideration" dimension reflected that he had developed a work atmosphere of mutual trust, respect for subordinates' ideas, and consideration of subordinates' feelings. Such a leader encourages good superior-subordinate rapport and two-way communication. A low "consideration" score indicates that the leader is more impersonal in his dealings with his subordinates.

A high "initiating structure" score indicates that the leader structures his role and those of his subordinates toward the attainment of goals. He is actively involved in planning work activities, communicating pertinent information, and scheduling work.

One research study attempted to compare foremen with different "consideration" and "initiating structure" scores on various performance measures.[18] The first measure was obtained from proficiency ratings made by plant management. Other measures were unexcused absenteeism, accidents, formally filed grievances, and employee turnover. Indices for

[17] See any of the following for excellent presentations of the two-dimensional theory: E. A. Fleishman, "The Measurement of Leadership Attitudes in Industry," *Journal of Applied Psychology,* vol. 37 (June, 1953), pp. 153–58; E. A. Fleishman and D. A. Peters, "Interpersonal Values, Leadership Attitudes and Managerial Success," *Personnel Psychology,* vol. 15 (Summer, 1962), pp. 127–43; and Abraham K. Korman, "Consideration, Initiating Structure, and Organizational Criteria—A Review," *Personnel Psychology,* vol. 19 (Winter, 1966), pp. 349–61.

[18] E. A. Fleishman, E. F. Harris, and H. E. Burtt, *Leadership and Supervision in Industry* (Columbus, Ohio: Bureau of Educational Research, Ohio State University, 1955).

each of these measures were computed for each foreman's work group for an eleven-month period.

Foremen who worked in production divisions were compared to foremen in non-production divisions on "consideration" scores, "initiating structure" scores and proficiency estimates. In the production divisions there was a positive relationship between proficiency and "initiating structure" and a negative relationship with "consideration." In other words, the foremen who were rated by their superiors as most proficient scored high on "structure" and low on "consideration." In the nonproduction divisions the relationships were reversed.

After comparing the leadership scores and foreman proficiency ratings, the researchers examined leadership scores and the performance measures —unexcused absenteeism, accidents, formally filed grievances, and employee turnover. In general, it was determined that high structure and low consideration were related to more absenteeism, accidents, grievances, and turnover.

A number of other studies have supported the general findings cited above, while other research findings present contradictory evidence.[19] Despite these differences, it certainly is true that the Ohio State researchers have stimulated the interest of laymen and researchers in systematically studying leadership. More effort along the lines of the Ohio State studies is needed if some of the mysteries of leadership in an organization are to be uncovered.

The Managerial Grid Theory

Thus far, we have examined continua, personal opinions, and research findings concerning leadership behavior. Another P-B theory which is based on research findings, but is related directly to management development programs, is the managerial grid concept. Blake and Mouton proposed that leadership styles can be plotted on a two-dimensional grid.[20] This grid is briefly presented in Figure 10–5.

Five specific leadership styles are indicated in Figure 10–5. Of course these are only a few of the many possible styles of leadership that can be and are utilized.

> 1,1–*Impoverished*—a minimum effort to accomplish the work is exerted.
>
> 9,1–*Task*—the leader concentrates on task efficiency but shows little regard for human resources.
>
> 1,9–*Country Club*—the leader focuses on being supportive and con-

---

[19] For a number of studies which dispute some of the findings of the Ohio State researchers, see Korman, *op. cit.*

[20] Robert R. Blake and Jane S. Mouton, *The Managerial Grid* (Houston, Texas: Gulf Publishing, 1964).

siderate of employees. However, task efficiency is not a primary concern in this easygoing atmosphere.

5,5—*Middle of the Road*—adequate task efficiency and satisfactory morale are the goals of this style.

9,9—*Team*—the leader facilitates production and morale by co-ordinating and integrating work-related activities.

Ideally, the leader who is a (9,9) individual would be the most efficient in an organization. However, defining a (9,9) leader for every type of

FIGURE 10–5

Managerial Grid

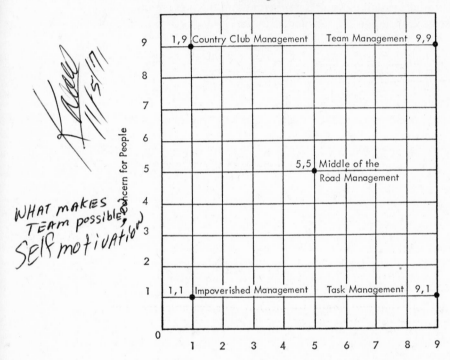

Concern for Production

job is an impossibility. But Blake and Mouton imply that a managerial development program can move leaders *toward* a (9,9) classification. They recommend a number of management development phases. It is assumed that the development experience will aid the manager in acquiring a more thorough concern for fellow employees and equip him with more expertise to accomplish task objectives such as productivity and quality. Four of these phases are outlined briefly below:

Phase 1: Laboratory-seminar groups. Conferences are used to introduce the leaders to the grid approach and philosophy. The training of the leaders in the conferences is conducted by line managers of the firm who are already familiar with the Blake and Mouton introduction. A key part of the phase is to analyze and assess one's own leadership style.

Phase 2: Teamwork. Each department works out and specifies its own (9,9) description. This phase is an extension of Phase 1, which included leaders from different departments in the conference groups. Thus, in the second phase, managers from the same department are brought together.

Phase 3: Intergroup Interaction. This phase involves intergroup discussion and analysis of (9,9) specifications. Situations are created whereby tensions and conflicts that exist between groups are analyzed by group members.

Phase 4: Goal Setting. Goal setting on the part of the leaders in the program is discussed and analyzed. Such problems as profits, cost control, and safety are placed in a goal-setting context (e.g., one participant vows to reduce direct expenses 20 percent over the next six-month period).

The managerial grid approach relates task effectiveness and human satisfaction to a formal managerial development program. This program is unique in that (1) line managers, not academicians or consultants, run the program, (2) a conceptual framework of management (the grid) is utilized, and (3) the entire managerial hierarchy of the firm undergoes development, not just one group level (e.g., first-line supervisors).

A Synopsis of the Personal-Behavioral Approach

Some readers may suggest that, instead of discussing an approach, we should talk about approaches. However, examination of the various P-B theories discussed in this section indicates that similar concepts are discussed, but different labels are utilized. For example, the continuum, the benevolent-autocrat proposition, Likert, the Ohio State researchers, and the managerial grid approach utilize two broadly defined concepts, which are summarized in Table 10–1.

Each of the five approaches summarized in Table 10–1 focuses upon two concepts; however, some differences should be emphasized. First, the leadership continuum is based primarily upon personal opinions. Although the opinions of the originators are respected, they must be supported with research evidence before more faith can be placed in each particular theory. Second, Likert implies that the most successful leadership style is employee-centeredness. He suggests that we need look no further to find the best leadership style. The critical question is whether the employee-centered style works in all situations. Instead of reporting studies and opinions which dispute Likert's claim, the Ohio

TABLE 10-1

Personal-Behavioral Approach

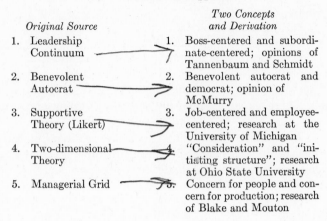

Original Source		Two Concepts and Derivation	
1.	Leadership Continuum	1.	Boss-centered and subordinate-centered; opinions of Tannenbaum and Schmidt
2.	Benevolent Autocrat	2.	Benevolent autocrat and democrat; opinion of McMurry
3.	Supportive Theory (Likert)	3.	Job-centered and employee-centered; research at the University of Michigan
4.	Two-dimensional Theory	4.	"Consideration" and "initiating structure"; research at Ohio State University
5.	Managerial Grid	5.	Concern for people and concern for production; research of Blake and Mouton

State researchers found that, from a production standpoint, the leader with a high "initiating structure" score was preferred by the executives of the company. Thus Likert's claim, or any other claim, that one best leadership approach has been discovered is subject to debate.

Finally, two of the theories can be fitted together to present a diagrammatic analysis of leadership. However, merging the other theories is difficult because of the differences in definitions and contentions of the originators.

The Ohio State theory and the managerial grid approach can be integrated into an overlay theory of leadership, "overlay" meaning that they are merged into one.[21] Perhaps more integrative work along the lines of the overlay (Figure 10-6) would provide the student of management with a better understanding of the P-B theories of leadership. This is not to suggest that an ultimate theory of leadership has been discovered, but that the endless list of styles causes semantic difficulties by referring to the same basic leadership behavior with different terminology.

Situational Theory

Recently, an increasing number of behavioralists have begun to focus their attention on an adaptive theory of leadership. That is, a leadership approach that is flexible enough to adapt to different situations. Included

---

[21] The merging idea was originally proposed and presented by Paul Hersey and Kenneth H. Blanchard, *Management of Organizational Behavior* (Englewood Cliffs, N.J.: Prentice-Hall, Inc., 1969), p. 68.

in this effort is a belief that the best leader is one who is able to adjust his individual style to a particular group at a specific point in time to handle a given situation. Thus, the primary ingredients of a situational theory are the leader himself, the group, and the situation.

Symbolically, the situational approach to leadership is expressed as

FIGURE 10–6

Overlay of Two Leadership Theories

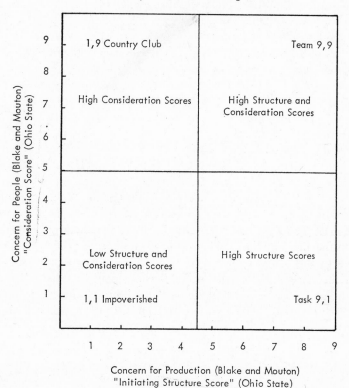

Concern for Production (Blake and Mouton)
"Initiating Structure Score" (Ohio State)

$L = f$ (LP, GP, and S), that is, leadership is a function of the leader's personality, the group's personality and the situation. The situation variable is of major importance since it affects what a leader can accomplish. The combat sergeant barking orders might be successful in a combat situation, but his counterpart in industry barking out higher production orders to employees may be a complete failure.

The situational theory advocates propose that the ideal leader is a person who is able to adapt his style to cope with the situation at hand and the personality of his subordinates. The leader is similar to the night club entertainer who is faced with a different audience, in a different city, at different times of the year, and on different stages with lighting and acoustical differences. One of the most complete analyses of situational or reality-based leadership is offered by Fiedler.

Fiedler Theory of Leadership. The recent work of Fiedler has focused upon adaptive leadership style. With a considerable body of research evidence behind him, Fiedler has developed a situational model of leadership.[22] Three important leadership dimensions are specified since they are assumed to be situational factors that influence the leader's effectiveness. The dimensions identified are:

1. *Leader-member relations*—This refers to the degree of confidence the subordinates have for the leader. It also entails the loyalty shown and attractiveness of the leader.
2. *Task structure*—This refers to the degree to which the followers' jobs are routine versus being ill-structured and undefined.
3. *Position Power*—This refers to the power inherent in the leadership position. It includes the rewards and punishments which are typically associated with the position, the leader's official authority (based on ranking in managerial hierarchy), and the support which the leader receives from his superiors and the overall organization.

By utilizing the three-dimensional model and empirical findings, Fiedler has specified the type of leadership style that is most appropriate in different situations. He has assembled data which relate leadership style to the three-dimensional measures of conditions favorable or unfavorable to the leader. The measure of leadership style adopted is one which discriminates between leaders who tend to be permissive, considerate, and foster good interpersonal relations among group members (Permissive) and leaders who tend to be directive, controlling, more oriented toward task than toward people (Directive). For example, considerate and permissive leaders obtain optimal group performance in situations where the task is structured, but the leader is disliked and must be diplomatic. This type of leadership style is also effective in situations where the leader is liked, but the group is faced with an ambiguous and unstructured task. When the situation is ambiguous and the task is structured, directive leadership is more effective.

In effect, the Fiedler model suggests that leaders who are directive and leaders who are permissive can function best in certain types of situations. Instead of stating that a leader must adopt this or that type of style, Fiedler identifies the type of leader that functions best in a situation. If a leader is to be effective in most situations, it would seem that Fiedler is suggesting that flexibility is appropriate. That is, the leader must examine

---

[22] Fred E. Fiedler, *A Theory of Leadership Effectiveness* (New York: McGraw-Hill Book Co., 1967).

the situation and decide whether to provide structured or unstructured instructions concerning the problem or goal.

In Table 10–2, some of Fiedler's findings about the relationship among the three dimensions to leadership style for such task groups as bomber crews, management groups, high school basketball teams, and open hearth crews are concisely presented.

TABLE 10–2

Summary of Fiedler Investigations of Leadership

| Condition | Group Situation | | | Leadership Style Correlating with Productivity |
	Leader-Member Relations	Task Structure	Position Power	
1	Good	Structured	Strong	Directive
2	Good	Structured	Weak	Directive
3	Good	Unstructured	Strong	Directive
4	Good	Unstructured	Weak	Permissive
5	Moderately Poor	Structured	Strong	Permissive
6	Moderately Poor	Structured	Weak	No Data
7	Moderately Poor	Unstructured	Strong	No Relationship Found
8	Moderately Poor	Unstructured	Weak	Directive

A review of Table 10–2 indicates a strong correlation between good task performance and a Directive style under conditions 1, 2, 3, and 8, and a strong correlation between good task performance and a Permissive style under conditions 4 and 5. These results indicate that for various situations a particular leadership style achieves the best task results.

In effect, Fiedler has presented a theory of leadership which takes into account the leader's personality as well as such situational variables as the task to be completed and the behavioral characteristics of the group of employees which the leader must influence. Of course, much more research is needed before the theory gains widespread acceptance or even partial agreement from among those studying leadership. However, it appears that Fiedler has provided an excellent starting point for research in the 1970s.

THE IDEAL STYLE IS NONEXISTENT

After reading the previous sections of this chapter, it becomes evident that the "one best way" of leadership is not only elusive but has led to confusion. There is no "one best way" to lead people. In practice, leaders are seldom totally autocratic or totally democratic. The matter of leadership style is a complex web of factors. Such items as the past experiences of the leader, the organizational climate, and the personality of the leader are often mentioned in the management literature as being most important in influencing leadership behavior. The behavioral management literature, however, is beginning to stress the importance of empirical findings in proposing theories of leadership. This contemporary concern with empirical support of propositions about leadership has led the present authors to suggest a concise model for leadership.

The model of leadership offered is primarily a descriptive device that only attempts to show a number of important factors that should be considered when analyzing leadership effectiveness. The model hopefully serves as a brief integrative graphical presentation.

Leadership Framework

The leader should consider a number of important organizational and environmental variables as illustrated in Figure 10–7.[23] In the context of the leadership framework, the effective leader is an individual who influences followers in such a manner that high productivity is achieved, high group morale exists, low absenteeism, turnover, and accident rates are the rule, and the development of followers is achieved. Figure 10–7 only specifies three personal qualities which contribute significantly to a leader's ability to influence others. This is not intended to be a complete list of relevant factors in the leader network. The three qualities selected, however, are suited for most leadership styles and are especially compatible with the situational theory of leadership. They are also related as shown by the dashed line to the perception factors identified.

Awareness of Self. One of the most important factors in the situational approach to leadership centers around leadership self-awareness.[24] Any leader of people should be aware of his impact upon those whom he leads. We are not assuming that he can predict accurately in every situation how his leadership style will affect followers. However, we are suggesting that the leader should attempt to learn more about his influence upon others.

Many of us maintain and develop inaccurate images of our personalities and interaction styles. For example, a leader may perceive himself

[23] The model illustrated in Figure 10–7 does not include every relevant behavioral or environmental factor. It only intends to provide the reader with a manageable guideline for considering some of the most relevant leadership factors.

[24] In Chapter 12, sensitivity training will be discussed. One of the purported advantages of sensitivity training is that it improves the self-awareness of participants.

FIGURE 10–7
An Integrative Perspective of Leadership

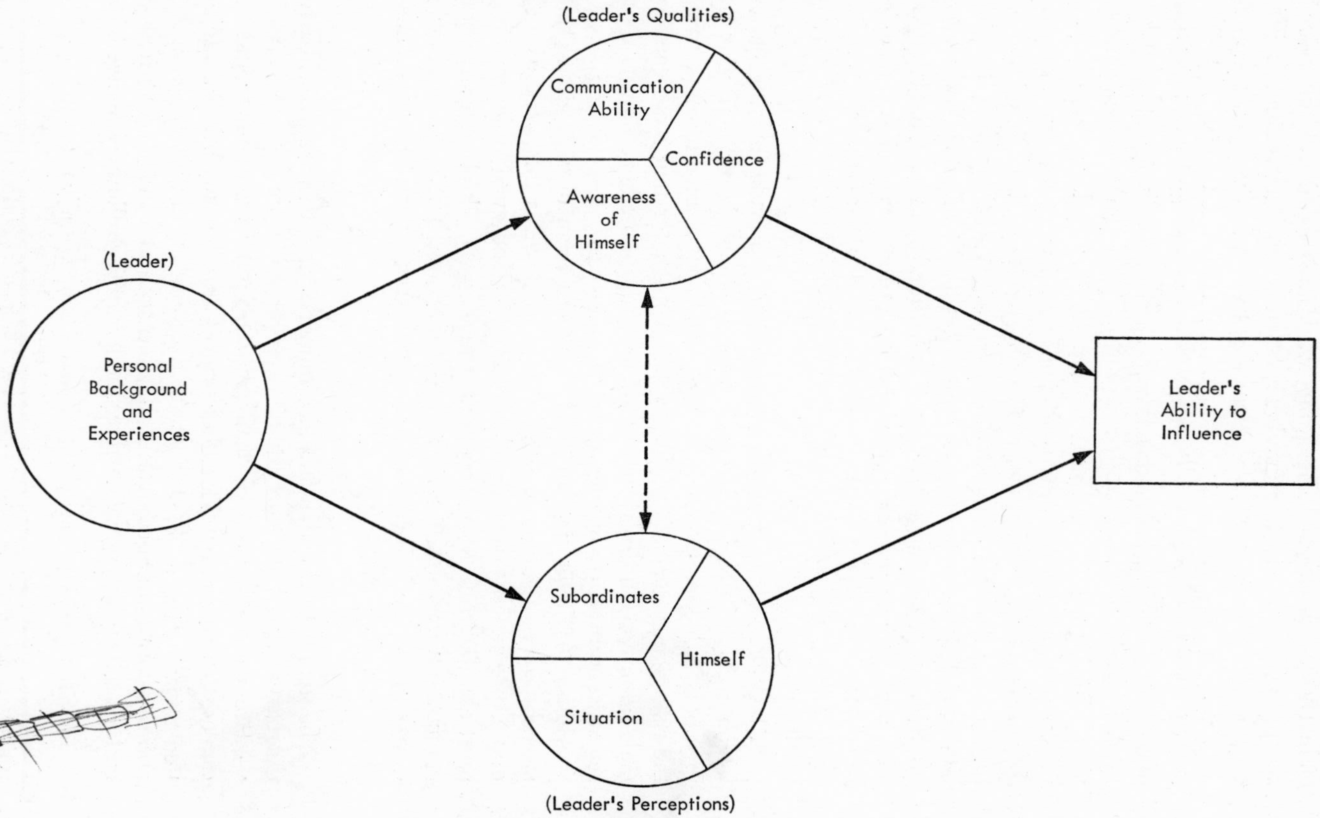

as being soft-spoken and easygoing, while his subordinates consider him sharp-tongued and ill-tempered. This type of counter evaluation or perception of the leader often reduces a group's effectiveness. It causes ineffectiveness because the leader continues to assume that he is one person and the group views him as the complete opposite, and the result is often conflict, misunderstanding, and low morale.

Confidence. Leaders differ significantly in the personal confidence which they have in their ability to lead others. The leader that lacks confidence would have difficulty in diagnosing different situations and adapting his style to cope adequately with the situation. These difficulties result in the leader failing to perform certain functions that could lead to desirable results. For example, a leader with little confidence in himself will often assume that followers cannot adequately perform their job tasks. This may lead to the leader exercising close supervision over his subordinates. The closeness of supervision may prove disruptive because of the type of job being completed, the personality and type of personnel in the work group, and the large size of the work group.

A lack of confidence could also result in the leader making decisions which are not adequate or are viewed as being harmful by the group members. In effect, the confidence of a leader is related to some extent to the risk-taking aversions of the leader. The leader that lacks confidence makes decisions in many instances that compromise his followers' morale, rewards, and status ranking among other groups.

Ability to Communicate. Every leader in an organizational setting must be able to communicate his objectives to his followers. The autocratic, production-oriented, people-oriented, and every other leader type must communicate his expectations to followers. The leader who fails to communicate with followers may become impotent as an influencer of others. This results because failing to communicate leads to chaos in general and an inability to coordinate necessary follower activities in particular.

The emphasis of the authors' model is on the leader's ability to diagnose himself and his total leadership environment. Perhaps what we are suggesting is that leadership training programs should stress diagnostic and adaptability skill learning. It should not be concluded that managers can be easily trained to diagnose accurately work situations and to adopt the appropriate leadership style. This type of training difficulty is succinctly summed up by Fiedler in the following manner:

> Industrial psychologists and personnel men typically view the executive's position as fixed and immutable and the individual as highly plastic and trainable. When we think of improving leadership performance, we generally think first of training the leader. Yet, we know all too well from our experience with psychotherapy, our attempts to rehabilitate prison inmates, drug addicts

or juvenile delinquents—not to mention our difficulties with rearing our own progeny—that our ability to change personality has its limitations.[25]

If leaders are to become diagnostically skilled and flexible to the degree of changing their leadership style, depending upon the circumstances at hand, patience is essential. The organization must be willing to plan, develop, and fund development programs which are time-consuming.

SUMMARY

Inevitably, organizations require leaders to utilize the abilities of their followers so that goals may be accomplished. Although an organization may have the necessary requisites for the attainment of goals, if it does not have a leadership team that can influence followers, the probability is high that the firm will not survive in the long-run. Consequently, it is obvious that effective leadership is the lifeblood of organizational survival.

The behavioral school has recognized the importance of leadership in organizations. This fact is disclosed by the extensive research and literature in the behavioral area devoted to the what, why, and how of leadership. The efforts of behavioralists have resulted in numerous theories of leadership. The theories are spun from concepts of influence, power and authority. To highlight the crux of these theories, the French and Raven analysis was employed in this chapter because it focuses upon the relationship between organizational factors (e.g., managerial hierarchy) and individual characteristics.

After establishing the fact that influence is the crux of leadership, a number of behavioral leadership theories were presented. The theories presented provide the reader with an indication of (1) the differences of opinion among behavioralists, (2) the different methodologies employed to study leadership, (3) the similarities between various theories, and (4) the fact that increasing research on the situational approach seems to be the contemporary thrust in the leadership area.

The final tone of the chapter offers the premise that there is no "one best way" to lead. It is felt that more emphasis should be given the situational approach. The key to this approach seems to be the diagnostic skill of the leader. That is, the leader who can ascertain the personality of his followers, knows his own behavioral patterns, and understands the organizational requirements is viewed as having a better chance of succeeding in influencing his subordinates.

DISCUSSION AND REVIEW QUESTIONS

1. What appears to be the trend in the behavioral school for conducting empirical research on leadership behavior?

---

[25] Fiedler, *op. cit.*, p. 247.

2. How could the incremental influence concept of Katz and Kahn be related to the trait theory of leadership?

3. What are some of the factors about motivation that a situational leader should know?

4. Why should a leader be aware of his impact on followers?

5. What are the similarities and differences found when Likert's approach to leadership is compared to the Ohio State theory of leadership?

6. What are some of the terms used in this chapter that are nearly synonymous with democratic leadership and autocratic leadership? Are there any terms that mean exactly the same thing?

7. Why is the diagnostic skill of the leader so vital to the situational approach to leadership?

8. Which of the personal-behavioral approaches is most similar to the situational theory of leadership? Why have you selected this approach?

9. Is it feasible to alter the job so that a particular type of leader will be more effective? Discuss an actual or hypothetical situation where it would be best to alter the job to suit the leader.

10. What is the major difference between influence and authority of a leader?

ADDITIONAL REFERENCES

Bowers, D. G. and Seashore, S. "Predicting Organizational Effectiveness with a Four-Factor Theory of Leadership," *Administrative Science Quarterly*, 11 (1966), 238–63.

Campbell, J. P., Dunnette, M. D., Lawler, E. E., III, and K. E. Weick, Jr. *Managerial Behavior, Performance, and Effectiveness*. New York: McGraw-Hill Book Co., 1970.

Cartwright, D. "Power: A Neglected Variable in Social Psychology," in *The Planning of Change*, W. G. Bennis, K. D. Benne, and R. Chin (eds.). New York: Holt, Rinehart, and Winston, Inc., 1966.

Dalton, M. *Men Who Manage*. New York: John Wiley & Sons, Inc., 1959.

Fiedler, F. "Engineer the Job to Fit the Manager," *Harvard Business Review*, 43 (1965), 115–22.

Ghiselli, E. "Individuality as a Factor in the Success of Management Personnel," *Personnel Psychology*, 13 (1960), 1–10.

Hunt, J. G. "Breakthrough in Leadership Research," *Personnel Administration*. 30 (1967), pp. 38–44.

Jacques, E. *Measurement of Responsibility*. London: Tavistock Publications, 1956.

Jay, A. *Management and Machiavelli*. New York: Holt, Rinehart, & Winston, Inc., 1967.

Likert, R. *The Human Organization*. New York: McGraw-Hill Book Co., 1967.

Maslow, A. H. *Eupsychian Management*. Homewood, Ill.: Richard D. Irwin, Inc. and The Dorsey Press, 1965.

Piotrowski, Z. A. and Rock, M. R. *The Perceptanalytic Executive Scale: A Tool for the Selection of Top Managers.* New York: Grune & Stratton, Inc., 1963.

Reddin, W. J. *Managerial Effectiveness.* New York: McGraw-Hill Book Co., 1970.

Sales, S. "Supervisory Style and Productivity: Review and Theory," *Personnel Psychology,* 19 (1966), 275–86.

Sayles, L. *Managerial Behavior.* New York: McGraw-Hill Book Co., 1964.

Smith, P. B., Moscow, D., Berger, M. and Cooper, C. "Relationships between Managers and Their Work Associates," *Administrative Science Quarterly,* 14 (1969), 338–45.

chapter eleven

Organizational Design

INTRODUCTION

Classical and behavioral theorists agree that proper organizational design is necessary if a firm is to successfully grow and remain competitive. Unless some form of systematic structuring of an organization is developed, management theorists, in general, believe that uncoordinated and unsynchronized activities will become the rule rather than the exception. These negative consequences of poorly structuring an organization can be minimized if some program of design is followed.

The major difference of opinion between classical and behavioral theorists focuses upon the programs of structuring which are being recommended. Classical theory devotes special attention to the anatomy of the organization, while behavioral theory stresses people-related factors. In this chapter, a behavioral critique of the classical interpretation of the structural variables is offered. In addition, research findings concerning a number of organizational variables are presented.

A BEHAVIORAL MANAGEMENT CRITIQUE

One of the major limitations of classical design theory is that many of the contentions are offered in the form of broad generalizations. These sweeping statements involving the principles of management are grounded upon deductive reasoning and personal observations. They also fail to consider the theory and research findings offered by the behavioral sciences. The behavioral approach to organizational design does not have what can be considered a cornerstone of principles such as the classical approach. Consequently, the behavioral critique of classical organization design will be centered upon four major classical management principles —division of labor, unity of command, line and staff, and span of control. A philosophical approach to organizational processes is presented in the behaviorally oriented Theory Y approach.

Theory Y—Behavioral Overtones

The behaviorally oriented counterpart of Theory X is called Theory Y. The Theory Y set of assumptions concerning organizational processes can be referred to as a people approach. That is, the human element is considered as an important element in the organization setting instead of just a simple cog, as is the case in the Theory X framework.

Assumptions of Theory Y. The underlying assumptions of the Theory Y approach are postulated as follows:

1) *The employees of the firm do not inherently dislike work.* The exercise of physical and mental effort on the job is a natural human phenomenon.

2) *Employees do not want to be rigidly controlled and threatened with punishment.* If an employee is committed to specific objectives, he will exercise self-control in attempting to attain these objectives.

3) *Employees under proper conditions do not seek to avoid responsibility.* If the organizational atmosphere and working conditions are functioning effectively, the average employee will seek responsibility.

4) *Employees desire security but also want to satisfy social, esteem, and self-actualization needs.* In motivating employees the security factor is important but it is not the only consideration. The whole man must be considered and this means that the employee's creativity, imagination, and intellectual potentialities must be considered.

The gist of the Theory Y type assumptions sets the stage for the behavioral approach to organizational design.

DIVISION-OF-LABOR CRITIQUE

The classicists emphasized the economic gains to be realized through specialization (Chapter 5). Unlike the classicists, the behavioralists emphasized noneconomic factors which contribute to the eventual negative returns to continued division of labor. If a job is broken down into fewer and fewer operations for an employee, eventually boredom, monotony, dissatisfaction, or some combination of these, and other negative factors will set in. Thus lower productivity and poor overall efficiency will eventually be the rule rather than the exception. Consequently, many behavioral comments concerning division of work have centered upon the depersonalization of the job which may lead to psychological alienation of many workers toward their job and the organization.

To support the alienation premise, the behavioral approach employs many research studies. One which is found time and time again in the behavioral literature is the Walker and Guest study.[1] These researchers were concerned with the social and psychological problems associated with mass production jobs in an automobile assembly plant. They found that many workers disliked numerous factors associated with their specialized jobs. It was determined that mechanical pacing, repetitiveness of operations, and a lack of a sense of accomplishment were job factors which employees in general disliked.

Walker and Guest also found a positive relationship between the number of operations performed and the overall interest an employee had in the job. These findings are summarized in Table 11–1.[2]

TABLE 11–1
Employee Interest and Job Variety

Number of Operations Performed	Number Reporting Work as Very or Fairly Interesting	Number Reporting Work as Not Very or Not at All Interesting	Total Employees
1	19	38	57
2–5	28	36	64
5 or more	41	18	59
Total	88	92	180

Source: Charles R. Walker and Robert H. Guest, *The Man on the Assembly Line* (Cambridge: Harvard University Press, 1952), p. 54.

Walker and Guest outlined some of the problem areas identified by behavioralists when discussing division of labor. The next phase of the critique centers upon techniques which behavioralists often suggest to overcome or minimize the psychological problems associated with division of labor.

Behavioral Suggestions for Overcoming the Psychological Problems of Division of Labor

A number of organizationally related strategies which display concern for the employees are suggested as possible minimizers of worker alienation once work is divided into fewer and fewer operations. Some of the most popular behavioral suggestions are covered in this section.

[1] Charles R. Walker and Robert H. Guest, *The Man on the Assembly Line* (Cambridge, Mass.: Harvard University Press, 1952).

[2] *Ibid.*, p. 54.

Job Enlargement. The behavioral literature contains many different job enlargement strategies. These strategies focus upon the opposite of dividing work—they are a form of despecialization or increasing the number of tasks which an employee performs. For example, a job is structured in such a manner that instead of performing three tasks the employee performs six tasks.

Although, in many instances, an enlarged job requires a longer training period, it is assumed that satisfaction of the worker increases because boredom is reduced. The implication, of course, is that the job enlargement will lead to more productivity and improved overall efficiency.

To support their contentions concerning job enlargement, the behavioralists call upon such studies as the often-quoted I.B.M. findings.[3] A parts manufacturing unit of the Endicott plant of I.B.M. reorganized a number of jobs in an attempt to improve worker morale. The job of machine operator after the reorganization included setting up the job, sharpening tools, inspecting the work, and operating the equipment.

The conclusions and findings of the I.B.M. study suggest that the job enlargement strategy increased worker morale, lowered production costs, increased the interests of employees, and improved the quality of output. It was also possible to eliminate an entire level of management in the organizational structure because, under the new job enlargement program, employees had greater responsibilities and authority.

Another study which involves the effects of job enlargement is the Maytag Company study.[4] It was concerned with changing the job design on a mass-production assembly line. During different phases of the study, the job was changed. The different phases studied were as follows:

Phase I: Six operators assembled a washing machine pump on a conveyor line.

Phase II: The assembling of the pump was a four-man operation.

Phase III: The work previously done on the conveyor line was done at four individual *one-man work benches.*

Throughout each of these changes, the time required to assemble the pump decreased. The least time-consuming design for assembling involved the one-man work benches. This suggests that reducing assembly line delays and enlarging the job may increase productivity in some instances.

The job enlargement strategy and research support presented are not to be viewed as a solution for all the ills of excessive division of work. It is only offered as a behaviorally oriented program to offset some of the negative factors associated with job specialization. Of course, too much

[3] C. R. Walker, "The Problem of the Repetitive Job," *Harvard Business Review,* vol. 28 (May, 1950), pp. 54–58.

[4] M. D. Kilbridge, "Reduced Costs through Job Enlargement: A Case," *The Journal of Business,* vol. 33 (October, 1960), pp. 357–62.

job enlargement may be as disruptive to the organization as too much specialization.

Job Rotation. Another strategy which some behavioralists believe can reduce the employees' alienation toward performing a smaller number of tasks is referred to as job rotation. In some nonmanagerial and managerial positions, it is feasible to rotate an individual from one job assignment to another. The person switches jobs periodically so that boredom and disinterest are hopefully reduced. Job rotation provides more flexibility to management because jobs do not have to be redesigned, as is the case in job enlargement. Also it allows management to select the most opportune time to rotate a person.

Participation Approaches. In many organizations, it may be possible to provide decision-making opportunities to employees at lower levels in the organization. In the classical theory schema, authority for decision-making is centered primarily among top-level executives; but, the participation concept offered by behavioralists redistributes some of the decision-making authority throughout the organization. The rationale behind the redistribution of authority is that people frequently feel more inclined to accept decisions which they have helped to make.

One example of a participation approach in management is the "multiple management" program at McCormick and Company.[5] This plan involves allowing junior executives to form what is called a junior board of directors. The junior board is used as a monitoring group for decisions made by the senior board of directors and top-level executives and makes decisions which supplement the top-level decisions.

Another example of worker participation in the decision-making process is the approach utilized at the Glacier Metal Company of Great Britain.[6] The approach is referred to as a "consultative hierarchy." The approach was specifically designed for three reasons: (1) provide for worker representation in making operating and general policy decisions; (2) improve communications between workers and management; and (3) provide workers with a feeling of involvement in the consultative hierarchy.[7]

The consultative hierarchy is composed of a network of committees representing all interest groups and levels of personnel in the company. The committees make decisions concerning job design, promotion, salary, retirement plans, and appeals procedures among other things.

---

[5] Charles P. McCormick, *Multiple Management* (New York: Harper & Row, 1938).

[6] See E. Jacques, *The Changing Culture of a Factory* (London: Tavistock Publications, Ltd., 1951); E. Jacques, *Equitable Payment* (London: William Heinemann, Ltd., 1961); and E. Jacques, *Measurement of Responsibility* (London: Tavistock Publications, Ltd., Cambridge, Mass.: Harvard University Press, 1956).

[7] Jacques, *The Changing Culture of a Factory, op. cit.*

Many other participation methods are suggested by the behavioralists. The theme of most of the others (as is the case in the McCormick and Glacier examples) is that involvement through participation may lead to more positive commitments by the worker to company objectives, even in situations where division of labor is intense.

UNITY-OF-COMMAND CRITIQUE

In viewing organizational relationships realistically, it is easy to understand why it is difficult to rigidly adhere to the unity-of-command principle. Even one of the most identified classical theorists, Henri Fayol, recognized the need to sometimes bypass the strict chain of command and suggested an organizational arrangement which enabled individuals to bypass the command hierarchy. His suggestion is referred to in Chapter 5 as the "Fayol Bridge."

The "Fayol Bridge" and the "Functional Foremanship" concept of Taylor can be viewed, not as behavioral examples of concepts which prove the unity-of-command principle invalid, but as examples emanating from classical theory which show that rigid unity-of-command practices are not generally found in organizations. It is more realistic to state that, typically, a worker will have one superior who is most dominant in influencing his behavior. The argument of the behavioralists concerning unity of command does not revolve around the reasonableness of the concept, but instead is centered upon the practicalities of everyday organizational life.

LINE-AND-STAFF CRITIQUE

It is implied in classical design theory that the line-and-staff organizational arrangement offers the best potential for growth, profitability, and overall organizational attainment of objectives. The difficulty is not what is discussed by the classical theorists, but how it is presented, and what is missing. In presenting the typical classical line-and-staff discussion, a manufacturing firm is normally utilized to provide insight to the reader. The operations of a manufacturing organization can be separated into activities which relate directly to the achievement of objectives (line) and activities which relate indirectly to the attainment of objectives (staff). Thus, the line-and-staff distinction is orderly. This orderly distinction, however, is more difficult to establish for nonmanufacturing and nonbusiness organizations.

It must be made clear that not only have classical theorists contributed to the confusion in presenting an understandable interpretation of line and staff, but so have the behavioralists. Presentations by both classical theorists and behavioralists concerning line-and-staff design have been discussed in terms of (1) attainment of objectives; (2) authority relationships (e.g., line has authority, while staff has little or no direct authority); or (3) functions.[8]

The main thrust of the behavioralists has been directed toward conflict and resolution of conflict involving line-and-staff personnel. The behavioralists point out that line-and-staff personnel are different in personal characteristics and this may aggravate the relationships between line and staff.[9] The comparison between the backgrounds of line-and-staff personnel offered by Dalton indicates that staff men are generally younger, are more educated, and come from different social backgrounds than line men.[10]

Another line-and-staff comparative analysis is the "cosmopolitan" and "local" classification of Gouldner.[11] The professional is described as a "cosmo" and is assumed to be less loyal to the employing organization and more committed to the specialized skills of his profession (e.g., accountant, operations researcher, industrial engineer). The line manager can be compared to the "local" and is assumed to have greater company loyalty and more concern for general knowledge rather than specific knowledge.

The behavioralist studies such phenomena as the reasons for line-staff conflict, methods which can minimize conflict so that it does not disrupt operations, personality and background differences of line-and-staff personnel. Thus, the emphasis is on the human element and not structural variables associated with line and staff. If the line-and-staff approach to organization is to be effective, understanding the mechanics involved is not worth much without knowledge about line-and-staff problems and personnel. The classical approach without interpreting necessary behavioral problems such as conflict is incomplete as is the behavioral approach without coping with the logic and mechanics of line-and-staff structure offered by the classical theorists.

SPAN-OF-CONTROL CRITIQUE

The behavioralists contend that the classicists' approach to span of control is too artificial in that they often state in specific quantitative figures what is the "ideal" ratio of subordinates to a superior. They believe that it is not realistic to utilize formulas and opinions concerning what a manager's span of control should be if he is located at a particular level

---

[8] Alan C. Filley and Robert J. House, *Managerial Process and Organizational Behavior* (Glenview, Ill.: Scott, Foresman and Co., 1969), p. 260.

[9] M. Dalton, "Changing Line-Staff Relations," *Personnel Administration,* vol. 28 (March–April, 1966), pp. 3–5.

[10] *Ibid.*

[11] A. W. Gouldner, "Cosmopolitans and Locals: Toward an Analysis of Social Roles—I and II," *Administrative Science Quarterly,* vol. 2 (September, 1957), pp. 281–306.

in the organizational hierarchy. A better approach than quantifying potential relationships according to behavioralists is to consider people, the environment, and the influence of various spans of control upon the overall organization structure and performance.

The behavioralists believe that small spans of control recommended by classical theorists impose organization structures which foster close supervision. If an organization has narrow spans of control, it typically has more levels of supervision and takes on a distinct tall pyramidal appearance. For example, assume that a company has forty-eight nonmanagers and the span of control is eight. There would be six supervisors directing the workers and two senior supervisors directing three supervisors each. This type of structure is illustrated in Figure 11–1.

FIGURE 11–1

Narrow Span of Control

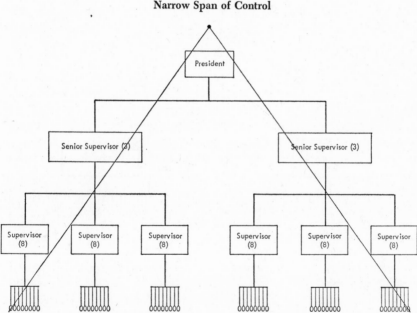

In the organization depicted in Figure 11–1, there are three levels of management: president, senior supervisor, and supervisor.

If the same number of workers (48) were supervised by two superiors, an organization with only two managerial levels could be structured. The organizational design resulting from widening the span of control to 24 is presented in Figure 11–2. By increasing the span of control from eight to twenty-four, one level of management and six managerial positions were eliminated from the organization.

The critique of the behavioralists does not center on organization chart presentations (i.e., Figures 11–1 and 11–2) but on the results of narrow spans of control. They suggest that a narrow span of control (Figure 11–1) allows a manager to exercise close supervision because of the small number of subordinates reporting directly to him. The narrow span of control leads to the bureaucratic structure which is graphically presented as a tall pyramid. Furthermore, it is the behavioralists' contention that the wider span forces management to utilize more general supervision.

The second factor given serious consideration in analyzing span of control by the behavioralist is the "manager." The capabilities of the manager must be considered in discussing spans of control. Individual managerial abilities must be studied before stating that a span of control should be some specific number. Such characteristics as the personality of the manager, the manager's attitudes toward delegating authority to subordinates, the manager's willingness to utilize staff assistance, and the

FIGURE 11–2

Wide Span of Control

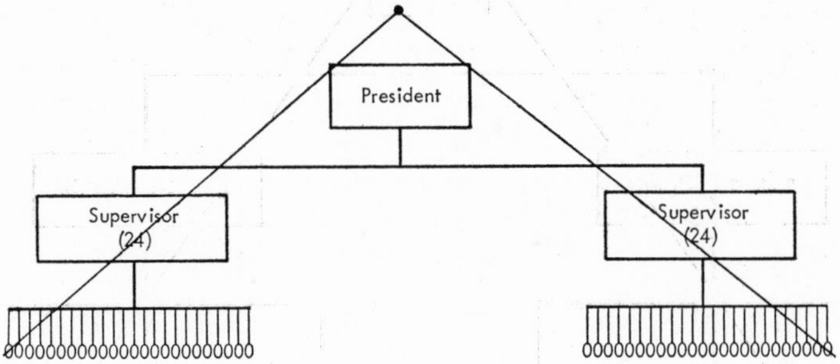

manager's experience are some of the critical areas of concern suggested by behavioralists.

The behavioralists are also very concerned about various characteristics of subordinates in studying span of control. The attitudes, personalities, experience, training, and abilities of the subordinates influence the choice of an effective span of control.

The third factor given emphasis by behavioralists includes the environment of the job. The type and nature of the work to be performed has some bearing on developing spans of control. If the work is routine in nature and involves little uncertainty in reaching decisions only minor attention of the manager may be required.[12] This would enable the utiliza-

---

[12] Justin G. Longenecker, *Principles of Management and Organizational Behavior* (Columbus, Ohio: Charles E. Merrill Co., 1969), p. 209.

tion of a wide span of control. At the other extreme would be jobs that are nonroutine in nature and decision making is often concerned with ill-defined problems. This type of work may necessitate a narrower span of control so that the manager can oversee the work.

The need to coordinate the activities of subordinates in performing their work should also be considered. If the work of one person or one group of workers has a significant influence on other persons or groups, the span of control must be narrower. For example, in food processing operations in a cereal packaging department, it may be necessary to co-ordinate the activities of six different groups on an automated line. Each station on the line, other than the first, is dependent upon the work performed at the previous station.

DECENTRALIZATION

The term decentralization has often been associated with the behavioral school of organizational design. It is placed into a behavioral context because such terms as "democratic," "less authoritarian," and "more autonomy" are used on numerous occasions when decentralization examples are cited. Instead of prolonging the argument about whether decentralization is a classical or behavioral phenomenon, the present authors have decided to present only some of the behaviorally-oriented virtues being espoused by advocates of decentralization in this section.

Structure

There are basically two methods of decentralizing an organization structure. One is leaving the decentralized units as integral divisions. In general, this is the approach followed by General Motors, the integral and viable divisions being Buick, Oldsmobile, Chevrolet, Pontiac, Cadillac, Allison, and Frigidaire. The other is to decentralize the organization by use of a subsidiary of affiliate company arrangement. The most publicized example of this decentralized arrangement are the Standard Oil Companies. Each company has its own president and board of directors. Basically, each Standard Oil company is operating autonomously.

In both the divisional and subsidiary arrangements, the major organizational unit develops, manufactures, and distributes its own products; purchases its own materials; recruits, selects, trains, and develops its own group of employees; and purchases its own equipment. The principal point is that appropriate authority is pushed further down into the divisional units and subsidiaries so that the various manufacturing, motivational, purchasing, and distribution problems can be resolved on a decentralized basis.

The People Factor

Since the behavioral school expends significant effort on learning how people respond to various organizational phenomena, it is best to review some of the consequences of decentralized operations on managers. If this is the main focus, then it would be appropriate to study managerial decentralization as a concept which involves the manager's assigned formal authority and freedom to make decisions. In a simplistic sense, an organizational structure is more decentralized than a typical classical organizational structure if:

1. Decisions are made at lower levels in the management hierarchy.
2. There are fewer controls and checks on decisions made by managers.

These two guidelines are only used as criteria for evaluating or comparing organizations on a centralization-decentralization scale. That is, if two organizations are contrasted and it is found that in one company the decisions concerning production, personnel, and finance matters involving expenditures of $100,000 or more are being made at the very top level of the firm but, in the second company, it is found that similar decisions are being made at the middle level of the managerial hierarchy, it could be assumed that on the basis of the decisions analyzed, the second firm has a more decentralized organizational design.

Why Decentralization?

There is no universal agreement within the behavioral school about why it is better to decentralize operations. The following items are only partially agreed upon by the many different scholars analyzing the decentralization approach. They may or may not be true depending upon such factors as the size of the firm, desire for autonomy of employees, the availability of competent managers, government regulations, and other important factors.

First, advocates assume that decentralization encourages the professional development of managers. The main point is that as decision-making authority and responsibility are pushed down in the organization, the manager must adapt and prove himself if he is to advance in the company. That is, the manager must become a generalist who knows something about each factor he must cope with in the decentralized arrangement.

Second, because managers in a decentralized structure often have to adapt and deal with difficult decisions, they are excellently trained for promotions into positions of greater authority and responsibility. Managers can be readily compared with their peers on the basis of actual decision-making performance. In effect, the decentralized arrangement leads to a more equitable performance appraisal program. This can lead to a more satisfied group of managers because they perceive themselves as being evaluated on the basis of results not personalities. It should be remembered, however, that developing performance criteria for any manager is an extremely difficult task.

Third, the decentralized arrangement leads to a competitive climate within the organization. The managers are motivated to contribute in this competitive atmosphere since they are being compared with their peers on various performance measures.

Finally, in the decentralized pattern, the manager is able to exercise more autonomy and this satisfies the desire of man to participate in problem-solving. This freedom is assumed to lead to managerial creativity, ingenuity, and action that contributes to the growth and development of the firm and the manager himself.

These are only four of the factors associated with the virtues of decentralization. They should not be classified as literal truisms being proposed by behavioralists. They are only cited as examples of some of the often-mentioned advantages of decentralized operations. These advantages do not come free of costs. Certainly, the behavioralists are aware that organizational and people costs may have to be incurred if a firm shifts its organizational pattern from a more centralized arrangement to a decentralized design. Some of the costs are:

1. Managers must be trained to handle decision making and this may require expensive formal training programs.
2. Since many managers have worked in centralized organizations, it is very uncomfortable for them to delegate authority in a more decentralized arrangement. These old attitudes are difficult to alter and often lead to resistance and disruptive conflict.
3. To alter accounting and performance appraisal systems so they are compatible with the decentralized arrangement is costly. Administrative costs are incurred because new or altered accounting and performance systems must be tested, implemented, and evaluated.

These are, of course, only some of the costs that the behavioral school considers when discussing and analyzing the pros and cons of decentralizing. Like most managerial concepts, there is definitely no clear-cut answer about whether decentralization is better or worse for an organization. It would appear that considering each organizational factor (e.g., manpower, size, and products) intensely is a prerequisite for reaching design decisions concerning decentralization.

It should now be obvious that centralization and decentralization are the opposite ends of a continuum. The effort of behavioral design experts does not focus upon whether one is good or one is bad because neither is an ideal. The real effort of research and interest is on how much centralization and how much decentralization is most suitable for a company with a certain type of personnel, product line, technology, size, and in various locations. The behavioralists view more opportunities for growth and development of employees—the people—in an organization with significant amounts of decentralization.

The behavioral approach to decentralized organizational design is certainly not to be accepted blindly. In fact, the behavioral school of management suggestion is to first consider the complexities and costs associated with various degrees of decentralization. For example, when an organization decentralizes to a greater extent, they are faced with improving their control mechanisms. That is, in order for the policy makers to know what is transpiring in decentralized units, they must have effective control systems. When a financial, production or quality control system is implemented such items as forms, manpower, and communication networks are typically utilized. These items increase the cost of operations. Thus, when a firm increases its decentralization, it must face up to the reality of considering the extension of control mechanisms and increased cost of operations.

A PICTORIAL REVIEW

A graphical representation of the classical structure and forms of the behavioral advocated structures should clarify the organizational design approaches. The classical approach is succinctly presented in Figure 11–3. Examples of behavioral type designs are presented in Figure 11–4. Both of these figures attempt to capture the main flavor of the two opposing design philosophies and sets of assumptions. Basically, they show that the classicists are identified with the taller, many-layered structure and the

FIGURE 11–3

The Pyramid

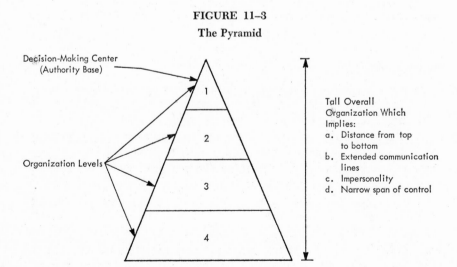

FIGURE 11-4

Behavioral Modifications of the Pyramid

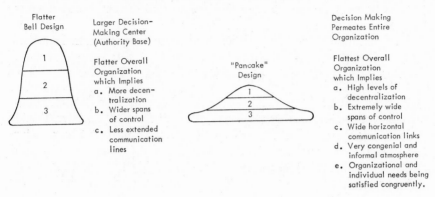

behavioralists with the flatter, fewer-layered and more decentralized structure.

STUDIES CONCERNING ORGANIZATIONAL DESIGN

The classical approach and the behavioral approach to designing an organization continue to remain main topics of debate and controversy. Empirical research concerning organizational design is not conclusive enough today to support any specific organizational design strategy. In fact, the number of research studies involving organization structure *per se* is limited.

There are three popular methods of research employed in studying organizational design.[13] These methods can also be applied to the study of the principles of classical theory such as division of labor, span of control, line and staff separation, and unity of command. The three methods are as follows:

1. The researcher attempts to relate the behavior of individuals to such phenomena as organization structure and various applications of the principles.
2. The researcher attempts to explain the features of organizational structures and the principles of organizational theory.
3. The researcher conducts comparative research which is concerned with the similarities, dissimilarities and consequences of various organization structures and approaches to designing organization structure.

---

[13] William Scott, "Field Methods in the Study of Organizations," in James March (ed.), *Handbook of Organizations* (Chicago: Rand McNally, 1965), pp. 261–304.

Each of the three research approaches is valuable in providing insights into organizational design from a classical and a behavioral viewpoint. Thus, a number of studies are presented in this section which employ the three research methodologies to investigate the impact of organizational structure upon morale, job satisfaction, and organizational success.

The Sears, Roebuck Research of 1950

Worthy studied the morale of over 100,000 employees at Sears, Roebuck and Company during a 12-year period.[14] He was concerned with determining the morale of Sear's employees with respect to six major factors of their work environment: (1) the company in general, (2) the local organization, (3) the local management, (4) immediate supervision, (5) fellow employees, and (6) job and working conditions.

The results of the Worthy research program are basically the following:

1. The more complex the organizational structure, the greater the probability that poor management-employee relationships will result.
2. Dividing work into fewer and fewer units and dividing departments into subdepartments often results in low output and low morale. Those groups which are most consistent in contributing to the organization (e.g., salesmen) and display the highest morale complete tasks in their entirety.
3. Over-functionalization requires close and constant supervision at the work level to maintain production. A consequence of closely supervising employees is rigid control systems which negatively affect morale and productivity.
4. Over-functionalization does not allow personnel to operate except in closest coordination with others, and the system is often so complex that this coordination cannot occur spontaneously.
5. The overly complex, overly functionalized organizational structure typically requires the type of leader who uses pressure as a supervisory device.

Next, Worthy compared and contrasted various organization structures. The implication of his analysis is that organizations with fewer levels and wider spans of control yield a less complex organizational system. The wide span of control literally forces management to delegate authority. In addition to delegation, the flattening technique (widening span of control) requires a better trained management team, shortens communication networks, and shortens the administrative distance between the levels of management. Figure 11–5 highlights conceptually the analysis of Worthy.

---

[14] James C. Worthy, "Organizational Structure and Employee Morale," *American Sociological Review*, vol. 15 (April, 1950), pp. 169–79.

FIGURE 11–5

The Pyramid versus the Flat System

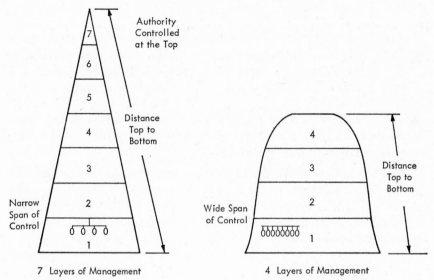

7 Layers of Management   4 Layers of Management

According to Worthy, the executives at Sears found that the flatter organization structure with maximum decentralization develops self-reliance, initiative, and decision-making abilities. He advocates the flatter organizational structure for Sears, Roebuck and Company.

Porter and Lawler Study of Attitudes in Tall and Flat Organizations

A study conducted by Porter and Lawler in 1964 concentrated upon the job attitudes of managerial personnel in tall and flat organization structures.[15] A flat organization structure was one in which there are few levels of management relative to the total size of the organization. The tall organization structure was viewed as one having many levels of management relative to the total size of the organization.

Porter and Lawler utilized a need satisfaction questionnaire to ascertain the job satisfaction of managers in the tall and flat structures. They were concerned with the security, social, esteem, autonomy, and self-actualization need satisfactions of the managers studied. Over 1,500 managers participated in this study. The major findings of the investigation are briefly summarized as follows:

[15] L. W. Porter and E. E. Lawler, "The Effects of Tall versus Flat Organization Structures on Managerial Job Satisfaction," *Personnel Psychology*, vol. 17 (Summer, 1964), pp. 135–48.

1. In firms employing fewer than 5,000 employees, managerial satisfaction was greater in the flat than in the tall organization structure for some needs.
2. In firms employing 5,000 employees and over, the managers in the tall organization structure generally reported more need satisfaction.
3. In the flatter organization structure, more satisfaction of the self-actualization need was found. However, in the taller organization structure, there was more satisfaction of the security and social need categories.
4. Thus, reviewing their findings Porter and Lawler conclude that there is no clear overall superiority of a flat organization structure over a tall organization structure.

The conclusions of Worthy support the behavioralists' contentions regarding the advantages of the flat structure over the tall structure. The Porter and Lawler research, however, prevents one from making sweeping generalizations that a flat organization structure produces more favorable job satisfaction.

The Woodward Studies of Industrial Organization

A complete and insightful study of organization structures was conducted by Joan Woodward.[16] She and research associates studied 100 firms in Great Britain. All the firms studied manufactured goods and offered them for sale, but the nature of their markets and market share goals differed considerably.

By a combination of research methods (e.g., surveys, interviews) various data and information were collected. Some of the information obtained was:

1. history, background and objectives of the firm,
2. information on the manufacturing processes and methods employed,
3. forms and routines through which the firm was organized and operated,
4. organization chart,
5. labor structure and cost,
6. qualifications of managers, and
7. assessment of the success of the firm in their respective industries.

Woodward developed a system for classifying firms as above average, average, and below average in success. In constructing the success criterion such factors as the state of the industry in which the firm operated (e.g., new and expanding, old and contracting), the percentage of the

---

[16] Joan Woodward, *Industrial Organization: Theory and Practice* (London: Oxford University Press, 1965). This presentation of a concise summarization of Woodward's work was stimulated by Filley and House, *op. cit.*, pp. 78–81.

total volume of the industry the firm contributed, five-year profit figures and investment figures, the fluctuation of the firm's shares on the Stock Exchange, the reputation of the firm, the salaries it pays, and the union opinion about the firm were some of the items considered.

The researchers after delving into the investigation, became aware of the many variations in manufacturing methods utilized by the firms studied. This led to classifying the firms into three groups:[17]

1. unit and small-batch,
2. large-batch and mass production, and
3. long-run process production.

The three groupings suggested differences in technological complexity of operations. The simplest complexity involved the production of goods for a single customer in the form of unit or small-batch manufacturing operations. The middle range of technological complexity involved the production of large batches of goods on a mass-production scale. While the highly technological complexity category included the production of goods utilizing interrelated processes such as chemicals.

The successful firms in the high and low technological scales (i.e., long-run process and unit and small batch) tended to adhere more closely to the behavioralist's suggestions concerning organizational design. There was greater delegation of authority and more permissive management.

In the successful firms line-and-staff organization was most developed in the middle ranges of technological complexity. In all the successful large batch production firms, there was a clear definition of duties and responsibilities and adherence to the unity of command principle.

In the final analysis, Woodward's research and findings suggest that although there is no one best way of structuring an organization, there seems to be a particular form of structure most appropriate for each technical situation. The organization engaged in large batch production appears to operate more successfully if it is organized along classical theory lines. However, the other two classifications based on technology are most successful, if a less classical and more behavioral orientation is utilized.

SUMMARY

A behavioral perspective of designing an organization system has been presented in a concise form. There is both agreement and disagreement between the classical and behavioral design approaches. The classical theory of design is associated with such concepts as Theory X management; "ideal" bureaucratic structures, intense division of labor at the job level and departmentalization at the organizational level, unity of com-

---

[17] Woodward, *op. cit.*, p. 39.

mand, orderly line and staff distinctions, and narrow spans of control which foster tall organization systems. The main theme of the classical approach is upon structural mechanics or the anatomy.

The behavioralists relate their organization design strategies to the human element more specifically than the classical theorists. They stress Theory Y, despecialization of job tasks, line-and-staff conflict analysis and procedures to reduce this conflict, wider spans of control which foster flatter organizational structure, more general supervision and more decentralization.

When empirical research evidence is closely scrutinized, it appears that the classical approach to organization design is not perfectly applicable to all situations and organizations. It is also evident that a pure behavioral approach to design which includes participation by workers and flatter organization structure is also not suited for some situations and organizations. The limited amount of sound research evidence does not allow conclusive statements to be made concerning which type of organizational design is best for a particular organization. The few good research studies available in the management literature suggest that the type of managerial and nonmanagerial personnel, the type of work being performed, the size, and production processes of the organization are some of the myriad of variables that should be given more than passing attention in designing an organization. When management experts more clearly specify the significant organizational factors influencing the success of a particular design, they will be in a better position to design effective organizations. This is a monumental order and there certainly is no one specific classical or behavioral design approach that will be recommended. Instead a *blending* of classical and behavioral concepts would seem to be appropriate when designing organizations.

DISCUSSION AND REVIEW QUESTIONS

1. Do you consider General Motors Corporation a decentralized organization? Why?

2. Discuss the applicability of the classical theory of division of labor in the 1970s. Will high degrees of specialization be found in organizations in the 1970s? Where?

3. Why do some scholars of management theory refer to the behavioral perspective of organizational design as a motivation-oriented approach?

4. What is the major difference between the unity of command concept and the chain of command concept?

5. What is meant by the term administrative distance? What would the behavioralist viewpoint be concerning the decreasing of the administrative distance between top management and nonmanagers?

6. Can generalizations about satisfaction attained by managers in tall and flat structures in various industries be made based upon the Porter and Lawler research results? Why?

7. When structuring an organization, what are some of the behavioral factors that should be considered and analyzed?

8. What is the classical viewpoint concerning the line-and-staff concept? What are the similarities in the classical and behavioral viewpoints concerning line and staff?

9. Are the advantages of participation consistent with the classical theory of organizational structure? Why?

10. If a manager understands the Theory Y assumptions, can he predict the behavior of the work force he is dealing with? Why?

ADDITIONAL REFERENCES

ARGYRIS, C. *Integrating the Individual and the Organization.* New York: John Wiley and Sons, Inc., 1964.

CHANDLER, A. D., JR. *Strategy and Structure.* Cambridge, Mass.: The M.I.T. Press, 1962.

ETZIONI, A. *A Comparative Analysis of Complex Organizations.* Glencoe, Ill.: Free Press, 1961.

EVAN, W. M. "Organizational Lag," *Human Organization,* 25 (1966), 51–53.

FISCH, G. G. "Line-Staff Is Obsolete," *The Harvard Business Review,* 39 (1961), 67–79.

HULIN, C. L. and BLOOD, M. R. "Job Enlargement, Individual Differences, and Worker Responses," *Psychological Bulletin,* 69 (1968), 41–55.

KRUPP, S. *Pattern in Organization Analysis: A Critical Examination.* New York: Holt, Rinehart, and Winston, Inc., 1961.

LAWRENCE, P. and LORSCH, J. *Organization and Environment.* Division of Research, Graduate School of Business, Harvard University, 1967.

LEAVITT, H. J. and WHISLER, T. L. "Management in the 1980s," *Harvard Business Review,* 36 (1958), 41–48.

MARCH, J. G. and SIMON, H. A. *Organizations.* New York: John Wiley and Sons, Inc., 1958.

PUGH, D. S., HICKSON, D. J., HININGS, C. R., and TURNER, C. "Dimensions of Organization Structure," *Administrative Science Quarterly,* 13 (1968), 65–105.

RUBENSTEIN, A. H. and HABERSTROH, C. J. (eds.). *Some Theories of Organization.* Homewood, Ill.: Richard D. Irwin, Inc., and The Dorsey Press, 1966.

RUSHING, W. A. "The Effects of Industry Size and Division of Labor on Administration," *Administrative Science Quarterly,* 12 (1967), 273–95.

TALACCHI, S. "Organization Size, Individual Attitudes and Behavior: An Empirical Study," *Administrative Science Quarterly,* 5 (1960), 398–420.

THOMPSON, J. D. *Organizations in Action.* New York: McGraw-Hill Book Company, 1967.

chapter twelve

Organizational Change

INTRODUCTION

The manager must continually consider the necessity for change. If he were able to design a perfect, optimum organization and if the environment in which the firm operates were stable and unchanging, there would be little pressure for organizational change. But neither is the case. Organizational change[1] is a pressing problem for the modern manager; and in recent years, a great deal of literature has appeared which focuses on the need for *planning* for change. Some companies have instituted staff units whose mission is organizational planning.[2] The planning units are specific responses to the need for systematic, formalized procedures to anticipate and implement changes in the structure, technology, and personnel of the firm.

In this chapter the processes of organizational change are discussed. We will use a model which describes the important factors of the change

---

[1] "Organizational change" is broadly interpreted for purposes of this discussion. Some management students restrict the term to changes in the formal structure, but we will include changes in employee behavior and technology.

[2] Paul E. Holden, Carlton A. Pederson, Gayton E. Germane, *Top Management* (New York: McGraw-Hill Book Co., 1968), pp. 66–68.

FIGURE 12–1

A Model for the Management of Change

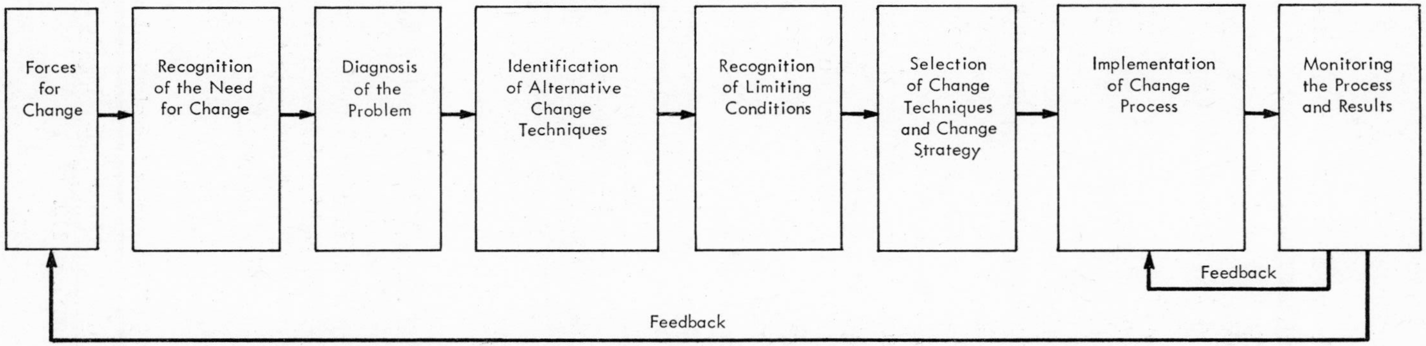

process. The discussion will also provide the student with the opportunity to integrate and to refine his understanding of the classical and behavioral schools of management, since both make contributions to the management of change. As we shall see, concepts from both schools must be blended to manage change successfully.

A MODEL FOR MANAGING CHANGE

The management of change implies a systematic process which can be broken down into subprocesses or steps. The model which we propose is described in Figure 12–1. The model consists of eight subprocesses which are linked in a logical sequence. A manager considers each of them, either explicitly or implicitly, to undertake a change program. The prospects for initiating successful change are enhanced when the manager explicitly and formally goes through each successive step. For this reason, each step is discussed in a separate section of this chapter.

It is our purpose to describe change alternatives, but not to propose that some alternatives are superior to others. No one change technique or change strategy can be judged superior on *a priori* grounds.[3]

The well-equipped manager is one who recognizes the multiplicity of alternatives. He is not predisposed to one particular approach to the exclusion of all others. At the same time, the manager avoids the pitfalls of stagnation. The sign of decay, as Greiner has observed, is "managerial behavior that (*a*) is oriented more to the past than to the future, (*b*) recognizes the obligations of ritual more than the challenges of current problems, and (*c*) owes allegiance more to department goals than to overall company objectives."[4] Thus the management of change implies a flexible, forwardlooking stance for the manager. This attribute is essential for using the change model outlined in Figure 12–1.

The model presumes that forces for change continually act upon the firm; this assumption reflects the dynamic character of the modern world. At the same time it is the manager's responsibility to sort out the information that he receives from the firm's control system and other sources which reflect the magnitude of change forces. The information is the basis for recognizing the need for change; it is equally desirable to recognize when change is *not* needed. But once the manager recognizes that something is malfunctioning, he must diagnose the problem and identify relevant alternative change techniques. The change technique selected

[3] Jeremiah J. O'Connell, *Managing Organizational Innovation* (Homewood, Ill.: Richard D. Irwin, Inc., 1968), pp. 10, 142–45.

[4] Larry E. Greiner, "Patterns of Organization Change," *Harvard Business Review*, vol. 45 (May–June, 1967), p. 119.

must be appropriate to the problem, as constrained by limiting conditions. One example of a limiting condition which we have discussed in an earlier chapter is the prevailing character of group norms. The work groups may support some of the change techniques, but may sabotage others. Further limiting conditions include leadership behavior, legal requirements, and economic conditions.

The fact that a change program can be thwarted underscores the fact that the choice of change *strategy* is as important as the change technique itself. One well-documented behavioral phenomenon is that people tend to resist change or at least to be reluctant to undergo change. An appropriate strategy for implementing change is one which seeks to minimize resistance and maximize employee commitment. Finally, the manager must implement the change and monitor the change process and change results. The model includes feedback to the implementation phase and to the forces-for-change phase. These feedback loops suggest that the change process itself must be monitored and evaluated. The mode of implementation may be faulty and lead to poor results, but responsive action could correct the situation. Moreover, the feedback loop to the initial step recognizes that *no* change is final. A new situation is created within which problems and issues will emerge; a new setting is created which will itself become subject to change. The model suggests no "final solution"; rather, it emphasizes that the modern manager operates in a dynamic setting wherein the only certainty is change itself.

The process by which the solution to one problem creates new problems is widely recognized. Blau and Scott refer to it as the "dialectic processes of change,"[5] and they illustrate the dilemma by a number of examples. They observe that assembly line techniques increase productivity but that, at the same time, employee absenteeism and turnover increase. Assembly line work is monotonous and routine; it alienates workers and creates discontent; morale declines and personnel problems emerge. Thus a whole new set of difficulties is created by the solution itself. This phenomenon must be taken into account as a manager considers changes.

The thoughtful student will, no doubt, suggest that many successful changes have been implemented by managers who did not consciously and systematically go through each step of the model. Indeed there are many such cases. However, these managers may not be representative of the population of managers. They may very well be intuitive artists who have the experience and judgment to guide and implement change without a conscious effort. Such men are the geniuses of management. The

---

[5] Peter M. Blau and W. Richard Scott, *Formal Organizations* (San Francisco: Chandler Publishing Co., 1962), pp. 250–53.

rest of us might be well advised to follow a more systematic approach as outlined in this chapter.

FORCES FOR CHANGE

The forces for change can be classified conveniently into two groups, namely, external and internal forces. External forces work from without the firm; they are beyond the control of the manager. Internal forces operate inside the firm and are generally within the control of management.

External Forces

The manager of a business firm has historically been concerned with reacting to changes in the *market place*. Competitors introduce new products, increase their advertising, reduce their prices, or improve their customer service. In each case a response is required unless the manager is content to permit the erosion of profit and market share. At the same time changes occur in customer tastes and incomes. The firm's products may no longer have customer appeal; customers may be able to purchase more expensive, higher-quality forms of the same product.

The enterprise system eliminates from the economic scene those firms which do not adjust to market conditions. The isolated-from-reality manager who ignores the signals from the market will soon confront the more vocal and louder signals of discontented stockholders. By that time, however, the appropriate change may well be dissolution of the firm—the final solution.

Another source of market forces is that of the supply of resources to the firm. A change in the quality and quantity of human resources can dictate changes in the firm. For example, the adoption of automated processes can be stimulated by a decline in the supply of labor. The techniques of coal mining and tobacco farming have changed greatly during recent years due to labor shortages. We can also understand how changes in the materials supply can cause the firm to substitute one material for another. Rayon stockings and synthetic rubber tires were direct outgrowths of World War II–induced shortages of raw materials. We need not catalog the whole range of possible changes in the resource markets which stimulate organizational change. The potential is great, however, and must be recognized.

The second source of external change forces is *technology*. The knowledge explosion since World War II has introduced new technology for nearly every business function. Computers have made possible high-speed data processing and the solution to complex production problems. New machines and new processes have revolutionized the way in which many products are manufactured and distributed. High rates of obsolescence have encouraged many firms to adopt payback criteria as low as two years, so that they will not be caught with an obsolete piece of equipment. Computer technology and automation have affected not only the technical conditions of work, but the social conditions as well. New occupations have been created and others have been eliminated. Slowness in adopting new technology which reduces costs and improves quality will show itself in the financial statements sooner or later. Technological advance is a permanent fixture in the business world and, as a force for change, will continue to demand attention.[6]

Finally, the third external force consists of *environmental* changes. The business manager must be "tuned in" to great movements over which he has no control but which, in time, control his firm's fate. The 1950s and 1960s witnessed a distinct increase in social activity. The drive for social equality posed new issues for managers, which had not been previously confronted. Sophisticated mass communications and international markets created great potentials for business, but also posed a great threat to those managers unable to understand what was going on. Finally, to add to the problem, the relationship between government and business became much more involved as new regulations were imposed. These pressures for change reflect the increasing complexity and interdependence constituting modern living. The traditional function of business is being questioned and new objectives are being advanced. No doubt the events of the future will intensify environmental forces for change.

Internal Forces

The forces for change which occur within the organization can be traced to *process* and *people* causes. Process forces include breakdowns in decision-making, communications, and interactions. Decisions are either not being made, are made too late, or are of poor quality. Communications are shortcircuited, redundant, or simply inadequate. Tasks are not undertaken or not completed because the person responsible did not "get the word." A customer order is not filled; a grievance is not processed; or an invoice is not filed; and the supplier is not paid because of inadequate or nonexistent communications. Interpersonal and interdepartmental conflicts reflect breakdowns in the human interactional process.

Low levels of morale and high levels of absenteeism and turnover are symptoms of problems that must be diagnosed. A wildcat strike or a walkout may be the most tangible sign of a problem, yet such tactics are

---

[6] Thomas J. Watson, Jr., "Technological Change," in Arthur O. Lewis, Jr. (ed.), *Of Men and Machines* (New York: E. P. Dutton & Co., Inc., 1963), pp. 295–309.

usually employed because they rouse the management to action. There is in most organizations a certain level of employee discontent; a great danger is to ignore the complaints and suggestions. But the process of change includes the *recognition* phase, and it is at this point that management must decide to act or not to act.

RECOGNITION OF THE NEED FOR CHANGE

Information is the basis on which managers are made aware of the magnitude of the change forces. In our discussion above, we have hinted at some of the important sources of information. Certainly the most important information comes from the firm's preliminary, concurrent, and feedback control data. Indeed, the process of change can be viewed as a part of the control function, specifically the corrective-action subfunction. Analyses of financial statements, quality control data, and budget and standard cost information are important media through which both external and internal forces reveal themselves. Declining profit margins and market shares are tangible signs that the firm's competitive position is deteriorating and that change may be required. These sources of feedback control information are highly developed in most firms because of their crucial importance.

The need for change goes unrecognized in many organizations until some major catastrophe occurs. The employees strike or seek the recognition of a union before management finally recognizes the need for action. Whether it takes a whisper or a shout, the need for change must be recognized by some means; and the exact nature of the problem must be diagnosed.

DIAGNOSIS OF THE PROBLEM

Before appropriate action can be taken, the symptoms of the problem must be analyzed to discover the problem itself. Experience and judgment are critical to this phase unless the problem is readily apparent to all observers. Ordinarily, however, persons in management can disagree as to the nature of the problem. There is no magic formula which is available for accurate diagnosis. The objectives of this phase can be described by three questions:

1. What is the problem as distinct from the symptoms of the problem?
2. What must be changed to resolve the problem?
3. What outcomes (objectives) are expected from the change, and how will such objectives be measured?

The answers to these questions can come from information ordinarily found in the company, such as financial statements and departmental reports. Or it may be necessary to generate *ad hoc* information through the creation of committees or task forces. Meetings between managers and employees provide a variety of points of view which can be sifted through by a smaller group. Technical operational problems may be easily diagnosed, but more subtle human relations problems usually entail extensive analysis. One approach to diagnosing the problem is the attitude survey.

Attitude surveys can be administered to the entire work force or to a sample of the population. The survey permits the respondents to evaluate and rate (1) management, (2) pay and pay-related items, (3) working conditions, (4) equipment, and (5) other job-related items. The appropriate use of such surveys requires that the questionnaire be completed anonymously so that employees can express their views freely and without threat, whether real or fancied. The objective of the survey is to pinpoint the problem or problems as perceived by the members of the organization. Subsequent discussions of the survey results at all levels of the organization can add additional insights into the nature of the problem.

The approach which management uses to diagnose the problem is a crucial part of the total strategy for change. As will be seen in a later section, the manner in which the problem is diagnosed has clear implications for the final success of the proposed change.

Finally, the diagnostic step must specify *objectives* for change. Given the diagnosis of the problem, it is necessary to define objectives to guide as well as to evaluate the outcome of the change. The objectives can be stated in terms of financial and production data, such as profits, market shares, sales volume, productivity, scrappage, or the like. Or they can be stated in terms of attitude and morale data as derived from employee-survey information. Whatever the objectives, they must be explicit and, if possible, measurable.

ALTERNATIVE CHANGE TECHNIQUES

The choice of the particular change technique depends upon the nature of the problem which management has diagnosed. Management must determine which alternative is most likely to produce the desired outcome, whether it be improvement in the knowledge, attitudes, skills, or job performances of the organization's personnel. As we have noted, diagnosis of the problem includes specification of the output which management desires from the change. In this section, we will describe a number of change techniques. They will be classified according to the major focus of the technique, namely, to change structure, people, or technology.[7]

---

[7] See Harold J. Leavitt, "Applied Organizational Change in Industry: Structural, Technological and Humanistic Approaches," in James G. March (ed.), *Handbook of Organizations* (Chicago: Rand McNally and Co., 1965), pp. 1144–1168.

This classification of approaches to organizational change in no way implies a distinct division among the three types. On the contrary, the interrelationships among structure, people, and technology must be acknowledged and anticipated.

An important contribution of the behavioral school is the documentation of the impact of structure on attitudes and behavior. Overspecialization and narrow spans of control can lead to low levels of morale and low productivity.[8] At the same time, the technology of production, distribution, and information processing affect, indeed may *determine,* the structural characteristics of the firm,[9] as well as attitudes and sentiments.[10] The fact that the interrelationships among structure, people, and technology are so pronounced might suggest a weakness in our classification scheme; but in defense of it, the techniques described below can be distinguished on the basis of their *major* thrust of focus—structure, people, or technology.

Structural Change

Changes in the structure of the organization ordinarily follow changes in strategy.[11] Logically, the organizing function follows the planning function since the structure is a means for achieving the goals established through planning. Structural change in the context of organizational change refers to managerial action which attempts to improve task performance by altering the formal structure of task and authority relationships. At the same time, we must recognize that the structure creates human and social relationships which gradually can become ends for the members of the organization. These relationships, when they have been defined and made legitimate by management, introduce an element of stability.[12] Members of the organization may resist efforts to disrupt these relationships.

Structural changes affect some aspect of the formal task and authority definitions. As we have seen, the design of an organization involves the definition and specification of job content and scope, the grouping of jobs

[8] Rensis Likert, *The Human Organization* (New York: McGraw-Hill Book Co., 1967).

[9] Joan Woodward, *Industrial Organization* (New York: Oxford University Press, 1967); and Frank J. Jasinski, "Adapting Organization to New Technology," *Harvard Business Review,* vol. 37 (January–February, 1959), pp. 79–86.

[10] Harriet O. Ronken and Paul R. Lawrence, *Administering Changes: A Case Study of Human Relations in a Factory* (Boston: Division of Research, Harvard Business School, 1952).

[11] Alfred Chandler, *Strategy and Structure* (Cambridge, Mass.: M.I.T. Press, 1962).

[12] R. K. Ready, *The Administrator's Job* (New York: McGraw-Hill Book Co., 1967), pp. 24–30.

in departments, the determination of the size of groups reporting to a single manager, and the provision for staff assistance. Within this framework, the communication, decision-making, and human interaction processes occur. We can see, then, that changes in the nature of jobs, bases for departmentalization, and line-staff relationships are the foci of structural change.

Changes in the nature of jobs include any revision in the prescribed ways for performing assigned tasks. The origins of such changes are the implementation of new methods and new machines. Work simplification and job enlargement are two examples of methods changes. The former narrows job content and scope, whereas the latter widens them. Scientific management introduced significant changes in the way work is done through the use of motion and time studies. These methods tend to create highly specialized jobs. Job enlargement, however, moves in the opposite direction, toward despecialization.

One application of job change which led to significant increases in productivity and decreases in absenteeism occurred at Texas Instruments Incorporated.[13] In 1965, a group of women who had been assembling radar equipment according to methods defined by the engineering department were given the responsibility for devising their own methods, manufacturing processes and goals. The women had full access to cost and engineering information and staff personnel. After implementation of the group's own methods and goals, the assembly time per unit dropped from 138 hours to 86 hours. At this point a second goalsetting session was held, and the women suggested that they did not need a supervisor; they could, in their own judgment, exercise self-control. The women did keep their supervisor informed, but they self-directed their activities. The assembly time for the unit was finally reduced to 36 hours.

In this instance of job change, the employees were encouraged to evaluate their own task performance. They responded by not only enlarging the job along the horizontal dimension—by adding additional tasks, but also along the vertical dimension—by assuming the responsibility for their own supervision. The degree of general applicability to other manufacturing situations is, of course, a matter of on-site determination; the case does suggest the positive gains from job change which can be realized.

Changes in the bases for departmentalization occur in response to a variety of stimuli. One analysis of the response of firms to growth of their markets reports a number of changes. In a study of 30 California-based financial, service and manufacturing firms which experienced marked

[13] Charles L. Hughes, "Applying Behavioral Science in Manufacturing Supervision: Case Report," *Proceedings of the Ninth Annual Midwest Management Conference* (Carbondale, Ill.: Bureau of Business Research, Southern Illinois University, 1966), pp. 85–89.

growth during the period 1947–1955, McNulty found a considerable increase in the relative importance of product departmentalization relative to other bases.[14] The use of product bases indicates efforts to move toward decentralized forms of organization like those found in General Motors and in General Electric. But the ambivalence of the firms in the study is demonstrated by the tendency to create "taller" rather than "flatter" organizations. With decentralization, one expects to find relatively wider spans of control. McNulty's study suggests that the problems of rapid market growth are such that management is reluctant to relinquish too much control over the situation.

Changes in line-staff relationships include two techniques. The first and the usual approach is to create staff assistance as an *ad hoc* or permanent solution. McNulty reported that one response of manufacturing firms to the problem of market expansion is the creation of separate staff and service units.[15] These units provide the technical expertise to deal with the production, financial, and marketing problems posed by expansion. The location of these units in the company, whether at corporate or plant level, is related to the issues of centralization-decentralization and departmentalization bases.

An illustrative case is a company which has grown quite rapidly since its entry into the fast-foods industry. Its basic sources of field control are area directors who supervise the operations of sales outlets of a particular region. During the growth period the area directors had considerable autonomy in making the advertising decisions for their regions. They could select their own media, format, and budget within general guidelines. But, as their markets became saturated and as competitors appeared, corporate officials decided to centralize the advertising function in a staff unit located at corporate headquarters. Consequently, the area director's freedom to maneuver in his region was limited and an essential aspect of his job was eliminated.[16]

A final illustration of changes in line-staff relationships is based upon the case which O'Connell described.[17] A large insurance company engaged the services of a management consulting firm to analyze the problem created by a deteriorating market position. The consulting company recommended that the firm undertake a program of decentralization effected through the transformation of a staff position to that of a line

[14] James E. McNulty, "Organizational Change in Growing Enterprises," *Administrative Science Quarterly*, Vol. 7 (June, 1962), pp. 1–21.

[15] *Ibid.*

[16] See Herbert A. Simon *et al.*, *Centralization versus Decentralization in Organizing the Controller's Department* (New York: The Controllership Foundation, 1954) for another discussion of the key issues to be resolved in the decision to locate staff units, in this case, an accounting unit.

[17] O'Connell, *op. cit.*

manager. This recommendation was based upon the consultants' belief that the company must have its best personnel and resources available at the branch office level to increase premium income. Accordingly, the consultant recommended that assistant managers be converted to first-level supervisors reporting to branch managers. The transformation required a significant change in the work of assistant managers and in the work of managers throughout the organization.

These examples illustrate the range of alternatives open to managers who must consider changes in the structure. Certainly we have not exhausted the possibilities. The point that should be made in concluding this discussion, however, is not that the list is incomplete, but that students and managers must recognize the interrelationships of structural parts. A change in job content does not take place in a vacuum; on the contrary, the change affects all other directly related jobs, supervisory and nonsupervisory alike. The management of structural change must be guided by the *holistic* point of view that all things are connected.

Behavioral Change

This class of change refers to efforts to redirect and improve employee attitudes, skills, and knowledge bases. The objective is to enhance the capacity of the individual to perform his assigned task in coordination with others. The early efforts to engage in behavioral change date to scientific management work improvement and employee training methods. These attempts were primarily directed at improving employee skills and knowledge bases. The employee counseling programs which grew out of the Hawthorne studies were (and remain) primarily directed at improving employee attitudes.

The training programs for managers have typically emphasized supervisory relationships. These programs attempt to provide supervisors and foremen with basic technical and human-relations skills. Since supervisors and foremen are primarily concerned with overseeing the work of others, the content of these traditional programs emphasizes techniques for dealing with people problems: how to deal with the malcontent, the loafer, the troublemaker, the complainer. The programs also include conceptual material dealing with communications, leadership styles, and organizational relationships. The vehicles for training include roleplaying, discussion groups, lectures, and organized courses offered by universities.[18] A number of programs include materials about the managerial grid, democratic leadership, and other ideas derived from the behavioral school.

Training continues to be an important technique for introducing people changes. Training has taken on quite a different form in some appli-

---

[18] Ernest Dale and L. C. Michelon, *Modern Management Methods* (New York: The World Publishing Company, 1966), pp. 15–16.

cations from that which developed in classical management theory. In contemporary management a popular behavioral change approach is sensitivity training.

Sensitivity training is a change technique which attempts to make the participant more aware of himself and of his impact on others. "Sensitivity" in this context means sensitivity to self and to relationships with others. An assumption of sensitivity training is that the causes of poor task performance are the emotional problems of people who must collectively achieve a goal. If these problems can be removed, a major impediment to task performance is consequently eliminated. Sensitivity training stresses "the *process* rather than the *content* of training and . . . *emotional* rather than *conceptual* training."[19] We can see that this form of training is quite different from traditional forms which stress the acquisition of a predetermined bundle of concepts with immediate application to the work place.

The process of sensitivity training includes a group of managers (Training group or T-group) who in most cases come together at some location other than their place of work. Under the direction of a trainer, the group usually engages in a dialogue which has no agenda and no focus. The objective is to provide an environment which produces its own learning experiences.[20] As each member engages in the dialogue, he is encouraged to learn about himself as he deals with others. He explores his motives and his feelings as revealed through his behavior toward others in the group and through the behavior of others toward him. The T-group is typically unstructured. As Marrow points out in a report of his own sensitivity training, "It [sensitivity training] says 'Open your eyes. Look at yourself. See how you look to others. Then decide what changes, if any, you want to make and in which direction you want to go.'"[21]

The role of the trainer in the T-group is to facilitate the learning process. According to Kelly, the trainer's mission is "to observe, record, interpret, sometimes to lead, and always to learn."[22] The artistry and style of the trainer are critical variables in determining the direction of the T-group's sessions. He must walk the uneasy path of unobtrusive leadership. He must be able to interpret the roles of participants and encourage them to analyze their contributions without being perceived as a threat

[19] Henry C. Smith, *Sensitivity to People* (New York: McGraw-Hill Book Co., 1966), p. 197.

[20] L. P. Bradford, J. R. Gibb, and K. D. Benne, *T-Group Theory and Laboratory Method* (New York: John Wiley & Sons, Inc., 1964).

[21] Alfred J. Marrow, *Behind the Executive Mask* (New York: American Management Association, 1964), p. 51.

[22] Joe Kelly, *Organizational Behaviour* (Homewood, Ill.: Richard D. Irwin, Inc., and the Dorsey Press, 1969), p. 419.

himself. Unlike the group therapist, the T-group trainer is dealing with people who are considered normal, but who have come together to learn. The ordinarily prescribed role of the trainer is that of "permissive, non-authoritarian, sometimes almost nonparticipative" leadership.[23]

The critical test of sensitivity training is whether the experience itself is a factor leading to improvement in task performance. It is apparent that, even if the training induces positive changes in the participant's sensitivity to self and others, such behavior may be either not possible or not permissible back in the work place. The participant must deal with the same environment and the same people as before the training. The open, supportive, and permissive environment of the training sessions is not likely to be found on the job. Even so, proponents of sensitivity training would reply that it makes the participant better able to deal with the environment and to understand his own relationship to it. We should also recognize that sensitivity training may well induce negative changes in the participant's ability to perform his organizational task; the training sessions can be occasions of extreme stress and anxiety. The capacity to deal effectively with stress varies among individuals and the outcome may be dysfunctional for some participants.

The empirical evidence to date on the effectiveness of sensitivity training as a change technique suggests mixed results.[24] The manager must critically examine this technique in terms of the kinds of changes he desires and those which are possible. Our model suggests the existence of conditions which limit the range of possible changes. In this light the manager must determine whether the changes induced by sensitivity training are instrumental for organizational purposes and whether the prospective participant himself is able to tolerate the potential anxiety of the training.

The recognition that structure must be compatible with behavior and vice versa has stimulated the search for a means to relate the two. A notable contribution is that of Professor Rensis Likert. He proposes on the basis of considerable research that the most effective organizational form is one which can be clearly distinguished from others; he furthermore proposes that management should make a conscious effort to change to the superior form,[25] which he terms System 4.

System 4 Organization relates people change and structural change. According to Likert an organization can be described in terms of eight

[23] Leavitt, *op. cit.*, p. 1154.

[24] See Robert J. House, "T-Group Education and Leadership Effectiveness: A Review of the Empirical Literature and a Critical Evaluation," *Personnel Psychology*, vol. 20 (Spring, 1967), pp. 1–32; and John P. Campbell and Marvin D. Dunnette, "Effectiveness of T-Group Experiences in Managerial Training and Development," *Psychological Bulletin*, vol. 70 (August, 1968), pp. 73–104.

[25] Rensis Likert, *The Human Organization* (New York: McGraw-Hill Book Co., 1967).

operating characteristics. They are (1) leadership, (2) motivation, (3) communication, (4) interaction, (5) decision-making, (6) goal setting, (7) control, and (8) performance. The nature of each of these characteristics can be located on a continuum through the use of a questionnaire which members of the firm (usually managers) complete. The

FIGURE 12–2

Organizational Profile for Two Manufacturing Firms

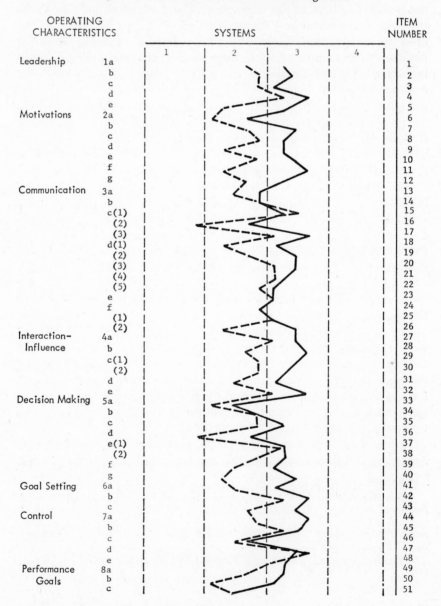

OPERATING CHARACTERISTICS		SYSTEMS				ITEM NUMBER
		1	2	3	4	
Leadership	1a					1
	b					2
	c					3
	d					4
	e					5
Motivations	2a					6
	b					7
	c					8
	d					9
	e					10
	f					11
	g					12
Communication	3a					13
	b					14
	c(1)					15
	(2)					16
	(3)					17
	d(1)					18
	(2)					19
	(3)					20
	(4)					21
	(5)					22
	e					23
	f					24
	(1)					25
	(2)					26
Interaction–Influence	4a					27
	b					28
	c(1)					29
	(2)					30
	d					31
	e					32
Decision Making	5a					33
	b					34
	c					35
	d					36
	e(1)					37
	(2)					38
	f					39
	g					40
Goal Setting	6a					41
	b					42
	c					43
Control	7a					44
	b					45
	c					46
	d					47
	e					48
Performance	8a					49
Goals	b					50
	c					51

latest form of this questionnaire is included in the Appendix to this chapter. The arithmetic means (averages) of each response category are calculated and plotted to produce an organizational profile. Figure 12–2 presents superimposed profiles for two plants located in southeastern Kentucky.

The horizontal dimension of the organizational profile describes four points on the continua for each of the eight operating characteristics which appear on the vertical dimension. Likert has labelled the four points as follows:

System 1—Exploitive-Authoritative,
System 2—Benevolent-Authoritative,
System 3—Consultative, and
System 4—Participative Group.

Likert no longer uses these value-laden labels since value-free descriptions of each of the systems are obviously desirable. He now defines each system in quantitative terms on the dimensions shown in Figure 12–2.

Close examination of the appendix will provide the student with the basic understanding for differentiating the four systems. We can summarize by observing that the System 4 organization is one in which managers (1) use the principle of supportive relationships; (2) use group methods for decision making and supervision; and (3) have high performance goals.[26] More specific characteristics of System 4 organization are:

1. *Leadership processes* which include perceived confidence and trust between superiors and subordinates and vice versa. Subordinates feel free to discuss job problems with their superiors, who in turn solicit their ideas and opinions.
2. *Motivational processes* tap a full range of motives through participatory methods. Attitudes are favorable toward the company and toward goals of the company.
3. *Communication processes* are such that information flows freely throughout the organization—upward, downward, and laterally. The information is accurate and undistorted.
4. *Interaction processes* are open and extensive; both superiors and subordinates are able to affect departmental goals, methods, and activities.
5. *Decision-making processes* occur at all levels of the organization through *group methods.*
6. *Goal setting processes* encourage group participation in setting high, yet realistic objectives.
7. *Control processes* are dispersed throughout the company with all par-

[26] *Ibid.,* p. 47.

ticipants seeking information to implement self-control; the emphasis of control is problem-solving, not blame-setting.

8. *Performance goals* are high and actively sought by superiors, who also recognize the necessity for making a full commitment to developing, through training, the human resources of the company.

The System 4 organization as described above has no counterpart in reality. Likert himself has studies of companies which *approach* System 4, but he has not discovered any companies which are pure System 4. He assumes that it is an "ideal-type," an ideal based on extrapolation toward which the most successful companies are moving. He expects soon to be able to define by quantitative dimensions an even more effective management system which he is labeling System 5.

The profiles of the two firms presented in Figure 12–2 demonstrate the kinds of differences that can occur in organizational processes. In Likert's terms, the firm represented by the dotted line is clearly a System 2 organization, whereas that represented by the solid line is a System 3 organization with tendencies toward System 2. The profiles (derived from Likert's questionnaire) were used in conjunction with attitude surveys to pinpoint the nature of suspected problems. The profiles suggested the need to examine motivational, communication, and decision-making processes since the most pronounced deviations occurred in these areas. Subsequent analysis of information contained in the attitude survey and interviews with the employees confirmed these observations that problems existed in the areas of motivation, communications, and decision making. The managements of both organizations believed that efforts to move toward System 4 organization should be undertaken.

The change toward System 4 involves measuring the present state of the firm through the use of the questionnaire. Subsequent training programs emphasize the concepts of System 4 management and their application to the present organization. The use of supportive, group-oriented leadership and the equalization of power to set goals, implement controls, and make decisions should ordinarily lead to higher earnings and productivity, according to Likert. These favorable results derive from positive changes in employee attitudes which are induced by the structural changes. As has been pointed out by others, "To obtain lasting change, one does not try to change people, but rather to change the organizational constraints that operate upon them."[27]

Technological Change

This category of change includes any application of new ways to transform resources into the product or service. In the usual sense of the word,

---

[27] Eliot D. Chapple and Leonard R. Sayles, *The Measure of Management* (New York: The Macmillan Company, 1961), p. 202.

technology means new machines—lathes, presses, computers, and the like. But we should expand the concept to include new techniques with or without new machines. From this perspective, the work improvement methods of scientific management can be considered as technological breakthroughs. However, in this section only those changes which are induced by the introduction of a machine or man-machine process are discussed. We have already suggested the implications of these new techniques in the discussion of changes in job content, Chapter 2.

The changes in organizational efficiency brought about by a new machine are calculable in purely economic and engineering terms. Whether the machine is a good investment is a matter of estimating its future profitability in relation to its present cost. These calculations are an important part of the managerial control function. Here, however, we are interested in the impact of the new machine on the structure of the organization and on the behavior of the people in the organization. As some scholars have observed, technology is a key determinant of structure.[28] They tentatively conclude that firms with simple and stable technology should adopt a structure that tends toward bureaucratic organization, whereas firms with complex and dynamic technology ought to tend toward the more open and flexible System 4 structure.[29] Thus it would appear that the adoption of new technology involves a concurrent decision to adapt the organizational structure to that technology. Whether or not an inexorable and deterministic relationship between technology and structure exists, the fact remains that the introduction of technological innovation has far-reaching effects within the firm.

In order to catalog the impact of technological change on structure and behavior, Floyd C. Mann analyzed a number of actual cases and concluded that the adoption of new machines in the factory involves:

1. major changes in the division of labor and the content of jobs;
2. changes in social relations among workers;
3. improved working conditions;
4. the need for different supervisory skills;
5. changes in career patterns, promotion procedures, and job security;
6. generally higher wages;
7. generally higher prestige for those who work; and
8. around-the-clock operations.[30]

---

[28] Woodward, *op. cit.*, and Jasinski, *op. cit.*, among others.

[29] Burns and Stalker make this point in their analysis of the ways European electronic firms responded to technological change. They use the terms "mechanistic" to refer to relatively tight, highly structured organizations and "organic" to refer to relatively loose, flexibly structured organization. Tom Burns and G. M. Stalker, *The Management of Innovation* (London: Tavistock Publications, 1961).

[30] Floyd C. Mann, "Psychological and Organizational Impacts," in John T. Dunlop (ed.), *Automation and Technological Change* (Englewood Cliffs, N.J.: Prentice-Hall, Inc., 1962), pp. 50–55.

The degree and extent of these observed changes in structure and behavior depend upon the magnitude of the technological change. Obviously, the introduction of a new offset printing press will not cause the great dislocations and changes which Mann observes, but the complete automation of a previously man-paced manufacturing process would include many, if not all of them.

A widespread structural adaptation to the necessity for utilizing technological innovation with minimum delay is referred to as project or program management. In this organizational form, the responsibility for achieving the goals of a short-run project is assigned to a project manager. He may then draw upon the expertise of functional experts in production, engineering, finance, or any other, as necessary. The project manager usually has complete authority over all the activities and personnel necessary to carry out the project, including personnel who ordinarily report to a functional department head. This organizational form permits horizontal communications and authority relationships necessary to complete the project but maintains the traditional and permanent vertical relationships. However, the existence of a dual authority system introduces the potential for problems associated with dual command.

The decision to adopt a technological approach to organizational change must include consideration of the potential structural and behavioral impacts. These impacts must, in turn, be reconciled with conditions which limit the scope and magnitude of the proposed change.

RECOGNITION OF LIMITING CONDITIONS

The selection of the change technique is based upon diagnosis of the problem, but the choice is tempered by certain conditions that exist at the time. Filley and House identify three sources of influence on the outcome of management development programs which can be generalized to cover the entire range of organizational change efforts, whether structural, behavioral, or technological. They are the leadership climate, formal organization, and organizational culture.[31]

Leadership climate refers to the nature of the work environment which results from "the leadership style and administrative practices" of superiors. Any change program which does not have the support and commitment of management has a slim chance of success. Managers must be at least neutral toward the change. We also understand that the style of leadership itself may be the subject of change; for example, sensitivity training and System 4 are direct attempts to move managers toward a certain style—open, supportive, and group-centered. But, it must be recognized that the participants may be unable to adopt such styles if they are not compatible with their own superiors' style.

The *formal organization* must also be compatible with the proposed

[31] Alan C. Filley and Robert J. House, *Managerial Process and Organizational Behavior* (Glenview, Ill.: Scott, Foresman and Company, 1969), pp. 423–34.

change. This includes the effects on the environment that result from the philosophy and policies of top management, as well as "legal precedent, organizational structure, and the system of control." Of course, each of these sources of impact may itself be the focus of the change effort; the important point is that a change in one must be compatible with all others. For example, a change in technology which will eliminate employees contradicts a policy of guaranteed employment.

The *organizational culture* refers to the impact on the environment resulting from "group norms, values, and informal activities." The impact of traditional behavior, sanctioned by group norms but not formally acknowledged, was first documented in the Hawthorne studies. A proposed change in work methods or the installation of an automated device can run counter to the expectations and attitudes of the work group. If such is the case, the change strategist must anticipate the resulting resistance.

The implementation of change, which does not consider the constraints imposed by prevailing conditions within the present organization, may amplify the problem that initiated the change process. Even if implemented, the groundwork for subsequent problems is made more fertile than what could ordinarily be expected. Taken together, these conditions constitute the climate for change and can be positive or negative.

THE STRATEGY FOR CHANGE

The selection of a strategy for implementing the change technique has consequences in the final outcome. Greiner analyzes reported changes and relates various change strategies to the relative success of the change itself.[32] He identifies three approaches which are located along a power continuum with *unilateral* authority at one extreme and *delegated* authority at the other extreme. In the middle of the continuum are approaches which he terms *shared* authority.

Unilateral approaches can take the form of an edict from top management which describes the change and the responsibilities of subordinates in implementing the change. The formal communication may be a memorandum or policy statement. It is, in any form, a one-way, top-down communication.[33] Shared approaches involve lower-level groups in the process of either (1) defining the problem and alternative solutions, or (2) defining solutions only after higher level management has defined the problem. In either case, the process engages the talents and insights of all members of the company at all levels. Finally, delegated approaches re-

---

[32] Greiner, *op. cit.*

[33] Greiner identifies replacement of key personnel and structural changes as two other forms of unilateral change. For our purposes, personnel and structural changes are change techniques, not strategies for implementing change. Techniques specify *what* is to be done; strategies specify *how* it is to be done.

linquish complete authority to subordinate groups. Through freewheeling discussions, the group is responsible for the analysis of the problem and proposed solutions. According to Greiner, the relatively more successful instances of organizational change are those which tend toward the shared position of the continuum. Why is this the case?

As has been observed, most instances of organizational change are accompanied by resistance from those who are involved in the change. The actual form of resistance may range in extreme from passive resignation to deliberate sabotage.[34] The objective of the strategy is to at least minimize resistance and at most maximize cooperation and support. The manner in which the change is managed from beginning to end is a key determinant of the reaction of people to change.

The strategy which emphasizes shared authority has the greatest likelihood of minimizing resistance to change. This is the case because it takes into account the "American culture pattern of equivalence between self-reliance and self-respect."[35] Change imposed from the top—unilateral authority—runs the danger of *creating* resistance even though the proposed change may benefit the participants in every conceivable way by any objective standards. As has been recognized by the behavioral school of management, an important means for overcoming resistance to change is to involve those who will be affected by the change in the decision to make the change.

The process of shared authority is composed of six phases. According to Greiner, each of these phases accompanies each instance of reported successful change. The six phases in logical sequence are:

1. Pressure and Arousal. Instances of successful change are stimulated by strong pressure on the top management of the firm. This pressure ordinarily exerts itself in the form of unmistakable and unambiguous signals that something is wrong and needs attention.

2. Intervention and Reorientation. Because there is a tendency to seek answers in traditional solutions, the intervention of an outsider is necessary to reorient the management away from routine approaches and toward nonroutine approaches. The outsider may be a new management appointee, a corporate staff official, or a consultant. The outsider brings a different perspective into the situation and serves as challenger to the status quo. At this point, top management must commit itself to change.

3. Diagnosis and Recognition. The entire organization from top to bottom joins together to diagnose and specify the problem. Greiner observes that the less successful changes use either unilateral or delegated approaches in this step. The former fails because management pre-

[34] Arnold S. Judson, *A Manager's Guide to Making Changes* (New York: John Wiley and Sons, 1966), p. 41.

[35] Paul C. Agnew and Francis L. K. Hsu, "Introducing Change in a Mental Hospital," *Human Organization,* vol. 19 (Winter, 1960), p. 198.

sumes that they alone know the problem and its solution and thus ignore the necessity for involving participants. The latter fails because subordinates question the sincerity of managers who totally abrogate their authority. The involvement of all concerned members of the organization and, at the same time, maintenance of the necessary authority relationships approaches a "balance between maximized feelings of independence and the need for enforcing policy and authority."[36]

4. Intervention and Commitment. The outsider actively encourages management and nonmanagement personnel to invent new solutions to its diagnosed problems. All members share in this step. Through the sharing experience, a high degree of commitment to the change can be expected—provided that top management makes a commitment to the proposed new solution.

5. Experimentation and Search. The solution is not implemented on a grand scale; rather, it is implemented on a small scale at various points throughout the organization. The objective is to test the validity of the solution on an experimental basis. This tactic avoids large errors by permitting a test run—a "shakedown" cruise.

6. Reinforcement and Acceptance. As the experimental attempts provide positive signals that the change is proceeding as planned, there is a reinforcement effect which encourages the participants to accept the change and to enlarge, potentially, the scope of their own efforts. "People are rewarded and encouraged" by the success of the experimental changes, thus validating the efficacy of broader application of the change.

The strategy for implementing change as described above involves superiors and subordinates in the entire process. But, we should recognize that there is no guarantee that the strategy will work in all firms. Indeed, some very basic preconditions must exist before employees can meaningfully participate in the change process. They are:[37]

a) An intuitively obvious factor is that employees must want to become involved. For any number of reasons, they may reject the invitation. They may have other, more pressing, needs, getting on with their own work, for example. Or, they may view the invitation to participate as a subtle (but not too subtle) attempt by managers to manipulate them toward a solution already predetermined. If the leadership climate or organizational culture has created an atmosphere of mistrust and insincerity, any attempt to involve workers will be viewed by them in cynical terms.

b) The employees must be willing and able to voice their ideas. Even if they are willing, they must have some expertise in some aspect of the analysis. Certainly the technical problems associated with computer

---

[36] Agnew and Hsu, *op. cit.,* p. 198.

[37] Based upon Judson, *op. cit.,* pp. 109–13.

installation or automated processes are beyond the training of the typical assembly-line worker; yet he may have valuable insights into the impact of the machinery on his and his co-workers' jobs. But even if he has the knowledge, he must be able to articulate his ideas.

c) The manager must be secure in his own position. If he is insecure, then he would perceive any participation by his employees as a threat to his own authority. He might view employee participation as a sign of his weakness or as undermining his status. He must be able to give credit for good ideas and to give explanations for ideas of questionable merit. As is evident, the manager's personality and leadership style must be compatible with the shared-authority approach if it is to be a successful strategy.

d) Finally, the manager must be openminded to employees' suggestions. If he has predetermined the solution, the participation of employees will soon be recognized for what it is. Certainly, the manager has final responsibility for the outcome, but he can control the situation by specifying beforehand the latitude of the employees: He may define objectives, establish constraints, or whatever, so long as the employees know the rules prior to their participation.

If any of the conditions which limit effective participation are present, the use of shared or delegated authority approaches must be viewed with caution. As we have seen, the same factors which limit the range of viable alternative change techniques also limit the range of alternative change strategies. Leadership style, formal organization, organizational culture, along with characteristics of the employees are key variables which constrain the entire change process. It should be recognized that the nature of the problem itself affects the choice of strategy. If, for example, the problem is one which requires immediate action, a unilateral approach may be the only means since alternative approaches consume time. We can summarize by observing that the appropriate change strategy depends upon three factors: the problem, the participants, and the organizational setting.

IMPLEMENTING AND MONITORING THE PROCESS

The implementation of the proposed change has two dimensions— *timing* and *scope*. Timing is the selection of the appropriate point in time to initiate the change. Scope is the selection of the appropriate scale of the change. The matter of timing is strategic and depends upon a number of factors, particularly the company's operating cycle and the groundwork which has preceded the change. Certainly if a change is of considerable magnitude, it is desirable that it not compete with ordinary business operations. Thus the change might well be implemented during a slack period. On the other hand, if the problem is critical to the survival of the firm, then immediate implementation is in order. The scope of the change depends upon the strategy. The change may be implemented throughout the firm and it becomes an established fact in a short period of time. Or, it may be phased into the organization level by level, department by department. The strategy of successful changes, according to Greiner, makes use of a phased approach, which limits the scope, but provides feedback for each subsequent implementation.

The provision of feedback information is termed the *monitoring* phase. From Figure 12–1 we see that information is fed back into the implementation phase. It is also fed back into the forces for change phase because the change itself establishes a new situation which will create problems. The monitoring phase has two problems to overcome: (1) the acquisition of data which measure the desired objectives, and (2) the determination of the expected trend of improvement over time.

The acquisition of information which measures the sought-after objective is the relatively easier problem to solve, although it certainly does not lend itself to naive solutions. As we have come to understand, the stimulus for change is the deterioration of performance criteria which management traces to either structural, behavioral, or technological causes. The criteria may be any number of objective indicators, including profit, sales volume, productivity, absenteeism, turnover, scrappage, or costs. The major source of feedback for those variables is the firm's usual information system. But, if the change includes the expectation that employee attitudes and morale must be improved, the usual sources of information are limited, if not invalid. As Likert has shown, it is quite possible for a change to induce increased productivity at the expense of declining employee attitudes and motivation.[38] Thus, if the manager relies on the naive assumption that productivity and employee morale are directly related, the change may be incorrectly judged successful when improved cost and profit reports come to his attention.

To avoid the danger of over-reliance on productivity data, the manager can generate *ad hoc* information which measures employee attitudes and morale. The benchmark for evaluation would be available if an attitude survey had been used in the diagnosis phase. The definition of acceptable improvement is difficult when evaluating behavioral data since the matter of "how much more" positive should be the attitude of employees is quite different than the matter of "how much more" productive they should be. Nevertheless, if a complete analysis of results is to be undertaken, behavioral measurements must be combined with productivity measurements.

The second problem of the monitoring phase is the determination of

---

[38] Likert, *op. cit.*, pp. 84–91.

the trend of improvement over time. The trend itself has three dimensions: (1) the first indication of improvement, (2) the magnitude of improvement, and (3) the duration of the improvement. In Figure 12–3 three different patterns of change for a particular performance or behavioral measure are illustrated. In the change illustrated by the solid line, improvement is slight during the early periods of time, but rises and maintains itself at a positive level. The dashed line illustrates a marked increase, but followed by a deterioration and a return to the original position. The dotted line describes a situation in which the early signs indicate a decrease, but followed by a sharp rise toward substantial

FIGURE 12–3

Three Patterns of Change in Results through Time

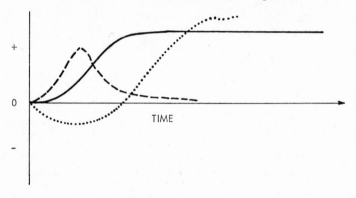

improvement. The figure illustrates only three of a number of possible change patterns. A well devised change strategy should include an analysis of what pattern can be expected. The actual pattern can then be compared to the expected.

Ideally, the pattern would consist of an index which measures both the performance and behavioral variables. Figure 12–4 illustrates a model which describes the necessary information for such an index. The solid line is the expected pattern through time. It shows a movement into acceptable behavior prior to a movement into acceptable performance. The expected pattern may of course assume any configuration. The dashed line is the plot of actual change through time. It reflects not only what is happening, but also the impact of corrective action which management takes to keep the change program on course. If the expected pattern is valid as originally conceived, the management's objective is to minimize the oscillations around the planned results.

In general, the monitoring phase is a specific application of manage-

FIGURE 12–4

Expected and Actual Pattern of Results*

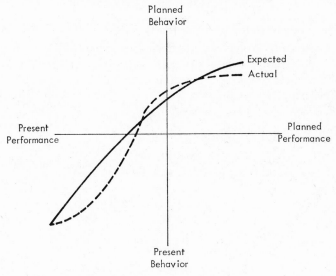

* Based upon O'Connell, *op. cit.*, p. 156.

ment control. Before it can be effective, management must provide for a measurement of the objective, information to compare actual results with planned results, and action to correct any deviations.

SUMMARY

This chapter concludes the discussion of the behavioral science contributions to management theory and practice. In the context of a model which describes the process of managing organizational change, a number of behavioral science concepts are shown to have considerable relevance. Motivation, attitudes, work groups, and leadership styles are key concepts in an overall change framework which stresses the dynamic nature of the managerial process. Indeed, since change itself has become such a pervasive fact of the modern world, it is appropriate and logical to cast management in a framework which emphasizes change. At the same time, the management of change does not imply random and unplanned responses to a changing environment. On the contrary, we have stressed the need for systematic analyses of all facets of the proposed change program.

The literature which reports changes undertaken in various organizations indicates the critical need for planning, organizing, and controlling the change process. We have emphasized that the manner in which the change is implemented bears heavily on the ultimate outcome. In fact, we should recognize that a change technique may fail because of ineffective implementation. We have also stressed the necessity for evaluating techniques and strategies in the context of the particular organization. Thus, even though there is evidence that certain strategies (e.g., shared authority) and certain techniques (e.g., sensitivity training) are appropriate in many instances, their validity in the specific instance is a matter of on-site analysis.

REVIEW AND DISCUSSION QUESTIONS

1. Review your understanding of the change model by using it to evaluate a change which you implemented recently in your approach to getting a college degree.
2. Which step in the change model is most important for the ultimate success of a particular proposed change?
3. Which step in the change model is most difficult and most likely to be ignored because of its difficulty?
4. What are the dangers of the indiscriminate use of sensitivity training?
5. A young manager states: "It took me 30 years to develop a set of ego-defense mechanisms that enable me to live and function in this crazy world. I refuse to participate in any training program whose objective is to tear them down." Comment.
6. Why is the creation of staff departments such a widespread reaction to organizational problems?
7. "The successful manager is one who knows how to play the role of a change agent." Comment.
8. How can supervisors and foremen provide management with feedback information which monitors a change process?
9. What changes do you believe are necessary within your own college or university? Why do you think so? What is your evidence? What are the limiting conditions? What are the objectives? How would you evaluate your proposed changes once implemented?
10. Even though structure should follow strategy, can you find instances where strategy followed structure?

ADDITIONAL REFERENCES

ARGYRIS, C. *Interpersonal Competence and Organizational Effectiveness.* Homewood, Ill.: Richard D. Irwin, Inc. and The Dorsey Press, 1962.

BENNIS, W. G., BENNE, K. D., and CHIN, R. *The Planning of Change.* New York: Holt, Rinehart, and Winston, Inc., 1961.

COCH, L., and FRENCH, J. R. P. "Overcoming Resistance to Change," *Human Relations,* 1 (1948), 512–32.

DALTON, G. W., LAWRENCE, P. R., and GREINER, L. E. *Organizational Change and Development.* Homewood, Ill.: Richard D. Irwin, Inc., and The Dorsey Press, 1970.

DICKSON, W. J. and ROETHLISBERGER, F. J. *Counseling in an Organization.* Boston: Harvard University Division of Research, 1966.

GINZBERG, E., and REILLEY, E. W. *Effecting Change in Large Organizations.* New York: Columbia University Press, 1957.

GOULDNER, A. *Patterns of Industrial Bureaucracy.* Glencoe, Ill.: The Free Press, 1964.

GUEST, R. H. *Organizational Change: The Effect of Successful Leadership.* Homewood, Ill.: Richard D. Irwin, Inc., 1962.

JACQUES, E. *The Changing Culture of a Factory.* London: Tavistock Publications, Ltd., 1951.

LIPPITT, R., WATSON, J. and WESTLEY, B. *The Dynamics of Planned Change.* New York: Harcourt, Brace and World, Inc., 1958.

MINER, J. B. *Personnel Psychology.* New York: The Macmillan Co., 1969.

PAINE, F. T. "Management Perspective: Sensitivity Training: The Current State of The Question," *Academy of Management Journal,* 8 (1965), 228–32.

SEASHORE, S. E. and BOWERS, D. G. *Changing the Structure and Functioning of an Organization.* Ann Arbor, Michigan: University of Michigan Survey Research Center, 1963.

SOFER, C. *The Organization from Within.* London: Tavistock Publications, Ltd., 1961.

TRIST, E. L., HIGGIN, G. W., and POLLACK, A. B. *Organizational Choice.* London: Oxford University Press, 1965.

APPENDIX

The Likert Instrument for Determining the Organizational Profile*

1. Leadership processes used

a. Extent to which superiors have confidence and trust in subordinates

| Have no confidence and trust in subordinates | Have condescending confidence and trust, such as master has in servant | Substantial but not complete confidence and trust; still wishes to keep control of decisions | Complete confidence and trust in all matters |

b. Extent to which subordinates, in turn, have confidence and trust in superiors

| Have no confidence and trust in superiors | Have subservient confidence and trust, such as servant has to master | Substantial but not complete confidence and trust | Complete confidence and trust |

c. Extent to which superiors display supportive behavior toward others

| Display no supportive behavior or virtually none | Display supportive behavior in condescending manner and situations only | Display supportive behavior quite generally | Display supportive behavior fully and in all situations |

d. Extent to which superiors behave so that subordinates feel free to discuss important things about their jobs with their immediate superior

| Subordinates do not feel at all free to discuss things about the job with their superior | Subordinates do not feel very free to discuss things about the job with their superior | Subordinates feel rather free to discuss things about the job with their superior | Subordinates feel completely free to discuss things about the job with their superior |

* Rensis Likert, *The Human Organization* (New York: McGraw-Hill Book Co., 1967), pp. 197–211, reproduced by permission. Copies of the instrument can be obtained from the Foundation for Research on Human Behavior, P. O. Box 1248, Ann Arbor, Michigan.

Item				
e. Extent to which immediate superior in solving job problems generally tries to get subordinates' ideas and opinions and make constructive use of them	Seldom gets ideas and opinions of subordinates in solving job problems	Sometimes gets ideas and opinions of subordinates in solving job problems	Usually gets ideas and opinions and usually tries to make constructive use of them	Always gets ideas and opinions and always tries to make constructive use of them
2. Character of motivational forces a. Underlying motives tapped	Physical, security, economic needs, and some use of the desire for status	Economic needs and moderate use of ego motives, e.g., desire for status, affiliation, and achievement	Economic needs and considerable use of ego and other major motives, e.g., desire for new experiences	Full use of economic ego, and other major motives, as, for example, motivational forces arising from group goals
b. Manner in which motives are used	Fear, threats, punishment, and occasional rewards	Rewards and some actual or potential punishment	Rewards, occasional punishment, and some involvement	Economic rewards based on compensation system developed through participation; group participation and involvement in setting goals, improving methods, appraising progress toward goals, etc.

APPENDIX (*Continued*)

c. Kinds of attitudes developed toward organization and its goals	Attitudes usually are hostile and counter to organization's goals	Attitudes are sometimes hostile and counter to organization's goals and are sometimes favorable to the organization's goals and support the behavior necessary to achieve them	Attitudes usually are favorable and support behavior implementing organization's goals	Attitudes are strongly favorable and provide powerful stimulation to behavior implementing organization's goals
d. Extent to which motivational forces conflict with or reinforce one another	Marked conflict of forces substantially reducing those motivational forces leading to behavior in support of the organization's goals	Conflict often exists; occasionally forces will reinforce each other at least partially	Some conflict, but often motivational forces will reinforce each other	Motivational forces generally reinforce each other in a substantial and cumulative manner
e. Amount of responsibility felt by each member of organization for achieving organization's goals	High levels of management feel responsibility; lower levels feel less; rank and file feel little and often welcome opportunity to behave in ways to defeat organization's goals	Managerial personnel usually feel responsibility; rank and file usually feel relatively little responsibility for achieving organization's goals	Substantial proportion of personnel, especially at higher levels, feel responsibility and generally behave in ways to achieve the organization's goals	Personnel at all levels feel real responsibility for organization's goals and behave in ways to implement them

f. Attitudes toward other members of the organization	Subservient attitudes toward superiors coupled with hostility toward peers and contempt for subordinates; distrust is widespread	Subservient attitudes toward superiors; competition for status resulting in hostility toward peers; condescension toward subordinates	Cooperative, reasonably favorable attitudes toward others in organization; may be some competition between peers with resulting hostility and some condescension toward subordinates	Favorable, cooperative attitudes throughout the organization with mutual trust and confidence
g. Satisfaction derived	Usually dissatisfaction with membership in the organization, with supervision, and with one's own achievements	Dissatisfaction to moderate satisfaction with regard to membership in the organization, and one's own achievements	Some dissatisfaction to moderately high satisfaction with regard to membership in the organization, supervision, and one's own achievements	Relatively high satisfaction throughout the organization with regard to membership in the organization, supervision, and one's own achievements
3. Character of communication process				
a. Amount of interaction and communication aimed at achieving organization's objectives	Very little	Little	Quite a bit	Much with both individuals and groups

	Downward	Mostly downward	Down and up	Down, up and with peers
b. Direction of information flow				
c. Downward communication				
(1) Where initiated	At top of organization or to implement top directive	Primarily at top or patterned on communication from top	Patterned on communication from top but with some initiative at lower levels	Initiated at all levels
(2) Extent to which superiors willingly share information with subordinates	Provide minimum of information	Give subordinates only information superior feels they need	Give information needed and answers most questions	Seek to give subordinates all relevant information and all information they want
(3) Extent to which communications are accepted by subordinates	Viewed with great suspicion	Some accepted and some viewed with suspicion	Often accepted but, if not, may or may not be openly questioned	Generally accepted, but if not, openly and candidly questioned

d. Upward communi-cation

	Very little	Limited	Some	A great deal
(1) Adequacy of upward communication via line or organization				
(2) Subordinates feeling of responsibility for initiating accurate upward communication	None at all	Relatively little, usually communicates "filtered" information and only when requested; may "yes" the superior	Some to moderate degree of responsibility to initiate accurate upward communication	Considerable responsibility felt and much initiative; group communicates all relevant information
(3) Forces leading to accurate or distorted upward information	Powerful forces to distort information and deceive superiors	Many forces to distort; also forces for honest communication	Occasional forces to distort along with many forces to communicate accurately	Virtually no forces to distort and powerful forces to communicate accurately
(4) Accuracy of upward communication via line	Tends to be inaccurate	Information that boss wants to hear flows; other information is restricted and filtered	Information that boss wants to hear flows; other information may be limited or cautiously given	Accurate

(5) Need for supplementary upward communication system

| Great need to supplement upward communication by spy system, suggestion system, and similar devices | Upward communication often supplemented by suggestion system and similar devices | Slight need for supplementary systems; suggestion systems may be used | No need for any supplementary system |

e. Sideward communication, its adequacy and accuracy

| Usually poor because of competition between peers, corresponding hostility | Fairly poor because of competition between peers | Fair to good | Good to excellent |

f. Psychological closeness of superiors to subordinates (i.e., friendliness between superiors and subordinates)

| Far apart | Can be moderately close if proper roles are kept | Fairly close | Usually very close |

(1) How well does superior know and understand problems faced by subordinates

| Has no knowledge or understanding of problems of subordinates | Has some knowledge and understanding of problems of subordinates | Knows and understands problems of subordinates quite well | Knows and understands problems of subordinates very well |

(2) How accurate are the perceptions by superiors and subordinates of each other?

Often in error | Often in error on some points | Moderately accurate | Usually quite accurate

4. Character of interaction-influence process

a. Amount and character of interaction

Little interaction and always with fear and distrust | Little interaction and usually with some condescension by superiors; fear and caution by subordinates | Moderate interaction, often with fair amount of confidence and trust | Extensive, friendly interaction with high degree of confidence and trust

b. Amount of cooperative teamwork present

None | Relatively little | A moderate amount | Very substantial amount throughout the organization

c. Extent to which subordinates can influence the goals, methods, and activity of their units and departments
(1) As seen by superiors

None | Virtually none | Moderate amount | A great deal

APPENDIX (Continued)

(2) As seen by subordinates	None except through "informal organization" or via unionization	Little except through "informal organization" or via unionization	Moderate amount both directly and via unionization (where it exists)	Substantial amount both directly and via unionization (where it exists)
d. Amount of actual influence which superiors can exercise over the goals, activity, and methods of their units and departments	Believed to be substantial but actually moderate unless capacity to exercise severe punishment is present	Moderate to somewhat more than moderate, especially for higher levels in organization	Moderate to substantial, especially for higher levels in organization	Substantial but often done indirectly, as, for example, by superior building effective interaction-influence system
e. Extent to which an effective structure exists enabling one part of organization to exert influence upon other parts	Effective structure virtually not present	Limited capacity exists; influence exerted largely via vertical lines and primarily downward	Moderately effective structure exist; influence exerted largely through vertical lines	Highly effective structure exists enabling exercise of influence in all directions
5. Character of decision-making process **a.** At what level in organization are decisions formally made?	Bulk of decisions at top of organization	Policy at top, many decisions within prescribed framework made at lower levels but usually checked with top before action	Broad policy decisions at top, more specific decisions at lower levels	Decision making widely done throughout organization, although well integrated through linking process provided by overlapping groups

b. How adequate and accurate is the information available for decision making at the place where the decisions are made?

Information is generally inadequate and inaccurate	Information is often somewhat inadequate and inaccurate	Reasonably adequate and accurate information available	Relatively complete and accurate information available based both on measurements and efficient flow of information in organization

c. To what extent are decision makers aware of problems, particularly those at lower levels in the organization?

Often are unaware or only partially aware	Aware of some, unaware of others	Moderately aware of problems	Generally quite well aware of problems

d. Extent to which technical and professional knowledge is used in decision making

Used only if possessed at higher levels	Much of what is available in higher and middle levels is used	Much of what is available in higher, middle, and lower levels is used	Most of what is available anywhere within the organization is used

APPENDIX (*Continued*)

e. Are decisions made at the best level in the organization as far as

(1) Availability of the most adequate and accurate information bearing on the decision

| Decisions usually made at levels appreciably higher than levels where most adequate and accurate information exists | Decisions often made at levels appreciably higher than levels where most adequate and accurate information exists | Some tendency for decisions to be made at higher levels than where most adequate and accurate information exists | Overlapping groups and group decision processes tend to push decisions to point where information is most adequate or to pass the relevant information to the decision-making point |

(2) The motivational consequences (i.e., does the decision-making process help to create the necessary motivations in those persons who have to carry out the decision?)

| Decision-making contributes little or nothing to the motivation to implement the decision, usually yields adverse motivation | Decision making contributes relatively little motivation | Some contribution by decision making to motivation to implement | Substantial contribution by decision-making processes to motivation to implement |

Item				
f. To what extent are subordinates involved in decisions related to their work?	Not at all	Never involved in decisions; occasionally consulted	Usually are consulted but ordinarily not involved in the decision making	Are involved fully in all decisions related to their work
g. Is decision making based on man-to-man or group pattern of operation? Does it encourage or discourage teamwork?	Man-to-man only, discourages teamwork	Man-to-man almost entirely, discourages teamwork	Both man-to-man and group, partially encourages teamwork	Largely based on group pattern, encourages teamwork
6. Character of goal setting or ordering — a. Manner in which usually done	Orders issued	Orders issued, opportunity to comment may or may not exist	Goals are set or orders issued after discussion with subordinates of problems and planned action	Except in emergencies, goals are usually established by means of group participation
b. To what extent do the different hierarchical levels tend to strive for high performance goals?	High goals pressed by top, generally resisted by subordinates	High goals sought by top and often resisted moderately by subordinates	High goals sought by higher levels but with occasional resistance by lower levels	High goals sought by all levels, with lower levels sometimes pressing for higher goals than top levels

c. Are there forces to accept, resist, or reject goals?	Goals are overtly accepted but are covertly resisted strongly	Goals are overtly accepted but often covertly resisted to at least a moderate degree	Goals are overtly accepted but at times with some covert resistance	Goals are fully accepted both overtly and covertly
7. Character of control processes				
a. At what hierarchical levels in organization does major or primary concern exist with regard to the performance of the control function?	At the very top only	Primarily or largely at the top	Primarily at the top but some shared feeling of responsibility felt at middle and to a lesser extent at lower levels	Concern for performance of control functions likely to be felt throughout organization
b. How accurate are the measurements and information used to guide and perform the control function, and to what extent do forces exist in the organization to distort and falsify this information?	Very strong forces exist to distort and falsify; hence measurements and information are often incomplete and inaccurate	Fairly strong forces exist to distort and falsify; hence measurements and information are often incomplete and inaccurate	Some pressure to protect self and colleagues and hence some pressures to distort; information is only moderately complete and contains some inaccuracies	Strong pressures to obtain complete and accurate information to guide own behavior and behavior of own and related work groups; hence information and measurements tend to be complete and accurate

c. Extent to which the review and control functions are concentrated

Highly concentrated in top management	Relatively highly concentrated, with some delegated control to middle and lower levels	Moderate downward delegation of review and control processes; lower as well as higher levels perform these tasks	Review and control done at all levels with lower units at times imposing more vigorous reviews and tighter controls than top management

d. Extent to which there is an informal organization present or opposing goals of formal organization

Informal organization present and opposing goals of formal organization	Informal organization usually present and partially resisting goals	Informal organization may be present and may either support or partially resist goals of formal organization	Informal and formal organization are one and the same; hence all social forces support efforts to achieve organization's goals

e. Extent to which control data (e.g., accounting, productivity, cost, etc.) are used for self-guidance or group problem solving by managers and non-supervisory employees, or used by superiors in a punitive, policing manner

Used for policing and in punitive manner	Used for policing coupled with reward and punishment, sometimes punitively; used somewhat for guidance but in accord with orders	Used for policing with emphasis usually on reward but with some punishment; used for guidance in accord with orders; some use also for self-guidance	Used for self-guidance and for coordinated problem solving and guidance; not used punitively

APPENDIX (Concluded)

8. Performance goals and training

a. Level of performance goals which superiors seek to have organization achieve

Seek average goals	Seek high goals	Seek very high goals	Seek to achieve extremely high goals

b. Extent to which you have been given the kind of management training you desire

Have received no management training of kind I desire	Have received some management training of kind I desire	Have received quite a bit of management training of kind I desire	Have received a great deal of management training of kind I desire

c. Adequacy of training resources provided to assist you in training your subordinates

Training resources provided are only fairly good	Training resources provided are good	Training resources provided are very good	Training resources provided are excellent

chapter thirteen

Management Science
Foundations

INTRODUCTION

In this section of the book we shall examine the third major school of thought in management—the Management Science school. The idea of applying scientific methodology to large-scale management problems is not new. In fact, the central idea can be traced back as far as the 18th and 19th centuries.[1] During that period, Eli Whitney, the inventor of the cotton gin, was using a scientific approach to develop a model of manufacturing costs to enable more efficient use of the cotton gin. However, the recognized field of management science has formally existed for only the last 20 years. It was during this period that the individuals, now associated with this field, began to have a noticeable impact on the solution of complex military and business problems through the use of engineering and mathematical skills. Also during this period, such professional societies as the Institute of Management Sciences and the Operations Research Society of America were formed. It is such groups as these that we associate with the management science school of thought.

Boundaries of Management Science

As is often the case with an emerging body of knowledge, there is much confusion over just what it includes. Since its early development is

---

[1] For an excellent discussion of the historical background of management science, see Robert E. Schellenberger, *Managerial Analysis* (Homewood, Ill.: Richard D. Irwin, Inc., 1969), Chapter 3.

rarely a consciously planned effort, there may even be numerous approaches to studying the same phenomena which differ little except, perhaps, in name. This appears to have been the case with management science. Numerous synonyms for the term management science appear, such as managerial analysis, operations research, operational research, operations analysis, and systems analysis. We shall assume that they are all the same, since they all share in common the desire to apply scientific analysis to managerial problems in all types of organizations. Hence we place them all in the management science school of thought.

The activities of management scientists have been characterized by an emphasis on the mathematical modeling of systems. Applications by operations research specialists, mostly confined to the production segment of the business, began after World War II. During World War II, these individuals had successfully solved a number of military problems ranging from those of a logistical nature (equipment and troop movements) to developing strategy for submarine warfare.[2] As a result, after the war, operations research caught on quickly in some of the more progressive firms in the United States. Such companies as E. I. DuPont de Nemours and H. J. Heinz pioneered the use of early operations research applications. However, it was not until a few of those bolder firms had tried it with success that civilian operations research made any major headway in the United States.

It is not coincidental that computer technology developed in a parallel fashion with the field of management science. Undoubtedly there would be negligible interest in the field of management science (except perhaps for some applied mathematicians), if it were not for the vast data-generating capacity and computational ability of high-speed computers. The electronic computer has gone through its own developmental stages from a point where it could only process routine data to the point where it can now effectively assist in the conduct of management science studies. This increasing availability, understanding, and use of the electronic computer has made it possible to turn heretofore theoretical mathematical models into everyday here-and-now practical decision aids.

While it is difficult to place clear boundary lines around the field of management science, it is possible to distinguish certain characteristics of its approach. It is generally agreed that most management science applications possess the following characteristics:[3]

1. *A Primary Focus on Decision Making.* The principal end result of the analysis must have direct implications for management action. In

---

[2] An excellent reference on this subject is E. S. Quade (ed.), *Analysis for Military Decisions* (Chicago: Rand McNally & Co., 1964).

[3] Harvey M. Wagner, *Principles of Management Science* (Englewood Cliffs, N.J.: Prentice-Hall, Inc., 1970), p. 5.

other words, it must aid the manager to better perform his functions of planning and controlling.

2. *An Appraisal Resting on Economic Effectiveness Criteria.* A comparison of the various feasible actions must be based on measurable values that reflect the future well-being of the firm. Examples of such measured variables include costs, revenues, and rates of return on investment.

3. *Reliance on a Formal Mathematical Model.* These models are actually possible solutions to the problems, which are stated in mathematical form. The procedures for manipulating the data must be so explicit that another analyst can derive the same results from the same data. This *replicability* requirement is not new to the reader who saw in the previous section that this was also a major requirement of the behavioral science approach to management. In fact, replication is the keynote of scientific analysis.

4. *Dependence on an Electronic Computer.* This is actually a requirement necessitated by either the complexity of the mathematical model, the volume of data to be manipulated, or the magnitude of computations needed to implement the model. In the chapters in this section we shall examine simplified mathematical models in which all computations can be performed by hand. However, the reader will see that even repetitious use of these simplified models would be greatly aided by a computer. Obviously, when the models are applied in a real situation where the number of variables is great, a computer is a necessity.

The Role of Mathematical Models in Management Science

Thus far, we have made several references to mathematical models. In fact, they are the major characteristics of the management science approach. However, we have purposely avoided defining what a mathematical model is until now. Before doing so, let us examine two points.

In the previous section of the book we saw that experimentation is an important part of the scientific approach. It is through experimentation that the scientist either accepts or rejects his hypotheses. However, it is rare, if ever, that the company can perform what would be considered a *bona fide* scientific experiment to test the feasibility of taking a particular action. The practicalities of the business world preclude any manager from doing this. In other words, a manager cannot usually experiment with his inventory to determine which level minimizes carrying costs and ordering costs, or he cannot experiment with his advertising budget to determine which combination of media (e.g., radio, TV, magazines) produces the most favorable sales results. However, an accurately constructed mathematical model enables the decision maker to experiment with possible solutions without interrupting the ongoing system. If the model accurately depicts the ongoing system, it will provide the decision maker with the results of his proposed solution. In other words, it will react as the real system would react; and, therefore, the decision maker can simulate the behavior of the real system. It is this experimental role of mathematical models which makes them useful to business decision makers.[4]

While there are several different types of models, the emphasis on mathematical models in the management science school should be clear. In order to utilize scientific analysis, one must be "quantitatively oriented." Because, one of the major characteristics and prerequisites of scientific inquiry is quantitative measurement. Thus the models examined in this section of the book are quantitative or mathematical in nature.

Understanding the role of mathematical models in the management science school, we can define exactly what a mathematical model is: *A mathematical model is a simplified representation of the relevant aspects of an actual system or process.*

At this point, the value of a simplified representation of a business process may be questioned. This is why we have included the two words "relevant aspects" in our definition. It is obvious that the value of any model depends on how well it represents the system or process under consideration. A highly simplified model that accurately describes a system or process still provides a more clearly understood starting point than a vague conception which a manager creates in his mind. Such a model forces the manager to consider systematically the variables in the problem and the relationships among the variables. Thus, forcing the manager to formalize his thinking reduces the possibility of overlooking important factors or giving too much weight to minor factors.

In reality, the reader is probably more familiar with models for decision making than he thinks. The accounting equation, $A = L + C$, is a mathematical model. It is a mathematical model showing a simplified relationship between assets, liabilities, and capital. It does not resemble the actual system physically; but it does behave as the real system behaves. It is an abstraction of the financial condition of a particular enterprise at a *given moment of time*. On the other hand, the income statement is also a mathematical model in that it is an abstraction of the operations of a business *over a period of time*.

In conclusion, instead of studying the actual system, the manager studies a mathematical model of the system. This enables him to manipulate variables in order to determine the effects such changes will have on the overall performance of the actual system. The manager can, therefore, experiment on the properly constructed model and predict the effect such changes will have. Thus, the complexity of the task facing the manager

---

[4] For an additional discussion of management's use of mathematical models, see Russell L. Ackoff and Patrick Rivett, *A Manager's Guide to Operations Research* (New York: John Wiley and Sons, Inc., 1963).

and the impossibility of experimenting on the actual system make the use of mathematical models highly desirable. However, this same complexity makes the task of building accurate models extremely difficult. Since the hallmark of the management science approach is the construction of mathematical models, the remainder of this chapter will be devoted to this topic.

MANAGEMENT SCIENCE AND THE MANAGEMENT FUNCTIONS

Before proceeding in this section of the text, one final comment is in order concerning the relationship between management science and the management functions of *planning* and *controlling*. Before the advent of mathematical models and the electronic computer, managers were faced with the problem of planning and controlling their firm's operations. And they would still have to perform these functions, if the field of management science did not exist today. The point we are trying to make is that management science *is not* management. Mathematical models are useful only insofar as they are an *aid* to the manager as he performs the functions of planning and controlling. One of the goals of management science is to enable the manager to be a better planner and/or controller.

In addition, the reader should not construe our discussions in this section of the book as implying that mathematical models can provide the entire basis for *all* management decisions. This is inconceivable. We saw in the prior section (Behavioral School of Management) that there are many kinds of management decisions that should not or cannot rest solely on the manipulation of quantitative data. In fact, we shall see that successful implementation of a mathematical model must apply behavioral as well as mathematical science, because the resultant solution must be implemented by human beings.

TYPES OF MATHEMATICAL MODELS

Before a manager can understand, evaluate, and utilize mathematical models, he must be aware of the major types of these models. Mathematical models may be classified by the *purpose* of the model (descriptive or normative) or by the *types of variables* included in the model (deterministic or stochastic).

Descriptive and Normative Models

A *descriptive model* is one which describes how a system works. That is, it describes things as they are and makes no value judgments about the particular phenomena being studied. Many times a model is constructed solely to be a description of a real-world phenomenon in mathematical terms. This model can then be used to display the situation more clearly or to indicate how it can be changed. Descriptive models display the alternative choices available to the decision maker and, in some cases, help the decision maker determine the consequences or outcomes of each alternative. However, a descriptive model *does not* select the best alternative.

A *normative model* is one which is specifically constructed to select the best from among alternatives based on some previously determined criteria which are also included in the model. *It tells how the system should be, in order to achieve a particular objective.* These models are also referred to as optimizing models[5] and decision models.

The two classifications—descriptive and normative—describe the purpose of the particular model. These classifications can be further broken down based on the types of variables included in the model.

Deterministic and Stochastic Models

A model is *deterministic* when the law of chance plays no role. In other words, the model contains no probabilistic considerations. All of the factors taken into account in the model are assumed to be exact or determinate quantities and the solution is determined by this set of exact relationships. The linear programming model discussed in Chapter

FIGURE 13–1

Types of Mathematical Models

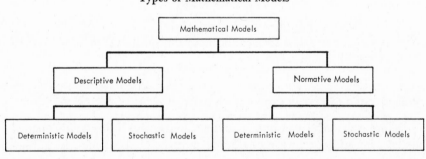

16 is a deterministic model because all relationships are exact and all cost data are known. In other words, in a deterministic model, we assume conditions of certainty.

Once chance or random variables are introduced, the model is said

---

[5] Clifford H. Springer, Robert E. Herlihy, and Robert I. Beggs. *Advanced Methods and Models* (Homewood, Ill.: Richard D. Irwin, Inc., 1964), p. 12.

to be a *stochastic model.* A stochastic model is based on the mathematics of statistics. Conditions of uncertainty are introduced in the model based often on observations of real events. Stochastic models may be referred to as probabilistic models. We can summarize what we have said thus far in Figure 13–1 which indicates that a mathematical model may be either descriptive or normative in purpose and contain either deterministic or stochastic variables.

In the remainder of this section, the reader will be introduced to various management science models. Before proceeding however, let us briefly examine some of the more popular mathematical models in the management science school.[6]

MANAGEMENT SCIENCE MODELS

Allocation Models

Allocation models are used in a variety of business situations in which numerous possible candidates or activities are all competing for limited resources. These models enable the decision maker to allocate scarce resources to maximize some given objective. The resources may be available time in certain departments, which the production manager must allocate over several different products in order to maximize profit. The resource may be advertising dollars which the marketing manager must allocate over several different advertising media in order to gain the most exposure for his product(s). In each case, the manager wishes to find the optimum way to allocate the scarce resources, given certain objectives and constraints.

One of the most widely used allocation models is the linear programming model. We shall see later that linear programming expresses the objective to be achieved in the form of a mathematical function, the value of which is to be maximized or minimized. Constraints are introduced in the form of equalities and/or inequalities. The constraints reduce the number of feasible alternatives. A powerful linear programming procedure known as the simplex method searches the alternatives in order to find the particular one that maximizes or minimizes the value of the objective function. We shall see that the linear programming model is normative in purpose and contains deterministic variables.

---

[6] Several of these models are discussed in this section of the text. If the reader wishes additional sources, the various models are also covered in excellent fashion in Richard I. Levin and C. A. Kirkpatrick, *Quantitative Approaches to Management* (New York: McGraw-Hill Book Co., 1965); Harold Bierman, Charles Bonini, and Warren Hausman, *Quantitative Analysis for Business Decisions* (Homewood, Ill.: Richard D. Irwin, Inc., 1969); and Martin K. Starr, *Management: A Modern Approach* (New York: Harcourt Brace Jovanovich, Inc., 1971).

Brand-Switching Models

One of the most important measuring devices, used by marketing executives in determining the success or failure of their efforts, is the share of the market secured by a product. Obviously, a marketing manager is constantly seeking ways to increase his product's share of the market or to at least prevent the existing share of the market from declining. In order to do this, the executive must have some idea of the behavior of consumers both in terms of their brand loyalty and their switching from one brand to another. Brand-switching models provide management with such information. Brand-switching models can be considered descriptive in purpose and containing stochastic variables.

Waiting-Line Models

In the production department, workers standing idle at the service facility waiting in line to requisition needed tools or raw materials cost money. In such a situation, the manager faces a dilemma. He would like to minimize worker idle time, but on the other hand, he cannot afford to provide a great number of service facilities. Thus he must strike a balance between the costs of additional facilities and worker idle time. In other business operations there are many examples of processes which generate waiting lines. These lines are often referred to as queues. For example, housewives often wait in long lines in a supermarket, while the husband may have to wait in line at a fuel pump in a service station. In many instances, customers become irritable when faced with long periods of waiting; and, if it becomes excessive, the business may lose customers. Waiting-line models, which are descriptive in purpose and contain stochastic variables, enable managers to reach effective decisions for facilities planning.

Inventory Models

In short, inventory models provide answers to two questions: "How much?" and "When?" Just as the firm is concerned with obtaining goods to be sold at the most favorable price, it must also be concerned with the point at which orders are placed for repeat goods and the quantity of each order. On one hand, enough inventory must be available at all times to insure that there are no lost sales or loss of customer goodwill due to stockouts; but on the other hand, frequent orders result in increased costs such as storage costs resulting from carrying an excessive average inventory. Ordering and carrying costs behave in such a way that one increases while the other decreases. In all cases, ordering costs decrease while storage costs increase as a function of average inventory levels. The inventory model which is normative in purpose and contains deterministic variables enables the manager to determine the economic order quantity (EOQ) and the optimum reorder point.

It should be noted that when the manager is confronted with uncertainty, such as lead time and usage rates, the inventory model can be modified to include probabilistic elements. However, we shall not be concerned with that in this text.

Simulation Models

In many situations management problems are so complex that they cannot be depicted by a standard mathematical model. Simulation involves constructing a model which replicates some aspect of the firm's operation; then performing step-by-step computations with the model; thus duplicating the manner in which the actual system might perform. An individual simulation can be thought of as an experiment upon a model. Numerous trials or experiments are performed until a workable satisficing solution, rather than an optimal solution, is reached. This experimental nature of simulation is an important advantage because the system can be studied under a wide variety of conditions which might be impossible using the actual real world system. In this respect, all mathematical models involve some degree of simulation. Simulation models are descriptive in purpose and contain stochastic variables.

CONSTRUCTING MATHEMATICAL MODELS

At this time, we shall examine the steps that can be taken to insure a logical approach for formulating and constructing mathematical models. While several approaches are available we suggest the following series of steps:[7]
1. define and formulate problem,
2. construct model,
3. solve model,
4. test solution,
5. develop necessary controls for the solution, and
6. implement solution.

Define and Formulate Problem

This first step in the model-building process lays the foundation for all of the following steps. If a problem is ill-defined or loosely formulated, any model constructed on such a weak foundation will be of little or no

---

[7] See C. W. Churchman, R. L. Ackoff, and E. L. Arnoff, *Introduction to Operations Research* (New York: John Wiley and Sons, Inc., 1957), Chapter 1. Also, see James H. Donnelly, Jr. and John M. Ivancevich, *Analysis for Marketing Decisions* (Homewood, Ill.: Richard D. Irwin, Inc., 1970), Chapter 2.

value. A problem that is well defined and formulated is one in which all of the elements are clearly delineated. This includes determination of the objective(s) to be achieved, identification of alternative courses of action, and all components of the particular problem.

The types of problems faced by managers vary in complexity. Some may be relatively definable with easily identifiable variables which behave with a high degree of certainty. On the other hand, a problem may contain a great number of interrelated variables which are probabilistic in nature. Thus we can array problems on a continuum from relatively simple and organized to complex and disorganized, with varying degrees

FIGURE 13–2

Problem Solving Continuum

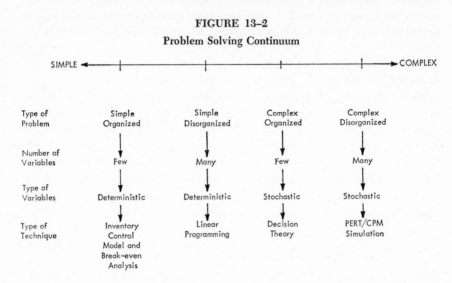

of disorganization for each type. This allows us to delineate four general classes of problems.[8] These are demonstrated diagramatically in Figure 13–2.

1. Simple and Organized. These problems have only a small number of variables which contain no probabilistic considerations (i.e., they are deterministic). An example of such a model is the inventory model in which all variables are exact or deterministic quantities.

2. Simple but Disorganized. These types of problems contain many variables, but all of the variables are deterministic. Linear programming

---

[8] This discussion adapted from: *Tentative Recommendations for the Undergraduate Mathematics Program of Students of the Biological, Management and Social Sciences* (Berkeley, California: Committee on the Undergraduate Program in Mathematics, 1964), p. 12. Also see Max D. Richards and Paul S. Greenlaw, *Management Decision Making* (Homewood, Ill.: Richard D. Irwin, Inc., 1966), Chapter 19; and Donnelly and Ivancevich, *op. cit.,* Chapter 2.

models are used under these conditions. Such models have a wide variety of use for several types of management problems which fall into this classification.

3. Complex and Organized. These types of problems contain a small number of stochastic variables. Many management problems fall into this class. Decision theory is useful for problems of this type.

4. Complex and Disorganized. These types of problems contain a great number of stochastic variables. Constructing optimizing models for such problems is extremely difficult. One aid to managers facing such problems has been the electronic computer, which has increased management use of such techniques as PERT/CPM and simulation.

Unfortunately for the business manager, the majority of the problems he faces tend to be complex and disorganized. This is because most business problems consist of a large number of interrelated variables which are probabilistic in nature and few normative models deal with this class of problem.

What then can the manager do in order to gain the benefits of these types of models? The only alternative available is to attempt to reformulate complex disorganized problems into more simple and organized problems. In this way they become more manageable and more readily adaptable to normative models. Obviously this task is not an easy one because in our attempt to simplify a problem we may eliminate one or more important variables, thereby resulting in a model solution which is of little or no practical value. Generally, there are three ways in which complex problems can be redefined into more manageable ones.[9]

1. Assume Certainty. In some instances it may be permissible to assume certainty in a problem, although some of the variables may be stochastic in nature. This approach is often used when facing inventory problems. In such problems the assumption is made that the demand for the product is known.

2. Simplify Relationships. Here we assume that the relationships between variables are much simpler than they are in reality. When utilizing linear programming it is assumed that the relationships among variables are linear, when in fact they probably are nonlinear.

3. Isolate Operations. Here we attempt to isolate a particular operation or segment of the business. We then seek to optimize the output from that segment and assume that the remaining operations of the firm are not adversely affected.

Thus, the manager should, wherever feasible, seek to break down complex problems into more manageable problems where the likelihood is greater that some problem-solving technique can be used.

---

[9] Richards and Greenlaw, *op. cit.,* pp. 531–32.

Construct Model

After the problem has been clearly formulated and defined, the model construction phase begins. This involves expressing the elements of the problem in mathematical form. Clearly, this is a vital phase. What is important here is that the model constructed responds in the same fashion as the real system. Basically, there are three elements of a mathematical model:[10]

1. Components.   These are the parts of the model. They may be firms, households, warehouses, costs, media, and any other phenomena which is a part of the real system.

2. Variables.   These relate in one way or another to the components of the model. They are often classified as *input variables* which arise outside the component and must be fed into it (e.g., inventory, raw materials); *status variables* which describe the state of a component (e.g., salary, income, education, age); and *output variables* which are anything generated by a component (e.g., costs, demand).

3. Relationships.   These specify how the values of different variables are related to each other. For example, inventory models specify the relationship between ordering costs and carrying costs.

The manager is faced with the task of determining all of the relevant components which affect the functioning of the system under study and arriving at measurable variables to represent these factors. Finally, he must determine the relationships among the variables and express them in mathematical form.

Solve Model

Once the model has been constructed, the next step is to arrive at a solution to the model. For a normative model, this involves mathematical techniques for arriving at the best strategy or alternative. In the case of complex linear programming problems, this may involve numerous computations. For computations the electronic computer has been used very successfully. In the case of a descriptive model where usually there is no solution, the model can be termed "solved" when it accurately describes the system under study. This is arrived at by manipulating the model until this point is reached. Later in the text this shall be illustrated when we examine break-even and inventory control models which are descriptive in purpose.

Test Solution

Once the model is solved, the solution should be tested before it is applied to a large segment of the firm's operations. The reason for this

[10] Guy Orcutt, "Simulation of Economic Systems," *The American Economic Review,* vol. 50 (December, 1960), pp. 893–907.

should be clear; testing the solution enables management to determine the effect of the model on a small scale, and if any errors are discovered, the model can be altered accordingly and a new solution obtained. For example, the solution to an inventory problem could be tested on a small scale using perhaps one warehouse or store or the solution to a distribution problem tested using only one plant and one warehouse. In this way we can gain some insight into the value of the solution and adjust accordingly if changes are necessary. Then and only then should the solution be applied on a full-scale basis.

Develop Controls

Once the model is constructed and solved, there must be a provision for *concurrent* control. In other words, the model must be carefully and continually reexamined in order to insure that the variables and relationships have not changed. Whenever there is a change in any of the variables included in the model, it may be necessary to completely revise it. There are also many forces at work which affect management decisions but over which the manager has little or no control. Thus the need for tight *monitoring* of the model is vital.

Implement Solution

After the model has been solved and tested, the solution should be implemented by or recommended to the decision maker, in cases where staff analysts have constructed the model. In any case, the decision maker must be aware of the objectives, assumptions, omissions, and limitations of the model. After this is done, further reformulation of the problem may result because of some previously overlooked factor which is deemed important. Before the solution is finally implemented, all personnel who will utilize the solution produced by the model should be made aware of the basic rationale behind the model and the advantages to be gained by implementing the solution. The manager must keep in mind at all times the behavioral ramifications involved in implementing change. These were discussed in Chapter 12. A well-constructed model may not provide its true benefit if individuals in the organization resist implementation or pay only token service to the solution provided by the model. Thus behavioral factors can vitally affect the success of management science problem solutions and must be considered by the manager.

SUMMARY

In this section of the book, the student will be introduced to the third major block of material in the field of management. Thus far, he has examined the classical school, which was concerned with the anatomy of formal organizations and the functions of the manager, and the behavioral school with its emphasis on human relations and the scientific approach to the study of human behavior. In the following chapters, he will be introduced to the management science school, with emphasis on mathematical models. While several models could be discussed, we have chosen those techniques which describe generally the nature of the management science school.

This section will begin with a discussion of decision theory which is the systematic study of decision problems and will set the stage for the discussion of other management science models—break-even models, inventory control models, linear programming models, and network models.

DISCUSSION AND REVIEW QUESTIONS

1. Discuss the similarities and differences between the behavioral science school and the management science school.

2. Evaluate the following statement: "Since a mathematical model cannot possibly include every variable that affects a problem, then it cannot be of much value as a decision aid."

3. When facing complex problems, it is often wise to break the problem down into more manageable problems which lend themselves to the use of some problem-solving technique. Create a problem which a manager might face and break it down into more manageable subproblems.

4. Mathematical models may be classified on the basis of *purpose* and on the *types of variables* included in the model. Clearly define each classification and give examples of each.

5. Assume you are the athletic director at your school. You have been bombarded with complaints about the distribution of tickets to students for basketball games. Tickets are distributed beginning four hours before each game. This creates long lines at ticket windows and much discomfort on rainy days. In addition, crowds form in the lobby, which makes seating by game time very difficult. You have decided to try and improve this system. You decide first to construct a model of the system. What would be the components, variables, and relationships in your model? Develop some alternative solutions.

6. Clearly define and discuss briefly the steps that can be taken to insure a logical approach to formulating and constructing a mathematical model.

7. In the text we said that problems could be arrayed on a continuum from very complex to very simple with varying degrees of complexity and disorganization in between. We delineated four general classes of problems using this scheme. Discuss each class in detail.

8. Generally, there are three ways in which complex problems can be redefined into more manageable ones. Discuss each one in detail.

9. After several semesters at your school, you are tired of becoming extremely irritated at registration time (long lines, closed courses, general bedlam).

You have decided that something must be done. You contact the registrar's office and offer your services as a consultant. Since they are desperate for any help they can receive, they accept your offer. You suggest that some kind of model needs to be developed. How would you go about developing this model? What would be some of the major considerations?

ADDITIONAL REFERENCES

ACKOFF, R. L. and SASIENI, M. W. *Fundamentals of Operations Research.* New York: John Wiley and Sons, Inc., 1968.

CABELL, R. W. and PHILLIPS, A. *Basic Operations Research Methods.* New York: John Wiley and Sons, Inc., 1961.

CHU, K. *Quantitative Methods for Business and Economic Analysis.* Scranton, Pa.: International Textbook Co., 1970.

CHURCHMAN, C. W., ACKOFF, R. L. and ARNOFF, E. L. *Introduction to Operations Research.* New York: John Wiley and Sons, Inc., 1957.

FORRESTER, J. W. *Industrial Dynamics.* Cambridge, Mass.: Massachusetts Institute of Technology Press, 1961.

MILLER, D. W. and STARR, M. K. *Executive Decisions and Operations Research.* Englewood Cliffs, N.J.: Prentice-Hall, Inc., 1970.

MORRIS, W. T. *Management Science.* Englewood Cliffs, N.J.: Prentice-Hall, Inc., 1968.

SCHODERBEK, P. P. *Management Systems.* New York: McGraw-Hill Book Co., 1967.

THIERAUF, R. J. and GROSSE, R. A. *Decision Making through Operations Research.* New York: John Wiley and Sons, Inc., 1970.

WAGNER, H. M. *Principles of Operations Research.* Englewood Cliffs, N.J.: Prentice-Hall, Inc., 1969.

chapter fourteen

Management Science Framework for Decisions

INTRODUCTION

The management science school emphasizes that decision making is a necessary and critical phase of managing within any business organization, government agency, or educational institution. Scholars of management science stress that the crux of the manager's daily, monthly, and yearly activities is making decisions. When planning for future plant expansion, a manager is involved in the decision-making process. When deciding to promote one of six candidates, a manager is making a necessary decision. When deciding to place a particular price tag on a new product, he is involved in a critical pricing decision. The list of necessary managerial decisions is endless.

Although the manager is engaged in other activities besides decision making, a main theme of the management science school is focusing upon the "how" and "why" of decisions. A decision theory framework has been utilized in the management science and contemporary management literature.

The decision theory area has been misunderstood because of semantic conflicts and false impressions projected by various writers. The term "decision theory" has been associated with sophisticated mathematical formulas and theories. Thus many students of management believe that a background in high-powered mathematics and statistics is necessary to fully comprehend the usefulness of decision theory. The discussion in this chapter indicates that the decision theory framework can be appreciated without an in-depth background in mathematics and statistics.

Objectives, Optimization, and Suboptimization

The business manager today operates in an environment that is competitive, becoming more international, and scrutinized more closely by the government, unions, and the public. Each of these environmental factors and many others influence the ability of the manager to achieve specific objectives. The objective of management cannot be neatly classified as profit maximization. Although profit is a necessary objective of business corporations, it is only one of many. The decision-making activities of managers are directed toward achieving such often stated objectives as: (1) improving market share; (2) developing human resources; (3) creating a favorable public image; (4) producing and marketing a quality product; and (5) generating profit.

In the everyday activities of business decision making, a manager often finds himself facing a situation in which he optimizes one objective, while he suboptimizes other objectives. In an economic sense, the manager has reached the optimum state, when marginal revenue is equal to marginal costs. Whenever marginal revenue is not equivalent to marginal costs, suboptimization has occurred. The decision maker is faced with making decisions where other factors besides marginal cost and marginal revenue must be considered. For example, the morale of employees may be adversely influenced by making one decision rather than a second. Another example would be a case in which the attainment of a short-run objective such as reducing maintenance expenses may lead to the long-run consequence of increased production costs. In this case, the short-run goal was optimized at the cost of suboptimizing a long-run goal.

The multiplicity of objectives, optimization, and suboptimization can be examined in a decision theory framework. That is, the decision-making activities of a manager can be systematically studied. In this type of analysis, some of the variables involved in managerial decision making are brought into sharp focus.

Decision-Making Variables

Normally the manager is operating within an environment in which some variables are controllable and others uncontrollable. The business manager is able to control what strategy (S_i) will be selected. That is, he can initially establish a number of possible inventory levels for the month of August. Then after considering such factors as available storage space, transportation possibilities, and costs of the inventory, he will select the best inventory level. He literally controls which strategy (S_i)

will be adopted. Thus, in a decision-making context, the one major variable that is controllable is the actual choice of a strategy.

Two variables which significantly influence the consequences of selecting a strategy are the states of nature (SN_i) and competitive actions (CA_i). The term, states of nature, is used to designate the possible events which may actually occur. The most predictable state of nature facing mankind is death. The event, death, will definitely occur at some time for all human beings. The term, strategy, in a decision theory context is used to designate the action selected by a manager to cope with the occurrence of possible events. These uncontrollable factors (states of nature and/or competitive actions), plus the strategy selected, interact to yield a highly desirable, a highly unattractive, or an unclear and vague end-result. The actual end-result is the criterion which determines the degree of optimization that results from the decision.

The states of nature are completely uncontrollable from the vantage point of the manager. For example, a manufacturer of children's toys knows that the accuracy of his production forecasts will depend in large measure upon the state of the overall economy. Similarly, the executive of a tobacco corporation is faced with the problem of how much of each of the firm's products should be produced. Of course, the production forecasts are influenced by economic conditions and the government campaign against certain tobacco products.

Typically, there are a large number of possible states of nature that can occur. It would be impossible to list them all and to determine the effects that each might have on a problem-solving situation and outcome. Normally, the manager would consider only those states of nature which are most likely to occur. He would not become entangled in an endless list of uncontrollable variables which might occur. The opinions and experiences of the manager and his assistants decreases significantly the number of states of nature that are given serious consideration.

Another uncontrollable variable is the competitive action of market opponents. In a business environment, the total sales revenue received from the sale of a product, the return on capital investment, and the type of work force hired in a community will be affected by the actions of competitors. The actions and reactions of competitors are, of course, difficult to determine. Thus the activities of competitors in response to a particular strategy are perceived as being uncontrollable.

Utility of Decision

Each decision made by a manager is designed to achieve some objective or set of objectives. The outcome of each decision reached yields some form of utility to the decision maker. The form which the utility of an outcome takes may be psychological or economic. It is possible to consider utility as a subjective measure of the worth of the payoff to the manager making a decision.

The main concept to remember when discussing utility is that the reward received from each individual outcome is subjective. That is, each decision maker has his own conception of what each outcome provides him in the form of psychological gratification and/or economic benefits. To date, in the management science literature there exists no practical method which can compare in an orderly and systematic fashion the utilities of different managers. If, however, it were possible to accurately determine the utility derived by a manager for each outcome, the utility concept could then be expressed mathematically. The outcomes could be viewed as the "payoff" to the manager, which results from the interaction of strategies, states of nature, and competitive actions. This relationship in decision theory is often presented as

$$U = f(S,SN,CA)$$

which is read U is a function (f) of S,SN,CA, where U designates utility, S designates the strategy, SN designates the state of nature, and CA designates competitive actions. The two important factors to consider are that the three major variables—namely the strategy, states of nature, and competitive action—are highly interrelated and the utility of the "payoff" as perceived by the individual manager is a subjective phenomenon. The opinions, attitudes, beliefs, experiences, and intuitions of human beings may result in different selections of strategy among managers because of their different perceptions and expectations of the utility of the payoff. In a monetary sense then, the payoff in dollars can have a different utility to managers faced with similar problems.

The Value of a Payoff Matrix

In analyzing decision making in general and utility of payoffs in particular, a useful mechanism is the payoff matrix. The matrix presents, in a two-dimensional array, the payoff which results for each combination of strategy and states of nature or competitive actions. The payoffs can be expressed in monetary terms, behavioral indices, or whatever notation is applicable to the decision being considered.

To illustrate the payoff matrix procedure, only a monetary payoff (MP) will be considered in this chapter. The payoff is the amount which the manager will receive for each strategy and state of nature or competitive action combination. Table 14–1 is a schematic representation of a payoff matrix. The MP_{11} payoff matrix amount is that value the manager would receive if strategy S_1 were selected and state of nature SN_1 occurred.

The payoff matrix does not eliminate the need to make a decision. It

TABLE 14–1

Symbolic Payoff Matrix

	States of Nature				
Strategies	SN_1	SN_2	SN_3	...	SN_x
S_1	MP_{11}	MP_{12}	MP_{13}	...	MP_{1x}
S_2	MP_{21}	MP_{22}	MP_{23}	...	MP_{2x}
S_3	MP_{31}	MP_{32}	MP_{33}	...	MP_{3x}
.	.	.	.		.
.	.	.	.		.
.	.	.	.		.
S_y	MP_{y1}	MP_{y2}	MP_{y3}	...	MP_{yx}

does, however, aid the manager in organizing pertinent data upon which a decision will be based.

THE PAYOFF MATRIX AND CONDITIONS OF DECISION MAKING

In decision theory discussions, it is assumed that decisions can be made under three slightly different sets of conditions. These conditions are specifically related to the states of nature or competitive actions as perceived by the manager. The three conditions are: (1) certainty, (2) risk, and (3) uncertainty.

Certainty

When a manager knows exactly which state of nature or competitive action will occur, he is making a decision in a certainty environment. This would mean that the manager would be able to make perfectly accurate decisions, time after time, which would allow him to attain his objective(s). Of course, this type of decision-making environment is difficult, if not impossible, to find.

In reaching certainty decisions, the manager would only have to utilize a part of a typical payoff matrix. He would have to examine a number of different strategies, but only the payoffs related to the one state of nature which will occur. If the manager knew what the profit for his new burnished-gold wall plaque would be for each price and he wanted to generate the largest possible monetary return, he could reach a decision after examining Table 14–2.

Examination of the payoffs leads to the monetarily motivated decision to charge $40 for the wall plaque. This price tag would enable the manager to achieve the largest return under the certainty conditions of this particular decision.

TABLE 14–2
Payoff Matrix for Wall Plaque

Strategies (Prices)	State of Nature (Profit)
$S_1 = \$30$	\$400
$S_2 = \$40$	\$600*
$S_3 = \$50$	\$550
$S_4 = \$60$	\$540
$S_5 = \$70$	\$410

* Largest possible monetary return.

Risk

The realities of business decision making indicate that managers do not know exactly (i.e., probability of 1.00) that a particular state of nature or competitive action is going to occur. In situations where the manager does not know for certain the probability of occurrence of the states of nature or competitive actions, he is attempting to make a decision in a risk environment. In this environment, the manager has faced the same or similar set of circumstances and can construct a frequency distribution for the occurrence of states of nature or competitive actions.

In risk-oriented decision making, the concepts of conditional value (CV) and expected value (EV) are utilized. The *conditional value* is the payoff which is conditioned by the occurrence of a state of nature or competitive action. The *expected value* is the conditional value (CV_i), multiplied by the probability of occurrence (p_i). The expected value of three possible outcomes is symbolically presented as

$$EV = CV_1(p_1) + CV_2(p_2) + CV_3(p_3),$$

where $p_1 + p_2 + p_3 = 1$, since either CV_1, CV_2, or CV_3 must occur.

A simple problem of conditions of risk will illustrate how the probabilities of occurrence are employed and how the manager can move from use of conditional values to the use of expected values. As stated previously, in risk-oriented decision-making, the manager has some previous experience with a similar set of circumstances. Assume that the manager of the Tru-Grip Tire Store is attempting to determine how many 7.75x14, Tru-Grip snow tires he should stock for the winter season. For the past ten years, he has compiled a demand record for this type of snow tire. The frequencies of demand are summarized in Table 14–3.

The stocking action for this coming season is based upon a selling price of \$20 per tire, a cost per tire of \$16, and the past sales record. The manufacturer charges such a reasonable price for the tire (\$16) that they will purchase unsold tires back for only \$2.00 each. This \$2.00 figure constitutes a salvage value.

TABLE 14–3

Historical Record of Tire Demand

Tires Demanded	Years Demanded	Frequency
180	3	0.3
190	4	0.4
200	2	0.2
210	1	0.1
		1.00

The conditional values can be determined by using the following formula:

$$CV = (P \times Q_D) - (C \times Q_S) + \$2.00(Q_{ns})^1$$

If 200 tires are demanded (Q_D) and 200 tires are stocked (Q_S), the formula is applied as follows:

$$CV = (\$20 \times 200) - (\$16 \times 200) + \$2(0)$$
$$CV = \$4000 - \$3,200 + 0$$
$$CV = \$800.$$

When 200 tires are demanded and 210 tires are stocked, the conditional value is

$$CV = (\$20 \times 200) - (\$16 \times 210) + \$2(10)$$
$$CV = \$4,000 - \$3,360 + \$20$$
$$CV = \$660.$$

Each possible demand and stock combination is considered and the conditional values determined. The conditional values for each possible combination are presented in Table 14–4.

The manager after constructing a conditional value matrix would employ the historical data of demand to develop an expected value matrix.

TABLE 14–4

Conditional Values for Tire Decision
(in $)

7.75 × 14 Tire Supply	States of Nature (Demand)			
	180	190	200	210
180	720	720	720	720
190	580	760	760	760
200	440	620	800	800
210	300	480	660	840

---

[1] Q_{ns} designates quantity not sold.

The expected value for supplying 180 tires and having a demand of 180 tires would be calculated as follows:

$$EV = (CV_{180}) \times (P_{180})$$
$$EV = 720 \times 0.3$$
$$EV = 216.$$

Each of the other expected values for the various supply-demand combinations is determined in a similar manner. The expected values are summarized in Table 14–5.

TABLE 14–5

Expected Values for Tire Decision

	States of Nature (Demand)				
7.75 × 14 Tire Supply	(.3) 180	(.4) 190	(.2) 200	(.1) 210	Total Expected Value
180	216	288	144	72	720
190	174	304	152	76	706
200	132	248	160	80	620
210	90	192	132	84	498

The manager utilizing the historical demand frequency data, the conditional value matrix, and the expected value matrix has quantitative data to support a decision to stock 180 snow tires (7.75x14) for the coming winter season. This type of stocking decision would lead to the greatest expected return over the long-run. The success or astuteness of this stocking decision depends upon such factors as the actual demand for tires, the costs of purchasing the tires from the manufacturer, the salvage value, and many other market related factors. Thus, the risk inherent in this type of decision making clearly distinguishes this decision from the certainty (wall plaque) example cited previously.

Uncertainty

A number of individuals define decision theory as focusing primarily upon making decisions and improving the decision process under conditions of uncertainty.[2] The main thrust of this interpretation of decision theory is that the manager is faced with reaching a decision with no historical data concerning the probabilities of occurrence of states of

---

[2] The authors of this text, however, believe that decision theory applies to certainty and risk decision making. However, for an excellent discussion of decision theory in an uncertainty context, see Harold Bierman, Charles P. Bonini, and Warren H. Hausman, *Quantitative Analysis for Business Decisions* (Homewood, Ill.: Richard D. Irwin, Inc., 1969).

nature or competitive actions. In the uncertainty situation, the manager often resorts to the use of objective–subjective opinions about the probabilities of occurrence. The opinions are, of course, based upon past business experience of the manager and the manager's behavioral make-up. The behavioral factor is a personal characteristic. Some managers are pessimistic; some are optimistic; and others range somewhere along a pessimistic–optimistic continuum.

A number of different decision criteria have been proposed as possible explanations for the decision actions of different managers. These decision criteria include:

1. Maximizing the maximum possible payoff (e.g., profit)—the *maximax* criterion.
2. Maximizing the minimum possible payoff (e.g., profit)—the *maximin* criterion.
3. Minimizing the maximum possible regret to the decision maker— the *minimax* criterion.
4. Assuming equally likely probabilities for the occurrence of each possible state of nature or competitive action—the *insufficient reason* criterion.

Maximax Criterion

Hurwicz[3] suggested that it is best to think optimistically about the occurrence of events influencing a decision. If this philosophy is followed, the manager should select that strategy under which it is possible for him to receive the most favorable payoff. It is dangerous to employ this criterion because it ignores possible losses and the chances of making or not making a profit. In the situation in which the decision maker is completely optimistic, he would first examine the conditional value matrix. That is, he should maximize the maximum possible gain (maximax).

In order to study the various decision criteria under conditions of uncertainty, a sample problem will be consistently utilized. Assume that the management of the Jilby Food Company is considering two possible equipment investment decisions: (1) purchase the Jaco power packaging device now; or (2) purchase the Jaco power packaging device next year. The management has seriously considered two possible reactions of their main competitor if the purchasing decision is made now or next year. The competitor actions are classified as (1) purchase a competing machine now; or (2) wait until next year to purchase the new machine. The investment decision will effect the cost and profit situation of processing

---

[3] Leonid Hurwicz, "Optimality Criteria for Decision Making under Ignorance," Cowles Commission Discussion Paper, Statistics, No. 370, 1951 (mimeographed); and R. Duncan Luce and Howard Raiffa, *Games and Decisions* (John Wiley & Sons, Inc., New York, 1957).

cake mix products. The Jilby management develops a conditional value (profit) matrix (Table 14–6).

TABLE 14–6

Conditional Values for Jaco Machine
(in $ thousand)

Strategies	CA_1(Purchase Now)	CA_2(Purchase Next Year)
	Competitive Actions	
S_1*	82	48
S_2†	58	70

* Purchasing Jaco now.
† Purchasing Jaco next year.

The manager that is applying the maximax criterion would arrange the most favorable payoffs for each strategy as follows:

Strategy	Most Favorable Payoff
S_1	82
S_2	70

The manager would decide to purchase the Jaco machine now since the largest payoff ($82,000) is associated with this strategy choice.

It would be naive to assume that a manager in all situations would be completely optimistic. Thus Hurwicz developed the concept of the coefficient of optimism. This procedure allows the manager to take into account the most and least favorable payoffs and assign weights to them to correspond with his degree of optimism. For example, assume that the decision maker is 0.6 optimistic and 0.4 pessimistic about the occurrence of one competitor action versus another competitor action. Each strategy would then be examined separately with these two coefficients in mind. The mathematical procedure used to determine the sum of the weighted values for the two strategies in the investment problem is presented in Table 14–7.

TABLE 14–7

Application of Coefficients of Optimism and Pessimism
(in $ thousand)

Strategy	Most Favorable	Least Favorable	Coefficients Most Favorable 0.6	+	Least Favorable 0.4	=	Sum of Weighted Value
S_1	82	48	0.6 × (82) = 49.2		.4(48) = 19.2		68.4
S_2	70	58	0.6 × (70) = 42.0		.4(58) = 23.2		65.2

Examination of the calculations in Table 14–7 illustrates that it would be more favorable to select S_1 (purchase the machine now). In the present example, coincidentally both the completely optimistic and cautiously optimistic manager would decide to invest in the new power packaging machine now.

Maximin Criterion

There are managers who make decisions believing that only the worst possible outcome can occur. Wald proposed that this type of pessimism results in the belief that a manager should select that strategy which allows him to maximize the least favorable payoff.[4]

The manager with the pessimistic state of mind would examine Table 14–6 and isolate the minimum payoffs for each strategy. This separation and review would lead the manager to select S_2. He would not

Strategy	Least Favorable Payoff
S_1	48
S_2	58

purchase the Jaco machine this year, but would instead wait until next year.

In the maximax criterion case, it was assumed that a manager may be cautiously optimistic. That is, the most favorable and least favorable payoffs are weighted (probability introduced). Wald, however, in the maximin case, fails to analyze the partially pessimistic manager. The manager is thought to be completely pessimistic. This failure to weigh the degree of pessimism of the manager is a major weakness of the maximin analysis.

Minimax Criterion

If the manager selects a strategy, and a state of nature or competitive action occurs that does not enable him to receive the most favorable payoff, he experiences regret. The manager is regretful that his strategy selection did not lead to the best payoff. Savage introduced the minimax criterion to clarify the decision process which involves regret.[5]

Once the manager makes a strategy choice and the state of nature or competitive action has occurred, he receives the payoff. If the manager had known which of the various states of nature or competitive actions would occur, he would select the strategy that led to no regrets. Thus,

---

[4] A more complete discussion of the maximin criterion is presented in David W. Miller and Martin K. Starr, *The Structure of Human Decisions* (Englewood Cliffs, N.J.: Prentice-Hall, Inc., 1967), p. 116.

[5] L. J. Savage, "The Theory of Statistical Decision," *Journal of the American Statistical Association*, vol. 46 (March, 1951), pp. 55–67.

managerial regret is defined as the payoff for each strategy under every state of nature or competitive action subtracted from the most favorable payoff that is possible with the occurrence of this event. For example, in Table 14–8 the most favorable payoff under CA_1 is 82; if the manager selected S_1, he would have 0 regret for his decision ($82 - 82 = 0$). However, if S_2 were selected and CA_1 occurred, the regret to the manager would be 24 ($82 - 58 = 24$).

TABLE 14–8

Minimax Regret Matrix
(in $ thousand)

Strategies	CA_1	CA_2	Maximum Regret
S_1	0	22	22
S_2	24	0	24

A minimax regret matrix is presented in Table 14–8. When the manager is attempting to minimize his maximum regret, he would select S_1. This selection indicates that no matter which competitive action occurs, the manager will never have a regret of more than $22,000. If he selected S_2, he would have a regret of $24,000.

Insufficient-Reason Criterion

The three preceding decision criteria assumed that, without any previous experience, it is not worthwhile to assign probabilities to the states of nature or competitive actions. One well-known concept, however, is utilized in introducing probability into decision making under conditions of uncertainty. This is referred to as the insufficient-reason criterion.[6] This criterion states that, if the manager does not know the probabilities of occurrence for the various states of nature and competitive actions, he should assume that they are all equally likely to occur. In other words, assign equal probabilities to each competitive action. Symbolically, this is represented for a strategy, S_1, in the general case as follows:

$$EV_{s_1} = \frac{1}{n}(CV_{11} + CV_{12} + \cdots + CV_{1n}).$$

The symbol n in the formula designates the competitive actions and the CV's designate the conditional values under each of the competitive ac-

[6] This criterion is also referred to as Bayes' postulate. See Robert Schlaifer, *Probability and Statistics for Business Decisions* (New York: McGraw-Hill Book Co., Inc., 1959), p. 50.

tions for S_1. The insufficient reason criterion applied to Table 14–6 values yields for S_1

$$EV_{S_1} = \frac{1}{2}(82 + 48) = 65$$

and for S_2

$$EV_{S_2} = \frac{1}{2}(58 + 70) = 64.$$

The manager is faced with a close decision but would select S_1 because the largest expected payoff is 65 as opposed to 64 for S_2.

A Review of Strategy Choices

The four decision criteria used for the sample problem illustrate that both S_1 and S_2 are selected. The criterion being utilized affects the type of decision being made. The completely optimistic and cautiously optimistic manager would purchase the Jaco machine now. The pessimistic manager would wait until next year. The regret-oriented manager and the manager assigning equal probabilities would decide to purchase the machine now.

The sample problem employing only two strategies and two competitive actions indicates that when a manager must reach a decision under uncertainty conditions, there is no "one best" criterion to employ. The choice of a particular criterion is a personalistic phenomenon. In business organizations, all types of philosophies concerning decision making exist ranging from the complete optimist to the complete pessimist.

THE USE OF DECISION THEORY IN PRACTICE

In the preceding discussion of decision-making criteria, it was easy to see that the decision theory framework can provide the manager with a systematic method for analyzing problems.[7] This is one of the practical advantages of decision theory. It literally encourages the manager to discover and enumerate potential strategies, states of nature, and competitive actions.

The decision theory framework forces the manager to consider the relationships between organizational objectives and strategies, states of nature, and competitive actions. This type of examination allows the manager to cope in mathematical terms with many possible combinations of relationships. In fact, by placing the problem in a decision theory framework (i.e., using conditional value and expected value matrices), the manager is able to utilize computers in a systematic manner. The

---

[7] For another discussion of decision theory, see Stephen H. Archer, "The Structure of Management Decision Theory," *Academy of Management Journal,* vol. 7 (December, 1964), pp. 269–87.

development of computers and the use of a systematic decision theory framework has allowed the manager to study problems with enormous numbers of strategies, states of nature, and competitive actions.

In discussing the role of management, the management science school uses as its central focal point the decision-making process. Decision theory enables us to study systematically how managers think about decision making. The framework is only a step in the direction of attempting to understand how decisions are made and how decision making can be improved.

DISCUSSION AND REVIEW QUESTIONS

1. The stock of the Payoff Corporation has paid dividends of $1.60 per share in 13 of the last 20 dividend payments. The other seven times, it has paid $1.40. What is the expected dividend?

2. Discuss what is meant by the statement that each decision situation and outcome has a specific utility for each manager.

3. Briefly describe the type of manager that would be most inclined to employ a maximax criterion—a maximin criterion.

4. The manager of the Mary and Slim Cosmetics Company is planning to place a price tag on his new dandruff-ending hair rinse. The main competitor of Mary and Slim is the Baldy Clinical Corporation. Baldy is watching the commercial pricing program with interest. The manager of Mary and Slim has narrowed his price down to three possibilities and believes that Baldy may resort to one of three actions when the new hair rinse reaches the market. The three competitor actions are (1) lower the price of a close substitute (CA_1); (2) do nothing (CA_2); or (3) intensely advertise the Baldy current hair rinse product (CA_3). From these assumptions and his knowledge of the market place, the manager develops a conditional value table.

Conditional Values for Hair Rinse Product
(in $ thousand)

	Competitive Actions		
Strategies	CA_1	CA_2	CA_3
S_1 − $1.98	50	59	58
S_2 − $2.25	62	40	60
S_3 − $2.40	41	49	70

a) What would the maximax choice be?
b) What would the minimax choice be?
c) What would the maximin choice be?
d) What would the insufficient reason choice be?
e) If the decision maker is interested in optimizing profit, what would

his choice be if he subjectively assigned probabilities of 0.3 to CA_1, 0.4 to CA_2, and 0.3 to CA_3?

5. A dairy store manager observes the daily sales of skim milk for a 100-day period. He develops the table of sales presented below.

Skim Milk Sales

Quantities Purchased	Number of Days
40	20
50	15
70	15
100	30
120	20

The milk sells for $.30 a quart and the cost to the store manager of securing the milk from the dairy is $0.20.

a) If 70 units are stocked every day, what will be the firm's expected profit per day over the long run?

b) Using the data presented in the table, what quantity (40, 50, 70, 100, or 120) should be purchased every day to maximize long-run profits?

6. Why is it difficult to assume that many business decisions are made under conditions of certainty?

7. What decision-making factors are not presented in a payoff matrix?

8. An analysis and forecast of next year's sales results in the following probability distribution:

Total Demand	Probability
1000 units	0.20
1200 units	0.20
1400 units	0.40
1600 units	0.20

The price per unit is $58. The cost of the product is $38. If the product is not sold during the year, it is worthless.

a) Prepare a table of conditional values for the different events.

b) Prepare a table of expected values, and indicate the optimum choice if management is attempting to optimize profits.

ADDITIONAL REFERENCES

BAUMOL, W. J. *Economic Theory and Operations Analysis*, 2nd ed. Englewood Cliffs, N.J.: Prentice-Hall, Inc., 1966.

BROSS, I. D. F. *Design for Decision*. New York: The Macmillan Company, 1953.

HEIN, L. W. *The Quantitative Approach to Managerial Decisions*. Englewood Cliffs, N.J.: Prentice-Hall, Inc., 1967.

MAGEE, J. F. "Decision Trees for Decision-Making," *Harvard Business Review*, 42 (1964), 72–75.

MORGAN, B. W. *An Introduction to Bayesian Statistical Decision Processes*. Englewood Cliffs, N.J.: Prentice-Hall, Inc., 1968.

RAIFFA, H. *Decision Analysis.* Reading, Mass.: Addison-Wesley Publishing Co., Inc., 1968.

SCHELLENBERGER, R. E. *Managerial Analysis.* Homewood, Ill.: Richard D. Irwin, Inc., 1969.

SCHLAIFER, R. *Analysis of Decisions under Uncertainty.* New York: McGraw-Hill Book Co., Inc., 1967.

SHELLY, M. W., II AND RYAN, G. L. (eds.). *Human Judgments and Optimality.* New York: John Wiley & Sons, Inc., 1964.

chapter fifteen

Break-even and Inventory
Control Models

INTRODUCTION

The managerial team of any business firm is faced with many different kinds of cost problems that influence the daily operations of the organization; that is, the cost components must be studied, analyzed, and understood before goal-oriented decisions can be reached. Two specific quantitative models, which are increasingly being used by managers faced with cost-influenced decisions, are the break-even model and the inventory model. Both models and modifications of them deal with cost factors.

In this chapter the break-even model and an inventory control model will be examined. Thus the basic assumptions of management scientists who utilize the models in actual business decision making is made clear. As is true in working with most of the quantitative models found in the management science school, both of the models have limitations. The primary objective of this chapter is to present the logic, assumptions, and limitations associated with the break-even and inventory control models.

THE ECONOMIC AND ACCOUNTING INFLUENCE

The economist and accountant have contributed many ideas, principles, formulas, and models to each of the three schools of management. In the area of cost-and-profit analysis, the economic influence is certainly obvious. The economist and accountant have clarified the meaning of such terms as fixed costs, variable costs, total revenue, marginal revenue, and marginal costs. This clarification has proved beneficial in developing and utilizing quantitative models to analyze various types of business problems. An understanding of the meaning of these terms is essential, if the management science tools are to be employed effectively.

Fixed Costs

Every business sells a product or service and incurs costs in making the sale. A group of costs remains fixed regardless of the level of sales generated and are aptly designated as *fixed costs*. The insurance on a storage warehouse must be paid regardless of whether the warehouse is being fully utilized, or, the business must pay property taxes no matter how much of a product is produced. These costs and others are a function of the creation of capacity and of time.

If a firm plans to utilize warehouse space, it has planned for this by purchasing a warehouse. Because of present production levels, it may not be completely utilized. The firm has created the needed warehouse capacity and must pay for this creation. The warehouse is insured for a period of time (e.g., one year) and the fixed insurance premium must be paid regardless of the level of output.

As a business firm grows in size, the amount of fixed costs incurred also increases. The insurance premium and property taxes also rise. However, fixed costs do not remain *fixed* indefinitely but do vary from time to time. In addition, many fixed costs, although remaining fixed for normal variations in output, will vary if output is either exceedingly low or high. An example of such a situation would be hiring additional part-time salespeople during an unusually high peak demand season. These costs we can term "semifixed" costs. Thus, when we use the term "fixed" costs we are actually referring to the short run. In the long run, all costs are subject to variation.

Variable Costs

Economists and accountants have identified costs that move in close proportion to changes in output as *variable costs*.[1] In a manufacturing plant the amount of material used depends upon the number of units produced. This is also true with regard to the labor costs incurred in manufacturing the product—the more units of a product produced, the greater the total labor expenditure. Thus variable costs are related to the activity itself (e.g., production of a product) rather than to creating capacity or time, as is the case with fixed costs.

---

[1] Campbell R. McConnell, *Economics* (New York: McGraw-Hill Book Co., 1963), p. 244.

Total Revenue

The anticipated or actually generated total revenue is determined by using sales volume and price data. If a manager is forecasting total revenue, he would utilize the anticipated sales volume at each price level. If, however, total revenue is being determined after the product has been sold, the exact volume and price figures are used. In any case, the total revenue, price, and volume relationship can be expressed mathematically as

$$TR = Q \times P$$

where TR designates total revenue, Q designates anticipated or actual volume, and P designates anticipated or actual price.

Marginal Costs and Marginal Revenues

In analyzing the operations of a production, transportation, or quality control section of a business firm, the economist's concept of "marginalism" can be applied. The management scientist has utilized the basic precepts of the economist's marginal approach in developing various models such as the break-even model. The term marginal cost is used to specify the additional costs incurred by selling or servicing or producing one more unit of output. If the costs incurred by the firm are linearly related, the marginal cost concept is shown as a straight line. Figure 15–1 illustrates the linear representation.

FIGURE 15–1

Marginal Cost

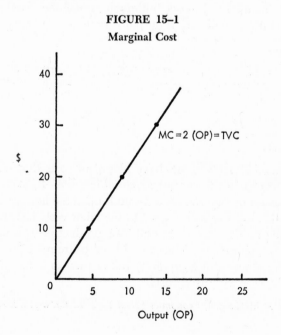

MC = 2 (OP) = TVC

Output (OP)

The relationship expressed in Figure 15–1 shows that the firm's marginal costs are $2 at all output levels. It should also be apparent that the total variable cost (TVC) is determined by multiplying the $2 marginal cost by the respective level of output. Of course, when costs are related non-linearly to production levels, the marginal costs will vary at different levels of output.

The marginal revenue amount designates the additional revenue generated as a result of taking a particular course of action, such as selling one more unit. In an economic theory framework, when marginal revenue equals marginal costs the firm is achieving maximum profit. Thus, if the business manager is concentrating on generating profits as one of his numerous goals, he would be concerned with the marginal cost–marginal revenue relationship. However, in utilizing the break-even and inventory models, the major focus is not upon the marginal concepts but upon the total cost and total revenue relationships. The economist and accountant have provided the basic marginal theory and classification schema which are valuable in utilizing most of the management science models. Without understanding the economists' concepts of cost and revenue, and the classification framework offered by the accountants, the assumptions and conclusions associated with the break-even and inventory models would have very little, if any, practical meaning to the operating manager. The accountant provides managers with accounting practices that enable a manager to plan and control inventory more efficiently.

THE BREAK-EVEN MODEL

At the end of an operating period a manager hopes that the income from the period's sales will be sufficient to cover production costs, marketing costs, administrative costs, and provide some amount of profit. However, if revenue for a particular period is sufficient only to cover the first three items, we can say that the seller in question has broken even or is operating at the break-even point. In other words, if the firm had been able to increase its sales volume by only one item more than the break-even point, it would have shown a profit for the period. The break-even point is the particular level of operations where *total revenue equals total cost.*[2]

In order to utilize break-even analysis we must utilize the cost and revenue components discussed originally by economists and accountants and transposed into a quantitative framework by management scientists. The management scientists study the cost, revenue, and volume relation-

---

[2] James E. Howell and Daniel Teichroew, *Mathematical Analysis for Business Decisions* (Homewood, Ill.: Richard D. Irwin, Inc., 1963), p. 80.

ships by employing representative symbols. The following symbols are generally used:

$$BE = \text{break-even point,}$$
$$P = \text{selling price per unit,}$$
$$VC = \text{variable cost per unit,}$$
$$TFC = \text{total fixed costs, and}$$
$$Q = \text{number of units.}$$

The break-even point occurs when sales produce a margin of income above variable costs that equals the amount required for fixed costs. If a firm produces annually 80,000 units of a product selling at $10 each, it would receive $800,000 in sales revenue. If the variable costs (VC) of producing the item is $6 per unit, it obtains a marginal income of $4 per unit, or $320,000. If the total fixed costs for the firm are $320,000, this year the firm has broken even.

Using the mathematical symbols and the margin of income discussion cited above allows us to derive two break-even model formulas. First we define the equation for total cost:

$$TC = VC \cdot Q + TFC.$$

Then we define total revenue:

$$TR = P \cdot Q.$$

At the break-even point the total cost equals the total revenue; therefore, equating these two equations yields:

$$P \cdot Q = VC \cdot Q + TFC$$

Solving for Q:

$$P \cdot Q - VC \cdot Q = TFC$$
$$(P - VC) Q = TFC$$
$$Q = \frac{TFC}{P - VC}$$

This is the break-even equation in units. Proof: by dimensional analysis:

$$\text{Units} = \frac{\$}{\$/\text{unit}} = \text{Units}$$

To get the break-even equation in terms of dollars, divide by the reciprocal of selling price.

$$\frac{Q}{\frac{1}{P}} = \frac{TFC}{\frac{P}{P} - \frac{VC}{P}}$$

$$P \cdot Q = \frac{TFC}{1 - \frac{VC}{P}}$$

Proof by dimensional analysis:

$$\frac{\text{Units}}{1} = \frac{\$}{\$/\text{unit}}$$
$$\frac{1}{\$/\text{unit}} = \frac{\$/\text{unit}}{\$/\text{unit}}$$
$$\$ = \frac{\$ \text{ units}}{\text{units}} = \frac{\$}{1} = \$.$$

Summarizing,

$$\text{Break-even Point in Units} = \frac{TFC}{P - VC}$$

$$\text{Break-even Point in Dollars} = \frac{TFC}{1 - \dfrac{VC}{P}}$$

Application of Break-even Analysis: Sales

Managers often use break-even analysis to cope with many different types of business problems.[3] For example, the manager of the Maxi Corporation may be concerned with the current state of the overall economy and is primarily interested in ascertaining how much the sales for electric can openers could decline before operations resulted in a loss. Assume that all other cost components of the model remain unchanged. The Maxi break-even data are presented as

Current Data
Price $= \$20.00/\text{unit}$
$VC = \$12.00/\text{unit}$
$TFC = \$80,000$
Quantity Sold $= 100,000.$

We know that

$$BE = \frac{TFC}{P - VC}$$

Thus,

$$BE = \frac{\$80,000}{\$20.00 - \$12.00};$$

$$BE = \frac{\$80,000}{\$8};$$

$$BE = 10,000 \text{ units.}$$

Since we know that 100,000 can openers are being sold annually and have determined that selling 10,000 can openers allows the firm to break even, the company can sell 90,000 fewer can openers and still not lose money. However, if they sell 90,001 fewer can openers they will incur an operat-

---

[3] Harold Bierman, Jr., Charles P. Bonini, and Warren H. Hausman, *Quantitative Analysis for Business Decisions* (Homewood, Ill.: Richard D. Irwin, Inc., 1969), p. 182.

ing loss. By utilizing the break-even point in dollars formula we reach a similar conclusion:

$$BE = \frac{TFC}{1 - \frac{VC}{P}}$$

$$BE = \frac{\$80,000}{1 - \frac{\$12.00}{\$20.00}}$$

$$BE = \$200,000.$$

If the company sells 100,000 units, the total revenue generated from sales would be $2,000,000. Thus, a reduction of $1,800,000 in revenue could occur before an operating loss is incurred. This, of course, constitutes a reduction in sales of 90,000 units ($1,800,000/$20 = 90,000).

Application of Break-even Analysis: Distribution

Managers are often faced with the problem of deciding how to distribute a particular product. To illustrate a distribution choice decision, let us work through a simple problem.

The Battel Pipe Manufacturing Company produces a stainless steel circular pipe rack which is distributed mostly through wholesalers to gift shops, cigar stores and variety stores. Originally the firm had planned to market the product as a novelty but then began to consider the product from a more practical viewpoint. After an extensive analysis of the potential market, the firm narrowed its distribution choice down to two alternatives. The management of Battel is initially interested in determining what the break-even points are for Alternatives I and II. These alternatives are:

I. Market the rack to *wholesalers* who would then distribute the product to large department stores on a national basis.

II. Market the rack directly to *cigar stores* on a national basis.

Cost data for the two alternatives are presented below:

Alternative I *(Wholesalers)*		*Alternative II* *(Cigar Stores)*	
Production Costs (fixed)	$20,000.00	Production Costs (fixed)	$20,000.00
Production Costs (per unit variable)	3.00	Production Costs (per unit variable)	3.00
Marketing Costs and Administrative Costs (fixed)	20,000.00	Marketing Costs and Administrative Costs (fixed)	40,000.00
Marketing Costs and Administrative Costs (per unit variable)	3.00	Marketing Costs and Administrative Costs (per unit variable)	1.00
Battel Price Charged Wholesalers	8.00	Battel Price Charged Stores	6.00

By utilizing the break-even formula the following results are determined:

Alternative I

$$\text{Break-even Point in Units} \ \ = \frac{\$40,000}{\$8.00 - \$6.00} = 20,000 \text{ units}$$

$$\text{Break-even Point in Dollars} \ \doteq \frac{\$40,000}{1 - \dfrac{\$6.00}{\$8.00}} = \$160,000$$

Alternative II

$$\text{Break-even Point in Units} \ \ = \frac{\$60,000}{\$6.00 - \$4.00} = 30,000 \text{ units}$$

$$\text{Break-even Point in Dollars} = \frac{\$60,000}{1 - \dfrac{\$4.00}{\$6.00}} = \$180,000$$

The above formulas have provided us with the break-even points in units and dollars for both of the alternative plans. Another way of examining the relationship of revenue, costs, and incomes for various volumes of sales is to employ the break-even chart.

The Break-even Chart

It is common practice to graphically present break-even relationships. The relationships for Alternative I are presented in Figure 15–2. By use of the graphical analysis we verify the formula findings. The break-even point is at 20,000 units or $160,000 sales revenue.

The total revenue line represents the relationship between price and volume. The area of fixed costs is marked off as a horizontal line which indicates the constant nature of the fixed expenditures. The total cost line begins at the same point as fixed costs and moves upward to the right for different output levels.

Figure 15–3 presents the revenue, cost, and income relationships for Alternative II. Once again, the break-even point determined graphically is identical to the unit and dollar figures found by using the break-even formulas.

Despite having formula and graphical answers to the distribution dilemma, the manager must still make a choice. The mathematics utilized do not preclude the necessity of the manager stating that the rack will be distributed via wholesalers or cigar stores.

Changes in Components and Decision Theory

The break-even formulas and graphical representations do not provide the manager with a complete understanding of the cost and revenue com-

FIGURE 15–2

Break-even Chart for Alternative I
(wholesalers)

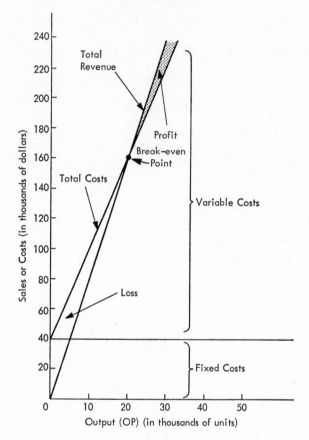

ponents. The manager, by using the traditional break-even procedures discussed above, is not giving adequate consideration to the various levels of sales that are possible. In general, in coping with break-even problems the manager does not know exactly what level of sales volume will be achieved. A method for dealing with the uncertainty of sales volume is to use a range of possibilities.

Let us assume that based on the assessment of the economy in general and the market for pipe racks in particular, the management of Battel estimates potential levels of sales for Alternatives I and II. In addition, the managerial team has estimated the probabilities of achieving the various levels of sales under both alternatives.

FIGURE 15–3

Break-even Chart for Alternative II
(cigar stores)

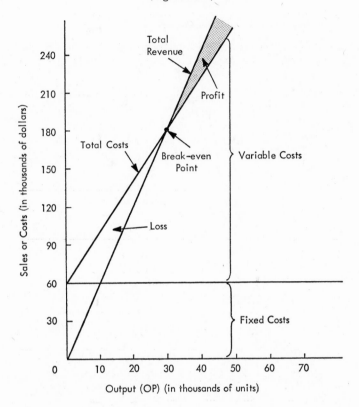

The range of sales and probabilities of occurrence for Alternatives I and II are as follows:

Alternative I

Level of Pipe Rack Sales	Probability of Occurrence
20,000	0.50
30,000	0.30
40,000	0.20

Alternative II

Level of Pipe Rack Sales	Probability of Occurrence
20,000	0.40
30,000	0.30
40,000	0.20
50,000	0.10

Using the sales data and the probability estimates will enable the Battel management group to determine the expected profit of each of the alternative plans. The reader will recall from Chapter 14 that the expected profit of a particular event equals the value of the event if it should occur multiplied by the probability of the event occurring.

Using the cost data for the alternatives would enable the manager to construct profit tables. Table 15–1 illustrates the sales level, revenue, cost, and profit relationship for Alternative I.

The profit data for Alternative II is presented in Table 15–2.

TABLE 15–1
Profit Levels of Alternative I

Level of Sales	Sales Revenue	Total Costs	Conditional Profit or Loss
20,000	$160,000	$160,000	$ –0–
30,000	240,000	220,000	20,000
40,000	320,000	280,000	40,000

TABLE 15–2
Profit Levels of Alternative II

Level of Sales	Sales Revenue	Total Costs	Conditional Profit or Loss
20,000	$120,000	$140,000	–$20,000
30,000	180,000	180,000	–0–
40,000	240,000	220,000	20,000
50,000	300,000	260,000	40,000

By utilizing the probability estimates in conjunction with the data provided in the profit level tables (15–1 and 15–2), the managers at Battel could determine the expected profit of each of the alternative plans. Tables 15–3 and 15–4 present the expected profits for the two alternatives.

If the Battel managers have faith in the probability estimates, the cost

TABLE 15–3
Expected Profit for Alternative I

Level of Sales	Conditional Profit	×	Probability of Sales	=	Expected Profit
20,000	$ –0–	×	.50	=	$ –0–
30,000	20,000	×	.30	=	6,000
40,000	40,000	×	.20	=	8,000
	Expected Profit of Alternative I				$14,000

TABLE 15–4
Expected Profit for Alternative II

Level of Sales	Conditional Profit	×	Probability of Sales	=	Expected Profit
20,000	−$20,000	×	.40		−$8,000
30,000	−0−	×	.30		−0−
40,000	20,000	×	.20		4,000
50,000	40,000	×	.10		4,000
	Expected Profit of Alternative II				−0−

data, and revenue data, and if profit is a significant criterion for decision making, they would select Alternative I. The pipe racks would then be distributed through the wholesalers since the expected profit for Alternative I is $14,000 as compared to an expected profit of zero dollars for Alternative II. One assumption made in selecting the wholesaler distribution channel is that if this type of choice was repeated many different times the expected profit achieved for Alternative I would average $14,000. However, selecting Alternative II over the long run would yield an average expected profit of zero dollars.

Assumptions and Limitations of the Break-even Model

In order for the break-even model to be properly applied to management problems, the decision maker should be aware of the following:

1) Break-even analysis is useful only over relatively short ranges of output. This is because it is assumed that there is a linear relationship among costs, volume, and revenue. Thus, it is not a valuable long-range decision making tool.

2) Since the break-even model (i.e., the symbolic equation formula) is a deterministic model, it is a static tool. That is, the relationships are representative of only a point in time. Therefore it would be more valuable in relatively stable situations than in highly dynamic or volatile situations. It provides a simplified presentation of the relationships between cost, revenue, and output.

3) Utilizing probabilities and a range of sales volume injects more realistic characteristics into the analysis. However, probabilities clearly indicate that the manager is operating under conditions of risk. The accuracy of the decision depends significantly on the accuracy of the probability estimates.

4) The break-even model should only be used as guide for decision making. Its presentation provides a conceptual tool for understanding the relationships between costs, revenue, and output. However, it should not be the determining factor in a decision.

The important point to recognize is that utilization of the break-even model is an aid to the manager. It is definitely not a technique which can be used mechanistically without considering its limitation to reach every-day business decisions.[4]

THE INVENTORY MODEL

The business manager is often faced with the problem of maintaining an adequate inventory.[5] The inventory could be dresses for the women's wear store manager; iron ore for the manufacturer of steel; stainless steel for the producer of pipe racks; or typists for the firm that sends typists to locations upon request. The adequate supply of raw materials, finished goods, or people is an integral part of the ongoing operations of an organization. In this section we will examine a decision-making approach that focuses upon controlling inventories so that costs are minimized. The examples cited will concentrate on finished goods, but the principles and concepts could be applied to raw material and human resource inventory control.

A basic reason for having finished goods in inventory is to separate manufacturing and distribution into independent, successive activities. The manager who must cope with inventory problems in a firm is usually concerned about inventory cost minimization. At times, decisions concerning the minimization of inventory costs and fulfilling customer demand for a product are at cross-purposes. For example, a manager may be concerned about the cost of carrying large inventories but desires to satisfy the buyer's demand for a product at the time of request. This is especially true in retail food stores. The store owner only has a specified amount of storage space for his food inventory. He may fear that by not having a requested product on hand, the customer will become dissatisfied and not return in the future. The desirable course of action is to systematically study the cost components of inventory and the demand for the items so that customer service and goodwill are maintained at a high level.

The Inventory Decision

The seller or manufacturer of goods must cope with two key inventory decisions if a complete and intelligent inventory program is to be developed. These mutually interrelated decisions are: (1) the size of each lot or batch of items to be purchased, and (2) the time to order or request

---

[4] For another discussion of break-even analysis as applied to distribution, see Frank J. Charvat and W. Tate Whitman, *Marketing Management: A Quantitative Approach* (New York: Simmons-Boardman Publishing Corp., 1964), Chapter 10.

[5] For a discussion of inventory systems, see J. W. Schmidt and R. E. Taylor, *Simulation and Analysis of Industrial Systems* (Homewood, Ill.: Richard D. Irwin, Inc., 1970), Chapter 4.

this quantity. By utilizing a basic technique (referred to as the economic order quantity model) which was developed by management scientists, the inventory decision process facing the manager can be made easier.

Cost Factors in Inventory Control

In resolving inventory control problems, the manager must initially identify the cost factors which affect the choices being considered. First, there are the *ordering costs* of getting a particular item into the firm's actual inventory. These costs are incurred each time an order is placed. They are clerical and administrative costs per order which also include the cost of receiving and placing into inventory the goods ordered.

FIGURE 15–4

Ordering and Carrying Cost Relationship

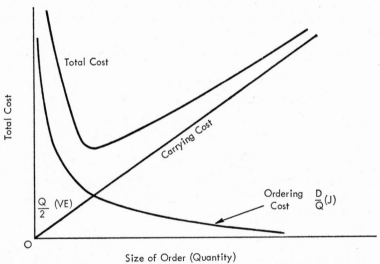

Size of Order (Quantity)

Second, there are the *carrying costs*. These include the interest on money invested in inventory, storage space, rent, obsolescence, payment of taxes and insurance on losses due to theft, fire and deterioration, and protection. The carrying cost component is usually expressed as an annual figure and as a percentage of the average inventory.

To minimize inventory costs, managers attempt to minimize ordering and carrying cost. These two costs are related to each other in opposing directions as shown in Figure 15–4.

The number of orders placed by the firm or manager for a given period of time is equal to demand (D) for the period divided by the size of each order quantity (Q). The total ordering cost per period (week, month, or year) is equal to the cost of placing each order (I) multiplied by the number of orders per period, $\frac{D}{Q}$, or $\frac{D}{Q}$ (J). It should be evident now that as the order lot size increases (e.g., from 5 to 6 or 25 to 30, etc.) fewer orders are required to meet the demand for a period, and consequently the ordering cost component will decrease. This is illustrated graphically by the downward sloping order cost curve in Figure 15–4.

The cost of carrying an item in inventory is calculated by multiplying the value of the item (V) by a percentage figure (E), which is management's estimate of taxes, insurance, etc., per period as a percentage of the value of inventory. The total carrying costs are equal to the cost of carrying one item (VE) multiplied by the average inventory $Q/2$. In the illustrative problem to follow carrying cost is shown as a linear function. However, realistically the carrying cost factors should and would not be prorated as a constant percentage.

An example will illustrate why average inventory is assumed to be $Q/2$. Assume that the Battel company orders 500 pipe rack holder units and uses 100 of them each week; at the midpoint of the first week it has on hand 450. Table 15–5 illustrates the number in inventory at the mid-

TABLE 15–5

Average Inventory Analysis

Week	Number in Inventory at Midpoint of Week
1	450
2	350
3	250
4	150
5	50
	1,250

point of the week over a period of five weeks. A total of 1,250 holder units were on hand at the time of tabulation over the five week analysis period. Thus, an average of 250 per week are found in inventory. The 250 total is found by utilizing the $Q/2$ formula or $500/2$ mathematical notation.

Trial and Error Methodology

A manager can use trial and error procedures to determine what size of order to place for inventory items. However, in attempting to select the most optimal size of inventory from a cost standpoint, a number of assumptions are usually made.

1) The demand for the item over the period is known with certainty.

Thus, we are developing the economic order quantity model (EOQ) under conditions of certainty.

2) The rate at which the inventory of the item is depleted is constant. Figure 15–5 below illustrates depletion at a constant rate. The average inventory is found under conditions of constant usage (e.g., selling same amount monthly for year, 50 or 100 or 200 items per month for full year).

3) The time necessary for acquiring an order of items after order is placed is exactly known (i.e., the lead time).

FIGURE 15–5

Constant Depletion

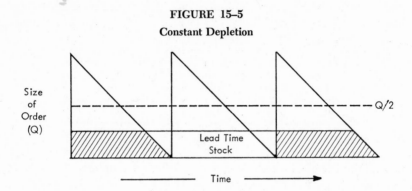

These assumptions are not completely realistic, but they allow us to study in an uncomplicated manner the development of the economic order quantity (EOQ) model. Further sophistication of the basic model can occur only if the simplified form is clearly understood.

An Ordering Problem in a Steel Corporation

A sample problem will once again serve as the vehicle for acquiring a working understanding of a quantitative tool applied to a business problem. Let us assume that a steel mill in South Chicago is attempting to solve a lot-size problem involving iron ingots. The manager desires to minimize total inventory cost per instructions of the plant manager. The yearly demand, which is constant, for the ingots is estimated as 1,000. The administrative and clerical cost of placing an order is $40. The manager estimates insurance and taxes to be 10 percent per year. The value of a single ingot is $20. Thus, the components involved are:

$$D = 1,000$$
$$J = \$40$$
$$E = 10 \text{ percent}$$
$$V = \$20$$

322   Fundamentals of Management: Functions, Behavior, Models

The manager could utilize a tabular format to reach an inventory ordering decision that would minimize the total inventory costs. The size of inventory order and cost relationships are shown in Table 15–6.

A review of the total cost data in Table 15–6 indicates that placing four orders of 250 each yields the lowest cost. However, note that the trial-and-

TABLE 15–6

Trial-and-Error Method

Number of Ingot Orders	Size of Order Q	Order Cost D/Q (J)	+	Carrying Cost Q/2 (VE)	=	Total Cost
1	1000	$ 40	+	$1000	=	$1040
2	500	80	+	500	=	580
4	250	160	+	250	=	410
10	100	400	+	100	=	500
20	50	800	+	50	=	850

error method could be tedious if many different numbers of orders are considered (e.g., 3, 5, 6, 7, 8, 9, and 11–19). To eliminate the tedious nature of the trial-and-error approach, management scientists have developed a specific economic order quantity (EOQ) model.

The EOQ Equation and Formula

The trial-and-error method involves experimentation and manipulation of costs before the decision maker arrives at the optimum cost. Instead of performing the tabular procedures every time an inventory program is being analyzed, it is possible to utilize what is referred to as the economic order quantity formula.

Referring back to Figure 15–4, we see that the minimum total inventory cost point is at the point directly above the intersection of carrying cost and ordering cost. Thus, the EOQ formula may be derived by using this relationship between total, carrying, and ordering costs. It should also be noted that for simplicity sake the relationship shown is linear. The first step in algebraic derivation is to set carrying and ordering cost equal to each other.

$$\frac{Q}{2}(VE) = \frac{D}{Q}(J)$$

Solving for Q yields:

$$Q(VE) = \frac{2DJ}{Q}$$

$$Q^2(VE) = 2DJ$$

$$Q^2 = \frac{2DJ}{(VE)}$$

$$Q = \sqrt{\frac{2DJ}{(VE)}}$$

The final equation is commonly referred to as the economic order quantity formula, which can be used to solve the type of inventory order size problem facing the management of the steel mill. Using the cost, demand, and estimation data in our problem we can determine the economic order size, $D = 1{,}000$, $J = \$40$, $E = 10$ percent, and $V = \$20$.

$$Q = \sqrt{\frac{2(1000)(\$40)}{(\$20)(.10)}}$$

$$Q = \sqrt{\frac{\$80{,}000}{\$2.00}}$$

$$Q = \sqrt{40{,}000}$$

$$Q = 200$$

Reviewing the trial-and-error method shows that the least costly inventory strategy is to place four orders to satisfy the overall ingot demand of 1,000. However, utilization of the more exact *EOQ* formula suggests that placing five orders of 200 each will achieve the least costly inventory program. Since the five-order strategy was not considered in the trial-and-error procedures, the manager was not able to really minimize inventory costs.

The *EOQ* model can also be used to take into consideration changes in demand for a product. Let us assume that the demand for ingots is 1,000 for the first ten months of the year, and 2,000 for the last two months of the year. For the January–October period, the *EOQ* calculations would be ascertained as follows:

$$D = 1{,}000$$
$$J = \$40$$
$$E = 10 \text{ percent}$$
$$V = \$20.$$

Thus,

$$EOQ = \sqrt{\frac{2(1{,}000)(\$40)}{(\$20)(.10)}}$$

$$EOQ = \sqrt{40{,}000}$$

$$EOQ = 200 \text{ units.}$$

The November–December inventory strategy would be determined as follows:

$$D = 2,000$$
$$J = \$40$$
$$E = 10 \text{ percent}$$
$$V = \$20.$$

Thus,

$$EOQ = \sqrt{\frac{2(2,000)(\$40)}{(\$20)(.10)}}$$

$$EOQ = \sqrt{\frac{\$160,000}{\$2.00}}$$

$$EOQ = \sqrt{80,000}$$

$$EOQ \cong 283.$$

The *EOQ* during the November–December peak period is approximately 283. This means that the manager must enter the decision process by determining whether seven or eight orders are appropriate. The human element is essential since $7 \times 283 = 1,981$ and $8 \times 283 = 2,264$, and the exact demand is 2,000. Thus, the *EOQ* decision for January–October was relatively clear-cut in that the demand of 1,000 could be satisfied exactly with five orders of 200 each. An exact *EOQ* is not the case with the November–December period. This example was used to show that despite the use of mathematical formulas, human judgment is still an important factor in many inventory control decisions.

The Quantity Discount Dilemma

A common inventory policy decision that managers face is determining the economic lot size if one or more price discounts can be obtained from a supplier when specific quantities are purchased. For example, the supplier informs the steel company that the per unit cost of an item would be reduced ten percent if the company, each time it places an order, requests 500 ingots.

An approach which may be used to aid in solving quantity discount problems is to compare the total annual cost of ordering and carrying inventory under nonquantity and quantity discount conditions. Let us continue using the original cost data information. The annual demand of ingots is 1,000; the value of each ingot is $20; the ordering cost is $40; the cost of carrying the inventory is ten percent of the value of inventory. The Exchange Supply Company offers the steel company a ten percent discount on purchases if they buy in lots of 500 or more. In order to compare the no-discount and discount situation we first would calculate the *EOQ* for the normal purchase situation.

$$Q = \sqrt{\frac{2DJ}{(VE)}}$$

$$Q = \sqrt{\frac{2(1,000)(\$40)}{(\$20)(.10)}}$$

$$Q = \sqrt{40,000}$$

$$Q = 200$$

The optimum number of ingots in each order is 200, and the price per ingot is $20; total value per order is $200 \times \$20 = \$4,000$. The average worth of the ingot inventory is $\dfrac{\$4,000}{2} = \$2,000$. The carrying cost is ten percent, and ten percent of $2,000 is $200. Each year five purchases are made to satisfy demand, and ordering cost is five multiplied by $40, or $200. The total annual cost under the *EOQ* conditions, or no discount, are as follows:

Ingot Value	($20 × 1,000) =	$20,000
Carrying Cost	(10% × $2,000) =	200
Ordering Cost	(5 × $40.00) =	200
	Total Annual Cost	$20,400

The total cost under the normal situation must now be compared to the quantity discount plan. If 500 ingots are purchased by the steel company each time they order, the cost of the ingots in each lot would be

$$(500 \times \$20 \times .90) = \$9,000.$$

Each order placed would be valued at $9,000; the average inventory value would be $4,500. The total cost calculations would be as follows:

Ingot Value	($18 × 1,000) =	$18,000
Carrying Cost	(10% × $4,500) =	450
Ordering Cost	(2 × $40.00) =	80
	Total Annual Cost	$18,530

Consequently, if the steel company accepts the ingot suppliers discount offer, a saving of $1,870 would be achieved.

Some Limitations of the EOQ Model

The most obvious limitation of employing the inventory model as presented is that conditions of certainty rarely exist in the real world. In our problem, we have assumed that the correct time to order is known. Many times transportation problems, order requisition difficulties, and other related problems make the lead time (e.g., time between placement of an order and actual delivery of the order) a highly unpredictable phenomenon.

The estimation of demand is another problem area. Throughout our discussion, demand was stated as a specific amount. The demand for any item at best can only be roughly estimated. There are so many variables, such as competitors' prices, economic conditions, social conditions, and substitutable items, that can influence demand that stating definitely that it is 1,000 units annually or 2,000 units for two months is too specific.

The cost components and estimates such as ordering cost per unit and carrying cost value as a percent of inventory are only subjectively based figures. Historical cost data, of course, improve the validity of the figures, but these data are by no means perfectly accurate.

Despite these limitations, the analytical approaches presented can aid the manager in reaching more effective inventory judgments. The reader should recognize that the inventory control methods discussed are analytical approaches which attempt to yield optimal decisions. The emphasis, of course, is on the word "attempt."

DISCUSSION AND REVIEW QUESTIONS

1. Under what situations would the material costs for a product not be completely variable? That is, when would material costs be semivariable?
2. Is the *EOQ* model able to adjust to changes in demand over a period of time? Why?
3. How can decision theory and break-even analysis be simultaneously used in analyzing cost–profit problems?
4. A student of management science is presented with the following sets of data.

Set 1	Set 2
BE units = 40,000	*BE* dollars = 300,000
Price = $10	Price = $15
VC/unit = $ 8	*VC*/unit = $12

If a complete break-even analysis is to be conducted on Set 1 and Set 2, what piece of information is needed in each case? Show all work.

5. If you knew at what point on a graph ordering costs and carrying costs intersect, what would you also know about the economic lot size?
6. Assume that the Battel Pipe Company probability estimates are as follows:

Alternative I

Level Pipe Rack Sales	Probability of Occurrence
20,000	0.80
30,000	0.10
40,000	0.10

Alternative II

Level Pipe Rack Sales	Probability of Occurrence
20,000	0.20
30,000	0.20
40,000	0.40
50,000	0.20

If the cost information in the chapter remains as presented for both alternatives, which distribution method would be selected? Show all work in reaching a solution.

7. The Slag Valley Construction Corporation uses 5,000 pressure valves annually. The cost accountants ascertain that the ordering costs for securing the valves from suppliers are $60.00. Each valve costs $10.00. The carrying charge for the valves is estimated to be approximately 20 percent per year of the value of the average inventory.

   a) Utilize the trial-and-error method to derive the economic order quantity for the following possibilities:
   Number of Valves in Order: 500, 1000, 2500, 5000
   b) Utilize the *EOQ* formula to determine the economic order size.
   c) If the Slag Valley Company purchases the valves in lot sizes of 1000 they will receive a 20 percent discount. Should the company accept the quantity discount plan? Why?

8. How are the following concepts related to each other?
   a) Marginal Cost .... Total Variable Cost
   b) Ordering Cost .... Carrying Cost
   c) Price .... Volume of Products Sold

ADDITIONAL REFERENCES

BAUMOL, W. J. *Economic Theory and Operations Analysis.* Englewood Cliffs, N.J.: Prentice-Hall, Inc., 1965.

BOCK, R. H. AND HOLSTEIN, W. K. *Production Planning and Control.* Columbus, Ohio: Charles E. Merrill Books, Inc., 1963.

BUFFA, E. S. *Production-Inventory Systems: Planning and Control.* Homewood, Ill.: Richard D. Irwin, Inc., 1968.

HADLEY, G. and WHITIN, T. M. *Analysis of Inventory Systems.* Englewood Cliffs, N.J.: Prentice-Hall, Inc., 1963.

STARR, M. K. and MILLER, D. W. *Inventory Control: Theory and Practice.* Englewood Cliffs, N.J.: Prentice-Hall, Inc., 1962.

chapter sixteen

Linear Programming

INTRODUCTION

In a previous chapter we indicated that linear programming models are one of the most widely used types of allocation models. However, the use of linear programming for management decision making is relatively new. In fact, its origin dates back to the years just following World War II. The person credited with developing linear programming was George B. Dantzig, who at the time worked for the United States Air Force as a civilian.[1] He was a mathematician and was assigned to work on logistics problems. While working on these problems, he found that many of them could be formulated into what we now know as a linear program. Dantzig formulated a mathematical procedure to solve these problems and entitled it the simplex algorithm. The term algorithm is defined as a rule or procedure for solving a mathematical problem that requires repetition of an operation.

Since World War II, linear programming models have been used increasingly to solve management problems. With the growth of the management science school and the simultaneous growth of the electronic computer, complex linear programming models are now being utilized on a wide scale. In this chapter we shall examine the fundamentals of linear programming.

---

[1] See G. B. Dantzig, "Maximization of a Linear Function of Variables Subject to Linear Inequalities," in T. C. Koopmans (ed.), *Activity Analysis of Production and Allocation* (New York: John Wiley and Sons, Inc., 1951).

FUNDAMENTALS OF LINEAR PROGRAMMING

Linear programming can be used whenever a problem exhibits the following two conditions: (1) Two or more activities compete for limited resources, and (2) it can be assumed that all relationships in the problem are linear. A linear relationship between two or more variables is one which is directly and precisely proportional. For example, a 20 percent change in one variable will result in a 20 percent change in the other variable(s).

We shall illustrate the fundamentals of linear programming by examining a problem. Assume that the production manager of the Apex Corporation has the choice of producing two different products (A and B). Furthermore, let us assume that both products must go through three departments (X, Y, and Z) in order to be completed. We can assume that Department X is production, Department Y is assembling, and Department Z is packaging. Both products require the same amount of time in Department X, but because of special features, Product B requires twice as much time in Department Y but less time in Department Z. The problem the production manager faces is to determine a production "program" for the two products.

In this particular problem, the products (A and B) are the competing candidates and the three processes (production, assembling, and packaging) are the limited resources. If profit is the objective, then the production manager hopes to design a program that will maximize profits. In linear programming this is formulated into a mathematical expression known as an objective function or profit function, whose value can be computed when the values of all the variables are determined. Finally, the capacity of the resources is limited and if we assume that no expansion plans are called for, then this limitation is expressed as a set of constraints which restrict the values that can be assigned to the competing candidates. Since we make the assumption of linearity, this set of constraints must be a set of linear constraints.

Thus the task of the linear programming model in this case is to "allocate" the limited resources (production, assembling, and packaging) among the competing candidates (Products A and B) in such a way as to maximize profit. Therefore, it should be clear that the linear programming model is *normative* in purpose since it selects the best alternative to optimize some objective and contains *deterministic* variables since all variables are assumed to be known with certainty. Note also that in order to utilize the linear programming model it is necessary to *assume certainty* and *simplify relationships* (assume linear relationships among variables) in the problem. Let us summarize the above problem in tabular format by introducing numerical values in Table 16–1.

A final key element of linear programming problem solving is the use

TABLE 16-1

Apex Corporation Resources

Department	Minutes Required per Unit Product A	Minutes Required per Unit Product B	Capacity per Day in Minutes
X	6	6	300
Y	4	8	320
Z	5	3	310
Profit Contribution per Unit	$10	$12	

of inequalities to express relationships. Equations are specific mathematical statements which are represented by an equals sign ($=$). For example, if profit is our sole objective in the above problem, we can express this in the following equation:

Profit = $10 (number of Product A sold) +
$12 (number of Product B sold)

However, most problems faced in business cannot be expressed in equations such as our objective function. More often the problem may require only that minimum or maximum requirements be met. For example, in the problem it is stated that the time needed in Department X (6 minutes) for one Product A times the number of Product A's produced plus the time required for one Product B (6 minutes) times the number of Product B's produced must be equal to or less than the 300 minutes of available time per day in Department X. In this case, we must utilize inequalities. The above inequality is expressed as follows:

$$6A + 6B \leq 300$$

In this case, any amount of time utilized which is equal to or less than 300 minutes per day would satisfy the inequality. When formulating inequalities the sign ($\leq$) stands for "less than or equal to" and the sign ($\geq$) stands for "greater than or equal to". Most constraints faced in linear programming problems are expressed as greater than or less than inequalities.

In order to develop an understanding of a typical linear programming problem we will work through a problem and solve it by (1) the graphical method and (2) the algebraic method. We shall also introduce the simplex method. Of the three methods, the simplex method is the most general and powerful method. However, an understanding of the graphical and algebraic methods will provide a foundation for better grasping the concepts and rationale of the simplex method. In addition, problems which have three or less candidates can be more easily solved by these two methods.

THE GRAPHICAL METHOD

Since it is not possible to present grapically more than three variables, only problems with three or less competing candidates can be solved by this method. Since the problem presented in Table 16–1 has only two competing candidates (Products A and B) it can be solved by the graphical method.

To begin solving the problem we must restate it in mathematical form. Since our goal is to maximize profit (P) we can state our objective as follows:

$$\text{Objective Function} = P = \$10A + \$12B$$

This equation is read: Profit equals $10 multiplied by the number of Product A produced plus $12 multiplied by the number of Product B produced. Assuming we produced 20 of each then profit would equal $10 (20) + $12 (20) or $440.

The next step is to express our constraints in mathematical form. The time used in the three departments cannot exceed the total time available per day in each of the departments. For example, the time needed to make one Product A times the number produced plus the time needed to make one Product B times the number produced must be equal to or less than 300 minutes in Department X. The constraints can be expressed as follows:

$$6A + 6B \leq 300 \text{ minutes in Department } X$$
$$4A + 8B \leq 320 \text{ minutes in Department } Y$$
$$5A + 3B \leq 310 \text{ minutes in Department } Z$$

Finally, every linear programming problem has a set of nonnegativity constraints. All this means is that there can be no such thing as negative production, since it has no physical counterpart. This means that the optimal solution must have positive values for A and B or: $A \geq 0$ and $B \geq 0$.

Summarizing our problem in mathematical form yields:

$$\text{Maximize } P = \$10A + \$12B$$

Subject to the following constraints

$$6A + 6B \leq 300$$
$$4A + 8B \leq 320 \quad \text{and} \quad \begin{matrix} A \geq 0 \\ B \geq 0 \end{matrix}$$
$$5A + 3B \leq 310$$

The next step is to designate on a two-dimensional graph Product A on the horizontal axis and Product B on the vertical axis. We are now able to plot the inequality $6A + 6B \leq 300$ by locating its terminal points and joining them by a straight line. These points are determined by assuming that all the available time is devoted to the production of one of the products. For example, if we did not produce any of Product B, we could produce 50 units of Product A. Similarly, if we produced no Product A, we would be able to produce 50 units of Product B. This is shown as follows:

$$\text{Let } B = 0 \qquad 6A + 6B \le 300$$
$$6A + 6(0) \le 300$$
$$\text{Point } B \qquad A \le 50 \text{ units of Product } A$$
$$\text{when no Product } B$$
$$\text{is produced.}$$

$$\text{Let } A = 0 \qquad 6A + 6B \le 300$$
$$6(0) + 6B \le 300$$
$$\text{Point } C \qquad B \le 50 \text{ units of Product } B$$
$$\text{when no Product } A$$
$$\text{is produced.}$$

The two points (B, C) are plotted on the graph shown in Figure 16–1.

FIGURE 16–1

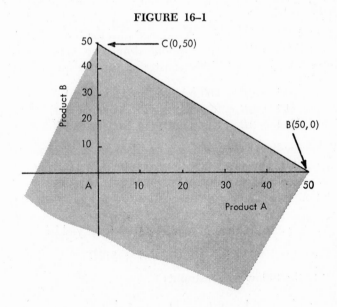

The region we are interested in is represented in Figure 16–1 by the shaded area. However, note that the shaded area includes negative values of A and B which would mean negative production. It is for this reason that we introduced the nonnegativity constraints $A \ge 0$, $B \ge 0$. These constraints restrict us to producing zero or more units of Products A and B. With the nonnegativity constraints included, the area of possible solutions is restricted to the first quadrant shown in Figure 16–2.

Note that any combination of Products A and B on line BC will use all

FIGURE 16–2

Department X Constraints

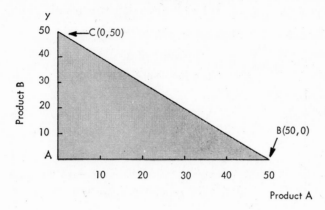

of the 300 minutes of available time in Department X. Also note that any combination of Products A and B which lies in the shaded ABC in Figure 16–2 can be produced without exceeding 300 minutes.

Let $B = 0$ $4A + 8B \leq 320$
$4A + 8(0) \leq 320$
$4A \leq 320$
Point D $A \leq 80$ units of Product A when no Product B is produced.

Let $A = 0$ $4A + 8B \leq 320$
$4(0) + 8B \leq 320$
$8B \leq 320$
Point E $B \leq 40$ units of Product B when no Product A is produced.

Let $B = 0$ $5A + 3B \leq 310$
$5A + 3(0) \leq 310$
$5A \leq 310$
Point F $A \leq 62$ units of Product A when no Product B is produced.

Let $A = 0$ $5A + 3B \leq 310$
$5(0) + 3B \leq 310$
$3B \leq 310$
Point G $B \leq 103$ units of Product B when no Product A is produced.

The constraint inequalities for Department Y (assembling) and Department Z (packaging) can be plotted in a similar manner.

The constraint equations for all three departments are plotted in Figure 16–3.

FIGURE 16–3

Department X, Y, and Z Constraints

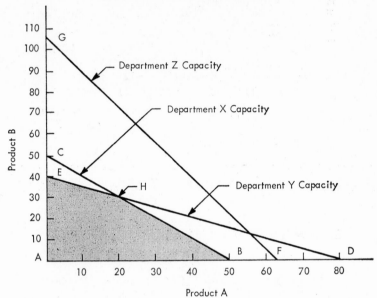

In order to complete either one unit of Product A or Product B, work must be done in all three departments. In other words, the best combination of both Products A and B must fall within the shaded area $ABHE$ in Figure 16–3. This combination will not exceed the maximum time in either Department X, Y, or Z. The shaded area in Figure 16–3 is referred to as a feasibility space.

The construction of Figure 16–3 is the first step in solving our problem by the graphical method. Our goal is to choose at least one point from the shaded area in Figure 16–3, which will maximize our objective (profit) function.

To achieve this, we are guided by our objective function. If it were possible to plot the objective function in Figure 16–3 and determine the direction of maximum increase, we could then continue to move it in this direction until we reached the farthest point on the boundary of the shaded area in Figure 16–3. We would then have the optimum solution.

Isoprofit Lines

Since our objective function $10A + $12B is not in the form of an equation, it cannot be graphed. However, this problem can be solved by selecting an arbitrary profit figure and determining how many units of Product A alone (or Product B alone) would be needed to earn such a profit. Any profit figure will suffice but we shall see it will be easier if the point selected falls within the feasibility space in Figure 16–3. Let us select a profit figure of $300. Since Product A contributes $10 we would have to produce 30 units in order to earn a profit of $300. If we produce only Product B, we would have to produce 25 units in order to earn a $300 profit since Product B contributes a profit of $12. If we locate these two points on our graph and join them we obtain the $300 isoprofit line. This appears as line XY in Figure 16–4.

The isoprofit line XY is, therefore, the locus of all points (all combinations of Products A and B) which yield a profit of $300. We could continue to construct these isoprofit lines for higher and higher profits as long as we remain within the feasibility space. We would be forced to stop when we reached a boundary line or corner point of the feasibility space. When this occurs, we have found one or more optimum solution(s).

FIGURE 16–4
$300 Isoprofit Line

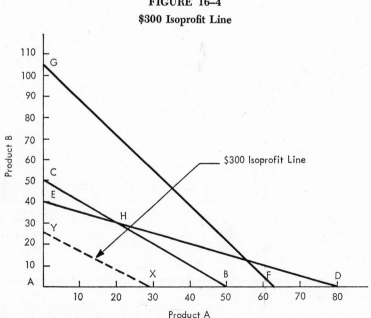

In our problem, we can see that the isoprofit line farthest from the origin and still within the feasibility space is at point H in Figure 16–4. Although there are an infinite number of solutions within the feasibility space, point H provides the optimum solution.

The coordinates of the point H can be read directly from the graph if it is constructed accurately or they can be found by solving simultaneously the equations of the two lines which intersect to form point H which is the only point common to both equations. The equations to be solved are:

$$\text{Line } BC \qquad 6A + 6B = 300$$
$$\text{Line } DE \qquad 4A + 8B = 320$$

To solve these equations simultaneously we
A) Multiply the first equation by 4.
B) Multiply the second equation by -3.
C) Add the results.

$$
\begin{aligned}
4(6A + 6B = 300) &= 24A + 24B = 1200 \\
-3(4A + 8B = 320) &= -12A + (-24B) = -960 \\
\cline{2-2}
12A &= 240 \\
A &= 20
\end{aligned}
$$

D) Substitute 20 for A in the second equation.

$$
\begin{aligned}
4A + 8B = 320 = 4(20) + 8B &= 320 \\
80 + 8B &= 320 \\
8B &= 240 \\
B &= 30
\end{aligned}
$$

E) Point H is, therefore, $(20, 30)$.

We can now test the four points that delineate the feasibility space in order to determine the highest dollar profit.

$$
\begin{aligned}
\text{Point } A \quad (0,0) &= 10(0) + 12(0) = \$0 \\
\text{Point } B \quad (50,0) &= 10(50) + 12(0) = \$500 \\
\text{Point } E \quad (0,40) &= 10(0) + 12(40) = \$480 \\
\text{Point } H \quad (20,30) &= 10(20) + 12(30) = \$560
\end{aligned}
$$

The point that provides us with the most profit is point H with a profit of $560.

We have shown that point H yields the highest profit contribution using either the isoprofit line or by solving simultaneously the equations of the two lines which intersect to form point H.

THE ALGEBRAIC METHOD

In this section we shall develop an algebraic solution to the linear programming problem we have just solved through the graphical method. This problem can be stated algebraically as follows:

$$\text{Maximize: } P = \$10A + \$12B$$
$$\text{Subject to: } 6A + 6B \le 300 \ \ (\text{Department } X)$$
$$4A + 8B \le 320 \ \ (\text{Department } Y)$$
$$5A + 3B \le 310 \ \ (\text{Department } Z)$$

As we have stated the problem, it cannot be solved algebraically. We must first convert the inequations into equations. The above inequations can be transformed into equations by the addition of nonnegative variables, e.g., S_x, S_y, S_z etc. Thus, we now have

$$6A + 6B + S_z = 300 \ \ (\text{Department } X)$$
$$4A + 8B + S_y = 320 \ \ (\text{Department } Y)$$
$$5A + 3B + S_z = 310 \ \ (\text{Department } Z)$$

The variables S_x, S_y, S_z are known as *slack variables* because they "take up the slack" and serve to form equations from the inequations of a linear programming problem. This is because the nature of the inequations being of the "less than or equal to" type, it is possible that the optimum combination of Products A and B may not necessarily utilize all of the available time in each department. Therefore, we add to each inequation a variable which will take up the time not used in each department. S_x is equal to the total available time in Department X less the time used there to produce both products. S_y is equal to the total available time in Department Y less the time used there to assemble both products and S_z equals the total available time used in Department Z less the time used to package both products. Mathematically, the slack variables can be expressed as follows:

$$S_x = 300 - 6A - 6B$$
$$S_y = 320 - 4A - 8B$$
$$S_z = 310 - 5A - 3B$$

Thus, by adding slack variables S_x, S_y and S_z we have converted the constraint inequations into equations. The slack variables will take on whatever value is needed to make the equation hold. For example:

1. Assume that in Department X we manufacture 10 Product A and 10 Product B.

$$S_x = 300 - 6(10) - 6(10)$$
$$S_x = 180 \text{ minutes of unused time in Department } X.$$

2. Assume that in Department Y we assemble 10 Product A and 10 Product B.

$$S_y = 320 - 4(10) - 8(10)$$
$$S_y = 200 \text{ minutes of unused time in Department } Y.$$

3. Assume that in Department Z we package 10 Product A and 10 Product B.

$$S_z = 310 - 5(10) - 3(10)$$
$$S_z = 230 \text{ minutes of unused time in Department } Z.$$

Since idle time in any of the three departments can have no profit or loss, the slack variables have no money value and can be included in our objective function with zero profit contributions as follows:

$$P = \$10A + \$12B + \$0S_x + \$0S_y + \$0S_z$$

In the graphical method we saw that all the points on or in the feasibility space represented various combinations of Products A and B which provided a profit. We can now also see that the coordinates (0,0) provide no profit whatsoever. Coordinates (0,0) indicate only unused capacity.

This feasible but nonprofit solution can be shown in the algebraic method by examining the slack variable equations:

$$S_x = 300 - 6A - 6B$$
$$S_y = 320 - 4A - 8B$$
$$S_z = 310 - 5A - 3B$$

These three equations indicate the relationship between the variables S_x, S_y, and S_z which represent unused time and A and B which represent products. Thus, our first solution can be stated as follows:

$$A = 0$$
$$B = 0$$
$$S_x = 300 - 6(0) - 6(0)$$
$$S_x = 300 \text{ minutes not used in Department } X$$
$$S_y = 320 - 4(0) - 8(0)$$
$$S_y = 320 \text{ minutes not used in Department } Y$$
$$S_z = 310 - 5(0) - 3(0)$$
$$S_z = 310 \text{ minutes not used in Department } Z$$

Our first solution is, therefore, technically feasible but it is certainly not attractive from a profit standpoint. In order to create any profit, we must institute one of the following possible programs:
1. produce only Product A,
2. produce only Product B, or
3. produce some combination of A and B which is technically feasible.

Produce Only Product A

In this case $B = 0$, $S_x = 0$, $S_y = 0$ and $S_z = 0$. Our equation system thus becomes:

For Department X:

$$6A = 300 \text{ or } A = 50$$

For Department Y:

$$4A = 320 \text{ or } A = 80$$

For Department Z:

$$5A = 310 \text{ or } A = 62$$

Since all three processes are needed to produce Product A, Department X provides the *limiting* capacity. Therefore, the maximum possible production of Product A is 50 units. In this case the profit will be:

Profit $= \$10(50) + \$12(0) + \$0(S_x) + \$0(120 \text{ min.}) + \$0(60 \text{ min.})$
    $= \$500$

Produce Only Product B

This means that $A = 0$, $S_x = 0$, $S_y = 0$, and $S_z = 0$. Our equation system thus becomes:

For Department X:

$$6B = 300 \text{ or } B = 50$$

For Department Y:

$$8B = 320 \text{ or } B = 40$$

For Department Z:

$$3B = 310 \text{ or } B = 103$$

In this case Department Y provides the limiting capacity. The maximum possible production of Product B is 40 units. This will yield a profit of:

Profit $= \$10(0) + \$12(40) + \$0(60 \text{ min.}) + \$0(S_y) + \$0(90 \text{ min.})$
    $= \$480$

Produce Both Products A and B

Any program we can devise that will produce a maximum profit utilizing some combination of Products A and B will be such that it utilizes as much of the available resources as possible. We must look for combinations in which either of the following occur:

1. $S_x = 0$, $S_y = 0$, or
2. $S_x = 0$, $S_z = 0$, or
3. $S_y = 0$, $S_z = 0$

If in our equation system we allow $S_x = 0$ and $S_y = 0$ we obtain the following:

$$A) \qquad 6A + 6B = 300$$
$$B) \qquad 4A + 8B = 320$$
$$C) \ 5A + 3B + S_z = 310$$

Solving equations A and B gives $A = 20$ and $B = 30$. Substituting these values into equation C gives:

$$5(20) + 3(30) + S_z = 310$$
$$S_z = 310 - 100 - 90$$
$$S_z = 120$$

This means that our solution of $A = 20$ and $B = 30$ will result in 120 minutes of idle time in Department Z. This program yields a profit of:

$$\$10(20) + \$12(30) = \$560$$

Since we have solved this problem by the graphical method, we know that this solution yields the highest profit. However, assuming that this is not known we must examine all the other combinations.

Let us assume now that S_x and $S_z = 0$

$$A) \qquad 6A + 6B = 300$$
$$B) \ 4A + 8B + S_y = 320$$
$$C) \qquad 5A + 3B = 310$$

Solving equations A and C gives $A = 80$ and $B = -30$. We then substitute these values into equation B.

$$4(80) + 8(-30) + S_y = 320$$
$$S_y = 320 - 320 + 240$$
$$S_y = 240$$

This solution is not acceptable because of the negative value of B which we know can have no physical counterpart since there is no such thing as negative production.

Let us assume now that S_y and $S_z = 0$

$$A) \ 6A + 6B + S_x = 300$$
$$B) \ 4A + 8B \qquad = 320$$
$$C) \ 5A + 3B \qquad = 310$$

Solving equations B and C gives $A = 54$ (rounded), $B = 13$ (rounded). Substituting these values into equation A yields:

$$6(54) + 6(13) + S_x = 300$$
$$S_x = 300 - 324 - 78$$
$$S_x = -102$$

This cannot possibly be a solution because it indicates that we are 102 units short of capacity in Department X. Thus by utilizing the algebraic method, we find that the company should produce 20 of Product A and 30 of Product B to optimize profit.

THE SIMPLEX METHOD

As we mentioned at the beginning of the chapter, the simplex method is the most widely applicable of the linear programming techniques. Both the algebraic and the graphical method are special cases of the general simplex method. In the following chapter, we shall examine the transportation model which is still another special case of the simplex method.

The major advantage of the simplex technique over the graphical and algebraic methods is that it is capable of handling any number of variables. Because of this, it usually requires a lengthy and involved computational procedure which we previously defined as an algorithm. It is necessary here to only outline the general characteristics of the simplex method.

The simplex method is similar to the graphical and algebraic methods in that conditions of certainty and linear relationships among variables are necessary in order for the simplex method to be used. Like the algebraic method, the simplex method requires that the problem be formulated in explicit quantitative terms, stating both the objective function and the constraints. Then an initial solution is developed which satisfies all of the constraints. Modifications in the initial solution are examined and the most favorable in terms of the objective function is incorporated into the second solution. This is repeated until no further improvements are possible. Thus the computational routine of the simplex algorithm is an iterative process. To iterate is to repeat mechanical and mathematical operations. Each iteration brings us closer to an optimal solution because each new solution yields a larger profit or lower cost than the previous solution. This method is clearly superior to trial-and-error methods.[2]

MANAGEMENT'S USE OF LINEAR PROGRAMMING

Linear programming is a management tool with many uses. In addition to the product-mix problems we have examined thus far in the chapter, there are numerous other allocation type problems in which the manager can make effective use of linear programming.[3]

Advertising Media-Mix

In most organizations, the manager must sooner or later face a media-mix problem. In other words, given an advertising budget

---

[2] For a complete treatment of the simplex method, see N. Paul Loomba, *Linear Programming* (New York: McGraw-Hill Book Co., 1964). This chapter draws upon Loomba's work.

[3] For an excellent discussion of various applications of linear programming, see Richard I. Levin and Rudolph P. Lamone, *Linear Programming for Management Decisions* (Homewood, Ill.: Richard D. Irwin, Inc., 1969), Chapter 9.

of so much money, how can he allocate this money over the various advertising media in order to achieve maximum exposure for his products. The reader can readily see that this type of problem lends itself to the use of linear programming. There are a number of competing candidates (e.g., ten magazines) all vying for limited resources, the advertising budget. It is the manager's task to "allocate" this budget in such a way as to maximize the exposure he receives for his product. Linear programming is currently in wide use in advertising agencies as an aid in solving this type of media-mix problem.

Distribution

Distribution is another operational area in which linear programming has been applied with a great deal of success. One particular area of success has been the use of linear programming to minimize transportation costs in moving products between different points in the marketing channel (manufacturers warehouses, wholesalers, and retailers). This type of problem will be examined in detail in Chapter 17.

There are a great multitude of other operational problems in which linear programming can be a valuable decision aid, for example,[4]

1. allocation of materials to machines in order to minimize production time,
2. allocation of cargoes to ships and aircraft,
3. allocation of coal to power stations to minimize shipping costs,
4. computing the right mixture of octane components in the blending of gasolines,
5. computing the most suitable animal feed mixes,
6. production scheduling, and
7. personnel assignment.

SUMMARY

In this chapter, we have seen that linear programming is a powerful decision-making tool for the manager. It has made possible the solution of many types of allocation problems which heretofore could only be dealt with (if at all) by trial-and-error methods. In addition, however, it has forced managers to more clearly delineate the variables and relationships affecting a decision problem. Thus forcing managers to formalize their thinking on specific problems enables the manager to visualize the key variables in a problem which brings organization and

---

[4] See S. Vajda, *Readings in Linear Programming* (New York: John Wiley and Sons, Inc., 1958); and T. H. Naylor and E. T. Byrne, *Linear Programming* (Belmont, Calif.: Wadsworth Publishing Company, Inc., 1963).

structure to a problem situation where little or none existed before.

The reader should not infer, however, that linear programming represents a remedy for the solution of all allocation decision problems. The employment of linear programming necessitates formulation of the decision problem in quantitative terms. This means in many cases the gathering of data and extensive calculations. In such a situation, the costs incurred in using linear programming may exceed any possible gains or savings that might be obtained from its use.

Earlier in the chapter, we indicated that linear programming can only be used for problems in which it can be assumed that the relationships between variables are linear. Many allocation problems may be such that linear programming approaches are not applicable. In addition, other important allocation problems involve such a degree of complexity that their solution is not possible via linear programming.[5]

Finally, we noted that the linear programming model is a deterministic model. This means that all variables are assumed to be known with certainty. While this is clearly a simplifying assumption, there will be many problems where such an assumption cannot be made, or if made, the solution obtained through the use of linear programming will be of little or no value.

In conclusion, it is important for the manager to understand not only how linear programming is used, but also the conditions under which its use is feasible. This is not to deter from the value of the tool but rather to strengthen the conditions under which it is used.

DISCUSSION AND REVIEW QUESTIONS

1. Using the graphical method, solve the following problem:
   Maximize: $20x + $10y$
   Subject to: $4x + 9y \leq 180$
   $$5x + 6y \leq 150$$
   $$5x + 14y \leq 175$$
   with $x \geq 0$, $y \geq 0$.

2. Using the algebraic and graphical methods, solve the following problem:
   Maximize: $10A + $12B$
   Subject to:
   Production $3A + 3B \leq 150$
   Printing $2A + 4B \leq 160$
   Assembling $2.5A + 1.5B \leq 155$
   with $A \geq 0$
   $$B \geq 0$$

---

[5] There are other techniques of linear programming applicable to such problems. The interested reader should consult Levin and Lamone, *op. cit.*

3. In a complete paragraph, describe exactly what is meant by linear programming.

4. What two conditions must a problem exhibit in order to enable the use of linear programming?

5. What is the simplex method? How does it differ from the graphical and algebraic methods? How is it similar?

6. Discuss some of the areas of business where linear programming has been used effectively.

7. Discuss the following statement: "Since conditions of certainty must exist in order for linear programming to be used, it is of little use to managers because conditions of certainty rarely, if ever, exist in the business world."

8. Discuss the following statement: "Linear programming should be applied to all allocation problems wherever it is feasible."

9. The Lockhart Company makes two products. Product A contributes $20 profit and Product B contributes $12 profit. Each product must go through two processes. Product A requires 12 hours in process X and 4 hours in process Y. Product B requires 4 hours in process X and 8 hours in process Y. There is a total of 60 hours available in process X and 40 hours available in process Y. Find the optimum combination of the two products which would maximize total profit. Use the graphical method.

ADDITIONAL REFERENCES

GASS, S. I. *Linear Programming: Methods and Applications*, 2nd ed. New York: McGraw-Hill Book Co., 1966.

LLEWELLYN, R. W. *Linear Programming*. New York: Holt, Rinehart, and Winston, Inc., 1964.

NAYLOR, T. H. and BYRNE, E. T. *Linear Programming*. Belmont, Calif.: Wadsworth Publishing Co., Inc., 1963.

SIMMONNARD, M. *Linear Programming*. Englewood Cliffs, N.J.: Prentice-Hall, Inc., 1966.

SMYTHE, W. R. and JOHNSON, L. A. *Introduction to Linear Programming, with Applications*. Englewood Cliffs, N.J.: Prentice-Hall, Inc., 1966.

SPIVEY, W. A. *Linear Programming: An Introduction*. New York: The Macmillan Co., 1963.

chapter seventeen

The Transportation Model

INTRODUCTION

The transportation method is a special class of linear programming problems which utilizes the basic approach of the simplex technique.[1] However, the transportation method is somewhat easier since it does not call for the development and manipulation of linear equations. Rather, it involves only addition, subtraction, and multiplication. In this chapter the transportation method will be examined by reviewing a problem that utilizes what is referred to as the "northwest corner" procedure. This is only one of a number of procedures that can be used by managers when they are faced with problems involving the shipment of goods or materials at a minimum total cost.

THE PROBLEM

The transportation problem may be stated as follows: Given a number of sources of supply and destinations, and the cost of shipping a product from the source of supply to each destination, select those routes that will minimize total shipping costs.

With data concerning the total capacities of the sources of supply, the total needs of the destinations, and the shipping cost per unit of the product, the transportation algorithm may be used to arrive at the optimum shipping program which results in the minimum total shipping costs. As

---

[1] Richard I. Levin and Rudolph P. Lamone, *Linear Programming for Management Decisions* (Homewood, Ill.: Richard D. Irwin, Inc., 1969), Chapter 6.

with the algebraic and simplex methods of linear programming, the basic transportation method can be used only with problems which display

1. conditions of certainty, and
2. linear relationships between the variables.[2]

This would mean that the shipping cost per unit is known in advance and this cost must remain constant regardless of the quantity of goods shipped. However, for the transportation algorithm an additional assumption—one-for-one substitution—must be made. This means that if a manager decides not to ship 100 units of a product from source x to destination y, he must be able to instead substitute 100 units from other sources to be shipped to destination y. It should be remembered that this is not a prerequisite of the graphical algebraic or simplex methods of linear programming.

Let us work through a sample problem so that the methodology can be clearly understood.

Utilizing the Transportation Model

The Frank Distributing Corporation is the distributor of air conditioning units. Frank owns three warehouses as follows:

Warehouse Locations	Air Conditioners
Phoenix	2000
Houston	1500
Portland	500

The corporation has the following monthly demand requirements from three customers:

Customer Location	Monthly Orders
Tampa	1800
Louisville	1500
Baltimore	700

The cost of delivery from each warehouse to each customer is determined largely on the basis of overland mileage. The per-unit delivery costs have been determined to be:

TABLE 17–1

Transportation Costs
(in $)

	Destination Demand		
Supply Source	Tampa	Louisville	Baltimore
Phoenix	15	12	24
Houston	7	8	15
Portland	27	18	21

---

[2] In more advanced treatments of the transportation algorithm, this assumption may be relaxed.

The management of Frank desires to deliver the air conditioners in good condition and in such a way that their transportation cost would be minimized. In this particular problem it would not be too tedious after acquiring problem-solving experience to arrive at the minimum transportation cost answer by careful inspection of Table 17–2 and the data on warehouses and customers cited above. If, however, Frank was an extremely large distributor with 50 warehouse facilities and 350 customers spread out all over the United States and overseas, then the complexity of the problem would make the inspection solution almost impossible. Thus, to acquire a working understanding of the transportation method, let us proceed to work out the above problem.

The Distribution Matrix

The first step in developing the initial feasible solution is to design a matrix indicating (1) all warehouse stocks and customer requirements and (2) the transportation costs for each unit in the upper portion of the matrix cell.[3] Such a matrix is presented in Table 17–2.

TABLE 17–2

Initial Distribution Matrix

Supply Source	Destination Demand			Total Supply
	Tampa	Louisville	Baltimore	
Phoenix	−15	−12	−24	2000
Houston	−7	−8	−15	1500
Portland	−27	−18	−21	500
Total Requirements	1800	1500	700	4000

The per-unit transportation costs are inserted in the subcell as negative values. The subcells represent costs and the Frank management is interested in minimizing total transportation costs. If the problem involved profit maximization, the cells would contain positive values.

The 4000 in the lower right-hand cell indicates that supply equals de-

---

[3] N. Paul Loomba, *Linear Programming* (New York: McGraw-Hill Book Co., 1964), p. 167.

mand. The figures in the requirements (demand) row and supply column are called *rim values*.

The next step is to assign shipments of air conditioning units in the lower left half of the cells in such a manner that the number of units shipped to the demand destination will exactly meet its requirements. One of the more widely known procedures used to reach an initial feasible solution in distribution problems is referred to as the *northwest corner method*. In Table 17–3 this would be the square (cell) in the upper left corner of the matrix. In the northwest corner cell, we place the smaller of the rim values for that row and column. The rim value for the

TABLE 17–3

Northwest Corner Initial Matrix

Supply Source	Destination Demand			Total Supply
	Tampa −15	Louisville −12	Baltimore −19	
0 Phoenix	−15 1800	−12 200	−24	2000
+4 Houston	−7	−8 1300	−15 200	1500
−2 Portland	−27	−18	−21 500	500
Total Requirements	1800	1500	700	4000

row is 2000 and for the column is 1800. Thus, we place 1800 in the northwest corner cell. This indicates that 1800 air conditioners are shipped from Phoenix to Tampa. Since the rim value of the column was less than that of the row, the next cell to be filled is the one to the right of the cell just filled. There are still 200 air conditioners available in Phoenix. The customer in Louisville has ordered 1500. Thus, we can place the 200 air conditioners in the Phoenix–Louisville cell. We have now depleted the Phoenix supply and cannot make another move to the right. We now drop down one cell and assign the necessary number of units to fill that cell, that is, the Houston–Louisville cell. Houston has 1500 air conditioners available and Louisville has an unsatisfied order for 1300. Thus, 1300 units of the Houston supply is allocated to Louisville.

We cannot make another move downward because Louisville's demand has been filled. Thus, we move one cell to the right, that is, to the

Houston–Baltimore cell. The remaining Houston supply of 200 air conditioners is used to fill part of the Baltimore demand of 700. Thus, we place 200 in the Houston–Baltimore cell. This leaves Baltimore with an unsatisfied demand for 500 air conditioners. However, Portland has exactly 500 air conditioners which have not been allocated. We assign these units to the Portland–Baltimore cell. This initial feasible solution is presented in Table 17–3.

The total shipping costs of the initial distribution arrangement can be computed. The units to be shipped are multiplied by their related costs and the products summed to obtain the total shipping cost. This is shown in Table 17–4.

TABLE 17–4
Total Transportation Cost

Supply:Demand	Units	× Cost per Unit($) =	Transportation Cost($)
Phoenix:Tampa	1800	15	27,000
Phoenix:Louisville	200	12	2,400
Houston:Louisville	1300	8	10,400
Houston:Baltimore	200	15	3,000
Portland:Baltimore	500	21	10,500
	Total Transportation Cost		53,300

The next step is to determine whether the initial solution of supply-and-demand shipments is the *optimum solution*. The optimum solution to the management of Frank is that solution which most nearly minimizes their total transportation costs. The formal test for optimization requires two steps: (1) determination of row and column values and (2) determination of the values of unoccupied cells.

Determination of Row and Column Values

In computing the r (row) and C (column) values, *only occupied cells are given consideration*. A basic rule to follow is: The sum of the row and column values is equal to the value in the subcell of an occupied cell.

A zero (any randomly selected number may be used) is placed to the left of the row of the northwest corner cell (e.g., the first occupied cell, Table 17–3). Following the basic rule:

$$0 + (-15) = -15$$

Therefore, the column value is -15, which is placed over the column (C_1). The next occupied cell to consider is row 1 (r_1), column 2 (C_2) or the Phoenix–Louisville shipment.

$$0 + (-12) = -12$$

The -12 value is placed over column 2 (C_2). The next row and column value to calculate is r_2. Since $C_2 = -12$, the value of row 2 is

$$-12 + (+4) = -8$$

The $+4$ is found because using the rule that the sum of the row and column values is equal to the value in the subcell of an occupied cell provides the problem solver with two known values the -12 and -8. Thus, column value (-12) + row value (unknown) equals the subcell value (-8). The row value which fulfills the requirements of the equation is $+4$.

Table 17–5 illustrates the necessary computations.

TABLE 17–5

Row and Column Value Computations

Occupied Cell	Row Value	+	Column Value	=	Subcell Value
r_1C_1	0		-15		-15
r_1C_2	0		-12		-12
r_2C_2	$+4$		-12		-8
r_2C_3	$+4$		-19		-15
r_3C_3	-2		-19		-21

The reader should note that a specific pattern must be adhered to when computing the row and column values, going from a known r or C value to the unknown r or C value.

Determination of Unoccupied Cells

The second formal step in testing for optimality of a solution is determination of the values of the unoccupied matrix cells. The rule used is: The value in the subcell is subtracted from the sum of the row and column values pertaining to the unoccupied cell being evaluated.

In Table 17–3, row 1, column 3 is unoccupied. To evaluate the cell, sum the row and column values,

$$0 + (-19) = -19$$

and then subtract the value in the subcell

$$-19 - (-24) = +5$$

The value of unoccupied cell r_1C_3 equals $+5$, and this computed value is placed in the cell. The values of each unoccupied cell may be computed in a similar manner. Table 17–6 illustrates the values of the unoccupied cells.

TABLE 17-6

Unoccupied Cell Computations

Cell	Row Value	+ Column Value	= Sum of r and C	− Subcell Value	= Unoccupied Cell Value
r_1C_3	0	−19	−19	−24	5
r_2C_1	4	−15	−11	− 7	−4
r_3C_1	−2	−15	−17	−27	10
r_3C_2	−2	−12	−14	−18	4

Table 17–7 presents the initial solution with row and column values and unoccupied cell values included in the matrix.

Interpretation and Improvement in Initial Matrix

Once the unoccupied-cell values are determined, the signs of the values indicate whether an optimum solution has been found. The signs are interpreted as follows:

1. A ($+$) value in an unoccupied cell indicates that a poorer solution will result if units are moved into that cell.
2. A ($-$) value in an unoccupied cell indicates that a better solution can be found by shifting units into the unoccupied cell.
3. A zero value in an unoccupied cell indicates that another solution of

TABLE 17-7

Initial Solution with Row, Column, and Unoccupied-Cell Values

Supply Source	Destination Demand			Total Supply
	Tampa −15	Louisville −12	Baltimore −19	
0 Phoenix	−15	−12	−24	2000
	1800	200	+5	
+4 Houston	−7	−8	−15	1500
	−4	1300	200	
−2 Portland	−27	−18	−21	500
	+10	+4	500	
Total Requirements	1800	1500	700	4000

equal value is available to the problem solver by moving units into the zero value cell.

Utilizing the sign interpretation and reviewing Table 17–7 reveals that an improved solution can be achieved by moving units into unoccupied cell r_2C_1; all other unoccupied cells have $(+)$ values and moving units into them would result in a poorer solution. If the problem solver is faced with a situation in which there is more than one negative cell, he could move into any one of the cells with negative values but ordinarily a move into the cell with the highest negative value will result in the most improvement since negative signs indicate total cost savings.

The cell selected to be moved into is indicated by placing a $(+)$ in it. In our problem, this is r_2C_1. The plus sign indicates that units are to be added to r_2C_1. However if units are added to r_2C_1, then the same number of units must be subtracted from either r_1C_1 or r_2C_2. If this is not done, then Tampa will get more air conditioners than it has ordered. Therefore, we place a $(-)$ sign in cell r_2C_2 to indicate the necessary reduction in units. This is necessary to maintain the rim values since we have said that the sum of the values in each column and row must be equal to the respective rim values.

However, if the value in r_2C_2 is reduced below 1300, then the sum of the units in row 2 will not equal 1500. Thus, we add units to the r_2C_1 cell. The occupied cell rule is that: The number of occupied cells must be equal to the number of rows plus the number of columns minus one $(r + C - 1)$. In this problem, there are three rows and three columns. Thus, there must be at least five occupied cells.

$$3 + 3 - 1 = 5$$

In order to meet this required condition one formerly unoccupied cell is to be occupied; one formerly occupied cell is to become unoccupied, and all other shifts must take place within the already occupied cells. Therefore, another $(+)$ sign must be placed in the matrix and the same logic dictates that a $(-)$ sign be placed in the table. Table 17–8 indicates the affected cells with the appropriate signs and dotted lines.

The problem solver must now decide how many units to move into cell r_2C_1. It is evident that the more units that are moved into r_2C_1, the more money we will save. The limiting factor becomes the smallest unit value in the cells in which we have placed $(-)$ signs. In Table 17–8, this is r_2C_2 which has 1300 units. Therefore, all cells containing $(+)$ or $(-)$ signs are adjusted by adding or subtracting 1300 units as the signs indicate.

The routine used to shift units in this example was to work with three occupied cells and one unoccupied cell in a square network. That is, three corners of the square were occupied $(r_1C_1, r_1C_2,$ and $r_2C_2)$. The other corner of the square was not occupied, r_2C_1. The method of work-

TABLE 17–8

Moving Toward Optimal Solution

Supply Source	Destination Demand			Total Supply
	Tampa −15	Louisville −12	Baltimore −19	
0 Phoenix	(−)------−15−−(+) −12		−24	2000
	∣1800	∣ 200	+5	
+4 Houston	(+)‾‾‾‾‾‾−7 ‾(−) −8		−15	1500
	−4	1300	200	
−2 Portland	−27	−18	−21	500
	+10	+4	500	
Total Requirements	1800	1500	700	4000

ing with a square or rectangle reduces the analyses to a systematic procedure. The improved solution is shown in Table 17–9.

All the row and column values must be recomputed to test the optimality of the improved solutions. These necessary computations are
summarized in Table 17–10 and Table 17–11. The four (+) values shown
in Table 17–9 indicate that an optimal solution has been reached.

TABLE 17–9

Improved Solution

Supply Source	Destination Demand			Total Supply
	Tampa −15	Louisville −12	Baltimore −23	
0 Phoenix	−15	−12	−24	2000
	500	1500	+1	
+8 Houston	−7	−8	−15	1500
	1300	+4	200	
+2 Portland	−27	−18	−21	500
	+14	+8	500	
Total Requirements	1800	1500	700	4000

TABLE 17–10

Row and Column Computations Improved Solution

Occupied Cell	Row Value	+ Column Value	= Subcell Value
r_1C_1	0	−15	= −15
r_1C_2	0	−12	= −12
r_2C_1	8	−15	= − 7
r_2C_3	8	−23	= −15
r_3C_3	2	−23	= −21

The total transportation costs of the improved solution are presented in Table 17–12.

The optimal solution shown in Table 17–9 results in lower transportation costs than the first solution. Recall that the total transportation costs for the first solution (Table 17–4) were $53,300. Thus, a savings of $5,200 ($53,300 − 48,100) is achieved by shipping the air conditioners as indicated in Table 17–12.

TABLE 17–11

Unoccupied Cell Computations Improved Solution

Cell	Row Value	+ Column Value	= Sum of r and C	− Subcell Value	= Unoccupied-Cell Value
r_1C_3	0	−23	−23	−24	+ 1
r_2C_2	8	−12	− 4	− 8	+ 4
r_3C_1	2	−15	−13	−27	+14
r_3C_2	2	−12	−10	−18	+ 8

The Frank management is able to minimize their transportation cost by shipping the air conditioners as shown by the improved solution. This problem required only one iteration which is unusual. Typically, the manager has to perform numerous iterations before reaching an optimal solution. In these instances, a computer is an invaluable aid in that it

TABLE 17–12

Total Transportation Cost

Supply:Demand	Units ×	Cost per Unit ($) =	Transportation Cost ($)
Phoenix: Tampa	500	15	7,500
Phoenix: Louisville	1500	12	18,000
Houston: Tampa	1300	7	9,100
Houston: Baltimore	200	15	3,000
Portland: Baltimore	500	21	10,500
Total Transportation Cost			48,100

reduces the tedious computational work that is necessary when solving the problem by hand.

A Synopsis of the Northwest Corner Method

1. Study the problem facing the manager (e.g., cost, items, and objectives).
2. Set up initial distribution matrix, allowing one column for each demand destination and one row for each supply source.
3. Set up northwest corner initial matrix and proceed to compute the initial solution.
4. Obtain the row and column values using the rule and formula: row value + column value = value in the subcell.
5. Evaluate unoccupied cells by using the rule and formula: row value + column value − (value in the subcell) = unoccupied-cell value.
6. Interpret signs of values in unoccupied cells and interpret their meaning.
7. Move units to the unoccupied cell with the largest negative value.
8. Repeat steps 4–7 until all unoccupied cells have positive values.
9. Present supply and demand combinations and the optimal total cost figure in a concise manner.

Introduction of a Slack Variable

Thus far, in our discussion of the transportation method, we have assumed that total supply was equal to total demand (requirements). In many problems, however, this condition will probably not be true. In other words, in most situations the firm either has more orders than it can fill or its available supply exceeds its orders. In both situations, the company will still be interested in obtaining the least cost distribution pattern. This objective can still be achieved by introducing a slight modification into the transportation method as we have presented it.

To illustrate a situation where supply and demand are not equal, let us assume that the Frank Distributing Corporation has more orders than it has air conditioners on hand:

Warehouse Locations	Air Conditioners in Stock
Phoenix	2000
Houston	1500
Portland	500
	4000

Customer Location	Orders
Tampa	1800
Louisville	1500
Baltimore	1200
	4500

We shall assume that the shipping costs per unit remain the same. It is obvious that at least one order will not be fully shipped. Thus, we must answer two questions: (1) Which order(s) will not be fully shipped? and (2) What is the least cost distribution pattern? To solve the problem, we utilize the same procedure as outlined previously except that a *slack variable* is introduced into the transportation matrix. In our problem, this is done by adding a row which represents a hypothetical warehouse (designated dummy) as shown in Table 17–13. If supply should exceed demand, an additional column for a dummy customer would be provided. The northwest corner method is then used to obtain the initial solution. This is shown in Table 17–13.

TABLE 17–13

Unequal Supply-Demand Situation Initial Solution

Supply Source	Destination Demand			Total Supply
	Tampa	Louisville	Baltimore	
Phoenix	−15 1800	−12 200	−24	2000
Houston	−7	−8 1300	−15 200	1500
Portland	−27	−18 500	−21	500
Dummy	0	0	0 500	500
Total Requirements	1800	1500	1200	4500

Note that in our initial solution, it is the customer in Baltimore whose order will not be fully shipped. This is because in the initial solution he is designated 500 units from the fictitious dummy warehouse which does not exist. However, note that the rim requirements have been met.

The costs have been entered in the subcells as usual. Note that zeros have been placed in subcells pertaining to the dummy warehouse. This is because the dummy warehouse will make no shipments, and therefore, will incur no costs. We compute the total cost of the initial solution as we did previously.

SUMMARY

In this chapter a simplified version of the simplex technique of linear programming was presented—the transportation method. This method deals with a special class of linear programming problems in which the objective is to transport a single product from various locations (supply) to different locations (demand) at a minimum total cost. The manager utilizes various supply, demand, and cost information to reach an optimum transport schedule. Thus it would be acceptable to state that the transportation method aids management in solving allocation of product-supply problems. An examination of the mechanics outlined in this chapter clearly illustrates that a computer may be used to solve transportation problems. However, specific steps of the method were presented so that a better understanding of the logic and method could be obtained.

DISCUSSION AND REVIEW QUESTIONS

1. Briefly discuss the following statements:
    a) "A computer is not needed for solving complex linear programming problems."
    b) "Supply of a product must always equal demand for a product before the transportation method can be used."
    c) "The rim values in a distribution matrix are definitely not constraints."
    d) "It is not necessary to know the subcell monetary amounts when utilizing the transportation method."
    e) "The transportation problem can be described accurately by referring to it as an assignment problem."
2. Would it be possible to utilize a "southeast corner" procedure to solve transportation type problems?
3. The Beltsville Products Corporation has three supply sources for their new pneumatic twist-off bottlecap machine. The machines are in demand from three purchasers located in Baltimore, Atlanta, and Milwaukee. The supply sources are as follows:

Supply Sources	Twist-off Machines on Hand
A	150
B	100
C	50

The demand requirements are as follows:

Demand	Machines Wanted
Baltimore	130
Atlanta	100
Milwaukee	70

The cost of delivery of the machines is a major concern to the Beltsville management who estimate the following cost schedule:

Supply	Destination Demand		
	Baltimore	Atlanta	Milwaukee
A	3	7	4
B	4	8	6
C	9	2	6

The manager in charge of developing a supply-demand mix which would minimize the total shipping cost is asked to set up a northwest corner matrix in its entirety and to evaluate the occupied and unoccupied cells.

a)   Set up the initial matrix and show all work in evaluating the occupied and unoccupied cells.

b)   Does this matrix provide an optimal solution? Why?

c)   What is the total transportation cost of the mix illustrated in the initial matrix?

4.   The Danny Company is a manufacturer of industrial equipment. They have three warehouses in the following locations:

Warehouse	Machines in Stock
New York	200
Chicago	150
Denver	50

The company has the following monthly demand for three customers.

Customer	Monthly Orders
Tampa	180
Portland	150
Salt Lake City	70

The cost of delivery from each warehouse to each customer is determined largely on the basis of overland mileage. The per unit delivery costs have been determined to be (in dollars):

Supply	Destination Demand		
	Tampa	Portland	Salt Lake City
New York	4	12	7
Chicago	5	8	2
Denver	8	5	3

The management would like to arrive at an optimal program which minimizes transportation costs. Utilize the northwest corner method and provide management with the optimal solution.

ADDITIONAL REFERENCES

BIERMAN, H., BONINI, C. P., and HAUSMAN, W. H. *Quantitative Analysis for Business Decisions.* Homewood, Ill.: Richard D. Irwin, Inc., 1969.

CHARNES, A., and COOPER, W. W. *Management Models and Industrial Applications of Linear Programming.* 2 Vols. New York: John Wiley & Sons, Inc., 1963.

DANTZIG, G. B. *Linear Programming and Extensions.* Princeton: Princeton University Press, 1963.

GASS, S. I. *Linear Programming: Methods and Applications.* New York: McGraw-Hill Book Co., 1966.

MILLER, D. W. and STARR, M. K. *Executive Decisions and Operations Research.* Englewood Cliffs, N.J.: Prentice-Hall, Inc., 1969.

WAGNER, H. *Principles of Operations Research with Applications to Managerial Decisions.* Englewood Cliffs, N.J.: Prentice-Hall, Inc., 1969.

chapter eighteen

Network Models

INTRODUCTION

One of the manager's major tasks is to allocate resources to fulfill the objectives of the organization. This may also include expansion, modification, or contraction of existing resource holdings. In the two previous chapters, we saw that the allocation of resources may be explicit as in the linear programming or transportation models. We also saw that with both models some data were available to aid the manager in reaching allocation decisions.

In this chapter, we shall examine certain techniques which may be used either to combine resources or to control activities in order to see that plans are carried out as stated. These techniques can be described under the general heading of *Network Models*. They are especially suited for projects which are not of a routine or repetitive nature and which will be conducted only once or a few times. In such projects there is a great need for some type of coordination, in order to insure that certain tasks that must be completed prior to another task are actually completed. Some idea is also needed of approximately how long the entire process will take. In summary, some method is needed to avoid unnecessary conflicts and delays by keeping track of all events and activities—and their interrelationships on a specific project. Network models provide the means to achieve this goal. As such, they are a valuable aid to the manager for both *planning* and *control* purposes.

NETWORK MODELS (PERT)

PERT stands for Program Evaluation and Review Technique. It was developed through the cooperation of the U.S. Navy and Booz, Allen, and Hamilton, a management consulting firm. The first major use was by the Navy Department for the construction of the Polaris missile submarine.[1] What exactly is PERT? It is a method by which conflicts, delays, and interruptions in a project are minimized by coordinating and synchronizing the various parts of the overall job in order to complete the project on schedule. It does not solve a manager's problems, but it does help him see what his problems are and what solutions are realistic.

PERT is especially useful to management in nonrepetitive problem areas—ones which the manager has not previously encountered in the past and is not likely to encounter again in the future. These are opposed to repetitive processes such as periodic reorders of inventory for which management has past experience, standards, and costs. However, management must still plan and control nonrepetitive operations. Obviously, this is more difficult because there is no past experience on which to rely. PERT is extremely helpful in such situations because it enables a manager to think through a project in its entirety and at the same time informs him of possible delays. As such, it usually leads to more optimum utilization of resources.

Fundamentals of PERT

PERT is developed around two fundamental concepts: activities and events. An *activity* is the work necessary to complete a particular event. An *event* is an accomplishment at a particular point in time and consumes no time. In PERT diagrams or networks, we designate an event with a circle and an activity as an arrow connecting the two circles. This is shown in Figure 18–1.

FIGURE 18–1
Two Events and One Activity

In Figure 18–1 there are two events which are assigned numbers connected by one activity which we designate with an arrow. Each of the two events occur at a specific point in time. Event 1 could represent the

---

[1] See William Fazur, "The Origins of PERT," *The Controller*, vol. 30 (December, 1962), pp. 34–36.

specific point in time "project begun" and event 2 could represent the specific point in time "project completed." The arrow connecting the two events represents the activity—the actual work done—and the time necessary to complete the work. Thus, the two events in Figure 18–1 designate the beginning and end of the activity. The activity is what requires time, not the events.

Above we referred to a PERT diagram or network. The term network is used when several events and activities are combined in a diagram. This diagram we shall refer to as a network. Figure 18–1 is a very simple PERT network involving two events and one activity. A more complex PERT network is presented in Figure 18–2.

FIGURE 18–2

Pert Network

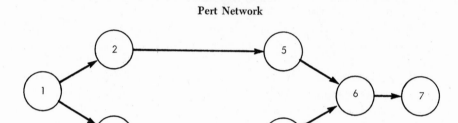

Examination of Figure 18–2 indicates that event 1 is the network beginning event since there are no activities leading to it, and event 7 is the network ending event since there are no activities leading away from it. Note also that event 1 is the beginning event for two activities, and event 6 is the ending event for two activities, as well as the beginning event for one activity.

The paramount variable in a PERT system is time—the basic measure of how long a project will take. Estimating how long each activity will take is extremely difficult since the manager has no experience to rely on in most cases. This results in uncertainty in making estimates of the time needed to complete the entire network. However, probability theory provides a means of reducing some of the uncertainty involved in our estimate of time.

ESTIMATING ACTIVITY TIME REQUIREMENTS

As we mentioned previously, PERT projects are usually unique and are, therefore, subject to a great deal of uncertainty. PERT is designed to deal specifically with this problem of uncertainty through the application of statistical analysis in determining the job time estimates.

For example, assume you are trying to estimate how long it will take to complete a term project for your management class. You know that you must collect and analyze certain information. If all goes well and you do not encounter any obstacles, you believe that you could complete the project in five weeks. However, if a situation occurred where you encountered numerous obstacles (dates, parties, illness, materials not available in the library, etc.), the chances would be greater that your term project would take much longer to complete. Thus you could estimate a variety of possible completion times for your term project.

Specifically, for PERT projects, three time estimates are required for each activity. The individual or group chosen to make each time estimate should be that individual or group who is most closely connected with, and responsible for, the particular activity under consideration. The three time estimates needed are:

Optimistic Time (*a*). This is the time the project can be completed in if everything goes exceptionally well and we encounter no obstacles or problems.

Most Likely Time (*m*). This is the most realistic estimate of how long an activity might take. This is the time we would expect to occur most often if the activity was repeated numerous times.

Pessimistic Time (*b*). This is the time that would be required if everything went wrong and we encountered numerous obstacles and problems.

Obviously, we cannot in PERT be concerned with three times for every activity. It would be extremely impractical to try to deal simultaneously with the most optimistic time, the most likely time and the most pessimistic time. Fortunately, a way has been developed which enables us to arrive at one time estimate. An *expected time* (t_e) and its standard deviation[2] (σ) can be estimated satisfactorily for each activity by using the following formulas:

$$t_e = \frac{a + 4m + b}{6}$$

$$\sigma = \frac{b - a}{6}$$

Let us examine this methodology in relation to the term project mentioned above. Assume that you estimate that eight weeks is the most likely completion time (*m*). However, you feel that there is a small chance (perhaps one time in ten) that the term project might be completed in two weeks. Therefore, the optimistic time (*a*) is 2. Finally, you feel there is also a slight chance things could go wrong and the project would take 10 weeks to complete. Therefore, the pessimistic time (*b*) is 10. The probability that the project will be completed in a given amount of time

---

[2] If necessary the reader can refresh his memory concerning the standard deviation and its properties by consulting any basic statistics text.

can be illustrated graphically as shown in Figure 18–3. We can see that there is a greater probability that the project will take eight weeks than any other time. This is shown as the highest point on the curve shown in Figure 18–3.

FIGURE 18–3

Probability Distribution

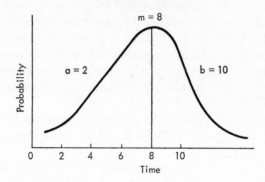

In order to compute the expected time (t_e) from the three time estimates that have been provided, we must determine what time will divide the total area under the curve in half. In other words, when there is a 50-50 chance of completing the project at that time. We use the previously mentioned formulas to arrive at the expected time and variation:

$$t_c = \frac{a + 4m + b}{6}$$

$$\sigma = \frac{b - a}{6}$$

Substituting our time estimates into the formulas yields:

$$t_e = \frac{2 + 4(8) + 10}{6}$$

$$= \frac{44}{6}$$

$$t_e = 7.33$$

and

$$\sigma = \frac{10 - 2}{6}$$

$$= \frac{8}{6}$$

$$\sigma = 1.33$$

Figure 18–4 indicates the 50-50 dividing line.

Note that in our formula for computing the expected time (t_e), the weight that is given to the most likely time is much greater than the weight given to the optimistic and pessimistic time, since each of them has only a small chance of occurring. Also, note that the optimistic and pessimistic time each receive the same weight.

FIGURE 18–4

Probability Distribution

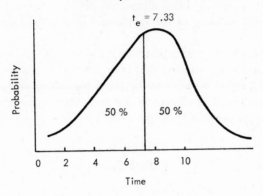

In conclusion, it should be clear that the expected time (t_e) may be either to the right or to the left of the most likely value (m) depending on the three time estimates. To illustrate an expected time value (t_e) to the right of the most likely time, let us now assume that we have the following three time estimates:

Optimistic Time (a) = 6 weeks
Most Likely Time (m) = 8 weeks
Pessimistic Time (b) = 16 weeks

Substituting these values into the formulas yields:

$$t_e = \frac{a + 4(m) + b}{6}$$

$$= \frac{6 + 4(8) + 16}{6}$$

$$t_c = 9$$

and

$$\sigma = \frac{b - a}{6}$$

$$= \frac{16 - 6}{6}$$

$$\sigma = 1.67$$

In this case, the expected time (t_e) lies to the right of the most likely time (m).

DEVELOPING PERT NETWORKS

There are four basic phases in constructing a PERT network.
1. Define each task that must be done.
2. Estimate how long each task will take.
3. Construct the network.
4. Find the critical path—i.e., the longest path, in time, from the beginning event to the ending event.

In this section we will solve a simplified problem using PERT in order to gain an understanding of the mechanics of constructing a PERT network.[3]

Assume you are the production manager for Fly-Hi Aircraft Company. The government has requested that your firm develop a prototype model of an aircraft engine which can be used in special purpose airplanes. Since the government is always in a hurry, you would like to have the model developed as quickly as possible. The first step is to define each

FIGURE 18-5

PERT Network

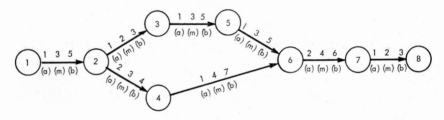

task that must be done. After consulting with the production and engineering departments, you conclude that the project consists of eight activities.
1. Develop engineering specifications for the engines.
2. Obtain test models of the engine.
3. Locate suppliers for component parts that will be needed for subassembly 2.
4. Develop production plans.
5. Begin subassembly 1.
6. Place orders for component parts and wait for receipt of component parts needed for subassembly 2.
7. Begin subassembly 2.
8. Begin final assembly.

The network for the project is shown in Figure 18-5 with the esti-

---

[3] For complete discussions of networking principles, see Louis R. Shaffer, J. B. Ritter, and W. L. Meyer, *Critical Path Method* (New York: McGraw-Hill Book Co., 1965); and K. G. Lockyer, *An Introduction to Critical Path Analysis* (New York: Pitman Publishing Corporation, 1964).

TABLE 18-1

Description of Activities and Events in Figure 18-5

Activity	Description	Prerequisite Activities	Event Description
1-2	Develop engineering specifications		2—Specifications completed
2-3	Obtain test models	1-2	3—Test models obtained
2-4	Locate suppliers of component parts	1-2	4—Suppliers located
3-5	Develop production plans	2-3	5—Plans completed
5-6	Begin subassembly 1	3-5	6—Subassembly 1 completed
4-6	Place orders for component parts and await receipt	2-4	6—Component parts received
6-7	Begin subassembly 2	5-6 and 4-6	7—Subassembly 2 completed
7-8	Begin final assembly	6-7	8—Engine completed

mates of the most optimistic (a), most likely (m), and most pessimistic (b) times. A detailed description of the activities and events in the network is provided in Table 18-1.

Our first task is to calculate the expected time for each activity in the network. In Table 18-2 the three time estimates are given and the expected time (t_e) is calculated using the formula

$$t_e = \frac{a + 4m + b}{6}$$

Figure 18-6 shows the PERT network with the expected time (t_e) values for each activity. Note that events 3 and 4 are branched. This is because activities 2-3 and 2-4 can be performed simultaneously.

TABLE 18-2

Calculation of t_e Values for Network

Activity	Most Optimistic Time (a)	Most Likely Time (m)	Most Pessimistic Time (b)	t_e (in Weeks)
1-2	1	3	5	3.0
2-3	1	2	3	2.0
2-4	2	3	4	3.0
3-5	1	3	5	3.0
4-6	1	4	7	4.0
5-6	1	3	5	3.0
6-7	2	4	6	4.0
7-8	1	2	3	2.0

FIGURE 18–6

Expected Time (t_e) for Each Activity

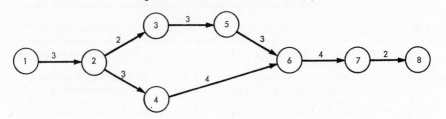

Calculation of Earliest Expected Date

Once the PERT network has been constructed and the expected time (t_e) has been calculated for each event we can turn our attention to calculating the *earliest expected date* (T_E) in which the project can be completed. The earliest expected date of an event is found by calculating the *longest* path from the network beginning event to the particular event in question, whether it is the network ending event or some other event.

Examination of the network reveals there are two paths through the network, path 1, 2, 3, 5, 6, 7, 8 which takes a total of 17 weeks; and path 1, 2, 4, 6, 7, 8 which takes a total of 16 weeks. Thus, if we begin at once, completion of the network can be expected no sooner than 17 weeks.

Let us suppose that the manager wants to determine how soon he can hope to complete a particular event which is not the network ending event. For example, when can he expect to have event 5 completed? To determine this we do exactly as we did previously; sum the paths from the network beginning event to the particular event in question and choose the longest path if there is more than one path. Thus, the (T_E) for event 5 is (path 1, 2, 3, 5) 8 weeks.

We can calculate the earliest expected date (T_E) for each event in the network by utilizing the same rule, by taking the longest path from

FIGURE 18–7

Earliest Expected Date for Each Event in Network

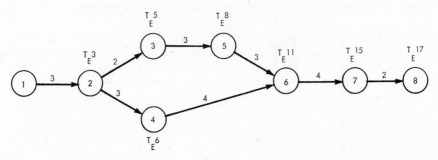

the network beginning event to each of the other events in the network. This is shown in Figure 18–7.

The importance of the *earliest expected date* (T_E) is that it provides us with the dates on which certain work will be completed. If the computed date is unsatisfactory it gives us the opportunity to adjust our operations.

Before leaving the calculation of (T_E) let us examine event 6. It is somewhat different since it has two events leading to it, path 1, 2, 3, 5, 6 which requires 11 weeks, and path 1, 2, 4, 6 which requires ten weeks. Therefore, the (T_E) of event 6 is 11 weeks because (T_E) is the longest path from the network beginning event to the particular event in question.

The Critical Path

We have just seen that the longest path through the network determines the earliest expected date of the network ending event. This longest path is more commonly referred to as the *critical path*. Thus, we can define the critical path as the most time-consuming path of activities from the network beginning event to the network ending event. In the above network it is path 1, 2, 3, 5, 6, 7, 8.

Latest Allowable Date

The latest allowable date is the latest date (T_L) on which an event can occur without creating a delay in the scheduled completion of the project. In Figure 18–7 we determined the longest path through the network by utilizing the earliest expected dates for each of the events. To calculate the $(T_L$'s) we subtract from the network ending event back to the event in question. (T_L) for an ending event is equal to the date directed by management for completion of the project. Let us assume that in this project we have a directed date of five months (20 weeks) in which the project must be completed. However, if a directed date was not specified, then $T_L = T_E$ for the network ending event. The (T_L) values for the entire network are shown in Figure 18–8.

By now the reader should note that when we calculated the $(T_E$'s) we found (by addition) the longest path from the network beginning event to the particular event in question. When calculating the $(T_L$'s) we subtract in order to find the longest path from the network ending event back to the particular event in question.

In Figure 18–8 we see that the (T_L) of an event is found by subtracting the expected time for the activity from the previous (T_L). For example, the (T_L) for event 3 is found by subtracting the (t_e) of activity 3–5 from the (T_L) of event 5, or $11 - 3 = 8$.

Examine event 2. Note that when two or more paths yield different values we always choose the smaller when calculating the (T_L) of an event. Remember, in calculating the (T_E) of an event we always choose the larger value. Calculating the (T_L) of event 2 we get:

$$\text{Path 2–3} = 8 - 2 = 6$$
$$\text{Path 2–4} = 10 - 3 = 7$$

FIGURE 18–8

Latest Allowable Date for Each Event in Network

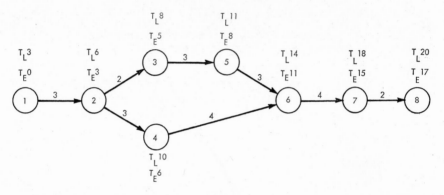

Since we choose the smaller value the (T_L) for event 2 is 6. This is obvious since Path 2, 3, 5, 6, 7, 8, involves 14 weeks and Path 2, 4, 6, 7, 8, involves 13 weeks. If we expect to complete the network in 20 weeks, event 2 must be completed within 6 weeks after the network beginning event in order to allow 10 additional weeks for the completion of the network.

Slack Time

Slack time is obviously time to spare in the completion of certain events. In Figure 18–8 we can see that event 6 does not have to occur until 14 weeks after the start of the network. However, event 4 is expected to be done in 6 weeks after the beginning of the network. Since activity 4–6 takes 4 weeks we can see that event 4 does not have to be achieved in 6 weeks. We could actually take 10 weeks to complete it and still meet our directed date of 20 weeks. Thus, there is slack on path 1, 2, 4, 6, 7, 8 and if we fall slightly behind we do not have to worry. Slack time is calculated by using the following formula:

$$\text{Slack Time} = S = T_L - T_E.$$

The calculations of slack time are shown in Table 18–3.

In Figure 18–8 and Table 18–3 we see that there is slack time on the critical path. Can such a situation exist? The answer is "yes" because we have allowed 20 weeks to complete the project, which is three more weeks than we actually need. However, note that the critical path has less slack (three weeks) than path 1, 2, 4, 6, 7, 8, which has four weeks. From a practical standpoint this indicates that we could fall three weeks behind somewhere on the events on the critical path and still not jeopardize our completion date. It also means that we can shift resources if possible to the critical, path, thereby perhaps shortening the time of the entire project. This is an important use of the slack time computation.

TABLE 18–3

Calculation of Slack Time for Events in Network

Event	T_L	—	T_E	= Slack Time
1	3	—	0	= 3
2	6	—	3	= 3
3	8	—	5	= 3
4	10	—	6	= 4
5	11	—	8	= 3
6	14	—	11	= 3
7	18	—	15	= 3
8	20	—	17	= 3

Before leaving this discussion we should mention that it is also possible to have a network in which the (T_L) of the network ending event is less than the (T_E) for the same event. This would occur when we have allowed the project less time than it is expected to take us to complete the project. In such cases which are atypical, the network has negative slack which would mean we are behind schedule. A case could also arise where $T_L = T_E$. This would be the case previously mentioned where there is no specified date for completion.

COMPUTING THE PROBABILITY OF ACHIEVING THE COMPLETION DATE

The reader will recall that when we began our discussion of PERT we pointed out that there was uncertainty involved in our estimates. The reason for this is that the entire PERT system is based upon estimates of time. Specifically, there were three estimates of time each with some degree of uncertainty attached to them. Even the (t_e) value is uncertain because it was calculated using the three time estimates. In this section we will examine methods for dealing with these uncertainties with the objective of estimating the probability that a project will be completed by (T_L). We shall use a simplified example to illustrate the procedure and then return to our more complex problem.

Earlier, in addition to calculating the expected time (t_e) we also provided a formula for calculating its standard deviation. The formula was:

$$\sigma = \frac{b - a}{6}$$

The reader should recall from an elementary statistics course that the standard deviation is a statistical measure which indicates the tendency for data to disperse around the mean. In PERT projects, it will aid us in calculating the probability of achieving the completion date of the project. In order to illustrate how this is done, let us examine the simplified PERT network in Figure 18–9.

FIGURE 18–9
PERT Network

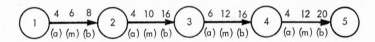

The most optimistic time, most likely time, and most pessimistic time estimates are listed for each activity. First, we shall compute the estimated time (t_e) and the standard deviation for each individual activity. Finally, we shall compute the standard deviation for the network ending event.

Our first step is to calculate the expected time (t_e) for each of the activities and determine the earliest expected date (T_E) for the network ending event. This is shown in Table 18–4.

TABLE 18–4
Expected Times for PERT Network in Figure 18–9

Activity	Most Optimistic Time (a)	Most Likely Time (m)	Most Pessimistic Time (b)	$\dfrac{a + 4m + b}{6} = t_e$
1–2	4	6	8	$\dfrac{4 + 24 + 8}{6} = 6.0$
2–3	4	10	16	$\dfrac{4 + 40 + 16}{6} = 10.0$
3–4	6	12	16	$\dfrac{6 + 48 + 16}{6} = 11.7$
4–5	4	12	20	$\dfrac{4 + 48 + 20}{6} = 12.0$

T_E (network ending event 5) $= 6.0 + 10.0 + 11.7 + 12.0$
$$T_E = 39.7 \text{ weeks}$$

TABLE 18–5

Standard Deviations for PERT Network in Figure 18–9

Activity	Most Optimistic Time (a)	Most Pessimistic Time (b)	$\dfrac{b-a}{6}$	Standard Deviation (σ)
1–2	4	8	$\frac{4}{6}$	.67
2–3	4	16	$12\frac{2}{6}$	2.00
3–4	6	16	$10\frac{0}{6}$	1.67
4–5	4	20	$16\frac{6}{6}$	2.67

Our next step is to calculate the standard deviations for each individual activity. This is shown in Table 18–5.

Now that we have the standard deviations for each of the individual activities we would like to obtain some probability measure that will indicate what our chances are of finishing on time. In order to obtain this we must calculate the standard deviation for the network ending event. To calculate the standard deviation for the ending event in a series we take the square root of the sum of the individual activity standard deviations squared. This is expressed mathematically as:

σ for Network Ending Event
$$= \sqrt{\Sigma(\sigma)^2}$$
$$= \sqrt{(0.67)^2 + (2.0)^2 + (1.67)^2 + (2.67)^2}$$
$$= \sqrt{(0.449) + 4.0 + 2.79 + 7.13}$$
$$= \sqrt{14.37}$$
$$\sigma T_E = 3.8 \text{ weeks (rounded).}$$

We now have two specific measures for this network:
1. the earliest expected date (T_E) for the network ending event (39.7) weeks, and
2. the standard deviation of the network ending event (3.8) weeks. This can be written (σT_E).

The manager is keenly interested in the likelihood of meeting the scheduled completion date of the project (T_L). He would also prefer to have that likelihood expressed quantitatively in terms of probability. PERT procedures can provide this information.

The difference between the earliest expected completion date (T_E) and the latest allowable date (T_L) is divided by (σT_E) in order to express the difference in standard deviations $(\sigma T_E\text{'s})$ which has traditionally been denoted by the letter Z. Thus we have

$$Z = \frac{T_L - T_E}{\sigma T_E}.$$

Since the earliest expected date (T_E) is the sum of a series of means of probability distributions, (T_E) will tend to be distributed according to the normal probability distribution, and the Z value which we compute can be evaluated by using the Table of Areas under the Normal Curve shown in the Appendix to this chapter.

Assume that the network in Figure 18–9 must be completed in 44 weeks. We illustrate the (T_E) and (T_L) of the network ending event in Figure 18–10.

FIGURE 18–10

Probability Distribution of Network Ending Event

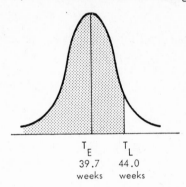

$$T_E \quad\quad T_L$$
$$39.7 \quad\quad 44.0$$
$$\text{weeks} \quad\quad \text{weeks}$$

In order to determine the number of standard deviations Z we are from the mean, we subtract the (T_E) value from the (T_L) value. This is actually slack time on this particular critical path. We then divide the slack time by the standard deviation of the network ending event in order to get the number of standard deviations the slack time represents. This is shown as follows:

$$Z = \frac{T_L - T_E}{\sigma T_E}$$

$$Z = \frac{44 - 39.7}{3.8}$$

$$Z = \frac{4.3}{3.8}$$

$$Z = 1.13$$

In order to determine what percentage of the curve is contained within 1.13 standard deviations from the mean we must consult the Appendix, the table of areas under the curve. We find that 1.13 standard deviations from the mean encompasses 0.3708 percent of the curve from the mean. We know that 50 percent of the area under the curve lies to the left of the mean. Thus, our chances of finishing before the latest allowable date

(T_L) is approximately 87 percent. The remaining difference (13 percent) is the probability that we will finish after the latest allowable date.[4]

Before proceeding, let us examine Figures 18–11 and 18–12. Figure 18–11 illustrates the existence of zero slack on the critical path. In this case, Z would equal zero and the probability of meeting the latest allowable date (T_L) equals 0.50. Figure 18–12 illustrates a case where

FIGURE 18–11

Probability Distribution
$(T_E = T_L)$

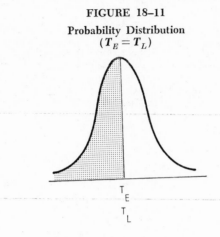

FIGURE 18–12

Probability Distribution
$(T_L < T_E)$

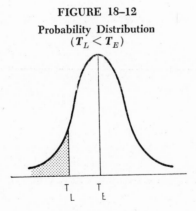

the (T_L) value lies to the left of the (T_E) value; that is, where we have negative slack on the critical path. In this case we know from the beginning that we have less time available to complete the job than we know we shall need. The shaded area in Figure 18–12 indicates the probability of finishing on time. Here, Z will be negative and the probability value is equal to 0.50 minus the value in the table. In this case the

[4] This calculation assumes that the task times along any path are independent.

probability of meeting the latest allowable date will be less than 0.50. The unshaded area in Figure 18–12 indicates the probability of being late which in this case is greater than 0.50.

Now let us return to our original problem (Figure 18–5) and calculate the probability of achieving the completion date. First, we must calculate the standard deviations for each individual activity on the critical path. This is shown in Table 18–6.

TABLE 18–6
Standard Deviations for Critical Path Activities

Activity	Most Optimistic Time (a)	Most Pessimistic Time (b)	$\dfrac{b-a}{6}$	Standard Deviation (σ)
1–2	1	5	$\frac{4}{6}$	0.67
2–3	1	3	$\frac{2}{6}$	0.33
3–5	1	5	$\frac{4}{6}$	0.67
5–6	1	5	$\frac{4}{6}$	0.67
6–7	2	6	$\frac{4}{6}$	0.67
7–8	1	3	$\frac{2}{6}$	0.33

Now that we have the standard deviation for each activity on the critical path we can calculate the standard deviation for the network ending event.

$$\sigma TE = \sqrt{\Sigma \sigma^2}$$
$$= \sqrt{(0.67)^2 + (0.33)^2 + (0.67)^2 + (0.67)^2 + (0.67)^2 + (0.33)^2}$$
$$= \sqrt{2.0}$$
$$\sigma TE = 1.4 \text{ weeks}$$

Our next step is to compute the slack time on the critical path. We divide the slack time by the standard deviation of the network ending event (σT_E) in order to get the number of standard deviations Z the slack time represents. This is computed as follows:

$$Z = \frac{T_L - T_E}{\sigma T_E}$$
$$= \frac{20 - 17}{1.4}$$
$$Z = 2.14$$

Examining the Appendix reveals that a Z value of 2.14 encompasses 0.4838 percent of the curve from the mean of a normal distribution. We know that 50 percent of the area under the curve lies to the left of the mean of a normal distribution. Thus, our chances of finishing before the latest allowable date (T_L) of 20 weeks is about 98 percent. This is shown as the shaded area under the curve in Figure 18–13.

In conclusion, the reader should see that PERT is an extremely valuable planning and control aid for management. It forces managers to think each major program and project through in its entirety. It aids them in identifying possible delays and conflicts before they occur. It helps in achieving earlier deadlines because of effective *concurrent* control.

FIGURE 18–13

Probability Distribution of Network Ending Event

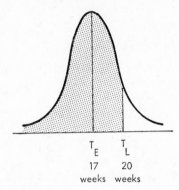

T_E T_L

17   20

weeks weeks

MANAGEMENT'S USE OF PERT

The PERT technique provides extremely useful information for planning and control purposes.[5] Thus, it is a valuable aid to the manager in performing these two important management functions.

PERT as a Planning Tool

Because it provides the manager with the interconnections of events and the estimated times for activities, PERT increases management's ability to plan an optimum network before starting work at whatever level or depth they feel is necessary. In other words, management can take a number of steps to reduce the total time needed to complete a project while the project is still in the planning stage. Time reductions can be brought about in a number of ways.[6] For example:

[5] For an excellent discussion of management's use of PERT, see Robert W. Miller, "How to Plan and Control with PERT," *Harvard Business Review*, vol. 40 (March–April, 1962), pp. 93–104.

[6] Based upon Harry Evarts, *Introduction to PERT* (Boston: Allyn and Bacon, Inc., 1964).

1. by reducing the expected time on the critical path by adding shifts or changing technology,
2. by eliminating some part of the project that previously might have been considered desirable but not necessary,
3. by transferring resources from slack to more critical paths,
4. by adding more resources,
5. by substituting a component if the time required to produce the component is too long, and
6. by changing some work to parallel activities when they had previously been planned in series.

PERT as a Control Device

It is easy to see that PERT is an effective internal control device. Because it provides time schedules for each activity, networks can be revised if unforeseen difficulties arise. This enables the manager to keep complete and effective control over a project. Resources can be shifted and activities can be rescheduled with a minimum of delay on the outcome of the project.

In addition to an internal control device, PERT may also be an effective external control device. For example, in projects where subcontractors are used, the necessity for meeting scheduled dates can be stressed by showing the subcontractor the negative effects a delay on his part will have on the entire project. When subcontractors are involved, it is vital that these firms meet their scheduled delivery dates. At the outset of the chapter we mentioned that PERT was used by the Navy Department in the Polaris project.[7] This vast project involved some 250 prime contractors and over 9,000 subcontractors. The failure of any one of these subcontractors to deliver a piece of hardware on schedule could have stalled the entire project. However, the use of PERT enabled the Polaris submarine to reach completion two years ahead of schedule. Thus, PERT can serve as both an internal and external control device.

Management Problems with PERT

While PERT has proven to be a valuable aid for management planning and control, there have also been several problems which some firms have encountered with it.[8] However, note that the majority of the problems have not been with PERT itself, but with management's application of it.

---

[7] See Fazur, *op. cit.*, pp. 34–36.

[8] Peter P. Schoderbek, "PERT—Its Promises and Performance," *Michigan Business Review*, vol. 17 (January, 1965), pp. 25–32. Also see H. S. Phelps, "What Your People Should Know about PERT," *Management Review*, vol. 5 (October, 1962), pp. 44–51.

1. *Acceptance.* In some firms line managers and technical personnel lack a full appreciation of PERT's benefits and limitations. This is due mainly to the failure of top management to support the implementation of it.

2. *PERT Misuse.* Unfortunately, PERT has at times been misused. Because of its value as a planning and control device, some overzealous managers have extended its application in some areas where it should not have been used.

3. *Resistance to Change.* This is an obstacle which stands in the way of the initial adoption of any new system. Thus, when the introduction of PERT results in alterations in work procedures, it is bound to be met with resistance unless management has undertaken the necessary preparations. The reader will recall the managerial approaches for coping with resistance to change were discussed in the previous section of the book.

NETWORK METHODS (CPM)

A method which is closely related to PERT is known as CPM (Critical Path Method). Next to PERT, this method of planning and controlling projects is probably the most widely used network method.

CPM departs from PERT in that CPM brings into the planning and control process the concept of cost. However, this is not to say that PERT completely omits the cost concept. In PERT we assumed that cost varied directly with time for all the activities of the project. In other words, when a reduction in time had been achieved, we assumed that a reduction in cost had also been achieved. When the earliest expected date (T_E) of the network was reduced, we assumed there had been a reduction in cost.[9]

Another area of departure between PERT and CPM is that CPM uses a single time estimate for each activity; whereas in PERT we used three. The user of CPM is assumed to have a more solid basis when estimating the time required for each activity.

Whether PERT or CPM is used will be determined by the needs of the program or the type of project. When time can be estimated accurately and costs can be determined in advance, CPM is probably the better of the two network methods. A good example of this type of project is a construction project where material and labor costs can be determined fairly accurately and in advance. However, when there is a high degree of uncertainty and/or the need for control over time outweighs control over costs, PERT is probably the better choice of the two.

Development of a CPM network follows the same principles as a

---

[9] When PERT was originally developed, it did not consider the direct relationship between cost and time. However, the latest versions of PERT present highly sophisticated cost analysis procedures.

PERT network so there is no need to repeat them. The real difference lies in estimating the times for each activity.[10]

For each activity in a CPM network there are two time estimates and two corresponding cost estimates. However, note that these two estimates refer to different kinds of estimates. Only one, the *normal time* estimate corresponds to the most likely time (t_e) in a PERT network. A *crash time* estimate is the time that would be needed if no costs were spared. *Normal cost* is, therefore, the cost necessary to finish the project in the normal time and *crash cost* is the cost necessary to complete the job in the *crash time*. We can depict this situation graphically in Figure 18–14.

FIGURE 18–14

Crash Time and Cost versus Normal Time and Cost

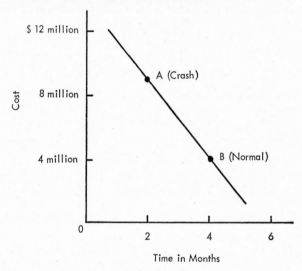

In Figure 18–14 the vertical axis represents the costs associated with completing a particular project and the horizontal axis depicts the time needed for completion. The graph indicates that a crash effort could complete the project in two months at a cost of $9 million while a normal effort would cost $4 million and take four months to complete. We refer to the line connecting the two points (*A* and *B*) as the approximated time-cost curve because we do not really know exactly how the time-cost relationship behaves without a great deal of research and cost analysis.

---

[10] See Edward W. Davis, "Resource Allocation in Project Network—A Survey," *Journal of Industrial Engineering*, vol. 4 (September, 1964), pp. 33–38 for a complete discussion of time estimation in CPM.

What we are actually doing here is assuming that a straight line is an accurate enough approximation of the actual relationship. In Chapter 13 we mentioned that one method used to simplify complex problems was to use linear approximations of actual relationships when in reality the true relationship is probably nonlinear. The purpose of doing this in CPM problems is to enable the manager to determine quickly the cost of speeding up a particular activity without engaging in time-consuming time-cost studies.

Let us illustrate the basics of CPM by examining the simple network Figure 18–15.

FIGURE 18–15
Normal Times for All Activities

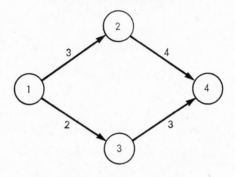

For any set of activities on the critical path of a given network, each will have its own cost per week of crashing and there will be a large number of alternative ways to crash the project with each having its own cost. For Figure 18–15 the normal times are shown on the network and the earliest expected date of the network ending event is 7 weeks. The critical path is path 1, 2, 4. Now let us calculate the cost of crashing the program. This is shown in Table 18–7.

TABLE 18–7
Calculation of Cost of Crashing Program

Activity	Time in Weeks		Cost		Cost to Crash
	Normal	Crash	Normal	Crash	
1–2	3	2	$4,000	$5,000	$1,000
1–3	2	1	3,000	3,750	750
2–4	4	3	3,000	3,500	500
3–4	3	2	5,000	6,500	1,500

In Table 18–7 the cost to crash is found by using the following formula:

$$\text{Cost to crash} = \frac{\text{crash cost} - \text{normal cost}}{\text{normal time} - \text{crash time}}$$

We can now construct a new network utilizing the crash time for each activity. By crashing all the activities we see that the earliest expected date for the network ending event is now 5 weeks. The critical path remains path 1, 2, 4 (see Figure 18–16). The cost of the project is now $18,750 (total of the crash cost column) as opposed to $15,000 under the normal time. However, the project is completed two weeks earlier. Our problem now becomes one of determining if we can crash the project without crashing every activity in the network. If this is possible we may be able to still reduce the earliest expected date of five weeks without increasing the total cost from $15,000 to $18,750.

FIGURE 18–16

Crash Times for All Activities

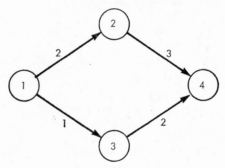

Examination of Table 18–7 indicates that activity 2–4 on the critical path is the least costly activity to crash. It can be reduced one week at a cost of $500. If this is done, then the earliest expected date would be six weeks, and the total cost of the program would be $15,500.

The remaining activity (1–2) on the critical path can be reduced one week at a cost of $1,000. Thus, the earliest expected date is five weeks with a total cost of $16,500.

Our network now is shown in Figure 18–17. Examination of Figure 18–17 now indicates that both paths 1, 2, 4 and 1, 3, 4 are critical paths. Each path requires five weeks to complete. Thus, any reduction of the time on one of the paths without a corresponding reduction on the other path will not reduce the earliest expected date (T_E) of the network ending event any further.

For example, why not crash activity 1–3 or 3–4? Remember that activities 1–2 and 2–4 have already been crashed and can be crashed no further.

Therefore, if we reduced the time of path 1, 3, 4 it would be a foolish expenditure of money, since path 1, 2, 4 would have the longest (T_E) and therefore remain as the critical path. Thus, by closer examination we have managed to reduce the (T_E) from seven weeks to five weeks with an expenditure of $1,500 rather than $3,750. The total cost is now $16,500 instead of $18,750 when all activities were crashed.

This discussion of CPM has utilized a very simplified problem. The reader can imagine that a more complex network made up of numerous activities would be more realistic. However, the example provided here presents the basic underlying rationale and approach of CPM. Finally, the reader can well imagine that for PERT or CPM problems involving numerous events and activities, the use of a computer greatly facilitates the analysis.[11]

FIGURE 18-17

Crash Times for Activities 1-2 and 2-4

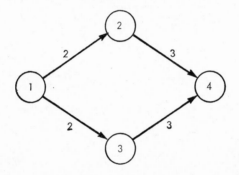

One final comment is in order concerning CPM and PERT as a control device. It is much more difficult to use CPM as a controlling device than it is to use PERT. Since CPM was initially developed as a static planning model, the reader can see that it is necessary to repeat the entire evaluation and manipulation phase each time changes are introduced into the network. PERT, therefore, is a much more flexible control device.

DISCUSSION AND REVIEW QUESTIONS

1. Why is PERT especially useful in nonrepetitive problem areas?
2. Cite some specific areas and types of problems that PERT would be useful in as a management tool.

---

[11] For an excellent, complete treatment of PERT and CPM, see Richard I. Levin and C. A. Kirkpatrick, *Planning and Control with PERT/CPM* (New York: McGraw-Hill Book Co., 1966).

3. Discuss the statement, "The paramount variable in a PERT network system is time."

4. Assume that you have been assigned a term project in one of your management courses. Data for the report will come from both primary and secondary sources. It is your task to collect both types of data. You have a total of ten weeks in which to complete the assignment. List the activities and their most optimistic, most likely, and most pessimistic times; and construct a PERT network for the project.

5. Assume that you have just received word to begin production on a special device that your company will produce for the government. You have developed the PERT network for the project, along with the time estimates for each activity. These are shown below. Assume you must complete the

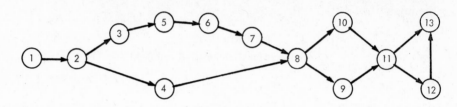

| Activity | Time Estimates (Weeks) | | |
	Most Optimistic Time	Most Likely Time	Most Pessimistic Time
1–2	1	2	3
2–3	2	4	6
2–4	2	4	6
3–5	1	3	5
4–8	2	4	6
5–6	4	7	10
6–7	1	2	3
7–8	1	2	3
8–9	1	2	3
8–10	1	2	3
9–11	2	3	4
10–11	3	4	5
11–12	1	2	3
11–13	4	6	8
12–13	1	1	1

project in 35 weeks. Compute the probability of achieving this date. Recall that this means you must first calculate the critical path and the (T_E) and (T_L) for each activity.

6. CPM is a valuable aid in certain kinds of projects. What characteristics do these problems have in common? Cite some example of where CPM might be used to advantage.

7. Answer in detail the following brief questions:
   A) Can there be slack time on the critical path?
   B) Can there be slack time on a noncritical path?
   C) Can there be any such thing as negative slack?
8. Place the following tasks in the form of a PERT network:
   A) Remove carburetor
   B) Rotate tires
   C) Put on snow tires
   D) Tune motor
   E) Clean and replace air filter
   F) Test drive car
   G) Remove air filter
   H) Complete tuneup

ADDITIONAL REFERENCES

BAKER, B. N. and ERIS, R. L. *An Introduction to PERT-CPM*. Homewood, Ill.: Richard D. Irwin, Inc., 1964.

HEIN, L. W. *The Quantitative Approach to Managerial Decisions*. Englewood Cliffs, N.J.: Prentice-Hall, Inc., 1967.

MARTINO, R. L. *Finding the Critical Path*. New York: American Management Association, 1964.

MILLER, R. W. "How to Plan and Control with PERT," *Harvard Business Review*, 40 (1962), 93–104.

MILLER, R. W. *Schedule, Cost and Profit Control with PERT*. New York: McGraw-Hill Book Co., 1963.

OLSEN, R. A. *Manufacturing Management: A Quantitative Approach*. Scranton, Pa.: International Textbook Co., 1968.

PAGE, J. C. and STOLLE, J. F. "Space Age Technique to Launch New Products (PERT Program)," *Sales Management*, 93 (1964), 22–27.

SHAFFER, L. R., RITTER, J. B., and MEYER, W. L. *Critical Path Method*. New York: McGraw-Hill Book Co., 1965.

APPENDIX

Table of Areas under the Normal Curve

z	.00	.01	.02	.03	.04	.05	.06	.07	.08	.09
0.0	.0000	.0040	.0080	.0120	.0160	.0199	.0239	.0279	.0319	.0359
0.1	.0398	.0438	.0478	.0517	.0557	.0596	.0636	.0675	.0714	.0753
0.2	.0793	.0832	.0871	.0910	.0948	.0987	.1026	.1064	.1103	.1141
0.3	.1179	.1217	.1255	.1293	.1331	.1368	.1406	.1443	.1480	.1517
0.4	.1554	.1591	.1628	.1664	.1700	.1736	.1772	.1808	.1844	.1879
0.5	.1915	.1950	.1985	.2019	.2054	.2088	.2123	.2157	.2190	.2224
0.6	.2257	.2291	.2324	.2357	.2389	.2422	.2454	.2486	.2517	.2549
0.7	.2580	.2611	.2642	.2673	.2704	.2734	.2764	.2794	.2823	.2852
0.8	.2881	.2910	.2939	.2967	.2995	.3023	.3051	.3078	.3106	.3133
0.9	.3159	.3186	.3212	.3238	.3264	.3289	.3315	.3340	.3365	.3389
1.0	.3413	.3438	.3461	.3485	.3508	.3531	.3554	.3577	.3599	.3621
1.1	.3643	.3665	.3686	.3708	.3729	.3749	.3770	.3790	.3810	.3830
1.2	.3849	.3869	.3888	.3907	.3925	.3944	.3962	.3980	.3997	.4015
1.3	.4032	.4049	.4066	.4082	.4099	.4115	.4131	.4147	.4162	.4177
1.4	.4192	.4207	.4222	.4236	.4251	.4265	.4279	.4292	.4306	.4319
1.5	.4332	.4345	.4357	.4370	.4382	.4394	.4406	.4418	.4429	.4441
1.6	.4452	.4463	.4474	.4484	.4495	.4505	.4515	.4525	.4535	.4545
1.7	.4554	.4564	.4573	.4582	.4591	.4599	.4608	.4616	.4625	.4633
1.8	.4641	.4649	.4656	.4664	.4671	.4678	.4686	.4693	.4699	.4706
1.9	.4713	.4719	.4726	.4732	.4738	.4744	.4750	.4756	.4761	.4767
2.0	.4772	.4778	.4783	.4788	.4793	.4798	.4803	.4808	.4812	.4817
2.1	.4821	.4826	.4830	.4834	.4838	.4842	.4846	.4850	.4854	.4857
2.2	.4861	.4864	.4868	.4871	.4875	.4878	.4881	.4884	.4887	.4890
2.3	.4893	.4896	.4898	.4901	.4904	.4906	.4909	.4911	.4913	.4916
2.4	.4918	.4920	.4922	.4925	.4927	.4929	.4931	.4932	.4934	.4936
2.5	.4938	.4940	.4941	.4943	.4945	.4946	.4948	.4949	.4951	.4952
2.6	.4953	.4955	.4956	.4957	.4959	.4960	.4961	.4962	.4963	.4964
2.7	.4965	.4966	.4967	.4968	.4969	.4970	.4971	.4972	.4973	.4974
2.8	.4974	.4975	.4976	.4977	.4977	.4978	.4979	.4979	.4980	.4981
2.9	.4981	.4982	.4982	.4983	.4984	.4984	.4985	.4985	.4986	.4986
3.0	.4987	.4987	.4987	.4988	.4988	.4989	.4989	.4989	.4990	.4990

part **IV**

CONTEMPORARY MANAGEMENT

Contemporary Management:
A Reality-Centered Approach

chapter nineteen

Contemporary Management: A Reality-Centered Approach

INTRODUCTION

A fundamental view of this book is that despite a lack of any specifically organized body of knowledge or universally accepted school of management, a science of management is slowly emerging. In the management field three overlapping schools—classical, behavioral, and management science—have been identified. Whether any of the three approaches are tenable and accurate is of course a moot question. The fact remains that an evolving science of management is forcing managers to examine, utilize, experiment, and discard various precepts of each of these three schools. This ferment in management is a result of, among other things, the pace of change in all fields of human activity—economic, social, technological, and international.

The pace of change has led writers to identify the next era of managing organizations in many different forms. Some of the future-oriented eras identified include (1) the information technology era, (2) the open systems era, (3) the computer age, (4) the comparative management era, and (5) the age of multinational management. The accuracy of these titles and the predictions of those espousing them cannot be assessed at this time. The evidence collected thus far, however, seems to indicate that the manager's chances of becoming obsolete are greater in the future. The rising probabilities of obsolescence are due to the geometrically accelerated changes in such areas as knowledge, techniques, and competitor actions continually impinging upon managers. The theme of this final chapter is that the manager who must cope with change should possess an understanding of the concepts included in each of the three management schools. This form of knowledge and competence should enable the manager to deal more effectively with the environment of the 1970s and thereafter.

REALITY-CENTERED MANAGING

The manager in the 19th century concentrated primarily on producing a product. Major decision-making emphasis was placed on building factories, installing equipment, hiring able employees, and producing a saleable product. This was the era of the supreme boss (owner) and subordinated labor force (employees). The days of being primarily concerned with producing products are over. Managing in such a way that production is the major focal point would not allow an organization to grow and remain stable in the contemporary environment.

In modern organizations of today we still find the boss (superior)–employee (subordinate) relationship, but many other factors are also apparent. The *union* is a force that must be included in the managerial actions involving adequate planning, organizing and controlling. Today the *government* is involved in organizational actions to a greater extent. For example, the government has played an active role in such areas as collective bargaining, strike settlements, hard-core unemployment programs, and financing the construction of plants in hard-pressed urban areas. The *public* is more vociferous and concerned about various actions of organizations. Public concern is especially evident in areas such as air pollution, conservation, and social responsibility. *International* competition is another factor that managers must cope with if they are to survive. The days of disregarding the steel manufacturer in Japan, the camera manufacturer in West Germany, and the oil producer in Kuwait are over.

In order to meet the increasing challenges offered by the union, government, public, and international competition, management must be *reality-centered*. That is, they must cope with problems and reach decisions concerning their operating boundaries of today and tomorrow. This type of competence requires the manager to use a number of different concepts, techniques, and models—unity of command, development of command work groups, utilization of job enrichment programs, and use of linear programming. These may be applied together to resolve a problem. The manager who is competent and flexible enough to use approaches from the three different schools of management is employing the reality-centered approach.

If the manager recognizes that useful concepts, techniques, and models exist in the three schools of management, this is a step in the direction of reality-centeredness. This is not to say that experience and/or wisdom will be totally useless in the modern era of management. Instead, the need for a balance of classical, behavioral, management science approaches, and experience is more realistic and contemporary. Sole reliance on classical principles, functions, processes, or behavioral suggestions such as participative management or management science models is as sterile and stagnant as relying solely on past experience. A blending of the schools of management and experience is what the reality-centered manager should attempt to accomplish. The task of blending would go far in making a manager more effective in the contemporary organization.

THE BLENDING OF THE THREE SCHOOLS OF MANAGEMENT

One of the major problems that must be overcome if executives are to adopt a reality-centered approach is that they must be able to visualize what various concepts, techniques and models can do to improve their organizations. The precepts suggested by such people as Taylor, Fayol, Urwick, Maslow, Herzberg, Bales, Fielder, Hurwicz, and Savage must be placed into a manageable framework. It has been suggested that each of the concepts, techniques, and models can be placed into one of two categories.[1] The first category includes factors that focus upon greater order, systematization, routinization, and predictability. This category will be referred to as the closed system (CS) factors. The second category includes factors that are primarily designed to develop greater openness, sharing, creativity, and individual initiative. This category will be designated as the open system (OS) factors.

Both the (CS) and (OS) factors are valuable ingredients for the reality-centered manager. Neither set is all right or all wrong for every management problem situation. It is best to perceive these two streams of factors as coexisting in the "technique kit" and knowledge base of the contemporary manager.

A Graphical Representation

In order to acquire a clearer understanding of the blending of factors from the three schools, a schematic diagram will be utilized. The factors specified in the diagram are not a complete referencing of all possible

---

[1] This classification scheme was developed by Paul R. Lawrence and Jay W. Lorsch, *Organization and Environment* (Homewood, Ill.: Richard D. Irwin, Inc., 1969). It is appropriate for our discussion concerning the blending of the three schools of management into a manageable framework.

items. Of course, space limitations constrain the total number of factors that can be specified.

Some factors from each of the three schools are presented in Figure 19–1. The purpose of Figure 19–1 is to illustrate how some of the factors discussed in the book move in one or both directions (closed or open). For example, planning can contribute to the routinization of a task by forcing the manager to develop plans that are in agreement with plans previously developed by a superior. However, in other instances, the manager may be allowed to plan his work activities, his sales budget, or his production schedule without adhering to rigid guidelines established by a superior. Therefore, planning is interpreted as a (CS) factor and an (OS) factor depending upon the situation.

If management by objectives (MBO) is examined closely it becomes apparent that the main objective is to have managers participate in the setting of goals. Theoretically, the (MBO) program will allow the manager to develop and grow on the job. He will be able to display greater individual initiative and creativity. Thus, (MBO) lends itself to the (OS) stream.

Examination of linear programming models suggests that they are designed to aid the manager in developing a program for the optimum allocation of resources. The utilization of linear programming focuses upon predicting the most optimum use of equipment or warehouses or personnel. Thus, this model meets the criteria of a closed system factor.

The two major categories (CS and OS) provide a manageable framework for classifying the numerous concepts of the three management schools. The advantage of having this type of framework is that instead of arguing about which managerial school is most accurate, the student of management focuses upon what each concept can accomplish most effectively. For example, a narrow span of control generally yields a routine orientation, while a wide span of control encourages a more open and creative orientation. There are certainly many gray areas when utilizing this classification system. That is, would a span of control of eight subordinates be considered a narrow or a wide span? The type of classification framework suggested does not deal with resolving debates about the degree of specialization, span of control, or planning. Its primary purpose is to offer a starting point for blending the concepts and techniques found in the three schools of management. Much more integrative and abstract work must be done before a comprehensive theory of reality-centered management is made operational.

The Contemporary Manager

The increasing number of concepts and techniques offered by the schools of management and the rapid pace of change around us require that a more sophisticated managerial cadre be called upon to make

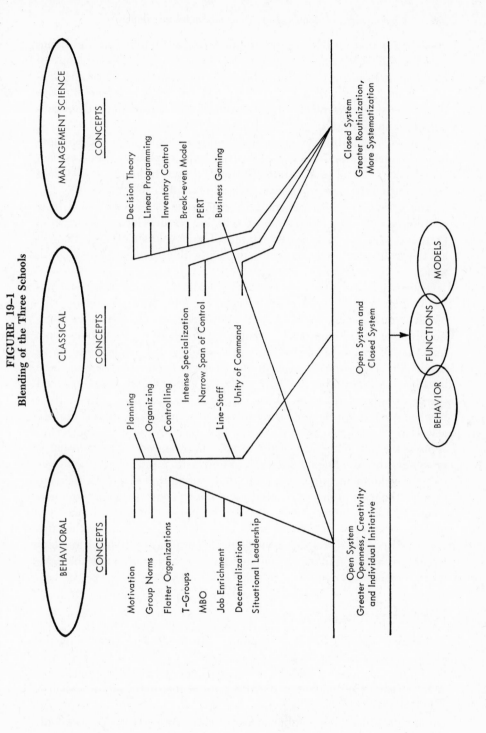

FIGURE 19-1
Blending of the Three Schools

BEHAVIORAL   CLASSICAL   MANAGEMENT SCIENCE

CONCEPTS   CONCEPTS   CONCEPTS

Motivation
Group Norms
Flatter Organizations
T-Groups
MBO
Job Enrichment
Decentralization
Situational Leadership

Planning
Organizing
Controlling
Intense Specialization
Narrow Span of Control
Line-Staff
Unity of Command

Decision Theory
Linear Programming
Inventory Control
Break-even Model
PERT
Business Gaming

Open System
Greater Openness, Creativity
and Individual Initiative

Open System and
Closed System

Closed System
Greater Routinization,
More Systematization

BEHAVIOR   FUNCTIONS   MODELS

organizational decisions. The need for an understanding of the boundaries established by classical scholars in presenting the functions of planning, organizing, and controlling is essential. Managers in contemporary organizations will need greater technical skills, conceptual skills, diagnostic skills, awareness of social and ethical issues, and a deep concern for human resources.

The skills and abilities required to perform effectively in a contemporary management position will be derived from a number of sources such as: (1) educational preparation; (2) professional training and development; and (3) actual experiences on the job and in society.

The education, development, and experience of managers will be a continuing process. The emphasis will be on developing managerial personnel with a situational orientation. The developmental process will aid the reality-centered manager in dealing with economic, technological, social, and international change.

The specifics of the exact type of educational background, developmental process, and experience spectrum is beyond the scope of this chapter. It is anticipated, however, that knowledge of economics, the functional areas of business (e.g., accounting, marketing, and production), quantitative methods, computers, and the behavioral sciences will prove invaluable. This is not to say that any manager can master each of these broad areas. It would certainly be virtually impossible to know in detail the theories, research, and techniques associated with each area. It is, however, feasible to assume that managers in organizations can nurture a working knowledge of some of the more relevant and pertinent concepts associated with each of the areas. The required comprehension is possible if the educational programs of universities and colleges, management development programs, and daily organizational activities encourage the preparation of reality-centered managers. A review of numerous curricula, seminar topics, textbooks, and organizational practices indicates that this encouragement is occurring. It seems likely that this trend will continue and that management will necessarily need to adopt a reality-centered philosophy and approach if they are to meet the challenges that are ever present.

FUTURE DEVELOPMENTS

The management literature abounds with predictions concerning the elements that are most likely to influence organizations and managers in the future. A sample of what the present authors view as potential future developments will be offered. The majority of the following discussion is less than a set of future-oriented predictions. Most of the future discussion points can actually be found in some of today's progressive organizations. Thus, the term future development is partially a misnomer.

Information Technology and Organizational Design

A number of management scholars have predicted the impact of what is called information technology on organizational design. This relatively new technology is composed of several related components. First, the high-speed computer that is able to process large amounts of information rapidly is a major element that managers must cope with on an ever increasing scale. Secondly, the utilization of statistical and mathematical methods similar to those used by management scientists are techniques that are compatible with the new technology. Finally, the utilization of simulation models in conjunction with high-speed computers to analyze complex organizational problems is emerging as an information technology standby.

It has been postulated that information technology will have a significant impact on the middle and top management of organizations. Whisler and Leavitt have prognosticated that in many instances the information technology thrust will lead to opposite conclusions from those proposed by individuals advocating and perpetuating "participative" management approaches.[2]

The main ingredients of the Whisler and Leavitt forecast are as follows:

1) Information technology should push upward in the organization structure the boundary between planning and performance. A significant portion of the planning currently being done by middle level managers will be given to such specialists as organizational analysts and operations researchers. These specialists will be located at the top managerial levels. In effect, the middle manager's job would become more structured, routine, and predictable. The middle manager would be operating within what we have referred to as a closed system.

2) Due to the availability of high speed computers, new mathematical and statistical techniques, and simulation devices, large corporations will move to recentralization of the planning, organizing and controlling functions. This recentralization trend will allow the top level managers to take on activities that call for more creativeness, innovation and openness.

3) The new technology and the movement toward recentralization will necessitate a reorganization of the middle management level. A number of middle manager jobs will literally be downgraded. That is, those managers will have less organizational status and receive less remuneration. Other middle management positions

---

[2] Harold J. Leavitt and Thomas L. Whisler, "Management in the 1980's," *Harvard Business Review*, vol. 36 (November–December, 1958), pp. 41–48.

will be upgraded and be considered within the revised organizational design as top management positions.

4) The line separating top and middle management will be drawn more clearly. Managers who are innovators, coordinators, and committors will be found at the top echelons.

These four major ingredients have led Whisler and Leavitt to predict that the organizational structure of the future would resemble a football balanced on the top of a bell. This form of structure is illustrated in Figure 19–2.

FIGURE 19–2

Whisler and Leavitt Predicted Structure

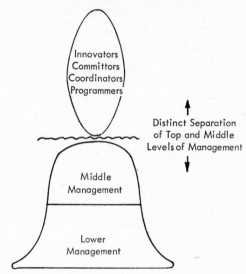

Anshen has viewed the new information technology as possessing the potential of enriching rather than shrinking the role of managers at the middle level.[3] The major points of difference between Whisler and Leavitt and Anshen concern the task of middle management and the role of the professional experts (top management).

It is Anshen's contention that because of the increased concern in the modern organization with problem identification, decision implementation, and new opportunities to find solutions, middle managers will be top managers in miniature. It is also Anshen's belief that the innovators or the professional experts in the Whisler and Leavitt framework will

---

[3] M. Anshen, "The Manager and the Black Box," *Harvard Business Review*, vol. 38 (November–December, 1960), pp. 85–92.

occupy positions of growing stature, responsibility, and influence in organizations. They will not, however, assume fundamental responsibilities of top level managers. He believes that it is tempting to admit ignorance and surrender decision making responsibilities to those espousing what appears to many managers as complex approaches, the new information technology jargon, and set of techniques. Professional experts are perceived by Anshen as possessing parochial judgments that are often not suited for the pace of dynamic decision making that is so essential in contemporary organizations.

Instead of adding fuel to the debate between those who view revolutionary changes and those who visualize evolutionary changes occurring because of information technology the present authors would like to offer the following considerations. It seems clear that the effects of information technology and advances in technology in general will result in a number of different organizational designs. Instead of predicting that organizations will follow a football-bell shape or any other specific design, it would be more realistic to propose that designs will differ. The viable organizations of the future will fall somewhere on a continuum ranging from highly routine production work to the creative work performed by trained scientists and professionals.[4] In fact, some organizations will perform tasks that range from routine to highly creative. Thus, it is possible that different designs may be appropriate for different divisions or units or departments of the same company. Some organizations will have dual hierarchies or as many as three, four, or five hierarchies. Perhaps one hierarchy would be for technical personnel, one hierarchy for support personnel, and one for those concerned with public image and environmental control.

The most essential point to consider is that the simple bureaucratic or nonbureaucratic dichotomy is not perfectly relevant in our changing society. It is best to consider the environment, the technology, the task, and the personnel of an organization as being closely linked to the design strategy pertaining to an organization. Thus, mixed and diverse designs will characterize contemporary organizations.[5]

The Multinational Firm

A major concern of management in the future will be the continued growth of the *multinational firm*—a firm with branches, divisions and

---

[4] For an excellent classification framework for studying organizations consult the ongoing research and work of Andrew Grimes, Stuart Klein, and Fremont Shull, "Matrix Model: An Empirical Test," *Proceedings for the Midwest Academy of Management*, 1970.

[5] For a number of insightful viewpoints of organizational design refer to James D. Thompson (ed.), *Approaches to Organizational Design* (Pittsburgh: University of Pittsburgh Press, 1966).

subsidiaries in foreign countries. Since the end of World War II, a growing number of United States corporations have transversed geographical boundaries and are investing private capital in overseas divisions, branches, and subsidiaries at an accelerated rate. It is estimated that approximately 4,200 American corporations currently operate in foreign nations.[6] During the decade 1955–1965, direct investment by U.S. corporations in Western Europe alone increased by approximately 360 percent to more than $12 billion.[7] This trend is expected to continue in the future.

United States corporations have invested in foreign countries for the same basic reasons they have invested capital in the domestic United States. These reasons vary from firm to firm, but most fall under the three interrelated goals of: (1) increasing long-term growth and profit prospects, (2) maximizing total sales revenue, and (3) improving overall market positions. Whatever the reasons, there is little doubt that the multinational firm will be commonplace in the near future. The complexity of the problem facing the management of a multinational firm is summarized succinctly in the following statement:

We must recognize that firms like IBM, World Trade, Royal Dutch/Shell are very complex, geographically decentralized systems embedded frequently in as many as a hundred different countries, in advanced, developing, in market-oriented, and command economies. They must be organized to serve billions of potential customers. AT&T has 679,100 employees and operates in the framework of the U.S. market with a 200 million population. General Motors has a somewhat higher number of employees and operates in as many countries as states with populations of more than a million. The management skills in General Motors . . . are rather different I would maintain.[8]

It is not difficult to see some of the problems a firm faces when it transcends national boundaries. One of the more obvious would be when it attempts to market its product or service in a foreign country. Depending on the cultural environment, different approaches would be necessary in advertising, pricing, and selecting channels of distribution for the firm's product. Just as important, although perhaps not as obvious, are the problems a manager faces when he attempts to perform the managerial functions of planning, organizing, and controlling in a foreign environment. These types of problems are currently being examined in an emerging field of study known as comparative management. Because of the importance of the *multinational firm* in the future growth and expansion of

---

[6] Juvenal L. Angel, *Directory of American Firms Operating in Foreign Countries* (New York: World Trade Academy Press, Inc., 1966).

[7] Richard A. Smith, "Nationalism Threatens U.S. Investments," *Fortune*, vol. 74 (August, 1965), p. 126.

[8] Howard V. Perlmutter, "Some Management Problems in Spaceship Earth: The Megafirm and the Global Industrial State," *Proceedings of the Academy of Management,* August, 1969, p. 76.

American industry, the reader should become familiar with the basic purposes of comparative management.

Comparative Management. Comparative management deals with problems of management and managerial efficiency in various countries. It seeks to detect, identify, classify, measure, and interpret similarities and differences. Essentially, the comparative method "focuses on how things *are*, rather than on how things *could be* (as in policy making) or on how they *should be* (the "principles") approach."[9]

The scholars engaged in comparative management research believe that the tasks facing a manager in the domestic environment differ greatly from those he faces in a foreign environment. This belief is exemplified in the following statement:

The subsidiary manager in Brazil may be a U.S. expatriate[10] who will have to learn Portugese, understand Brazilian politics, the economics of rapid inflation, and the difficulties of being considered a good citizen of Brazil. He will have to train local managers and learn to trust them, as well as his compatriots. This is a rather challenging task—not wholly different conceptually from the Pennsylvania manager—but different enough to make it possible for a manager to be a great success in Pennsylvania and a disaster in Brazil.[11]

Comparative management scholars also believe that existing management knowledge has some drawbacks in terms of orientation and application of two different types of cultures and economies. They contend that most existing studies of management have taken place within a framework where there has been little concern for the external environment in which the firm must operate. As long as the external environment is the same for all firms (e.g., all firms operating in the U.S.), this approach is valid. However, in the situations where the external environment differs, they believe that present management knowledge is inadequate. In such cases where environments do vary, as is the case between nations, they believe it is necessary to study the external pressures and constraints upon internal management. They contend that a manager may perform adequately in the internal management of his firm, but he is also substantially influenced by external factors in the particular country which directly influences how effectively he performs the managerial functions of planning, organizing and controlling.[12]

---

[9] J. Boddewyn, *Comparative Management and Marketing* (Glenview, Ill.: Scott, Foresman and Company), 1969. p. 3.

[10] The term *expatriate* is used to refer to those U.S. executives who have permanent assignments outside the geographic boundaries of the United States. The reader should also be aware that many U.S. firms attempt to employ local nationals whenever possible to manage overseas operations.

[11] Perlmutter, *op. cit.*, p. 76.

[12] Richard N. Farmer and Barry M. Richman, "A Model for Research in Comparative Management," *California Management Review*, vol. 7 (Winter, 1964), p. 56.

Introducing the External Environment. Several scholars have attempted to develop models for the analysis of management, taking into account the influence of external environments. These individuals have recognized that external cultural environments do affect the practice of management.

One promising approach is the model developed by Professors Farmer and Richman. Their model attempts to identify the effect of cultural factors on the various management functions. An adaptation of this model is shown in Figure 19–3.

FIGURE 19–3
Farmer-Richman Model for Analyzing Comparative Management

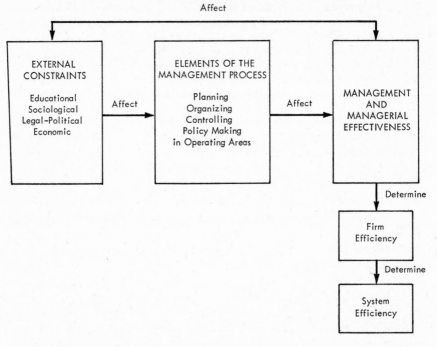

As noted in Figure 19–3, Farmer and Richman divide external and environmental constraints into four classes: educational, sociological–cultural, legal–political, and economic.

1) Educational constraints include such things as literacy level, the availability of specialized vocational and technical training, the prevailing attitude toward education, and the extent to which education matches requirements for skills and abilities. These educational factors may support or limit effective management.

2) Sociological–cultural constraints include a great number of factors.

Some of the most important are the general attitude of the society toward managers, the dominant views of authority and subordinates, the extent of union-management cooperation, and the dominant view of wealth and material gain.

3) Legal-political constraints include such things as defense policy and national security, foreign policy, political stability, and the flexibility of law and legal changes.

4) Economic constraints would include such factors as the basic economic system in the country, whether private or public ownership prevails, whether it is a competitive economy based on sound money and the extent to which the government controls economic activities.

From their identification of the various management functions and of a manager's external environment which influences the way he manages, Farmer and Richman constructed their model. While it is undoubtedly subject to revision in the future, the model does distinguish the managerial functions of planning, organizing, and controlling from the environment in which the managing occurs. Probably their major contribution is narrowing the concept of management to the managerial functions and separating from it consideration of external environmental factors which can influence actual practice in specific instances. In so doing, the model appears to be a useful means for evaluating management and for presenting what may make effective management differ between cultures.

While the entire field of comparative management is new and will undoubtedly undergo many changes as it progresses, the approach taken by Farmer and Richman has a great deal of usefulness. An additional advantage of their approach is that it can be a useful practical aid for firms operating in differing cultural environments. By specifying the areas of external constraints which may exist and identifying the elements within each area, they provide management in multinational firms with an orderly framework within which to perform the managerial functions of planning, organizing and controlling in varying environments.

Social Responsibility

Since the beginning of early history the wealthy and the powerful have often assumed responsibility for the welfare of those less fortunate around them. It is undoubtedly the lingering survival of this belief that today demands from the corporation the kind of social responsibility that has throughout history been expected of wealth and power. In the context of present times these expectations often take the following form:

Companies from AT&T to Xerox have been urged—and in many cases have willingly accepted—the challenges to educate our children, police our streets, clean up our polluted air and water, teach our disadvantaged citizens how to earn a living, rebuild our slums, and even tell us how to run our cities more efficiently.[13]

As problems such as these continue to mount, the manager of the future will be more and more faced with reconciling his responsibilities to two groups of individuals, stockholders and society in general. Because of its important influence in the future environment of the manager, this section will examine the issue of social responsibility.

In addition to the belief that power implies responsibility there are other reasons why the modern corporation has been asked to help in solving society's problems. First, more and more citizens are realizing that in addition to having the power, the modern corporation also has the technical know-how to solve the nation's problems. In addition, the federal government itself holds a similar viewpoint and has begun to actively solicit the aid of the modern corporation. For example, in 1968, the federal government announced a plan whereby private industry would be given the responsibility for hiring and training the majority of the nation's hard-core unemployed. Industry in turn would receive a measure of government subsidy.[14]

Many businesses are responding to this and similar challenges. Following are some specific instances where business has taken on responsibilities which can be considered social in nature.[15]

1. The city of New York's Mayor, John Lindsay called in McKinsey and Company to analyze the city's air pollution problems, and the Traffic Commission invited Sperry Rand, and later IBM, to help solve the city's growing traffic headache.

2. In California, Governor Ronald Reagan has borrowed business executives, whose salaries continue to be paid by their respective companies, as consultants in seeking ways to trim the costs of state government.

However, the move on the part of the corporation toward expressing an awareness of social responsibility has been subject to much debate. There are those who maintain that the large corporation administers a wealth that it does not own and, therefore, should not be forced to develop a social awareness over the use of assets that are owned ultimately by private citizens. There are others who seriously question whether it is proper to place public problems on the shoulders of corporate managers. They believe that these men who are highly skilled in business matters may not be so in matters of politics, the humanities, and the social sciences. In addition, they note that such men are in no way

[13] Hazel Henderson, "Should Business Tackle Society's Problems?" *Harvard Business Review*, vol. 46 (July–August, 1968), p. 77.

[14] *Ibid.*, p. 78.

[15] *Ibid.*, p. 78–79.

accountable to the voters for their decisions and could, in determining what is best for society, turn into paternalistic rulers. Finally, many people believe that business may suffer serious consequences by accepting too heavy a burden of social responsibility since capital and managerial talent may be drained by other activities which are alien to the profit motive.

The Manager's Dilemma. Thus, the corporate manager may find himself on the horns of a dilemma. When he attempts to become involved in society's problems he may be faced with a group of very angry stockholders who maintain that companies have no legal right to retain earnings for such uses and that the stockholders should decide how the money is spent since they are the rightful owners. On the other hand, when he attempts to maximize profit for the stockholders he may be faced with the wrath of other citizens who claim that he has no respect for the needs of society as a whole and that he is failing to safeguard the environmental conditions that provide for the survival and growth of the corporation.

As society and its problems become more complex, the corporation with its vast wealth of knowledge and capabilities will undoubtedly be looked upon more and more as a source of leadership. The manager of the future will be forced to reconcile the above two opposing viewpoints.

The root cause of the conflict over social responsibility appears to lie in the irreconcilability of two theories of the corporation[16]—the theory of the *traditional corporation* on the one hand, and the theory of the *metrocorporation* on the other. Both theories express extreme viewpoints.

The *traditional corporation* is an instrumentality of a single group—the shareholders—and has one clear cut purpose: conducting business for their maximal profit. The prior claim of the stockholders on earnings after taxes is unquestioned and management has to do no "balancing" of interests in distributing the earnings. This traditional view recognizes no public responsibilities except for legal ones and leaves the public interests to the care of the state. As we noted previously, the view has been attacked as being shortsighted and ultimately self-destructive.

The opposite model of the traditional corporation is the *metrocorporation,* which assumes limitless social responsibility. In this type of corporation, managers hold themselves accountable to many different segments of society. It is a major social institution with comprehensive aims, and it is far removed from the strict limited-objective of the traditional corporation: maximal profit for the stockholders. The metrocorporation emphasizes its rights and duties as a "citizen" in its relationships with the various groups in its environment. The dangers of this model were also previously pointed out: undue power for managers and the danger of

---

[16] This discussion is based upon Richard Eells and Clarence Walton, *Conceptual Foundations of Business* (Homewood, Ill.: Richard D. Irwin, Inc., 1961), pp. 468–76.

them becoming paternalistic rulers; incompetence in areas such as humanities and politics; and the suboptimization of corporate economic goals and functions.

Obviously, the above descriptions are two opposite extremes. The manager of the future will undoubtedly find a middle ground position between these extremes. The following statement should aid us in establishing this position.

The large business corporation is here to stay. It is an indispensible instrument for getting done some of the things that people want done. It is neither the exclusive instrument of one class of interests nor an indiscriminate roster of "social" interests. Like other large organizations, the corporation has to be tempered to the times; and as a viable instrument it must adapt to the changing requirements of our free, complex and interdependent society.[17]

Thus, it is necessary to find a position somewhere between the extremes of the traditional corporation and the metrocorporation which will take into account public expectations and not be in conflict with management's responsibilities to the stockholder. This model has been referred to as the *well-tempered corporation*.[18] This viewpoint holds that the claims of stockholders and creditors will more likely be met if a firm develops a position as a socially responsible company. This can only be done if management integrates the factors of production with respect to the primary interests of the owners and the prevailing norms of society. This will be a major task facing the manager of the future.

SUMMARY

Evidence that is presently available suggests that the manager's activities will become more difficult in the future than in the past. This increased complexity is a result of the forces of change that continually alter most of our patterns of behavior, perception, and ways of accomplishing job tasks. It is expected that because of changes in our economy, communities and world the manager will be reaching decisions in a continual state of uncertainty. The very survival of a manager operating in this dynamic environment may well depend upon his ability to comprehend and foster a reality-centered approach. The principles, concepts and models emerging from the three schools of management offer the contemporary manager many of the items for coping with his environment.

Contemporary managers who develop the skill to cope with change will undoubtedly find the future rewarding. The form of the rewards for performing effectively center, of course, around economic benefits and

---

[17] *Ibid.*, p. 474.
[18] *Ibid.*

sociological and psychological opportunities. Thus, although the challenges of the future are frightening in many respects, the opportunities available for the manager with proper training are unlimited.

DISCUSSION AND REVIEW QUESTIONS

1. What types of government control of industry do you foresee for the immediate future? Do you believe there should be more or less regulation?

2. It is generally assumed that computer experts still do not have much influence on the top policy makers in organizations. Do you believe that their status and power within the organization will change in the future? Why?

3. Many management scholars believe that new functions will be found in the organization chart of the future. These functions will be additions to the traditional functions such as finance, marketing, public relations, and production. Do you foresee any new areas on the organization chart of tomorrow? What will be some of the responsibilities of the executives heading up these new areas which you believe will emerge?

4. Develop a Figure 19–1(A) which will enlarge upon and extend the schools of management and the concepts presented in Figure 19–1.

5. Assume that you have been working for the XYZ Corporation for six years in their Chicago office. You have been offered and have accepted a promotion to division head in your field. However, the job opening is in the company's branch in Malaya. Upon arriving at your new assignment, would you approach the job any differently than if you have been given the same job in the firm's plant in Buffalo, New York?

6. Choose any foreign country with which you are familiar. Outline the major elements of its culture that in your judgment would influence the type of management you would expect in a typical firm.

7. Choose any management technique or approach (e.g., budgeting, participative management) and divide it into management fundamentals and those aspects which you feel would be influenced by cultural variables.

8. Assume that all corporations take on added social responsibilities. Whom do you feel will bear the additional costs, stockholders, employees? Or will prices increase?

9. A man calls at your home and represents himself as conducting an educational survey. When you admit him to your home, he proceeds to ask a few questions about the children in school, and then begins a sales talk about encyclopedias. Does this and other types of activities by business firms have any relationship to social responsibility?

10. A corporation in your city has just announced that it will contribute $25,000 to the Department of Marketing at your school to be used to study consumer buying habits in your state. How do you view this act? Is it altruistic? Is it motivated by a desire for profit?

ADDITIONAL REFERENCES

ANSHEN, M. and BACH, G. L. (eds.). *Management and Corporations, 1985.* New York: McGraw-Hill Book Company, 1960.

CHOWDHRY, K., and PAL, A. K. "Production Planning and Organization Morale," in A. H. Rubenstein and C. J. Haberstroh (eds.), *Some Theories of Organization.* Homewood, Ill.: Richard D. Irwin, Inc. and The Dorsey Press, Inc., 1960.

CLARK, J. W. *Religion and the Moral Standards of American Businessmen.* Cincinnati: South-Western Publishing Company, 1966.

CLAUSEN, E. A. "Marketing Ethics and the Consumer," *Harvard Business Review,* 45 (1967), 78–86.

DAVIS, K., and BLOMSTROM, R. L. *Business and Its Environment.* New York: McGraw-Hill Book Company, 1966.

KOONTZ, H. "Challenges for Intellectual Leadership in Management," *California Management Review,* 8 (1965), 11–18.

MCGUIRE, J. W. *Business and Society.* New York: McGraw-Hill Book Company, 1963.

MITCHELL, W. N. *The Business Executive in a Changing World.* New York: American Management Association, 1965.

NEGANDHI, A. R. and ESTAFEN, B. D. "A Research Model to Determine the Applicability of American Management Knowhow in Differing Cultures and/or Environments," *Academy of Management Journal,* 8 (1965), 309–18.

OBERG, W. "Cross-Cultural Perspectives on Management Principles," *Academy of Management Journal,* 6 (1963), 129–43.

PRASAD, S. B. (ed.). *Management in International Perspective.* New York: Appleton-Century-Crofts, Inc., 1967.

SUOJANEN, W. W. *The Dynamics of Management.* New York: Holt, Rinehart, and Winston, Inc., 1966.

WALTON, C. C. *Ethos and the Executive.* Englewood Cliffs, N.J.: Prentice-Hall, Inc., 1969.

GLOSSARY OF TERMS

Glossary of Terms

Acceptance Theory of Authority. A theory of authority which Barnard proposed according to which the ultimate source of authority is the decision of the subordinate to accept the superior's orders.

Accountability. The process by which a subordinate reports his use of assigned resources to a designated superior.

Activity. The work necessary to complete a particular event in a PERT network. It consumes time, which is the paramount variable in a PERT system. In PERT networks, three time estimates are used for each activity: an optimistic time, a pessimistic time, and a most likely time. In CPM networks only one cost estimate is used.

Administrative Duties. The 16 guidelines which Fayol believed should direct the manager in carrying out the organizing function. There is considerable overlap between his 16 Administrative Duties and his 14 Management Principles.

Allocation Models. This type of management science model is used in a situation where several possible candidates or activities are all competing for limited resources. It enables the user to allocate scarce resources in order to maximize some predetermined objective.

Anthropology. Examines all the behaviors of man which have been learned. This includes social, technical, and familial behaviors. It is often defined as the study of man and his works.

Authority. The legitimate right to use assigned resources to accomplish a delegated task or objective. The right to give orders and to exact obedience. The legal bases for formal authority are private property, the state, or a supreme being.

Base Time. The average time for the completion of a particular timing element. The average is calculated from a series of observations of a particular worker performing the task.

409

Behavioral Change. Planned change in the attitudes, skills, and knowledge of organizational personnel.

Behavioral Motivation Theory. The behavioral school of management advocates the pluralistic view of motivation which emphasizes that many different types of needs influence behavior, and that man is motivated by the desire to satisfy many needs.

Behavioral School of Management. A body of literature which is characterized by its concern for human behavior in the work environment. The school's primary means for acquiring knowledge is the scientific method with emphasis upon empirical research. The school of management thought which followed the classical school. The first phase may be identified as "human relations" theory. This phase became popular in the 1940s and early 1950s. The second phase was the "behavioral science" approach which came into popular use in the early 1950s.

Behavioral Science Approach. This approach to the study of management can be thought of as the study of observable and verifiable human behavior in organizations, using scientific procedures. It draws especially from psychology, sociology, and anthropology.

Brand-Switching Models. This type of management science model provides the manager with some idea of the behavior of consumers in terms of their loyalty and their switching from one brand to another.

Bureaucracy. A form of organization which has many of the characteristics of the classical organization design, i.e., it is highly structured and centralized, with narrow spans of control.

Carrying Costs. These are the costs incurred by a firm by carrying an inventory. They include such costs as the taxes and insurance on the goods in inventory, interest on money invested in inventory and storage space, and the costs incurred because of the obsolescence of the inventory.

Case Study. This type of study design attempts to examine numerous characteristics of a person or group over an extended period of time. Since the results achieved by a case study are usually based on a sample of one, the user cannot be certain as to their generality. Most case studies do not prove anything, but rather raise questions for future research.

Certainty Decisions. A decision is made in which the manager is certain about which state of nature or competitor action will occur. Thus, the probability that a particular event will occur is 1.00.

Classical Management Motivation Theory. The classical approach to motivation emphasized monetary incentives as a prime means for motivating the individual. This approach was undoubtedly strongly influenced by the classical economists who emphasized man's rational pursuit of economic objectives.

Classical School of Management. A body of literature which represents the earliest attempts to define and describe the field of management. The school's main focus is on formally prescribed relationships. Its primary means for acquiring knowledge are personal observation and case studies.

Closed System (CS) Factors. Management concepts and techniques which focus upon greater order, systematization, routinization, and predictability. Most of the management science techniques and many classical concepts fall into this category.

Coercive Power. This is the power of a leader that is derived from fear on the part of the follower. The follower perceives the leader as a person that can punish deviant behavior and actions.

Command Group. The command group is specified by the formal organization chart. The group of subordinates who report to one particular supervisor constitutes the command group.

Comparative Management. This emerging field of study deals with problems of management and managerial effectiveness in various countries. It seeks to detect, identify, classify, measure, and interpret similarities and differences.

Components. These are the parts of a management science model. They may be firms, households, warehouses, costs, or any other factor which is part of the system or process being modeled.

Concurrent Control. Techniques and methods which focus on the actual, ongoing activity of the organization.

Contributed Value. A measure of efficiency which relates value added to sales or profit.

Controlling Function. All managerial activity that is undertaken to assure that actual operations go according to plan.

Critical Path. This is the longest path in a PERT network, from the network beginning event to the network ending event.

Decentralization. This concept can be viewed as the pushing downward of the appropriate amount of decision-making authority. Each company practices a certain degree of decentralization. Thus, the concept is not an either/or precept but is instead one of degrees.

Decision Theory. This term is used to describe how managers in organizations can proceed to reach decisions under conditions of certainty, risk, and uncertainty. The descriptions include the use of some mathematics which can range from simple addition and subtraction to integral calculus.

Defense Mechanisms. When an individual is blocked in his attempts to satisfy his needs, he may evoke one or more defense mechanisms instead of adopting constructive strategies to solve his problems. Some of the most common are withdrawal, aggression, substitution, compensation, repression, regression, projection, and rationalization.

Departmentalization. The process of grouping jobs together on the basis of some common characteristic; typically, the basis is product, client, location, process, or function.

Descriptive Models. This type of model is one which describes how a system works. It describes things as they are and makes no value judgments about the particular thing being studied. It may display the alternative choices available to the decision maker but it does not select the best alternative.

Determinants of Personality. The formation of the human personality is influenced by the mutual interaction of many factors. Four general classifications of factors must be considered: constitutional determinants, group-membership determinants, role determinants, and situational determinants.

Deterministic Models. This refers to the type of variables included in the model. A model is deterministic when the law of chance plays no role. All the factors taken into account in the model are assumed to be exact or determinate quantities.

Dialectic Process of Change. A concept which recognizes that any change which management implements in reaction to a particular problem will create a new problem; the solution to a problem creates the environment within which new problems will emerge.

Differential Rate System. An incentive wage system devised by F. W. Taylor, which pays a fixed rate for all production up to standard, but a higher rate for all pieces once the standard is met.

Direction. A subfunction of control which refers to the manager's act of interpreting orders to a subordinate.

Discounted Rate of Return. The rate of return which equates future cash proceeds and the initial cost of the investment.

Distribution Matrix. A table showing the relationships between supply, demand, and costs used for analyzing transportation problems.

Earliest Expected Date (T_E). This is found by calculating the *longest* path from the network beginning event to the particular event in question, whether it is the network ending event or some other event.

Econometric Analysis. A technique which involves the specification of relationships among many variables and the verification of relationships through statistical techniques.

Emergent Leader. The leader who emerges from within the group. This person is a personification of the group's attitudes, values, beliefs, and opinions.

EOQ Model. This refers to the economic order quantity model. It is used to resolve size of order problems. If the manager is concerned with minimizing his inventory costs he could utilize the *EOQ* model to study the relationships between carrying costs, ordering costs, and demand.

Event. An accomplishment at a particular point in time on a network. It consumes no time.

Expected Time (t_e). This is one time estimate for each activity calculated by using the formula:

$$t_e = \frac{a + 4m + b}{6},$$

Where:

$$a = \text{optimistic time}$$
$$m = \text{most likely time}$$
$$b = \text{pessimistic time}$$

Experiment. This type of study design contains two key elements, namely, manipulation of some variable by the researcher and observation or measurement of the results.

Expert Power. The power which an individual possesses because followers perceive him to have a special skill or special knowledge or special expertise.

External and Environmental Constraints. Scholars engaged in comparative management research have recognized that external cultural environments do affect the practice of management. Many of these scholars have attempted to identify the affect of cultural factors on the various management functions. They divide external and environmental constraints into four classes:

1. Educational constraints. These include such things as literacy level, the availability of specialized vocational and technical training, and the prevailing attitude toward education.
2. Sociological-cultural constraints. These include such factors as the general attitude of the society toward managers, dominant views of authority and subordinates, and the prevailing attitudes toward wealth and material gain.
3. Legal-political constraints. These include such factors as defense policy and national security, foreign policy, and political stability.
4. Economic constraints. These include such factors as the basic economic system in the country, whether private or public ownership prevails, and the extent to which the government controls economic activity.

Feasibility Space. Only takes on physical meaning in a graphical solution, and then only in the two dimensional case for most people. Defines area which contains all combinations of all variables which satisfy the inequalities. Bounded by lines representing the structural constraints.

Feedback Control. Techniques and methods which analyze historical data to correct future events.

Felt Need. A felt need is the starting point in the motivation process. It is a deficiency of something within the individual that provides the spark which leads to behavior.

First-Line Management. The lowest level of an administrative hierarchy; managers at this level coordinate the work of nonmanagers, but report to a manager.

Fixed Costs. These are costs that remain fixed regardless of the level of sales generated or the number of units produced. Such costs as property taxes, depreciation, and insurance premiums are considered fixed.

Flat Pyramid Structure. The flatter organization structure theoretically is the type that reduces the layers of management, widens the span of control of managers at various levels, and is often more decentralized with regard to decision-making autonomy.

Forecasting. Projections of the future from which management derives budgets and plans.

Friendship Group. A group that is established in the work place because of some common group characteristic (e.g., the members like professional football), and that extends the interaction of members to include activities outside the workplace.

Frustration. This occurs when an individual is unable to satisfy his needs. Frustration may result in constructive problem-solving behavior or defensive behavior.

Functional Foremanship. The application of division of labor at the foreman level, as suggested by F. W. Taylor. It involves splitting the task of the foreman into eight subtasks and assigning each subtask to a separate individual.

Goal Priority. The relative importance of goals, both in the short and long run.

Goal Structure. Refers to (1) the delegation of authority to pursue subgoals and (2) the relationship among multiple goals.

Graicunas' Law. A mathematical formulation of the relationship between the number of subordinates (N) and the number of potential superior–subordinate contacts (C), viz.,

$$C = N(\tfrac{2^N}{2} + N - 1).$$

Group Cohesiveness. The attraction of members to the group in terms of the desirability of group membership to the members. In a straightforward manner, this is the "stick-togetherness" quality of a group.

Hawthorne Studies. Provided the impetus for the human relations approach to management. The studies were conducted by a group of researchers from Harvard University at the Chicago Hawthorne Plant of Western Electric. The general progression of the research took place in four phases: (1) Experiments in Illumination, (2) Relay Assembly Test Room Experiment, (3) Interview Program, and (4) Bank Wiring Observation Room Experiment.

Hierarchy of Needs. A widely adopted pluralistic framework of motivation. Developed by psychologist A. H. Maslow, the theory stresses two ideas:

1. Only needs not yet satisfied can influence behavior.
2. Man's needs are arranged in a hierarchy of importance. When one level has been satisfied, a higher level need emerges and demands satisfaction.

Maslow also distinguishes five general classes of needs: physiological, safety, social, esteem, and self-actualization.

Horizontal Specialization of Management. The process by which the natural sequence of a task is broken down into specialized subgroups and a manager is assigned the authority and responsibility for coordinating the subgroups.

Human Relations Theory. Brought to the attention of management the important role that individuals play in determining the success or failure of an organization. It embarked on the critical task of compensating for some of the deficiencies in classical theory. Basically, it took the premises of the classical school as given. However, it showed how these premises were modified as a result of individual behavior and the influence of the work group.

Incremental Influence. This concept was developed by Katz and Kahn. It refers to the influence of a leader over and above the influence base bestowed upon him because of his position in the organization.

Inequality. A functional relationship which allows latitude in variable values. Expresses either an upper or lower limit that combined variable values may take on.

Informal Group Norms. The agreement among group members to adhere to a level of production, a group attitude, or a group belief.

Insufficient-Reason Criterion. If a manager is operating under conditions of uncertainty, it is assumed that there is an equal probability that each of the possible states of nature or competitive actions may occur. Thus, equiprobabilities are assigned to each of the potential events and the total expected values are examined.

Interaction Analysis. The technique developed by R. F. Bales to study group interaction. Through the observation of groups working on solving a case, Bales determined that task and human relations specialists emerge. Based upon observing the group interactions and answers to questions as to what occurred within the group to solve the case, Bales developed an interaction profile.

Interest Group. A group that forms because of some special topic of interest. Generally, when the interest becomes weaker or a goal has been achieved, the group dissolves.

Intervening Variables. These are sometimes referred to as constructs. They are terms invented to describe internal and directly unobservable psychological processes which account for human behavior. Thus, *motivation* can be considered a construct or intervening variable. Intervening variables cannot be measured directly, but must be inferred from behavior.

Inventory Models. This type of management science model answers two questions relating to inventory management: "How much?" and "When?" It provides the manager with the point at which orders should be placed for repeat goods and the quantity of each order.

Investment Decisions. Decisions which commit present funds in exchange for potential future funds. These decisions are controlled through a capital budget.

Isoprofit Line. Used in graphical solution, traces the path of the objective function across the feasibility space, for an arbitrary profit (cost) level. The level which passes through that point of the feasibility space which is farthest to the right and upward is the profit (cost) at optimality.

Iteration. Associated series of steps to revise a simplex tableau in the process of searching for optimality.

Job Depth. The relative freedom that a job holder has in the performance of his duties.

Job Enlargement. This is a form of despecialization in that the number of tasks performed by the employee is increased. The increase in tasks theoretically makes the job more interesting and challenging and consequently work becomes more psychologically rewarding.

Job Enrichment. Suggested formally by Herzberg, this involves building into individual jobs greater scope for personal achievement, recognition, and responsibility. It is concerned with strengthening the motivational factors and is concerned only incidentally with maintenance.

Job Rotation. The procedure of moving a worker from one work station to another work station. The rotation supposedly reduces boredom among other things.

Job Scope. The relative complexity of the assigned task as reflected by its cycle time.

Latest Allowable Date (T_L). This is the latest date on which an event can occur without creating a delay in the scheduled completion of the project.

T_L for an ending event is equal to the date directed by management for completion of the project. If a directed date is not specified, then $T_L = T_E$ for the network ending event.

Leader-Member Relations. This is a dimension of leadership (Fiedler) that refers to the degree of confidence which followers have in their leader.

Leadership. A much defined but yet nebulous term. In the context of the behavioral school the term refers to the ability of a person to influence the activities of followers in an organizational setting. The emphasis is on the fact that the leader must interact with his followers in order to be influential.

Legitimate Power. This refers to the power which a leader has because of his ranking in the managerial hierarchy. For example, since the department manager is ranked higher than the foreman in the managerial hierarchy, he possesses more legitimate power.

Line Function. The activities of departments which contribute directly to the creation of the organization's output. In manufacturing, the line functions are manufacturing, marketing, and finance.

Maintenance Factors. Distinguished by Herzberg in his "two-factor" theory of motivation. Maintenance factors are those conditions of the job which operate primarily to dissatisfy employees when they are not present. However, their presence does not build strong motivation among employees. Herzberg distinguished 16 of these factors (e.g., salary, job security, work conditions).

Management. The process of coordinating individual and group activity toward group goals.

Management by Objectives. A management technique which consists of the following major elements:
1. Superiors and subordinates meet to discuss goals and jointly establish attainable goals for the subordinate.
2. The superior and subordinate meet again after the initial goals have been set to evaluate the subordinate's performance in terms of the preestablished goals.

Management Functions. The activities which a manager must perform as a result of his position in the firm. The text identifies planning, organizing, and controlling as the management functions.

Management Science. While it is difficult to place clear boundaries around this emerging discipline, we can say that most management science applications possess the following:
1. a primary focus on decision making,
2. an appraisal resting on economic effectiveness criteria,
3. reliance on a formal mathematical model, and
4. dependence on an electronic computer.

Management Science School. A body of literature which is characterized by its use of mathematical and statistical techniques to build models for the solution of technical operational problems. The school's primary means for acquiring knowledge is mathematical deduction.

Marginal Costs. A cost concept popularized by economists. These are the costs incurred by selling or servicing or producing one more unit.

Marginal Revenue. An economist-proposed concept that designates the additional revenue attained by selling one more unit.

Market Surveys. A set of techniques which enable the manager to estimate the attitude of consumers toward aspects of his product or service.

Mathematical Models. A mathematical model is a simplified mathematical representation of the relevant aspects of an actual system or process.

Maximax Criterion. The completely optimistic manager believes that only the most favorable result will occur when he makes a decision. The manager decides to maximize the maximum possible payoff.

Maximin Criterion. The pessimistic manager believes that he usually ends up with the worst possible outcome. Thus, he attempts to choose that strategy which enables him to maximize the least favorable payoffs.

Metrocorporation. This view is the extreme opposite of the *traditional corporation*. This view holds that the corporation has limitless social responsibilities and the managers hold themselves accountable to several groups in society.

Middle Management. The middle level of an administrative hierarchy; managers at this level coordinate the work of managers and report to a manager.

Minimax Criterion. The manager that believes that once a decision is made and an outcome occurs, there will be some regret. Therefore, he selects that strategy which allows him to experience the least regret.

Minus Values in Unoccupied Cells. This indicates to a manager that is attempting to minimize total cost that a better solution can be found by shifting more units into the unoccupied cell of a transportation matrix.

Mooney's Theory of Organization. A theoretical statement based upon Mooney's personal experience and his analysis of the forms which organizations have taken throughout history. According to Mooney, the underlying principle of all organizations is *coordination*, which is implemented through the *scalar* process. The result is a system of specialized tasks which Mooney terms the *functional* effect. Through deductive reasoning, he elaborates the framework to develop a logically complete three-by-three matrix.

Motion Study. The process of analyzing work in order to determine the preferred motions to be used in the completion of tasks. Motion study is a major contribution of scientific management, principally through the efforts of Taylor and Gilbreth.

Motivation. This term is defined as the inner state that activates or moves. It is derived from the Latin term for movement and can be described as all the inner striving conditions such as drives, desires, and motives.

Motivational Factors. Distinguished by Herzberg in his "two-factor" theory of motivation. Motivational factors are those job conditions which, if present, operate to build high levels of motivation and job satisfaction. However, if they are not present, they do not prove highly dissatisfying. Herzberg distinguished six of these factors (e.g., achievement, recognition, advancement).

Moving Budgeting. A form of budgeting which involves periodic updating through time.

Multinational Firm. A firm with branches, divisions, and subsidiaries in foreign countries. It is currently estimated that approximately 4,200 American firms operate in foreign nations.

Normal Time. Equal to the base time, multiplied by a rating factor which reflects the engineer's evaluation of the effort exerted by the worker being timed. If, for example, the engineer believes that the worker is faster than the ordinary or average worker, the base time will be increased by a factor of, say, 110%.

Normative Models. This type of model attempts to provide how things should be. It is one which is specifically constructed to select from among alternatives the best alternative based on some previously determined criteria, which are also included in the model. It tells how the system should be in order to achieve a particular objective.

Northwest Corner Method. This is a procedure whereby a number of units are assigned to the northwest corner cell of the initial distribution matrix. The amount assigned is usually the smaller of the demand and supply values that are related to the northwest corner cell.

Objective Function. Expression of the sole objective of the problem, maximize if profit, minimize if cost, made up of linear summation of the products of the quantity of each variable and the respective unit profit (cost).

Occupied-Cell Computation. In computing the row and column values for a distribution matrix only the occupied cells are considered. The rule for the row and column computations is that the sum of the row and column values is equal to the value in the subcell of an occupied cell.

Open System (OS) Factors. Management concepts and techniques which focus upon developing greater openness, sharing, creativity, and individual initiative. Most of the behavioral concepts and many classical concepts fall into this category.

Ordering Costs. A major cost component that is considered in inventory control decisions. Each time the firm orders items for inventory, they must formally contact the supplier. This preparation usually includes some clerical and administrative work in placing the order and labor to put the items in inventory. The clerical, administrative, and labor costs make up the ordering cost element in inventory control models.

Organizational Change. The process of diagnosing and implementing changes in the structural, behavioral, or technological components of an organization.

Organizational Psychology. Studies man's behavior and attitudes within an organizational setting, including the effect of the organization upon the individual and the individual's effect upon the organization.

Organization Structure. The formally defined framework of task and authority relationships. It is analogous to the biological concept of the skeleton.

Organizing Function. All managerial activity which results in the design of a formal structure of tasks and authority.

Overlay Theories. This refers to efforts to relate the managerial grid approach (Blake and Mouton) with the "initiating structure" and "consideration" (Ohio State) concepts. It is only a partial synthesis which is displayed schematically, but it shows many similarities in what two groups of individuals are espousing as theories of leadership.

Participative Approaches. A technique advocated by behavioralists which stresses the idea that employees throughout the firm should be allowed to participate in decision-making.

Payback Period. The length of time that it takes for an investment to pay for itself out of future funds.

Payoff Matrix. A two-dimensional array of data which indicates in tabular form the payoffs for various strategy, state of nature, or competitive action combinations.

Personal-Behavioral Theories. This refers to a group of leadership theories that are based primarily on personal and behavioral characteristics of leaders. Included in this category are theories based solely on authoritative opinion and theories based on extensive research in actual organizations.

Personality. The general sum of traits or characteristics of an individual. It is a very important determinant of individual behavior and motivation.

Planning Function. All managerial activities which lead to the definition of goals and to the determination of appropriate means to achieve those goals.

Plus Values in Unoccupied Cell. This indicates to a manager who is attempting to minimize total cost that a poorer solution will result if units are moved into the cell.

Preliminary Control. Consists of techniques and methods which attempt to maintain the quality and quantity of resources.

Principle–Process–Effect. A manner of logical reasoning which Mooney used to identify the essence of management. According to Mooney, it is possible to *deduce* the appropriate process and effect from an underlying principle; the effect is the specific result of a general principle.

Principles of Management. In classical management theory, "principles of management" refers either to rules of conduct which should guide manager's behavior or to the underlying laws of nature which determine the workings of the business organization.

Profitability Measures. Measurements of efficiency in the business firm; may be the ratio of net profit either to capital or to total assets or to sales.

Psychology. The study of human behavior. This behavioral science and many of its branches have provided many concepts and theories useful in the study of management.

Rate of Return. A general concept which refers to the ratio of annual returns to the initial cost of the investment.

Reality-Centered Movement. A view of management which recognizes a need for a balance of classical, behavioral, and management science approaches, as well as experience. The reality-centered manager would seek to blend both experience and the schools of management and recognize that in order to be effective in the contemporary organization he cannot rely solely on one approach.

Referent Power. This refers to the power of a leader based on his attractiveness. That is, the leader is admired because of some personal qualities and the follower identifies closely with these characteristics.

Resistance to Change. A behavioral phenomenon which reflects the reluctance of people to adopt new ways of doing things.

Reward Power. This refers to the power generated by the perception of followers that compliance with the wishes of leaders can lead to positive rewards (e.g., promotion).

Rim Values. These values represent the total demand and total supply amounts available in the problem. These values cannot be violated in developing a transportation schedule. Thus, they are constraints which the manager must consider.

Risk Decisions. These are decision situations in which the manager does not know for certain the probability of occurrence of the state of nature or competitive actions. However, he has some past experience and/or data upon which he can rely to develop probabilities. These probabilities are used with conditional values to determine expected values.

Sample Survey. In this type of study design, the collection of data is from a limited number of units which are assumed to be representative of the entire group.

Scalar Chain. The graded chain of authority through which all communications flow.

Sensitivity Training. A form of educational experience which stresses the process and emotional aspects of training.

Simulation Models. Simulation involves constructing a model which replicates some aspect of the firm's operation and by performing step-by-step computations with the model, duplicates the manner in which the actual system might perform. An individual simulation run can be thought of as an experiment upon a model.

Situational Theory. The situational theory of leadership advocates an approach in which the leader understands his own behavior, the behavior of his followers, and the situation at hand before he utilizes a particular style. The emphasis is on the diagnostic skills of the leader to size up the situation and then adjust his style.

Slack Time. This is the time to spare in the completion of an event. It is found by using the formula:

$$\text{Slack Time } (S) = T_L - T_E$$

Slack Variable. Variable introduced into constraint inequalities in order to form equalities. Their unit profit (cost) is zero.

Social Psychology. This branch of psychology deals with the behavior of individuals as they relate to other individuals.

Sociogram. A diagram which illustrates the interpersonal relationships existing within a group. By use of the sociogram it is possible to trace communication patterns within a group.

Sociology. Attempts to isolate, define, and describe human behavior in groups. It strives to develop laws and generalizations about human nature, social interaction, culture, and social organization.

Sociometric Analysis. The use of self-reports to find personal preference and repulsion patterns of members of work groups.

Soldiering. A term which was used during the scientific management era to refer to the observed practice of output restriction. That is, workmen were observed to be producing at a lower rate than what would ordinarily be expected.

Staff Functions. The activities of departments which contribute indirectly to the creation of the organization's output. Ordinarily, the staff personnel advise line personnel.

Standard Deviation. This is a measure of dispersion or variation. It is utilized in network models to aid in computing the probability of achieving the completion date. It helps to eliminate some of the uncertainty involved in network models.

Standard Time. The sum of the normal times for the several elements as increased to provide for unavoidable delays and rest periods.

Status Consensus. The agreement of group members about the relative status of members of the group.

Status Hierarchy. The ranking of a group member within the group, that is, the prestige rank order of group members forms the status hierarchy.

Stochastic Models. A model which contains stochastic variables is based on the mathematics of statistics and into which conditions of uncertainty are introduced. They are also referred to as probabilistic models.

Structural Change. Planned changes in the formally prescribed task and authority relationships.

Structure (in Group Context). The term "structure" refers to relatively stable relationships among members of a work group. It is basically the group culture which influences the group's reward system—norms among other things.

Suboptimization. In business decision making, the objectives which a manager is attempting to achieve are often dependent. Thus, the optimization of one can result in a lower degree of attainment for at least some of the multiple objectives. This lower degree of attainment is known as suboptimization.

Suboptimization of Goals. Refers to the fact that it is impossible to optimize multiple goals when each goal competes for limited resources.

Supervision. A subfunction of control which refers to the oversight of subordinate's work activity.

System 4 Organization. An organizational type which stresses open, supportive leadership and group methods for decision-making and goal-setting.

Tall Pyramid Structure. The taller structure projects the viewpoint of being a more rigidly controlled design. Theoretically, it fosters narrow spans of control, a large number of management levels, and more centralized decision making.

Task and Bonus Wage System. A method proposed by Henry Gantt wherein the worker is guaranteed a fixed daily wage for efforts to complete the assigned task (the standard). The worker receives a bonus for work exceeding the standard.

Task Group. A group of individuals working as a unit to complete a project, job, or job task constitutes a task group.

Task Structure. This refers to the degree of structure imposed on the follower's job. The job may be routine or ill-structured. If the job were routine it would be spelled out in detail—an inspector on the assembly line. While the job of the research scientist working on a medical cure for a dreaded disease has relatively little task structure.

Technological Change. Planned changes in the use of techniques and knowledge appropriate for the organization's purpose.

Theory X. A set of assumptions about the nature of man which, according to Douglas McGregor, underlies the classical management theory. The assumptions stress the indolent characteristics of man.

Theory Y. An approach to management which is based on precepts which are exactly the opposite of Theory X. They are:
1. Workers do not inherently dislike work.
2. Workers do not want to be controlled and threatened.
3. Workers under proper working conditions seek out additional responsibility.
4. Workers desire to satisfy other needs beside those related to job security.

Therbligs. The term used to identify fundamental work elements. It is equivalent to Gilbreth's, spelled backward with one letter transposed.

Time Series Analysis. A statistical technique for analyzing the relationship between a specified variable and time.

Time Study. The process of determining the appropriate elapsed time for the completion of a task or job. It was part of F. W. Taylor's effort to determine a fair day's work.

Timing Element. Identifiable breaks in the rhythm of completing a task which are appropriate for taking readings on the stop watch. The timing element may consist of a number of related Therbligs which are independent of the preceding and succeeding element.

Top Management. The top level of an administrative hierarchy; managers at this level coordinate the work of other managers, but do not report to a manager.

Traditional Corporation. This concept of the corporation views it as an instrumentality of a single group—the shareholders—and has one clear-cut purpose: conducting business for their maximal profit. This view recognizes no public responsibilities except for legal ones and leaves the public interest to the care of the state.

Trait Theory. The trait theory attempts to specify which personal characteristics (physical, personality, mental) are associated with leadership success in organizational settings. It relies on research that relates various traits to success criteria.

Trial-and-Error Method. This is a hit-or-miss procedure for resolving economic lot size problems. The manager would study costs and then reach a decision based on the relationships that were considered.

Uncertainty Decisions. These are decision situations in which no past experience or historical data is available. Thus, any one of a number of criteria are employed depending upon the personality of the manager.

Unity of Command. A management principle which states that each subordinate should report to only one superior.

Unity of Direction. The process of grouping all related activities under one superior.

Unoccupied-Cell Computation. The second step in testing for optimality of a solution is determination of the unoccupied matrix cells. These are computed by taking the value in the subcell and subtracting it from the sum of the row and column values.

Utility. This term is used to describe the degree of monetary and/or psychological satisfaction a manager achieves from the outcome of one of his decisions. In decision theory terms, utility is a function of the relationship of strategy, states of nature, or competitive actions.

Variable Budgeting. A form of budgeting which targets expected costs at various potential output levels.

Variable Costs. These represent costs that vary closely with changes in production. For example, as the number of units produced increases, the amount of material used also increases. Thus, the material used to produce a product would be an example of variable costs.

Variables. In a mathematical model these relate to the components of the model. They are classified as *input variables,* which arise outside the component and are fed into it; *status variables,* which describe the state of a component; and *output variables,* which are anything generated by a component.

Vertical Specialization of Management. The process by which the right to command is delegated downward so as to create a hierarchy of positions graded by degrees of assigned authority.

Waiting-Line Models. Waiting-line models enable the manager to reach optimal decisions in facilities planning. They help in striking a balance between the cost of additional facilities and some other factor such as idle time or customer ill will.

Well-Tempered Corporation. This view lies between the two extremes of the *traditional corporation* and the *metrocorporation.* This type of corporation takes into account public expectations, but also does not conflict with management's responsibilities to the stockholders. This viewpoint holds that the claims of stockholders and creditors will more likely be met if a firm develops a position as a socially responsible company.

Work Standards. The determination of the appropriate way and elapsed time for the completion of a task.

INDEXES

Name Index

427

Subject Index

Feedback control—*Cont.*
  quality control, 106, 109–10
  standard cost analysis, 106, 108–9
Feedback cycle in work group framework, 174
Feedback information in organizational change, 253–55
Feedback loops in organizational change, 233
Feudal system, management process in, 10–11
Field of management, 3 ff.; *see also* Management
  concept of management, 4–5
  fundamental points concerning, 16
  literature constituting, 3
  method, 3–4
  scope, 3–4
Field study of work group behavior, 180–81
Financial budgeting, 69–70
Financial management, 5
Financial resources, 65
  preliminary control of, 103–5
Financial statement analysis, 106–8
  function of, 106
  liquidity, measures of, 106–7
First-line management, 5, 8–9
  function, 23
Fixed costs, 307
Flat structures, study of, 225–26
Forecasting, 57, 65–68
  approaches to, 66–68
  defined, 49
  econometric models, 68
  hunches, 66
  issues to be resolved through, 66
  market surveys, 66
  sales, 66, 68
  time series analysis, 66–68
Formal organization, 248–49
Foundation for Research on Human Behavior, 121
Friendship group, 161
Frustration, 135
  personality and, 140
Functional definition, 48, 50, 75
Functional effect, 47–48, 50, 75
Functional foremanship concept, 27, 215
Functional process, human relations approach, 120
Functions of management; *see* Management *and specific topic*
Future developments in management, 394–404; *see also* Contemporary management

G

Gangplank principle, 44
Gantt Chart, 28
General Electric Company, 240
General management, 5
General Motors Corporation, 219, 240
Glacier Metal Company of Great Britain, 214
Glossary, 409 ff.; *see also specific terms*
Goal setting and ordering, 57–65
  clarity of goals, 61–63
  financial measures, 65
  implementation of goals, 61–65
  leadership development, 199
  long-run goals, 58
  marketing measures, 64
  measurement of goals, 61, 63–65
  physical measures, 65
  priority of goals, 58
  productivity measures, 64–65
  profit/net-worth ratio, 63
  profit-seeking as a goal, 59–61
  profit/total-asset ratio, 63
  profitability measures, 63–64
  short-run goals, 58
  structure of goals, 58–59
  studies of actual goals, 61
  subgoals, areas of, 62
  suboptimization of goals, 58–59
  timing of goals, 58
  ultimates, 58
  unity of goals, 61–63
"Goal Setting and Self Control" study, 146
Goals; *see* Goal setting and ordering
Government as management factor, 390
Graphical method of linear programming, 331–37
  simplex method distinguished, 341
Great Depression, 15, 38
Greek Empire, management process in, 10
Group pressure, 165–66
Group review and enforcement, 165–66

H

Hand motions; *see* Therbligs
Hawthorne Studies, 13, 241, 249
  Bank Wiring Observation Room Experiment, 116, 118
  chiseler, 118
  criticisms of, 118–19
  employee interviews, 116–18
  experiments in illumination, 116–17
  human relations theory, 116
  major contribution of, 118
  phases of, 116–17
  rate buster, 118

446   Subject Index

*This book has been set in 10 and 9 point Cale-
donia, leaded 2 points. Part numbers and titles
and chapter titles are in 18 point Cheltanham
Bold; chapter numbers are in 14 point Cheltanham Bold. The size of the type page is 27 by
45½ picas.*